Preventing the Sexual

Victimization of Children

D1523999

Preventing the Sexual Victimization of Children

Psychological, Legal, and Public Policy Perspectives

CHARLES PATRICK EWING

NORTH ARKANSAS COLLEGE LIBRARY
1515 Pioneer Drive
Harrison, AR 72601

OXFORD
UNIVERSITY PRESS

HV
6570
.E95
2014

OXFORD
UNIVERSITY PRESS

Oxford University Press is a department of the University of Oxford.
It furthers the University's objective of excellence in research, scholarship,
and education by publishing worldwide.

Oxford   New York
Auckland   Cape Town   Dar es Salaam   Hong Kong   Karachi
Kuala Lumpur   Madrid   Melbourne   Mexico City   Nairobi
New Delhi   Shanghai   Taipei   Toronto

With offices in
Argentina   Austria   Brazil   Chile   Czech Republic   France   Greece
Guatemala   Hungary   Italy   Japan   Poland   Portugal   Singapore
South Korea   Switzerland   Thailand   Turkey   Ukraine   Vietnam

Oxford is a registered trademark of Oxford University Press
in the UK and certain other countries.

Published in the United States of America by
Oxford University Press
198 Madison Avenue, New York, NY 10016

© Oxford University Press 2014

All rights reserved. No part of this publication may be reproduced, stored in a
retrieval system, or transmitted, in any form or by any means, without the prior
permission in writing of Oxford University Press, or as expressly permitted by law,
by license, or under terms agreed with the appropriate reproduction rights organization.
Inquiries concerning reproduction outside the scope of the above should be sent to the Rights
Department, Oxford University Press, at the address above.

You must not circulate this work in any other form
and you must impose this same condition on any acquirer.

Library of Congress Cataloging-in-Publication Data
Ewing, Charles Patrick, 1949–
Preventing the sexual victimization of children : psychological, legal, and public policy
perspectives / Charles Patrick Ewing.
    pages cm
Includes bibliographical references and index.
ISBN 978-0-19-989553-3
1. Child sexual abuse—Prevention.   2. Sex crimes—Prevention.   3. Sexually abused children.
I. Title.
HV6570.E95 2014
362.76'7—dc23
2013028790

9 8 7 6 5 4 3 2 1
Printed in the United States of America
on acid-free paper

For the latest love of my life,
Caroline Margaret Viapiano

CONTENTS

In 2011, I published *Justice Perverted: Sex Offense Law, Psychology, and Public Policy*. In that volume, I critically examined the major recent developments in the way the law deals with sex offenders, including those who offend against children and adolescents. I examined civil commitment of sex offenders, sex offender registration and notification requirements, child pornography statutes, and laws criminalizing and severely punishing those who use the Internet in efforts to sexually entice minors. All of these legal standards were put in place by Congress and state legislatures as part of a growing effort to prevent the sexual abuse and exploitation of children and adolescents. Unfortunately, as I noted repeatedly in *Justice Perverted*, none of these laws has demonstrated much, if any, preventive efficacy. Worse yet, a number of these legal initiatives appeared to increase rather than decrease the likelihood that sex offenders would reoffend. In other words, they have just the opposite effect from what was intended. Having spent much of my career as a psychologist working with both perpetrators and victims of sex offenses, I was saddened by what I learned and what I wrote about the failure of these laws.

Even though there is good reason to believe that the incidence of child sexual abuse is decreasing, and despite data showing that the recidivism rates for sexual offenders are quite low, there is still a pressing need for better and more cost-effective ways of preventing the sexual abuse and exploitation of minors. After discussing my previous book with many readers and colleagues interested in prevention, I realized that what I had done in that volume was too simple in a number of ways. First, it was simple in the sense that it was relatively easy to criticize legal initiatives that appear to have been put in place for political reasons and probably never had any real chance of being effective preventive tools. Second, it was simple in the sense that it was limited to preventive strategies aimed at perpetrators and largely ignored broader preventive efforts aimed at children, parents, and the community. Third, it was simple in that it ignored preventive efforts aimed at a number of increasingly important contexts in which child sexual abuse and exploitation frequently occurs (i.e., institutions, such as schools, churches, and youth-serving organizations) and child prostitution and the sexual trafficking of minors.

This book reiterates and updates what was written in *Justice Perverted* about preventive strategies aimed at perpetrators, but it takes a much broader look at the nature and extent of child sexual abuse and examines in much greater detail an array of programs, laws, and policies designed to prevent such abuse.

Chapter 1 provides a brief introduction to the nature and extent of the problem of child sexual abuse in the United States and elsewhere. This chapter then offers a short history of child sexual abuse and exploitation from Mesopotamia to the Digital Age, highlighting the importance of understanding the long history of this awful phenomenon. The chapter concludes with a discussion of the need to carefully examine the efficacy and cost-effectiveness of all current efforts to prevent child sexual abuse.

Chapter 2 explores the epidemiology and effects of child sexual abuse. This chapter begins with an extended analysis of the long-standing and unresolved controversy over the incidence and prevalence of child sexual abuse, then turns to an examination of data suggesting that child sexual abuse has been decreasing in recent years. Next, the chapter considers the characteristics of child sex abuse victims and their relationships to those who abuse or exploit them. Finally, this chapter critically examines nearly half a century of research dealing with the psychological effects of child sexual abuse.

Chapter 3 critically evaluates child sexual abuse prevention strategies aimed at parents, children, and the community. With regard to strategies directed toward parents, the chapter emphasizes educating parents about child sexual abuse and translating data on such abuse into information that is useful to them in their everyday lives. As for strategies directed at children, the chapter highlights efforts to teach children to protect themselves from sexual abuse; appropriate responses to and investigation of children's disclosures of abuse; and alterations to legal proceedings to make it more likely that sexually abused children will not be further traumatized and their allegations will be heard in court. Finally, with regard to interventions aimed at the community as a whole, the chapter explores two important issues: limiting the sexualization of children in contemporary society and overcoming the resistance of "bystanders" to intervene to protect children from sexual abuse.

Chapter 4 deals with many of the same topics that were examined previously in *Justice Perverted* (civil commitment of child sex offenders; registration of these offenders; community notification of their presence; restrictions on their housing and travel; and harsh criminal punishment for "online" offenders [i.e., those who possess child pornography or use the Internet to solicit sex from minors or "decoys" they believe are minors]). However, the chapter not only updates those issues but goes well beyond them and also critically examines recent efforts to extend or abolish statutes of limitation in cases of child sexual abuse, and sharply increase criminal penalties for convicted child sex offenders.

Chapter 5 considers ways of preventing the use of the Internet to sexually abuse and exploit children and adolescents. Specifically, the chapter examines efforts to prevent the Internet from being used to distribute images of child sexual abuse (commonly referred to as child pornography) and solicit sex from minors.

Chapter 6 examines efforts to prevent child sexual abuse in institutions, particularly schools, juvenile correctional facilities, daycare centers, churches, and youth-serving organizations. The chapter emphasizes that whatever the institution, prevention of child sexual abuse begins with understanding and communicating the nature of the risk. Although most of the preventive measures discussed in the chapter are educational in nature, many are practical or even physical (e.g., rearranging the layout of facilities to maximize transparency and minimize privacy, requiring that staff and/or volunteers never be alone with a child, and conducting fingerprint and criminal background checks on those who apply to work with children in these institutional settings).

Chapter 7 deals with the commercial sexual exploitation of minors, a global phenomenon in which children are forced into prostitution. The chapter examines the nature and scope of juvenile sex trafficking, explains why "child prostitution" is a misnomer, and critically examines both domestic and international efforts to prevent minors from being abused in this particularly egregious fashion.

Chapter 8 summarizes and synthesizes many of the ideas expressed in earlier chapters and offers a cautious but hopeful assessment of future efforts to prevent child sexual abuse and exploitation. This concluding chapter emphasizes the need to view preventing such abuse and exploitation as an ongoing and ceaseless process for which all people bear responsibility.

ACKNOWLEDGMENTS

As always, this book is the product of many hands, heads, and hearts. Greatest thanks are due my team of research assistants at SUNY Buffalo Law School, without whom it could not have been written. Dainia Jabaji, Michael Das, Adam Penna, Amanda Barnhardt, Lauric Clark, Rachel Pelleter, and Chifeng Jiang all left their own distinct marks on this work by scouting resources, critiquing my ideas, and giving me theirs. All received support from SUNY Buffalo Law School for their work and several were compensated by the Faculty Scholars Program, a unique scholarship initiative that enables the best law school applicants to begin their J.D. studies knowing that they will be able to work closely with a faculty member of their choice.

Thanks are also in order for Sarah Harrington, Senior Editor at Oxford University Press, for her wisdom, encouragement, and patience. She was ably assisted by Andrea Zekus, her colleague at Oxford University Press, who had the difficult job of trying to keep this book somewhere near to schedule.

I also appreciate the input of many colleagues, especially those who participated in the First Annual Symposium on Child Sexual Abuse at the Johns Hopkins/Bloomberg School of Public Health in 2012. The event was a great learning opportunity for me and helped shape many of the ideas in this book.

Last, but always first, my deepest appreciation goes to the one who makes it all possible: Dr. Sharon Harris-Ewing.

Preventing the Sexual
Victimization of Children

Introduction and
Historical Overview

Although reliable and accurate data are hard to come by, it is clear that the sexual exploitation of children is a major social problem in the United States and around the world. Depending upon how child sexual exploitation is defined and measured, wildly divergent estimates indicate that in the United States between 3 and 37 percent of males, and between 8 and 71 percent of females, are sexually abused in some manner during childhood or adolescence.[1] The federal government reports that in recent years more than 80,000 complaints of child sexual abuse have been received annually by authorities.[2] Many believe that this figure understates the scope of the problem because child sexual abuse is thought to be notoriously underreported. As the recent and still ongoing clergy sex abuse scandals have demonstrated, many victims of child sexual abuse do not come forward, if ever, until they are adults. Even accepting the lowest estimates of the incidence of child sexual abuse in the United States today, there can be little doubt that this is an extraordinarily serious problem.

In other nations, it appears that the problem of child sexual abuse is even more severe. In South Africa, for example, which has about a sixth of the United States' population, there were 23,000 reported cases of child rape in one recent year.[3] In India, where the national police agency has reported that 1.2 million children are involved in prostitution, a recent survey of 2,211 school children in a large city found that more than 20 percent said they had been exposed to severe forms of sexual abuse including sexual assault, being forced to sexually fondle another, being required to exhibit their private body parts, and being photographed in the nude.[4] In Japan, where the national government recently estimated that in one year there were only 590 reported cases of child sexual abuse, a retrospective survey of 665 college students found 54.7 percent reported having been the victim of some form of child sexual abuse (broadly defined to include such victimization as seeing an exhibitionist before the age of 13, being offered pornography before age 18, and engaging in sexual intercourse before age 13).[5]

However, statistics tell only part of the story of child sexual exploitation. Whatever the numbers may say, and no matter how controversial some of them may be, there is no denying that hundreds of thousands, if not millions, of children are sexually exploited each year. In some instances, the abuse is nonphysical: children are exposed to pornography, adult genitalia, and online sex chats and solicitations. However, in many cases the abuse is physical: children are sexually fondled, assaulted, sodomized and raped, forced into prostitution, and filmed and/or photographed to produce child pornography.

In response to this worldwide scourge, governments have passed strict laws, entered into international treaties, and established large bureaucracies aimed at curbing child sexual abuse and ameliorating its often devastating effects on victimized children and society as a whole. In virtually all of these efforts, governments have relied upon input from social scientists and mental health professionals. Over the years, these experts have shaped and implemented social, legal, and psychological responses to child sexual abuse in countless ways. More than any other group, they have identified the problem, defined its scope, gathered data, provided estimates, offered and implemented potential solutions, and evaluated and/or provided treatment to both the perpetrators and victims of child sexual abuse.

Although countless books and articles have been written about all of these efforts, few if any have sought to critically evaluate national and international efforts to reduce child sexual exploitation and ameliorate its effects. For the most part, input from social science and mental health experts has been accepted uncritically, as have the programs and laws that have been developed in reliance upon that advice. It is assumed that the epidemiological data, disparate though they may be, are relatively accurate in assessing the incidence and prevalence of child sexual abuse and providing a reasonable guide to the allocation of scarce preventive, investigative, and treatment resources. Similarly, it is often assumed that child sexual abuse is a clearly defined phenomenon that can be assessed, "diagnosed," or even proven solely by psychological means; that its effects are predictable; that generally effective psychological treatment is available for victims and perpetrators; and that severe legal sanctions (criminal and civil) levied upon its perpetrators will reduce the incidence of child sexual abuse.

This book questions what we actually know about the sexual exploitation of children, its nature, prevalence, incidence, victims, perpetrators, investigation, assessment, proof, treatment, prevention, and deterrence. Critically examining existing empirical evidence, this book demonstrates that much of what we think we know about child sexual abuse (and what governments have relied upon in shaping law and public policy in this realm) is not accurate or at least not substantiated by the evidence. The book argues that uncritical acceptance of inaccurate or questionable data has locked both law and psychology into many ineffective and counterproductive measures that fail to achieve the goal of reducing the incidence and impact of child sexual exploitation. Finally, the book offers a number of psychological and legal reforms that appear to stand a better chance of achieving that goal.

A BRIEF HISTORY OF CHILD SEXUAL ABUSE FROM
MESOPOTAMIA TO THE DIGITAL AGE

Although often regarded as a modern phenomenon, the sexual abuse and exploitation of children has occurred throughout the course of human history: "The
taboo against using children and adolescents as sexual objects is only a few hundred years old. In very early times the age distinctions between child, adolescent
and adult were not strong."[6]

In Mesopotamia, the cradle of civilization, prior to the Code of Hammurabi
(which dates to around 1772 BC), female children were sold into marriage, sometimes to more than one man. In Ancient Greece, beginning around the seventh
century BC, adult males often engaged in socially accepted sexual relationships
with boys, a practice known as pederasty; young Greek females in the same historical era who "lost their virginity, often against their will, would shame the
honor of their family and, as a result, were commonly sold as slaves for prostitution."[7] During the early Roman Empire, children were often abandoned or sold
into slavery. Some of these slave boys were castrated and sodomized by masters
who knew it was illegal to engage in homosexual relations with a free male and
"upper-class boys wore distinctive necklaces lest their fathers engage in sexual
behavior with them by mistake in public bathhouses."[8]

In the Byzantine Empire, the "rational continuation of the Roman empire"
(324-1453 BC), the law (which was usually not followed) required husbands to
wait until their wives reached the age of 12 before having sex with them. Sexual
abuse of a female child outside of marriage or engagement was punished variously
by fining the offender; dragging him through the streets; cutting off his nose; or
("in extreme cases") executing him.[9] Sexual abuse of boys was punished by dragging the adult offender naked through the streets, mutilating his penis and, more
often, "decapitation by sword."[10] Victims were placed in monasteries that "had the
characteristics of a modern reformatory."[11]

During the Middle Ages (500–1400) in Europe, sexual mores were dictated
largely by the Catholic Church, but the lives of children appear to have been no
better for it. Child slavery continued and often included sexual services. Children
who were indentured or served as apprentices "were easy prey for sexual perpetrators."[12] During the Renaissance (roughly the fourteenth to seventeenth century),
"both male and female children were seen as largely innocent in sexual matters
[but] sexual innocence for males was perceived to fall away at about age ten, while
for females it was lost two to four years later."[13] Although the Renaissance was
marked by cultural and scientific revolutions, that era "reintroduced the West
to the mores of the pagan classical world where paederasty was more widely
accepted and even extolled in myth."[14] "Public opinion during the Renaissance
held teachers to be 'notorious sodomites' and civil authorities, for instance in
Venice, tried to restrict teaching to public halls and daylight hours in an effort to
restrict temptation" to engage in sex with male pupils.[15] And "although most soci-
eties throughout this period considered [man-boy sex] a crime it was not always
punished harshly."[16] On the other hand, sex with a female child was considered

rape. Although punishment in proven cases generally involved execution, the age parameters of childhood were not clearly defined and, in any event, "the burden of proof fell heavily on the child."[17]

The sexual abuse and exploitation of children in America dates back to colonial times. "Tens of thousands of children were indentured from England and Scotland between 1600 and 1800" and "the French, Portugese, and Dutch also 'sent out' their unwanted children to Louisiana, the West Indies, Algeria, Africa, East Indies, and New York."[18] These indentured children "experienced sexual victimization at the highest level—some moving into prostitution after the indenture was completed."[19] Most of the colonies adopted laws banning incest and some prescribed execution as the penalty for this offense. However, "the goal of most colonial legislatures was not to punish fathers who had coercive sexual relationships with their minor daughters [but] to avoid complicated inheritance issues that arose when kin related by affinity married, such as a widower marrying his wife's sister."[20] Because incest laws were vaguely written, courts argued over whether they even applied to cases of intrafamilial child sexual abuse, and "few men who sexually assaulted their daughters were punished before the 1890s under a criminal law prohibiting incest."[21]

Even this early in American history there were, of course, rape laws. As early as 1787, New York criminalized rape of a female under the age of 10, specifying death as the punishment for a convicted offender. Although incest required only proof of sexual relations between a father and daughter, rape required proof that the victim had not consented to the sexual contact. Perpetrators of child sexual abuse could be charged with statutory rape, having sexual relations with a minor regardless of consent. However, it was not until the late nineteenth century that most states "recognized an 'age of consent,' an age below which the law presumes that a girl is developmentally incapable of consenting to sexual contact, regardless of her apparent willingness."[22]

At about the same time most American legislatures were beginning to deal with this issue, other major developments in the history of child sexual abuse were occurring in Europe. Between 1857 and 1878, Auguste Ambroise Tardieu, an early forensic physician, published studies of child sexual abuse in France. Tardieu documented thousands of sex crimes against children and reported that more than 75 percent of rapes and attempted rapes in France involved victims under 16. He also noted that most of these youngsters were girls younger than the age of 12. Around 1886, Sigmund Freud, the father of psychoanalysis, presented a group of papers on the cause of hysteria. These papers dealt with 18 patients who had been diagnosed with what was then called hysteria. Freud concluded that all of these women had been sexually abused as children by various caretakers, most often their fathers, and that this abuse caused their mental illnesses.[23] By 1897, however, Freud had repudiated this "theory of seduction": "Freud now believed that most, but not all, of the assaults he reported had never occurred. He instead suggested that the young child, needing to release sexual tensions, wished for the sexual attention from her father. He believed that these tensions were universal and unfolded in developmental stages."[24]

As the works of Tardieu and Freud were unfolding in Europe, American child protective agencies had become aware of, and were taking action against, child sexual abuse, particularly incest. Tardieu's work appears to have had little impact in America, but Freud's repudiation of his "seduction theory" may well have played an important role in changing the way child sexual abuse was dealt with in the United States: "In the early twentieth century the child-savers view of child sexual abuse changed significantly...By the 1920s...the *locus* of the problem was moved from home to streets, the *culprit* transformed from father or other authoritative male family member to perverted stranger, the *victim* transformed from innocent betrayed to sex delinquent. In other words, the fact that child sex abuse is overwhelmingly a family problem was obscured; instead it was pictured as rape by strangers on the street."[25] Apparently spurred by a handful of brutal sex crimes against children, the American news media began to vastly increase and sensationalize their coverage of these offenses in the late 1930s. As Freedman, an historian, wrote:

> Between 1937 and 1940, and again during the postwar decade, the New York Times, previously silent on the subject, averaged over forty articles per year on sex crimes. In 1937, magazines ranging from Science and the Christian Century to the Nation and the New Masses reported on the sex crime panic. After World War II news and family magazines, including Time, Newsweek, and Parents' Magazine, carried articles titled "Queer People," "Sex Psychopaths," and "What Shall We Do About Sex Offenders?" In its 1950 series on "Terror in Our Cities," Collier's magazine summarized the newspaper headlines in St. Louis ("The City that DOES Something About Sex Crime") in a representative composite. KINDERGARTEN GIRL ACCOSTED BY MAN—CLERK ACCUSED OF MOLESTING 2 GIRLS IN MOVIE—MAN ACCUSED BY 8-YEAR-OLD BOY OF MOLESTING HIM IN THEATRE—6-YEAR-OLD GIRL AT ASHLAND SCHOOL MOLESTED—LABORER ARRESTED FOR RAPE OF 10-YEAR-OLD GIRL—FINED FOR MOLESTING 2 BOYS, AGED 8 AND 10—ARRESTED ON SUSPICION OF MOLESTING 4-YEAR-OLD GIRL—YOUTH WHO MOLESTED BOY 4, IS FINED $500—9 CHARGES AGAINST MOLESTER OF GIRLS.[26]

At the same time media sources were trumpeting cases such as these, American psychiatrists appeared split on the causes of child sexual abuse. Freud's change of heart on his seduction theory likely altered the way many professionals, especially those in the mental health field, perceived child sexual abuse, particularly incest. For example, in 1937, in what may have been the first American study of victims of child sexual abuse, noted child psychiatrist Lauretta Bender and a colleague examined the cases of 16 boys and girls between the ages of 5 and 12 at New York's Bellevue Hospital. Bender and Blau recognized the existence of child sexual abuse but cautioned that "the child might have been the actual seducer rather than the one innocently seduced."[27] Meanwhile, however, most psychiatrists were interested more in the perpetrators than the victims of child sexual abuse. In the late 1930s, American psychiatrists began to tout the notion that persistent sex offenders were "psychopaths" with "no control over their sexual impulses," who, if simply incarcerated and left untreated, would "prey again upon women and children."[28] According to this growing psychiatric point of view, these offenders could be readily diagnosed, treated, and perhaps even cured under the proper medical regimen.

Together, the media and the psychiatric profession swayed not only the opinion of the public but that of many legislators. In 1937, Michigan passed the nation's first state "sexual psychopath" law; within two decades 25 other states followed suit. The idea behind these laws was that: "[A] man accused of rape, sodomy, child molestation, indecent exposure, or corrupting the morals of a minor—if diagnosed as a 'sexual psychopath'—could receive an indeterminate sentence to a psychiatric, rather than a penal, institution. The laws defined the sexual psychopath as someone whose 'utter lack of power to control his sexual impulses' made him 'likely to attack... the objects of his uncontrolled and uncontrollable desires.'"[29]

Although sexual psychopath laws remained in effect well into the 1970s (and in some cases beyond), the idea that children were not innocent victims of sexual abuse remained prominent. For example, in 1952, Bender and another colleague published a follow-up study of the 16 sexually abused children she had described in the 1930s. In their follow-up, they reported that "The original psychiatric evaluations repeatedly remarked on the children's unusually attractive and charming personalities, and it was frequently considered that these qualities had contributed to their appeal as sexual objects. In many, it was highly probable that the child had used his charm in the role of the seducer rather than that he had been the innocent one who had been seduced."[30]

A year later, famed sexologist Alfred Kinsey and his colleagues published the startling results of a groundbreaking survey of 4,441 adult women. Twenty-four percent of these women reported that, as children, they had been sexually abused by an adult male. Most of these women reported that these sexual experiences were frightening, but Kinsey and his colleagues could not understand this reaction: "It is difficult to understand why a child, except for its cultural conditioning, should be disturbed at having its genitalia touched, or disturbed at seeing the genitalia of other persons, or disturbed at even more specific sexual contacts."[31] While Kinsey "minimized his remarkable statistics, the largest body of data about child sexual abuse that had ever been collected," he and his colleagues expressed concern for alleged child sex offenders who were "imprisoned for accidental exposure of the genitalia while intoxicated, for nude swimming, or for the bestowal of 'grandfatherly affection.'"[32]

Numerous other nonrandom surveys of adults, conducted between 1940 and 1965, arrived at prevalence statistics similar to those of Kinsey and his colleagues. Three such studies reported that "between 17% and 28% of respondents were sexually abused as children."[33] Also, a number of studies conducted between 1942 and 1969 "confirmed the Kinsey findings that survivors recalled sexual contacts with adults as frightening, shocking, and emotionally upsetting, and also that these contacts led to sexual difficulties, depression, and other serious long-term effects."[34]

Although Kinsey's data on premarital and extramarital sex received wide attention, his findings regarding incest and child sexual abuse were "almost completely ignored."[35] It was not until the 1970s that experts and others began to challenge "the prevailing view that child sexual abuse was extremely rare and mostly confined to the economically disadvantaged or to particular ethnic or racial groups."[36]

That view was challenged most directly in 1978 when Diane Russell, a feminist sociologist, conducted a random sample survey of 930 women in the San Francisco area with regard to their experiences with child sexual abuse. Russell appears to have been the "first researcher to conduct a probability survey to ascertain the prevalence of incestuous and extrafamilial child sexual abuse."[37] Russell took pains to narrowly define child sexual abuse so that the data she obtained "would be taken seriously and not trivialized."[38] She defined incestuous abuse as "any kind of exploitive sexual contact or attempted sexual contact that occurred between relatives, no matter how distant the relationship, before the victim turned eighteen years old."[39] Sexual abuse outside the family was defined as follows: "Extrafamilial child sexual abuse involves one of more unwanted sexual experiences with unrelated persons, ranging from attempted sexual fondling to rape, before the victim turned 14 years, completed or attempted forcible rape experiences from the ages of 14 to 17 years (inclusive), and attempted or completed sexual fondling from the ages of 14 to 17 years (inclusive) by adult perpetrators (over 18 years of age) who were five or more years older than the victim."[40]

Despite the somewhat convoluted definitions used by Russell, her findings were striking. Sixteen percent of these women reported at least one incidence of incestuous abuse before the age of 18; 31 percent reported that they had experienced at least one incident of extrafamilial child sexual abuse before age 18; and overall, 38 percent reported at least one experience of incestuous and/or extrafamilial sexual abuse before turning 18. To the extent that Russell's findings could be generalized to American society at the time (and that is debatable), they suggested that more than a third of American women had been the victims of sexual abuse before they turned 18. While carefully detailing those findings, Russell also added to these numbers "incomplete data on noncontact experiences of incestuous and extrafamilial child sexual abuse" including unwanted sexual kisses, sexual hugs, and other nongenital touching" as well as "genital exposure experiences."[41] With these numbers added, she concluded that "54% of the 930 women...reported at least one experience of incestuous and/or extrafamilial child sexual abuse before 18 years of age."[42]

Within a decade of Russell's research a number of other random community surveys, as well as one national prevalence survey of child sexual abuse, had been conducted. In these studies, using various methodologies, 22–27 percent of women and 6–16 percent of men reported that they had been sexually abused as children.[43] In a random, nationwide telephone survey of 2,626 adults in 1985, 27 percent of women and 16 percent of men indicated that they had been sexually abused before the age of 18.[44] Sexual abuse was defined as an act the respondent believed was sexual abuse and included attempted or completed sexual inter-course; oral sex or sodomy; kissing, touching, or grabbing the respondent; rub-bing up against the respondent's body; someone taking nude photographs of the respondent; someone exhibiting parts of his or her body to the respondent; and performing a sex act in the presence of the respondent.[45]

All of these numbers were hard to ignore, but they were brought to public attention and their impact was significantly amplified (if not sensationalized) to a large extent by feminists and members of an emerging self-help move-ment in the 1970s and 1980s. For example, in 1976, Russell and one of her colleagues wrote that: "Every woman is a potential victim of rape: little girls, adolescents, single women, married women, middle-aged women—and even dead women...Women live in terror of rape from the most tender age. An incredible number of children are victims of sexual aggression even in their own families or from relatives. The climate of terror thus formed continues into adulthood and pushes women to look for 'protection' just where it can-not be secured: from men."[46] Later, psychiatrist Judith Herman would write in a chapter titled "Sex Offenders: A Feminist Perspective" that given the num-ber of child sexual abuse victims uncovered by these studies, "common sense would suggest that some comparable percentage of the male population has been doing the victimizing."[47]

The self-help movement for survivors of child sexual abuse emerged in the 1980s with the publication of best-selling books, such as *The Courage to Heal: A Guide for Women Survivors of Child Sexual Abuse* by Ellen Bass, which "combined personal narratives, explanations of the effects of abuse, and suggested healing exercises."[48] The book's premise was that although as many as one-third of women were sexu-ally abused as children, many are unable to remember the abuse. Readers, who numbered in the hundreds of thousands, were told: "There are many women who show signs of having been abused without having any memories"[49]; "If you are unable to remember any specific instances...but still have a feeling that some-thing abusive happened to you, it probably did"[50]; and "If you think you were abused and your life shows the symptoms, then you were."[51] The "symptoms" included feeling bad, dirty ashamed, powerless, victimized, endangered, unmoti-vated, vulnerable, and the need to be perfect.[52]

This best-selling self-help book (along with others of the same genre) went a long way toward making child sexual abuse a major social and political issue in the 1980s and 1990s: "[I]ts influence went far beyond the feminist survivors' movement. Virtually every participant in survivors' self-help groups of any politi-cal stripe read the book, and many other survivors did, too. It thus served as a link between the feminist survivors' wing, the larger self-help movement, and the mainstream culture."[53]

However, the same powerful aspects of the feminist and self-help movements that popularized the issue of child sexual abuse appear to have contained the seeds for what would ultimately be described as a "formidable backlash" against what some saw as a societal overreaction to child sexual abuse.[54]

In the 1980s and early 1990s, some law enforcement, social work, medical, and mental health professionals took extreme positions regarding child sexual abuse, such as suggesting that children never lie about allegations of molestation; when sexual abuse is suspected it almost certainly exists; certain childhood behaviors (not all of which are sexual) were indicators of child sexual abuse; and memories of child sexual abuse "recovered" long after the alleged abuse were generally evidence that such abuse actually occurred. Numerous sensational cases of child sexual abuse—often of a bizarre nature—purportedly committed by child care workers led to staggering criminal charges and hotly contested trials: "[A]llegedly abused children were talking about strange rituals, possibly satanic, involving the killing (and eating, in some cases) of animals. They told of eating excrement, drinking urine, and observing the murder (and cannibalizing, in some instances) of babies."[55] A number of these cases involved disclosures from children made in the face of allegedly biased and suggestive questioning from law enforcement personnel, social workers, or mental health professionals. Many eventually ended in acquittals or legal exonerations after conviction, but only after defendants were jailed for months or even years and their reputations and livelihoods were ruined. During the same era, there were many more questionable allegations of child sexual abuse raised in bitterly contested child custody proceedings around the country, with one parent seeking to gain legal leverage by accusing the other of abusing the child. Also, a host of adults brought lawsuits against their parents and others, usually family members, alleging that they had only recently recalled long repressed instances of childhood sexual abuse. Many of these claims were ultimately dismissed by the legal system, but not before families were torn apart and lives shattered. In some case, mental health professionals were even successfully sued for implanting false memories of child sexual abuse in adult patients.

The so-called backlash engendered by these developments ranged from bad press (books, articles, television shows, and films documenting numerous miscarriages of justice) to harsh political critiques of the child welfare system. Some claimed that as a result of a moral panic thousands of innocent individuals had been falsely accused of sexually abusing children (usually their own) and the most extreme critics likened the child welfare system's handling of child sexual abuse to Nazism, McCarthyism, and worse. One group, Victims of Child Abuse Laws (VOCAL), was especially active in fueling this backlash: "VOCAL has contended that a great many child sexual abuse allegations arise out of divorce and custody proceedings where one parent falsely and maliciously accuses the other to gain an advantage in court. The accuser then 'brainwashes' the child to testify accordingly. In other cases, VOCAL asserts, investigators are so sure the crime has occurred that they browbeat children until the abuse is 'admitted.' In the end the children *are* abused—but by the investigators, not the accused, says VOCAL."[56]

Some authorities in the field of child sexual abuse blamed the so-called backlash on accused child sex offenders and their attorneys and complained that it lacked any empirical basis, and that it was largely designed to defend adults accused of molesting children or to "otherwise minimize, rationalize, or deny the realities of childhood sexual abuse."[57] Significantly, even some of the strongest critics of the backlash conceded that it was not entirely without merit: "Although the backlash is characterized by extreme positions, lack of supporting research data and near total rejection of the knowledge and experiences of child sexual abuse, there is often an element of truth in its critique."[58] As one leading critic of the backlash acknowledged several years later: "We know and do things today that we could not envision a few years ago. We also believed things in the past that we know now were not accurate. To the extent that decisions were based on those data, it is likely that errors were made."[59]

The backlash forced many changes in the way legal, social service, and mental health professionals dealt with child sexual abuse and inspired major research initiatives. Some of this research was designed to test whether certain childhood behaviors and adult attitudes were in fact symptomatic of child sexual abuse victimization, whether children's suggestibility could result in false allegations of sexual abuse, and whether "recovered" memories of childhood sexual abuse were valid and reliable. However, the backlash was short-lived—not because its essential claims were disproven but because a new wave of concern about child sexual abuse in the 1990s overrode its influence.

Between 1989 and 1994, a highly publicized series of gruesome sex crimes committed against children effectively ended the backlash. In May 1989, in Tacoma, Washington, a man kidnapped, raped, strangled, and severed the penis of a 7-year-old boy who had been riding a bicycle near his own home. The boy survived and identified the perpetrator, who was known to the police for his previous offenses, including homicide, kidnapping, and the assault of two teenage girls, and had recently been released from prison because he had fully completed his latest sentence. Less than 4 months later, in Vancouver, Washington, two brothers were found stabbed to death in a city park. Both boys were tied up and one had been sodomized. About 2 months later, the body of another boy, age 4, was found by a lake in Vancouver. The boy had been repeatedly raped, strangled, and sexually abused postmortem. The man ultimately charged with all of these crimes was a 28-year-old pedophile with a long record of sex offenses against boys dating back to his teenage years. Upon being arrested, he admitted to killing all three Vancouver boys and to previously molesting approximately 30 children.[60]

Public outrage over these rare but horrible crimes, committed within such a limited geographic area and short time span, led the Washington legislature to pass in 1990 what would become the first of more than 20 modern laws aimed at allowing states and the federal government to indefinitely confine sex offenders believed to be dangerous even after they have served their full criminal sentences. In this reinvention of the "sexual psychopath," sex offenders, particularly those who offended against children, were dubbed "sexually violent predators" and many have been given what may amount to a life sentence of confinement in an extremely expensive and highly secure treatment facility.[61]

At the same time that outrageous crimes against children were leading to passage of these "sexually violent predator" laws, they were also prompting legislatures around the country to enact what have come to be called "Megan's laws."[62]

The push toward these laws, which deal exclusively with sex offenders, ironically began with a case in which there has never been any evidence of a sex crime. In 1989, an 11-year-old Minnesota boy was kidnapped from the street at gunpoint by a masked man. The boy was never seen again.[63] In response, his mother created a foundation and led a movement to press for laws requiring the registration of sex offenders. In 1994, Congress passed the Jacob Wetterling Crimes against Children and Sexually Violent Offender Registration Act, which effectively required every state to establish a sex offender registry by 1997.[64] Thereafter, every state required sex offenders to register with the authorities; ultimately every state made at least some of its sex offender registry available to the public. Today that information, often including not only the names and addresses of convicted sex offenders, but also other identifying details about them, is only a few mouse clicks away for anyone with access to a computer.[65] Many states and municipalities have taken the registry idea even further, prescribing where and under what conditions registered sex offenders may live, work, or travel.[66]

Most recently, the dawn of the Digital Age has impelled Congress and state legislatures to take legal steps calculated to protect children from sexual abuse conducted in whole or part via the Internet. For example, although child pornography has a history dating back to the ancient Greek culture, possession of child pornography has been considered a criminal offense only for several decades.[67] In the 1960s and 1970s, production and distribution of child pornography became an international commercial industry, leading to the relatively widespread availability of magazines, films, and photographs of children depicted in a sexual manner. In response to the growing availability of these materials, in the late 1970s and early 1980s, Congress and many state legislatures enacted laws prohibiting and criminally punishing the production and dissemination, but not the mere possession, of child pornography. It was not until 1991 that possession of child pornography was made a federal crime. Today, all 50 states and the District of Columbia have laws criminalizing the possession, manufacture, and distribution of child pornography.

Child pornography is defined by law as the visual depiction of a person under the age of 18 engaged in sexually explicit conduct. However, even a simple photograph of a naked minor may constitute child pornography if it is sufficiently sexually suggestive. In addition, for purposes of the child pornography statutes, federal law considers a person under the age of 18 to be a child. It is irrelevant that the age of consent for sexual activity in a given state might be lower than 18. Given that virtually all child pornographic images are today sent and received via the Internet or were created and/or stored at some point on media that travelled in interstate or foreign commerce, the federal law reaches virtually all child pornography offenders. Criminal penalties for possession of child pornography range from probation to life in prison. The courts have upheld the constitutionality of these statutes and penalties (including life imprisonment for mere possession of child pornography) based on their conclusions that child pornography constitutes a form of child sexual abuse, that children are sexually victimized not only in its making but in its distribution and repeated showing, and that those who possess but do not create child pornography create a market for this contraband and thus indirectly encourage the sexual abuse of children.

After recognizing the sexual abuse of children inherent in the production of child pornography and the contribution to such abuse made by those who merely possess child pornography, Congress and state legislators turned their attention to people who use the Internet in attempts to entice children and adolescents into sexual relationships. From 1990 through 2005, several federally funded surveys of youth and law enforcement helped shed light on the extent to which, and ways in which, children and adolescents are sexually victimized via the Internet. In a 1999–2000 survey that involved interviewing "a nationally representative sample of 1,501 youth ages 10 to 17 who use the Internet regularly," 19 percent of these youngsters reported having "received an unwanted sexual solicitation or approach in the last year," while 3 percent reported receiving an "aggressive sexual solicitation" via the Internet during that same time period.[68] Most of the offenders were reported to be youths or young adults and only two of the reported incidents resulted in relationships that "may have had sexual aspects."[69]

Later, based upon a national survey of 2,574 enforcement agencies, researchers estimated that there had been "2,577 arrests for Internet sex crimes against minors in the 12 months starting July 1, 2000."[70] Thirty-six percent of these arrests were for possession, distribution, and/or trade of child pornography only. Thirty-nine percent involved crimes with identified victims, including production of child pornography. Twenty-five percent of these arrests involved solicitations made to undercover law-enforcement officers posing as minors. In approximately half of the arrests involving crimes against identified victims, the offender used the Internet to initiate a relationship with the victim.

In another more recent federally funded national survey of youth conducted in 2005, 1,500 youths between the ages of 10 and 17 were interviewed. As opposed to 2000, when 19 percent of those surveyed reported having been sexually solicited online, only 13 percent reported having had such an experience within the preceding year.[71] At the same time, the number of surveyed youths reporting aggressive solicitations rose from 3–4 percent. Only four youths had "physical contact [they] would call sexual" during face-to-face meetings with adults they met online.[72] These youth were all 17 years of age, and the adults were all in their early 20s.

These studies were followed by legislation, at both state and federal levels, criminalizing the online sexual solicitation of minors. For example, the federal law, initially passed in 1996, specified a maximum prison sentence of 10 years for anyone using the Internet to persuade, induce, entice, or coerce any person under the age of 18 "to engage in prostitution or any sexual activity for which any person can be charged with a criminal offense."[73] In 1998, in "response to requests of victim parents and law enforcement to address public safety issues involving the most vulnerable members of our society, our children," Congress increased the maximum sentence to 15 years. In 2003, Congress raised the maximum sentence to 30 years and established a mandatory minimum sentence of 5 years.[74] In 2006, Congress passed the Adam Walsh Child Protection and Safety Act, which increased the mandatory minimum sentence to 10 years and the maximum sentence to life in prison.[75]

Finally, while Congress was busy increasing the minimum sentences for those who sexually prey on minors online, in 2003 they passed the PROTECT Act, aimed in part at curbing what some have called a global sex tourist industry in which Americans and citizens of other nations travel abroad to have sex with minors. The PROTECT Act made it a federal crime, prosecutable in the United States, for an American citizen or permanent resident alien "to engage in illicit sexual conduct in a foreign country with a person under the age of 18, whether or not the U.S. citizen or lawful permanent resident alien intended to engage in such illicit sexual conduct prior to going abroad."[76] Conviction under the PROTECT Act carries a prison sentence of up to 30 years.

Currently, more than a decade into the new millennium, America is witnessing another backlash against policies that were purportedly designed to protect children from sexual abuse and exploitation. For example, sexually violent predator laws, although upheld by most courts as constitutional, have been sharply criticized on practical grounds—namely that they require mental health experts to invent diagnoses and stretch recognized diagnoses in efforts to prove that convicted sex offenders are "mentally abnormal"; force such experts to make predictions of recidivism that have no empirical basis and fly in the face of the low base rate for recidivism among sex offenders; place sex offenders in unproven "treatment" programs that are little more than pretexts for continued secure confinement; and take a staggering toll on already limited taxpayer dollars that could be better used for other pressing purposes, such as the primary prevention of child sexual abuse.[77]

Likewise, sex offender registration, notification, and restriction laws are now being criticized as counterproductive and contrary to public safety. Critics say "[T]he proliferation of people required to register even though their crimes were not serious makes it harder for law enforcement to determine which sex offenders warrant careful monitoring. Unfettered online access to registry information facilitates—if not encourages—neighbors, employers, colleagues, and others to shun and ostracize former offenders—diminishing the likelihood of their successful reintegration into communities. Residency restrictions push former offenders away from the supervision, treatment, stability, and supportive networks they may need to build and maintain successful, law abiding lives."[78]

Finally, with regard to Internet-related sexual offenses against children, outside of members of the criminal defense bar and a few academics, there have been few powerful critics of recent laws requiring extremely harsh sentences for those who possess child pornography or solicit sex from minors online. However, among the most influential critics of these laws, particularly the sentencing aspects of the laws, are federal judges, some of whom have not only refused to impose maximum sentences in these cases but have also spoken publicly against these laws.

Sadly, although perhaps not surprisingly, given the checkered history of society's responses to child sexual abuse, while massive government resources have been devoted recently to what some have called the modern "war on sex offenders," this expensive "war" has largely ignored a growing and significant aspect of child sexual abuse that has emerged as a major international problem only in recent decades: commercial sexual exploitation of children. As the US Department of Justice has recently reported:

> The commercial sexual exploitation of children (CSEC) is sexual abuse of a minor for economic gain. It involves physical abuse, pornography, prostitution, and the smuggling of children for unlawful purposes...The number of known cases of CSEC is growing. Children are being kidnapped and sold into forced labor in the illegal sex industry. Some impoverished families are selling their children to traffickers in the hope of giving the children a better life. There are documented reports of children being held captive in basements and other slavelike conditions where they are beaten, malnourished, threatened, and sexually exploited.[79]

As already noted, American lawmakers have recently begun to tackle what many perceive as the growing menace of child pornography. However, their response (similar to what they relied upon in the so-called war on drugs) has largely been limited to ferreting out and massively punishing those who possess such contraband. The theory is that by punishing those who possess images of child sexual abuse, the government is limiting the demand for such images and thus ultimately reducing market incentives to create and distribute them. Unfortunately, there is little if any evidence to support this theory. For the most part, for various reasons that are explored in greater detail later in this book, the legal system has done little to apprehend and punish those who commercially manufacture and distribute images of child sexual abuse victimization, what is commonly called child pornography. Nor has much been done to crack down on commercial ventures (primarily Internet service providers) whose services are used to sell, buy, and trade these images.

Similarly, in the realm of what is generally referred to as child prostitution, remarkably little effort has been directed toward tracking down and prosecuting those who traffic in children at either the wholesale or the retail level: child sexual abusers ranging from international child sex traffickers to ordinary street pimps who control child "prostitutes" and the money paid for their sexual services. Remarkably, in many jurisdictions, when an adult pays to have sexual relations with a minor, it is the minor who is perceived as the criminal and charged with prostitution. Adult purchasers of child sex, who are clearly guilty of at least the crime of statutory rape, are often regarded as mere "johns" and prosecuted, if at all, simply for the very minor offense of soliciting a prostitute.

PREVENTING CHILD SEXUAL ABUSE

Those interested in preventing child sexual abuse ignore the history of this phenomenon at their peril—and that of the world's children. As it is often said, "Those who do not learn from history are doomed to repeat it."[80] Some commentators have noted that the history of efforts to prevent child sexual abuse has always been cyclical, alternating between periods of great concern and effort followed by some sort of backlash and/or loss of interest in the subject. To the extent that this is the case, and there seems to be a strong historical argument that it is (at least during the past half-century), it may well be so because of the frequently untested, often ineffective, and sometimes counterproductive ways in which society, government, and the helping professions have responded to child sexual abuse during those eras of great concern and effort.

To date, many programs aimed at curbing child sexual abuse have not been subjected to much, if any, systematic empirical scrutiny, and many that have been evaluated appear to be marginally effective, ineffective, or, worst of all, counter-productive. Moreover, many programs aimed at preventing child sexual abuse have been tertiary rather than primary or secondary in nature. Primary preven-tion targets all children and aims to keep abuse from happening; secondary pre-vention targets individuals or groups already at risk of child abuse victimization or perpetration and aims to reduce such risk; and tertiary prevention focuses on cases in which abuse has already occurred in an effort to reduce its negative con-sequences. Although all three types of prevention are important, primary preven-tion is more likely to achieve the goal of reducing the incidence and prevalence of child sexual abuse. Yet, most governmental efforts at preventing child sexual abuse have been secondary or tertiary in nature. Consider, for example, the efforts that have accompanied America's most recent wave of concern about child sex-ual abuse, such as indefinitely confining convicted sex offenders after they have served their criminal sentences; criminalizing and enhancing the punishment for possession of child pornography and online sexual solicitation of minors; requir-ing convicted sex offenders to register with the authorities, notifying the com-munity of their presence, and limiting where they can live, work, or even travel; and extending the reach of US jurisdiction to prosecute Americans who sexually abuse children abroad.

As the Executive Board of Directors of the Association for the Treatment of Sexual Abusers wrote in 2011:

> Sexual abuse is a serious national problem that cannot be solved solely by responding to abuse after it has been perpetrated. While the criminal justice and related systems may offer deterrence, incarceration, rehabilita-tion, and restitution, these efforts to foster community safety are imple-mented only after the detection and commission of a crime. After-the-fact interventions address the offender's crime and the victim's trauma with the burden of disclosure and prevention of further abuse placed on the victim. A complementary approach to prevent sexual abuse from being perpetrated in the first place is necessary. Public health prevention efforts encourage us to shift our focus from intervention and treatment following an assault to primary prevention, that is, the prevention of sexual abuse before it is perpetrated.[81]

All programs and efforts aimed at preventing child sexual abuse (whether primary, secondary, or tertiary) should be carefully examined to determine whether they are effective. Unproven and ineffective prevention efforts should be abandoned. Marginally effective and even broadly effective prevention efforts should be studied further to determine their cost-effectiveness (i.e., whether the results they bring about are justified when considered in the context of their social and monetary costs). Prevention efforts demonstrated to be both effective and cost-effective in reducing the incidence of child sexual abuse and exploitation should be given the highest priority for funding and implementation.

The Epidemiology and Effects of Child Sexual Abuse and Exploitation

Child sexual abuse has been recognized as a serious public health problem since at least 1985. It is useful to conceptualize child sexual abuse as a public health issue for several reasons. First, as discussed at length later in this chapter, child sexual abuse has been associated with many adverse health and mental health conditions among its victims. More importantly, the public health approach to any sort of pathology (whether physical, psychological, and/or social) is one that emphasizes, first and foremost, prevention. As noted in the preceding chapter, child sexual abuse is a "problem that cannot be solved solely by responding to abuse after it has been perpetrated."[1]

PREVALENCE AND INCIDENCE

Any sensible approach to prevention, but especially one grounded in public health, must begin with an assessment of the nature and extent of the problem, what public health specialists call prevalence and incidence. Prevalence is a measure of how much of a disease or condition exists in a given population at a particular point in time. Prevalence is often calculated by dividing the number of persons with the disease or condition at a particular time point by the number of individuals in the relevant population, then multiplying the dividend by 100, and expressing the result as a percentage. Prevalence is also sometimes expressed not as a percentage but as the number of cases per 100,000 population, particularly where the number of cases is low. For example, if cancer is measured in a population of 40,000 people and 4,700 people in that population have been diagnosed with cancer, the prevalence of cancer may be expressed as 0.1175, 11,750 per 100,000 persons, or 11.75 percent.[2]

Incidence is a measure of the rate of occurrence of new cases of a disease or condition in a specific time period (e.g., how many Americans developed cancer in the past year). Incidence is often calculated by dividing the number of new cases in the given time period by the relevant population. Where the number is large, it may be converted to a percentage; where it is relatively small, it is more likely to be expressed as a number per 100,000. For example, if 120 cases of cancer were diagnosed in a population of 40,000 during the past year, the annual incidence of cancer may be said to be .003, 0.3 percent, or 300 cases per 100,000.

For the past half century, clinicians, researchers, and advocates have tried to determine the prevalence and incidence of child sexual abuse. As was mentioned briefly in the preceding chapter, these efforts have resulted in wildly divergent numbers. This chapter examines this body of epidemiological research and the implications its results have for the prevention of child sexual abuse.

Determining the incidence and prevalence of child sexual abuse is critical to prevention for a number of reasons. To begin with, these data are likely to determine the amount of resources, if any, that will be directed toward prevention. For example, if child sexual abuse can be shown to have reached epidemic proportions (as some commentators have claimed), the investment in preventive efforts is likely to be substantial. However, if (as some others claim) the scope of child sexual abuse has been exaggerated, is of lesser proportions, or (as some now assert) is on the wane, it might be argued that preventive efforts should be correspondingly less substantial. Incidence and prevalence data regarding child sexual abuse also help specify those persons who are at risk, both as victims and abusers, and thus indicate where any prevention efforts should be directed. Such data may also dictate the methodology of preventive efforts. For example, if most child sexual abuse occurs in homes and is perpetrated by family members, caregivers, or acquaintances, as opposed to being perpetrated outside the home by strangers, preventive efforts should be allocated accordingly. Finally, accurate incidence and prevalence data are required to assess the efficacy of efforts to prevent child sexual abuse. If preventive efforts do not result in reduced incidence and prevalence over time, it might be argued that these efforts have largely failed and need to be replaced by potentially more effective strategies for prevention.

Incidence and prevalence studies have resulted in wildly divergent estimates of how many individuals have been sexually abused during any given period or over the course of their lifetimes. To begin to assess the true incidence and prevalence of child sexual abuse requires a critical analysis of the data that have fueled these estimates, the methods by which they were gathered, and other factors that lend to or detract from their credibility.

STUDIES OF INCIDENCE

Since the 1980s, the federal government has studied the incidence of child abuse, including child sexual abuse, as part of two initiatives, one conducted annually and the other periodically. Although these government-sponsored incidence studies are seriously limited in that they deal only with cases of child sexual abuse that have come to the attention of authorities, they represent the most extensive surveys ever conducted and are frequently cited.

National Child Abuse and Neglect Data System

The National Child Abuse and Neglect Data System (NCANDS) is a federally sponsored initiative that has collected and analyzed annual data on child abuse and neglect since 1988. After an allegation of abuse or neglect is received by a child protective service (CPS) agency, it is screened. Some of these referrals are screened out, whereas others are screened in. Screened in referrals are called reports, all of which receive responses. Responses include investigation of a child abuse or neglect complaint or an alternative, "which focuses primarily upon the needs of the family and may or may not include a determination regarding the alleged maltreatment."[3] NCANDS collects data on all cases in which child abuse or neglect complaints have received responses from a CPS agency in the United States (all 50 states, the District of Columbia, and the Commonwealth of Puerto Rico).

In its most recent report, NCANDS reported that during the period October 1, 2009 through September 30, 2010 (also known as federal fiscal year 2010), CPS agencies received an estimated 3.3 million referrals, involving the alleged abuse or neglect of approximately 5.9 million children. Based upon data from 45 states, NCANDS reported that 60.7 percent were screened in and 39.3 percent were screened out. Among the roughly 2 million reports that were screened in and received a CPS response, 90.3 percent received an investigation and 9.7 percent received an alternative response. Among the 1,793,724 reports that were investigated, more than 70 percent (1,262,118) were found to be unsubstantiated.

Looking at cases that received one or more responses (investigation or alternative) from a CPS agency, NCANDS used two separate sorting methods. They examined duplicate and unique counts: "The duplicate count of child victims counts a child each time he or she was found to be a victim. The unique count of child victims counts a child only once regardless of the number of times he or she was found to be a victim during the reporting year."[4] As NCANDS reported: "Examining the duplicate and unique counts of children who received a CPS response at the State level reveals the amount of duplication. Using a duplicate count, 3.6 million children received a CPS response at a rate of 47.7 children per 1,000 children in the population. Using a unique count, nearly 3 million children received a CPS response at a rate of 40.0 children per 1,000 children in the population."[5]

NCANDS reported that during federal fiscal year 2010, "the number of nationally estimated unique victims was 695,000."[6] Among that group, "Four-fifths (78.3%)...were neglected, 17.6 percent were physically abused, 9.2 percent were sexually abused, 8.1 percent were psychologically maltreated, and 2.4 percent

Table 2.1. NCANDS ESTIMATES OF CHILD SEXUAL ABUSE 2000–2010

Year	Estimated Number of Maltreated Children	Percentage of Maltreated Children Who Were Sexually Abused	Estimated Number of Children Sexually Abused
2010	695,000	9.2%	63,940
2009	702,000	9.5%	66,690
2008	772,000	9.1%	58,672
2007	794,000	7.6%	60,344
2006	905,000	8.8%	79,640
2005	899,000	9.3%	83,607
2004	872,000	9.7%	84,584
2003	906,000	9.9%	89,694
2002	896,000	9.9%	88,704
2001	903,000	9.6%	86,688
2000	879,000	10.1%	88,779

SOURCE OF DATA: National Child Abuse and Neglect Data System (2000–2010).[9]

were medically neglected. In addition, 10.3 percent of victims experienced such 'other' types of maltreatment as 'abandonment,' 'threats of harm to the child,' or 'congenital drug addiction.'"[7] Sexual abuse was defined as "a type of maltreatment that refers to the involvement of the child in sexual activity to provide sexual gratification or financial benefit to the perpetrator, including contacts for sexual purposes, molestation, statutory rape, prostitution, pornography, exposure, incest, or other sexually exploitative activities."[8]

Table 2.1 compares these data with those compiled by NCANDS for the previous 9 years. It is apparent based upon NCANDS data that since the beginning of the twenty-first century there has been a fairly steady annual decline in the number of child sexual abuse cases to which American CPS agencies have responded. NCANDS incidence data are clearly limited in that they include only cases of alleged child sexual abuse that have been brought to the attention of and responded to by CPS agencies.

Although there are no reliable data establishing what percentage of cases of child sexual abuse go unreported, both evidence and common sense suggest that not all such cases are reported to authorities and that, indeed, unreported cases may make up a substantial portion of all cases of child sexual abuse. Perhaps the most compelling evidence that many cases of child sexual abuse are never reported to authorities is the sometimes vast discrepancy between prevalence estimates (including those discussed below) and estimates based on incidence data from child welfare authorities, such as CPS agencies. One relatively recent Canadian prevalence study asked a large (*N* = 9,953) stratified sample of community respondents 15 and older whether they had been exposed to physical and sexual abuse when they were "growing up."[10] "Severe sexual abuse" involved experiencing any one or more of the following: having an adult threaten to have sex with the respondent, touch the sexual parts of the respondent's body, and try to have sex with or sexually attack the respondent.[11] In addition, "sexual abuse" was deemed to have occurred if an adult had exposed himself or herself to the respondent "more than once."[12] Only 8.7 percent of respondents deemed to have been "sexually abused" and 9.2 percent of those deemed to have been "severely sexually abused" reported any contacts with CPS.[13]

Although the definition of child sexual abuse used in this study, as in many other prevalence studies, is quite broad and encompasses noncontact abuse, the definition used by NCANDS is even broader, including exposure and statutory rape (i.e., sexual relations that might have been regarded as consensual, legal, and nonabusive but for the age of the parties). Also, whereas the Canadian study asked about experiences that occurred before the respondent turned 16 years of age, NCANDS data included acts committed against youngsters as old as 17. Thus, although the NCANDS data are certainly underinclusive (and thus underestimate the extent of child sexual abuse), they are also overinclusive to the extent that they deal with minors who may not always fit the common definition of "children" and because they include experiences that some may not regard as "child sexual abuse" (e.g., statutory rape).

Fourth National Incidence Study of Child Abuse and Neglect

Since 1979, the US government has periodically conducted what are perhaps the most extensive studies of the incidence of child abuse in the United States. These studies have collected incidence data on child abuse using a nationally representative sample of CPS agencies and other professionals. These include educational, medical, mental health, law enforcement, social service, and public health professionals. In the fourth and latest of these studies, reported in 2010, the Fourth National Incidence Study of Child Abuse and Neglect (NIS-4), researchers surveyed 122 counties with regard to incidents of child maltreatment (including sexual abuse) for two 3-month periods, either September 4 through December 3, 2005 or February 4 through May 3, 2006.[14]

NIS-4 examined information regarding three sets of children, all younger than 18, who were allegedly abused or neglected. This included reports of alleged child abuse made to CPS; alleged child abuse reports made to "other 'investigatory' agencies, such as law enforcement agencies, courts, or public health departments" but not to CPS; and alleged abuse recognized by "professionals in other major community institutions" but reported to neither CPS or other "investigatory" agencies.[15]

For purposes of statistical analysis, NIS-4 applied two definitional standards: the Harm Standard and the Endangerment Standard. The Harm Standard "is relatively stringent in that it generally requires that an act or omission result in demonstrable harm in order to be classified as abuse or neglect. It permits exceptions in only a few specific maltreatment categories, where the nature of the maltreatment itself is so egregious that one can infer that the child was harmed. The chief advantage of the Harm Standard is its strong objectivity. Its principal disadvantage is that it is so stringent that it provides a perspective that is too narrow for many purposes, excluding even many children whom CPS substantiates or indicates as abused or neglected."[16]

The Endangerment Standard "includes all children who meet the Harm Standard but adds others as well. The central feature of the Endangerment Standard is that it counts children who were not yet harmed by abuse or neglect if a sentinel thought that the maltreatment endangered the children or if a CPS investigation substantiated or indicated their maltreatment. In addition, the Endangerment Standard is slightly more lenient than the Harm Standard in allowing a broader array of perpetrators, including adult caretakers other than parents in certain maltreatment categories and teenage caretakers as perpetrators of sexual abuse."[17]

Sexual abuse, as defined in the NIS-4, "subsumes a range of behaviors, including [sexual] intrusion [with or without force], child's prostitution or involvement in pornography, genital molestation, exposure or voyeurism, providing sexually explicit materials, failure to supervise the child's voluntary sexual activities, attempted or threatened sexual abuse with physical contact, and unspecified sexual abuse."[18] With regard to intrusion and genital molestation, "the Harm Standard guidelines permit assuming that serious emotional harm occurred even if explicit symptoms are not yet observable."[19] However, "for the remaining abusive actions, the NIS definitions count children as sexually abused under the Harm Standard only if they experienced moderate injury or harm (physical, emotional, or behavioral) from that maltreatment."[20]

According to the federal report, issued in 2010, during the NIS-4 study period (2005–2006) an estimated 1,256,600 children were abused or neglected. While 44 percent (553,300) were estimated to be abused, 61 percent (771,700) were estimated to be neglected. It was further estimated that 135,300 or 1.8 children per 1,000 (24 percent of all the abused children) "experienced Harm Standard sexual abuse in the NIS–4 study year."[21] This number (135,300) "decreased from 217,700 in 1993 to 135,300 in 2005–2006 (a 38% decrease in the number of sexually abused children and a 44% decrease in the rate of sexual abuse)."[22] During the same 2005–2006 period, however, using the more inclusive Endangerment Standard, federal researchers found that an estimated 2,905,800 children had been abused or neglected and that 22 percent of them, 180,500 children, were sexually abused. This number (180,500) decreased from 300,200 in 1993, "reflecting a 40% decrease in number and a 47% decline in the rate."[23]

While "the principal purpose" of the NIS studies "was to go beyond cases of child maltreatment that come to the attention of the official child protective services system (CPS) and attempt to assess the overall national incidence of the problem of child maltreatment," their data also rely primarily upon reported cases of child sexual abuse.[24] As already noted, both evidence and common sense suggest that not all such cases are reported to authorities and that, indeed, unreported cases may make up a substantial portion of all cases of child sexual abuse. At the same time, the NIS data may be somewhat inflated because, like those from the NCANDS studies, they are capturing some cases that would not ordinarily be regarded as child sexual abuse. For example, these data also deal with "children" up to the age of 17 years. In many states, a 17 year old is regarded as capable of consenting to sexual contact; thus, consensual sexual activities that would be considered legal might still be considered child sexual abuse under the broad definitions used by NIS. Those definitions may also inflate the numbers of children who are sexually abused because they include cases in which adults have "fail[ed] to supervise the child's voluntary sexual activities."[25]

In all likelihood, however, any tendency toward inflation or exaggeration in the NIS data is mitigated by imposition of the Harm Standard. As noted earlier, NIS definitions count children as sexually abused under this standard only if they experienced sexual "intrusion" and/or "moderate injury or harm (physical, emotional, or behavioral) from that maltreatment."[26]

Developmental Victimization Survey

The Developmental Victimization Survey (DVS) was another government-sponsored effort to obtain 1-year incidence estimates of a "comprehensive range of childhood victimizations."[27] Unlike the annual NCANDS studies and the periodic NIS initiatives, the DVS looked directly to children and their parents as sources of information about the incidence of child abuse, including child sexual abuse. In the first wave of the DVS, conducted between December 2002 and February 2003, "a nationally representative sample of 2,030 children age 2 to 17 years living in the contiguous United States" was interviewed by telephone.[28] The sample was divided evenly by gender, 51 percent were age 2–9 years, and 49 percent were age 10–17 years.

DVS used an inventory of questions, known as the Juvenile Victimization Questionnaire (JVQ), which were designed to be "appropriate for self report by children as young as age 8."[29] A "caregiver version" of the JVQ was used with parents or other caregivers of younger children.[30] Included in the JVQ were the following questions regarding child sexual abuse:

19. In the past year, did a grown-up you know touch your private parts when you didn't want it or make you touch their private parts? Or did a grown-up you know force you to have sex?

20. In the past year, did a grown-up you did not know touch your private parts when you didn't want it, make you touch their private parts or force you to have sex?

21. Now think about kids your age, like from school, a boyfriend or girlfriend, or even a brother or sister. In the last year, did another child or teen make you do sexual things?

22. In the past year, did anyone try to force you to have sex, that is sexual intercourse of any kind, even if it didn't happen?

23. In the past year, did anyone make you look at their private parts by using force or surprise, or by "flashing" you?

24. In the past year, did anyone hurt your feelings by saying or writing something sexual about you or your body?

25. In the past year, did you do sexual things with anyone age 18 or older, even things you both wanted? (Only asked of children age 12 and older).[31]

The detailed results of the first wave of the DVS are depicted in Table 2.2. One child in twelve among this sample (82 per 1,000) reportedly experienced a sexual victimization (as defined above) in the year in question. This included 32 per 1,000 who reportedly experienced a sexual assault, and 22 per 1,000 who reportedly had been victims of rape, attempted rape, or verbal threats of rape without physical contact. Many of the perpetrators in reported flashing cases were peers of the victim, so the data were sifted "to separate out what is conventionally thought of as more stereotypical criminal flashing—that carried out by an adult."[32] Statutory sex offenses (voluntary sexual relationships with adults) "were limited here to relationships between adults (age 18 years and older) with youth age 15 or younger, in keeping with the statutes of many, but not all states."[33]

Other than being flashed by a peer, girls outnumbered boys as victims (by a wide margin) in every category of victimization examined in the DVS. Teenagers were victimized at more than three times the rate of children aged 6–12, and 10 times the rate of those 2–5 years old. Most of the perpetrators were juveniles and most were family members or acquaintances of the child victim. Adults were responsible for only 15 percent of sexual victimizations overall, 29 percent of sexual assaults, and 25 percent of attempted or completed rapes. Strangers accounted for only 7 percent of all sexual victimizations, 12 percent of sexual assaults, 11 percent of completed rapes, and 14 percent of attempted or completed rapes. Strangers constituted a high percentage (55 percent) of perpetrators in only one offense category: flashing by an adult.

Table 2.2. DEVELOPMENTAL VICTIMIZATION SURVEY (DVS), FIRST
WAVE RESULTS 2002–2003

Type of Reported Victimization	Number (Unweighted) in Sample of 2,030	Rate per 1,000
Any sexual victimization	154	82
Sexual assault	59	32
Rape completed	8	4
Rape attempted or completed	43	22
Sexual assault by known adult	11	6
Sexual assault by adult stranger	7	4
Sexual assault by peer	40	21
Flashing or sexual exposure by peer	57	26
Flashing or sexual exposure by adult	10	4
Sexual harassment	68	38
Statutory sexual offense	7	3

SOURCE OF DATA: Finkelhor et al. (2005).[34]

The second wave was conducted between December 2003 and May 2004. A total of 1,467 respondents (72.3 percent of the original sample) were reinterviewed using the JVQ. Additional data regarding the child, family, living circumstances, and other characteristics were also gathered. Data from the second wave indicated that the percentage of respondents acknowledging child sexual abuse (as defined in the JVQ) remained about the same as it had been a year earlier, at about 8 percent. However, a startling 39 percent of those who reported being sexually victimized during the year covered by the first wave also reported being revictimized sexually during the year covered by the second wave. Similarly high (in some cases, higher) rates of revictimization were also found for other types of child maltreatment. It also appeared that children who were victimized in one or more particular ways in Year 1 were at significant risk of being victimized in both the same and other ways in Year 2. As the authors of the second wave report noted, "virtually all types of victimization were associated with elevated vulnerabilities for all other kinds of subsequent victimizations."[35]

STUDIES OF PREVALENCE

The prevalence of child sexual abuse has been much more frequently studied than its incidence. Prevalence studies have generally been thought to be superior because, instead of relying upon limited official data (e.g., CPS reports or investigative findings), they are usually based upon self-reports from abuse victims. The usual paradigm for these studies involves surveys of adolescents or adults who are asked to respond to questions about their childhood experiences with child sexual abuse.

For example, in one of the earliest and most often cited prevalence studies of child sexual abuse, conducted in 1978, Diana Russell surveyed a probability sample of households in San Francisco. Russell began her study, which she says was the "first...probability survey to ascertain the prevalence of incestuous and extrafamilial child sexual abuse,"[36] with a sample of 2,000 addresses from which she "hoped to obtain 1,000 interviews with adult women."[37] Trained interviewers were sent to each address and ultimately 930 women were interviewed for an average of 1 hour and 20 minutes. Interviewers asked subjects whether, before they turned 14, they had (1) been upset by another exposing his or her genitals; (2) had anyone try or succeed in having any kind of sexual intercourse with them; (3) had anyone try or succeed in getting them to touch the other's genitals against her will; (4) had anyone try or succeed in touching her breast or genitals against her will; (5) had anyone feel, grab, or kiss her in a way she thought was sexually threatening; or (6) had any other "upsetting sexual experiences."[38] Subjects were also asked, without specifying any age limit, if they (7) ever experienced any unwanted sexual experience with a woman or girl; (8) ever had been the victim of rape or attempted rape; (9) ever had an unwanted sexual experience with an authority figure; (10) ever had any kind of sexual contact with a close relative; (11) ever had any kind of sexual contact with a more distant relative; (12) ever "narrowly missed" being sexually assaulted; (13) ever been in a situation of violence or threatened violence in which she was afraid of being sexually assaulted; and (14) ever had any other unwanted sexual experiences.[39] The results of Russell's survey are detailed in Table 2.3. According to Russell and Bolen, 16 percent of the sample reported "at least one experience of incestuous abuse before the age of 18 years" and "almost a third (31%)...reported at least one experience of sexual abuse by a nonrelative before the age of 18 years."[41]

Seven years after Russell's survey, a professional polling agency working with David Finkelhor and his colleagues conducted "the first national survey of adults concerning a history of childhood sexual abuse." A randomly selected group of 2,626 adults (1,145 men and 1,481 women) were interviewed by telephone for approximately half an hour. They were asked whether before the age of 18 they recalled having "any experience [they] would now consider sexual abuse: (1) 'like someone trying or succeeding in having any kind of sexual intercourse with you, anything like that'; (2) someone touching, grabbing, kissing or rubbing up against their bodies in a public or private place; or (3) someone taking nude photographs of them, exhibiting parts of his/her body to them, or performing some sex act in their presence; or (4) 'oral sex or sodomy—or anything like that.' "[43] According to

Table 2.3. RUSSELL'S SURVEY ON THE PREVALENCE OF CHILD SEXUAL ABUSE IN SAN FRANCISCO (1978)

Age	Incident	Percent Affirmative
<14	(1) Upset by exposure of other's genitals	27%
<14	(2) Successful or attempted intercourse	9%
<14	(3) Successful or attempted touching of other's genitals against her will	4.5%
<14	(4) Successful or attempted touching of her breast or genitals against her will	19%
<14	(5) Felt, grabbed, or kissed in a way she thought was sexually threatening	14%
<14	(6) Any other "upsetting sexual experiences"	9%
Ever	(7) Unwanted sexual experience with a woman or girl	8%
Ever	(8) Victim of rape or attempted rape	22%
Ever	(9) Unwanted sexual experience with an authority figure	31%
Ever	(10) Sexual contact with a close relative	15%
Ever	(11) Sexual contact with a more distant relative	10%
Ever	(12) "Narrowly missed" being sexually assaulted	12%
Ever	(13) Situation of violence or threatened violence with fear of being sexually assaulted	8%
Ever	(14) Any other unwanted sexual experiences	18%

SOURCE OF DATA: Russell and Bolen (2000).[40]

Finkelhor et al., child sexual abuse, so defined, was reported by 16 percent of the male respondents and 27 percent of the female respondents. The breakdown of their reports is shown in Table 2.4.

Before and since these studies were conducted, numerous other researchers attempted to determine the prevalence of child sexual abuse among various populations in the United States and around the world. Recently, Pereda and colleagues carried out a meta-analysis of this research, examining 65 such studies conducted between 1984 and 2007. These studies were conducted in 22 countries. Two of the studies were considered to be "outliers" because they resulted in prevalence rates of over 60 percent, one for child sexual abuse of men and the other for child sexual abuse of women. Pereda et al. report that "The analysis showed that 7.9% of men (7.4% without outliers) and 19.7% of women (19.2% without outliers) had suffered some form of sexual abuse prior to the age of eighteen."[45]

Pereda et al. acknowledged that both the criteria for defining "child" and those defining "sexual abuse" varied among these 65 studies. However, responding to the often expressed concerns that these criteria significantly influence prevalence data, they reported that "The present findings suggest that the definition of child sexual abuse (broad or narrow) used in a study does not influence the different prevalence rates found" and "[W]e found no significant differences in prevalence rates according to the cut-off age used to define childhood."[46] As they explained, "This finding could be due to the fact that the age at which most child sexual abuse takes place is generally...between 8 and 12. Therefore, sexual abuse would have already occurred regardless of the cut-off age used in the study provided that it was set at older than 12."[47] In only 3 of the 65 studies they examined was the cut-off age at or below 12 years.

Pereda et al. also responded to the concern that retrospective recall may not accurately measure the prevalence of child sexual abuse by arguing that this may result in an underestimate rather an overestimate of such prevalence: "Obviously, the use of self-report to assess personal experiences such as child sexual abuse, one that is

Table 2.4. AFFIRMATIVE RESPONSES TO QUESTIONS REGARDING CHILD SEXUAL ABUSE

Experience	Percent of Men	Percent of Women
(1) Sexual intercourse	9.5	13.6
(2) Touching, grabbing, kissing	4.5	19.6
(3) Exhibition, nude photos, sexual performance		
Photos	—	0.1
Exhibition	1.0	3.2
Sexual performance	0.3	0.3
Other	0.3	0.1
(4) Oral sex/sodomy	0.4	0.1

SOURCE OF DATA: Finkelhor et al. (1990).[44]

rarely spoken about, increases the risk of possible false negatives and this may be an obstacle in terms of obtaining an accurate measure. However, this risk is much greater than the relatively small number of victims who would make false allegations, and therefore, at all events, prevalence findings would be conservative."[48]

A STUDY OF INCIDENCE AND PREVALENCE

At least one major national study has examined both the incidence and prevalence of child sexual abuse among the same population. The federally sponsored National Survey of Children's Exposure to Violence (NatSCEV), conducted between January and May 2008, "measured the past-year and lifetime exposure to violence for children age 17 and younger across several major categories: conventional crime, child maltreatment, victimization by peers and siblings, sexual victimization, witnessing and indirect victimization (including exposure to community violence and family violence), school violence and threats, and Internet victimization."[49] Using a nationally representative sample of 4,549 children, researchers conducted telephone interviews of youths ages 10 to 17 and the adult caregivers of children 9 years and younger. Seven types of sexual victimization were studied, "including sexual contact or fondling by an adult the child knew, sexual contact or fondling by an adult stranger, sexual contact or fondling by another child or teenager, attempted or completed intercourse, exposure or 'flashing,' sexual harassment, and consensual sexual conduct with an adult."[50] Two types of "internet violence and victimization" were also measured: "internet threats or harassment and unwanted online sexual solicitation."[51]

Among the children surveyed directly or indirectly, 6.1 percent had been sexually victimized in the past year and 9.8 percent had been victimized over the course of their lifetimes. The results, broken down by category of child sexual abuse, are detailed in Table 2.5.

IS CHILD SEXUAL ABUSE INCREASING OR DECREASING?

As noted above, at least during the past decade or more, both the NCANDS and NIS estimates of the incidence of child sexual abuse in the United States have dropped substantially.

According to the latest NIS report, issued in 2010, reports of child sexual abuse in the United States that met the Harm Standard decreased in number by 38 percent and in rate by 44 percent between 1993 and 2005–2006, when NIS-4 was completed.[53] The same report indicated that reports of child sexual abuse meeting the less restrictive Endangerment Standard decreased in number by 40 percent and in rate by 47 percent over the same time period.[54] As depicted in Table 2.1, NCANDS estimates of the incidence of child sexual abuse went from 88,779 in 2000 to 63,940 in 2010, representing a 28 percent decrease in the first decade of this century. Examining

Table 2.5. NATIONAL SURVEY OF CHILDREN'S EXPOSURE TO VIOLENCE (NatSCEV)
RESULTS 2008

Type of Reported Victimization	Percentage Experiencing Within the Preceding Year	Percentage Experiencing in the Course of Lifetime
Any sexual victimization	6.1	9.8
Rape attempted or completed	1.1	2.4
Sexual assault by known adult	0.3	1.2
Sexual assault by adult stranger	0.3	0.5
Sexual assault by peer	1.3	2.7
Flashing or sexual exposure by peer	2.2	3.7
Flashing or sexual exposure by adult	0.4	0.6
Sexual harassment	2.6	4.2
Statutory sexual offense	0.1	0.4
Online sexual solicitation	1.5	2.4

SOURCE OF DATA: Finkelhor et al. (2009).[52]

NCANDS data from 1990 through 2008, Finkelhor, Jones, and Shattuck reported that "sexual abuse has declined 58 percent" over that period of time.[55]

Is child sexual abuse decreasing? There are at least two possible answers to this question. The first is that there has been an actual decrease in the incidence of child sexual abuse. The second is that there have simply been fewer reports and formal substantiations of child sexual abuse.

As Jones and Finkelhor have explained, "The most optimistic explanation is that incidents of child sexual abuse are decreasing."[56] Public awareness of the issue has increased; prevention programs have become more widespread; and more child sex abusers have been incarcerated, monitored in the community, or provided with some form of psychologically based treatment. As these authors observe, "All of these efforts could have the cumulative effect of reducing incidents of child sexual abuse."[57]

However, as Almeida et al. note, "In contrast, artifactual explanations for the decline include: (1) adoption of more conservative standards within CPS agencies (e.g., finding more allegations of CSA within divorce or custody disputes as questionable); (2) increased reluctance to report CSA on the part of victims or mandated reporters due to fear of backlash; (3) changes in data collection methods or definitions of CSA within CPS agencies; (4) exclusions by CPS workers of cases not involving primary caregivers; (5) increase in the caseload size due to resource restriction, which altered screening and investigative practices by CPS workers."[58] As Almeida et al. also point out, CPS workers in some states have dealt with increasing caseloads and declining resources by cutting back on the scope of their responsibilities, most notably in returning to their "traditional and statutory responsibilities" of "address[ing] threats to children's well-being at the hands of their caregivers."[59] As they further observe, this limitation is potentially significant because child sexual abuse is often inflicted by individuals who are neither relatives nor caregivers.

Whether the substantial decline in child sexual abuse reports and substantiations over the past couple of decades reflects a true decline in the incidence of this scourge or instead an artifact of changes in the way child protective systems deal with allegations of child sexual abuse remains an open question. Indeed, as Finkelhor and Jones conclude, "Although these are alternative explanations of the trend, they are not mutually exclusive. Any or all of these processes could be occurring simultaneously."[60]

Even assuming that there has been a true and substantial decline in the incidence of child sexual abuse since the early 1990s, the data from both incidence and prevalence studies, flawed and questionable though they may be, strongly suggest that large numbers of children are still being sexually victimized not only in the United States but around the world, and that major efforts to further reduce these numbers are well warranted. Moreover, for the most part, these data deal with child sexual abuse in only a small number of nations and, even in those nations, many if not most studies have not examined several forms of child sexual abuse that have come under scrutiny only relatively recently (e.g., child sex trafficking, child prostitution, online sexual solicitation of minors, child pornography, and sexual abuse committed by other children or adolescents).

Although better and more extensive data will be useful, if not fundamental, in developing broadly applicable and effective child sexual abuse prevention strategies, the available incidence and prevalence data, when taken as a whole, do seem sufficiently reliable to provide at least some rough answers to three important epidemiological questions: (1) Who are the victims of child sexual abuse? (2) Who are the perpetrators of child sexual abuse? (3) What are the medical, social, and psychological consequences of child sexual abuse?

WHO ARE THE VICTIMS AND PERPETRATORS OF CHILD SEXUAL ABUSE?

Most studies of the incidence and prevalence of child sexual abuse, whatever their methodology, share a number of basic and predictable common findings.

Gender

Not surprisingly, as documented in almost every published study, the overwhelming majority of child sex abuse victims are female and most child sex abusers are male.

Generally, the ratio of female to male victims of child sexual abuse has been estimated to be on the order of 3:1 but some studies report ratios as high as 5:1 and as low as less than 2:1. For example, in the NIS-4, "girls were sexually abused much more often than boys, under both the Harm Standard and the Endangerment Standard."[61] For girls the rate of sexual abuse was 3.8 per 1,000;

for boys it was 1 per 1,000. Looking solely at Harm Standard sexual abuse, the rate for girls was 3 per 1,000, five times greater than that for boys, 0.6 per 1,000.[62] In contrast, in the NatSCEV, girls were more likely than boys to be sexually abused but the ratios were less than 2:1. In the NatSCEV, 7.4 percent of girls and 4.8 percent of boys reported a sexual victimization within the past year; and 12.2 percent of girls and 7.5 percent of boys reported being sexually victimized during their lifetimes.[63]

In the Pereda et al. meta-analysis of 65 studies conducted in 22 countries between 1984 and 2007, the ratio of female to male victims was closer to 2.5:1.[64] It is noteworthy, however, that only 1 of these 65 studies, from South Africa, reported a higher number of male victims.[65] And even the authors of that study acknowledge that this finding may be peculiar to the geographic area studied and that their findings have not been replicated by any other published studies regarding child sexual abuse in South Africa.[66]

Some commentators have noted that sexual offenses committed against boys may be even more underreported than those committed against girls because of a perception that there is a greater stigma attached to being a male sex abuse victim. It has been suggested, for example, that some male victims may not report their sexual victimization because of "greater shame and the fear that they will be labeled as homosexual (if the aggressor was another man) or weak (if the aggressor was a woman), which may combine with the fact that they are more often accused of having provoked the abuse."[67] It has also been noted that the methodology used in some prevalence studies, particularly the definitions used or questions asked, may not sufficiently capture many instances of child sexual abuse because they are worded in ways that do not trigger a response from male victims.[68] It may well be that such terms as rape, sexual assault, and sexual intercourse are not viewed by some males as descriptive of the abuse they have suffered, even when they have been fondled or even sodomized orally or anally.

Perhaps the most important lesson to be taken from the consistent gender difference found in virtually every study of child sexual abuse is that, whereas girls are much more likely than boys to be sexually victimized, many boys are victimized, indeed probably many more than the data reflect.

There is near universal agreement that most child sex abusers are male. The proportions of male to female offenders vary among studies and estimates, but most agree that about 90 percent of child sex offenders are male. For example, in its National Incidence Studies of Missing, Abducted, Runaway, and Thrownaway Children, the US Office of Justice Programs estimated that in 1999, 95 percent of sexually abused children were victimized by a male.[69] In the NIS-4, "The prevalence of male perpetrators was strongest in the category of sexual abuse, where 87% of children were abused by a male compared to only 11% by a female."[70]

These numbers, however, may also be somewhat inaccurate because there may be a kind of reverse gender bias when it comes to reporting child sex offenses committed by women or girls. Some child and adolescent victims of child sexual abuse (particularly, but not necessarily, boys) may be disinclined or at least less inclined to see themselves as victims when the perpetrator is a female, whether peer or adult. Also, as just noted, it has been suggested that some males who have been sexually abused by females may not report their victimization because of fear of being labeled "weak" or being accused of "having provoked the abuse."[71]

Age

The relationship of children's ages to the likelihood that they will be sexually abused is unclear. As one recent summary describes it, "There are discrepancies about the risk factor of age. Some studies find no difference among age groups; others find that older children are more at-risk. There are no studies that suggest that very young children are most at risk."[72] Another summary concluded in 2003, "Risk for [child sexual abuse] rises with age. Data…indicate that approximately 10% of victims are between ages 0 and 3 years. Between ages 4 and 7 years, the percentage almost triples (28.4%)."[73] "Ages 8–11 years account for a quarter (25.5%) of cases, with children 12 years and older accounting for the remaining third (35.9%) of cases."[74]

These conclusions are reasonably well substantiated by the results of the 2008 NatSCEV. Table 2.6 breaks the incidence and prevalence reports of respondents down by age. As the table shows, child sexual victimization in general and most specific types of child sexual abuse were found to increase with age.

It is also worth noting that the above-described apparent declines in the incidence of child sexual abuse were "not uniform across age groups."[76] As the NIS-4 report indicates: "It is most evident among children ages 3 to 11 years and 15 to 17 years (where rates decreased by 42% to 68%). Children in puberty (12 to 14 years old) experienced only a small decline in their risk of Harm Standard sexual abuse (9%). [A]mong children ages 0 to 2, the incidence of Harm standard sexual abuse increased by 33%. However, this last result is less reliable, since fewer than 100 sample children support the component estimated rates."[77]

Most perpetrators of child sexual abuse are adults but a substantial minority of child sex offenses is committed by juveniles, most of whom are boys. In a recent "bulletin," the US Office of Justice Programs examined the FBI's National Incidence-Based Reporting System (NIBRS) data from 2004 to examine "the characteristics of the juvenile sex offender population coming to the attention of law enforcement."[78] NIBRS is a federal crime reporting system that is replacing the well-known FBI Uniform Crime Reports. The Uniform Crime Report "monitors only a limited number of index crimes and gathers few details on each crime event (except in the case of homicide), [but] NIBRS collects a wide range of information on victims, offenders, and circumstances for a greater variety of offenses."[80]

Based upon 2004 NIBRS data, researchers concluded that perpetrators younger than the age of 18 account for 35.6 percent of "those known to police to have committed sex offenses against minors."[81] They further estimated that: "Known juvenile offenders who commit sex offenses against minors span a variety of ages. Five percent are younger than 9 years, and 16 percent are younger than 12 years.

Table 2.6. NATIONAL SURVEY OF CHILDREN'S EXPOSURE TO VIOLENCE (NatSCEV) RESULTS 2008 BY AGE GROUPS

Type of Reported Victimization	Percentage Experiencing Within the Preceding Year By Age Group					Percentage Experiencing in the Course of Lifetime By Age Group			
	(0–1)	(2–5)	(6–9)	(10–13)	(14–17)	(2–5)	(6–9)	(10–13)	(14–17)
Any sexual victimization	0.0	0.9	2.0	7.7	16.3	1.5	5.0	9.42	7.8
Rape attempted or completed	0.0	0.1	0.1	1.3	3.8	0.3	0.8	1.6	8.3
Sexual assault by known adult	0.0	0.2	0.1	0.0	0.9	0.6	0.7	0.2	3.9
Sexual assault by adult stranger	0.0	0.2	0.1	0.2	0.7	0.3	0.1	0.2	1.8
Sexual assault by peer	0.0	0.2	0.6	0.9	4.0	0.3	2.6	1.4	7.7
Flashing or sexual exposure by peer	0.0	0.5	1.0	1.4	6.9	0.8	1.7	2.0	11.9
Flashing or sexual exposure by adult	0.0	0.2	0.3	0.3	1.1	0.2	0.5	0.3	1.9
Sexual harassment	0.0	0.0	0.2	5.6	5.6	0.0	0.4	6.5	11.6
Statutory sexual offense	0.0	0.0	0.0	0.0	0.6	0.0	0.0	0.0	1.9
Online sexual solicitation	0.0	0.0	0.0	1.7	4.8	0.0	0.0	2.5	8.1

SOURCE OF DATA: Finkelhor et al. (2009).[75]

The rate rises sharply around age 12 and plateaus after age 14. As a proportion of the total, 38 percent are between ages 12 and 14, and 46 percent are between ages 15 and 17. The vast majority (93 percent) are male."[81]

Victim-Offender Relationship

In most cases of child sexual abuse, the perpetrator is known to the victim. The clearest evidence of this understanding of the relationship between victim and perpetrator in child sexual abuse cases can be seen in the 2004 NCANDS report on child maltreatment. Although generally these annual reports do not provide such detail, the 2004 report breaks down the data on child sexual abuse and details the relationship of the perpetrator to the victim. These data, which are drawn from 37 states, are summarized in Table 2.7.

As the table shows, more than half (56.8 percent) of the perpetrators were parents (or other relatives). When parents and relatives are combined with other perpetrators who were probably known to the child victim before the abuse (12.97 percent), it appears that nearly 70 percent of perpetrators had some kind of relationship to the child at the time of the abuse. NCANDS data include only cases of alleged child sexual abuse that have been brought to the attention of, and responded to, by child protective agencies. Thus, these data are undoubtedly missing many cases of actual child sexual abuse and there is no way of knowing to what extent that skews the percentages of cases committed by various categories of perpetrators. Indeed, given that CPS agencies most often concentrate on cases of intrafamilial child abuse, it is reasonable to believe that the percentage of child sexual abuse cases represented in these data as having been perpetrated by parents or other relatives may be somewhat exaggerated.

Earlier, in 2000, federal researchers used data from the NIBRS to examine, *inter alia*, the relationship of child sexual abuse victims to their abusers in cases reported to law enforcement.[83] They reported that 27 percent of all perpetrators were related to their victims and that abusers of young victims were more likely to be family members. For example, 49 percent of those who victimized children younger than age 6 years were family members, compared with 42 percent of those who sexually abused youngsters 6–11, and 24 percent who abused juveniles ages 12–17. Sixty percent of all perpetrators were classified by law enforcement as acquaintances of the victim and 14 percent were classified as strangers. The younger the victims, the less likely it was that the perpetrator would be a stranger: strangers accounted for 3 percent of offenses against children younger than age 6 years, 5 percent of those against children ages 6–12, and 10 percent of those against juveniles ages 10–17. Generally, victim-offender relationships showed little difference by gender of the victim. However, for victims younger than 12, family members were the perpetrators in 40 percent of cases involving male victims but 47 percent of cases involving female victims.

THE EFFECTS OF CHILD SEXUAL ABUSE AND EXPLOITATION

As noted in Chapter 1, it was not until the late twentieth century that experts began to realize the extent to which children were subjected to sexual contact by adults. Moreover, although numerous studies conducted in the 1940s, 1950s, 1960s, and 1970s reported finding that in some cases these "contacts led to sexual difficulties, depression, and other serious long-term effects,"[84] the dominant view among experts appeared to be that these experiences, although perhaps morally reprehensible, were unlikely to result in much if any lasting harm to children.

The Gagnon Study (1966)

For example, in 1965, the noted sexologist John Gagnon reported on a study of 333 adult women who had been victims of child sexual abuse as children. Gagnon

Table 2.7. RELATIONSHIP OF CHILD SEXUAL ABUSE PERPETRATOR TO
VICTIM: NCANDS REPORT FOR 2004

Relationship	Number of Cases	Percent of Cases
Parent	13,957	29.1
Other relative	13,271	27.7
Foster parent	191	0.4
Residential facility staff	131	0.3
Child daycare provider	1,115	2.3
Unmarried partner of parent	3,150	6.6
Legal guardian	34	0.07
Other professionals	26	40.6
Friends or neighbors	1,302	2.7
Other (unspecified)	11,022	23.0
Unknown or missing	3,459	7.2

SOURCE OF DATA: National Child Abuse and Neglect Data System (2004).[82]

remarked that one of the major findings of the study was "the small number of negative outcomes that seem to result from these early intrusions into the 'normal' development of childhood sexuality."[85] Although he observed that "It might be expected that involving children in sexuality at these ages, especially with an adult partner, might distort the social as well as the sexual adjustment of the child," he reported that "[o]f the 333 persons with child-adult contacts, only 5 percent could be considered to have had adult lives that had been severely damaged for whatever reason."[86] Gagnon also noted that "Of these 18 adults only three in the interview related their current condition to the early sexual experience."[87] Finally, he reported that, regardless of the nature of the sexual abuse, roughly 75 percent of victims had "no apparent adult maladjustments, while 9 to 12 percent had only minor complaints, none of which incapacitated them from playing an adequate social and occupational role in the community. About 4 to 7 per cent of each of the groups showed major psychological or other disturbance related either to a deviant style of life or to some psychological problem."[88]

Cataloguing the Symptoms

More than a decade later, C. Henry Kempe, the renowned physician who coined the term "battered child syndrome," concluded that "Most sexual molestation appears to do little harm to normal children."[89] By then, however, influenced to a large degree by complaints from feminists and child protection advocates, a new wave of research had begun to catalog the various psychological, psychiatric, and social problems reported by child sexual abuse victims, their parents, and their therapists. Such difficulties ranged from "anxiety, feelings of isolation and stigmatization, poor self-esteem, tendency toward revictimization, [and] difficulty in trusting others" to "mood disorders to relationship and sexual problems, to eating disorders, self-mutilation, and alcohol and drug abuse, to psychosis."[90] As psychologist Susan Clancy has observed, "These long lists of symptoms were used to justify more professional interest, research funding, and insurance coverage for treatment. In keeping with the new perspective, these studies implied that sexual abuse directly caused these problems, but, as psychologists themselves often noted, this could not yet be proven."[91]

A Critical Review of the Early Literature

In 1986, psychologist Angela Browne and sociologist David Finkelhor published a highly regarded review of literature to date dealing with the impact of child sexual abuse. Their review began by noting that "[a]lthough clinical literature suggests that sexual abuse during childhood plays a role in the development of other problems ranging from anorexia nervosa to prostitution, empirical evidence about its actual effects is sparse."[92] They then examined the existing research regarding the initial effects (those occurring within 2 years of the abuse) and long-term effects of child sexual abuse victimization and concluded that it was not clear that these findings were representative of child sexual abuse victims generally or even those seen for clinical treatment or evaluation. After further cataloging the effects of child sexual abuse reported among adults in the literature (e.g., depression, anxiety, low self-esteem, substance abuse, relationship difficulties, and sexual dysfunction), Browne and Finkelhor observed, *inter alia*, that it appeared that child sexual abuse by fathers and stepfathers had a more negative impact than that perpetrated by others and that abuse that involved genital contact and/or force appeared to have more serious consequences. Finally, Browne and Finkelhor cautioned that research in this area was in its "infancy" and suffered from sample, design, and measurement problems that could invalidate their findings.[93]

The Next Decade (1987–1997)

In the decade or so after Browne and Finkelhor's seminal review, it appears that many authorities took for granted that child sexual abuse was causally related to multiple negative consequences for the victims of such abuse. Some research, however, was focused directly on that question and appeared to document associations between child sexual abuse victimization and subsequent negative life experiences, such as further sexual victimization[94]; subsequent physical and sexual victimization[95]; later domestic violence victimization[96]; self-harm and self-abuse[97]; shorter relationships and a higher number of sexual partners[98]; adult sexual risk behaviors[99]; suicide attempts and ideation[100]; and psychological problems including but not limited to anxiety, depression, substance abuse, antisocial behavior, sexual dysfunction, poor self-esteem, and eating disorders.[101]

Most of these studies were limited by their retrospective nature and failure to take into account the confounding effects of dysfunctional family functioning, considered by many to be associated with child sexual abuse.[102] Some authorities suggested that because of such confounding effects there was little if any evidence that child sexual abuse had any unique value as a predictor of the sorts of negative "consequences" attributed to it.[103] However, a number of these same studies did use multivariate statistical methods to sort out the influence of child sexual abuse and that of family and social background on later functioning of victims. These studies demonstrated that the strength of the association between child sexual abuse and adult problems was reduced but not eliminated when family and other social variables were taken into account.[104]

Additionally, some studies during this era tried to link specific aspects of child sexual abuse to more negative outcomes. For example, numerous studies found that adult victims of child sexual abuse were more likely to experience and/or report mental health problems if the abuse they suffered as children included penetration, injury, or physical violence.[105] Adult survivors of child sexual abuse were also found to suffer more adverse mental health effects when (1) they were abused at an early age,[106] (2) their abusers were biologically related to them,[107] (3) they had been sexually abused by more than one abuser,[108] (4) they had been more frequently abused,[109] and (5) the child sexual abuse they suffered occurred over a longer period of time.[110] At least one study also found that women in the community aged 18–30 who had been sexually abused on more than one occasion were significantly more likely than other women to report adult sexual dysfunction.[111]

The Rind Meta-Analyses

In 1998, psychologist Bruce Rind and his colleague reported the results of a meta-analysis of studies of child sexual abuse outcomes. Rind et al. acknowledged that the data from the 1980s and 1990s were consistent with what they called the "pathogenic view" of child sexual abuse: studies based mainly on clinical and legal samples that "generally concluded that CSA causes such diverse problems as depression, anxiety, low self-esteem, sexual dysfunction, dissociation, suicidal ideation, and PTSD, and that these effects are pervasive in the general population of persons who have experienced CSA."[112] However, Rind et al. further noted that these conclusions and the methods used to reach them were suspect for two reasons: because child sexual abuse had been consistently found to be confounded with other forms of child abuse and neglect, it could not be assumed that there was a causal relationship between child sexual abuse and the outcomes attributed to it; and the largely clinical and legal samples from which these conclusions were drawn might not generalize to the general population of child sexual abuse victims and may overestimate negative effects.[113]

"To address these shortcomings," Rind and his colleagues conducted meta-analyses of studies that focused on nonclinical and nonlegal samples of individuals reported to have been the victims of child sexual abuse to test four hypotheses: "(a) CSA causes harm; (b) this harm is pervasive in the population of persons with a history of CSA; (c) this harm is likely to be intense; and (d) CSA is equivalent for boys and girls in terms of its widespread and intensely negative effects."[114]

Rind I: The National Probability Samples

In the first of these meta-analyses, Rind et al. included only studies based on national probability samples. In sum, they found that:

> Prevalence rates for CSA for males and females were 11 percent and 19 percent, respectively. Although statistically significant, the association between CSA and adjustment was small: effect size r =.07 for males and r =. 10 for females. Females reported more negative effects and reactions than males did. Although 68 percent of females reported some sort of negative effect at some point in their lives since the CSA occurred, only 42 percent of males did. This difference was statistically significant and of medium-small magnitude, r = .23...Results contradicted or failed to support the four hypotheses.[115]

Rind II: The College Samples

In the second meta-analysis, Rind et al. focused on studies based on college student samples, which provided greater numbers of respondents, especially males. In sum, they reported that:

> Commonly expressed opinions, both lay and professional, have implied that CSA possesses four basic properties: causality (it causes harm), pervasiveness (most SA persons are affected), intensity (harm is typically severe), and gender equivalence (boys and girls are affected equally)...
>
> Review of the college samples revealed that 14% of college men and 27% of college women reported events classifiable as CSA, according to the various definitions used. Results from the college data do not support the commonly assumed view that CSA possesses the four basic properties outlined previously.
>
> CSA was associated with poorer psychological adjustment across the college samples, but the magnitude of this association (i.e., its intensity) was small, with CSA explaining less than 1% of the adjustment variance...Results also revealed that lasting negative effects of CSA were not pervasive among SA students, and that CSA was not an equivalent experience for men and women. These results imply that, in the college population, CSA does not produce pervasive and intensely negative effects regardless of gender...[116]

In explaining the implications of this second meta-analysis, Rind et al. added that:

> [T]he findings of the current review should not be construed to imply that CSA never causes intense harm for men or women—clinical research has well documented that in specific cases it can. What the findings do imply is that the negative potential of CSA for most individuals who have experienced it has been overstated.[117]

The Rind Backlash: "Dr. Laura," Congress, and the American Psychological Association

One might think that results such as those reported by Rind et al. would have been welcomed by anyone with a serious interest in the effects of child sexual abuse. In essence, these meta-analyses showed that being the victim of child sexual abuse did not necessarily result in serious or lasting psychological harm. That would seem to be good news, especially for the many people who have been sexually victimized as children.

Unfortunately, however, many commentators chose to see the glass as half-empty rather than half-full, and shoot the messengers, because they did not like—or perhaps understand—the message. Laura Schlesinger, a nationally syndicated radio talk show host with a doctorate in physiology, denounced the second of these meta-analyses, which was published in the *Psychological Bulletin*, one of psychology's most prestigious and competitive peer-reviewed journals. Schlesinger noted that she was a "real scientist,"[118] apparently as compared with Rind and his colleagues, and warned that "the public must be extremely cautious in accepting and relying on papers that appear to counter common sense, fundamentals of morality, and long-term understanding of what is socially desirable and basically healthy for any individual."[119] She further claimed that meta-analysis is not an acceptable scientific technique, that psychology is not a science, and that the findings of Rind et al. were "junk science at its worst."[119] She added that "the point of the article is to allow men to rape male children" and that the meta-analysis was "a not-so-veiled attempt to 'normalize' pedophilia."[120]

Schlesinger's condemnation of the study led others to pile on. One major conservative fund-raising group denounced the meta-analysis as giving "pedophiles the green flag."[121] Religious and lay magazines wrote of the study under headlines that included "Tossing the Last Taboo: Psychologists Praise Pedophilia" and "Tossing the Last Taboo: Psychologists Hail the Benefits of Pederasty."[122] Meanwhile, the only source that appeared pleased with the study was the North American Man Boy Love Association, a group that openly promotes pedophilia. North American Man Boy Love Association used its website to tout the meta-analysis.[123]

Before long the growing controversy over the work of Rind et al. caught the attention of Congress. One House member reviled the meta-analysis as "the Emancipation Proclamation of pedophiles," another professed that he was "appalled and outraged that an influential American psychological association would publish a study that advocates normalizing pedophilia," and a third stated that "the authors write that pedophilia is fine...as long as it is enjoyed."[124]

The American Psychological Association (APA), in whose journal the second Rind et al. meta-analysis was published, responded initially by defending the study as well conducted and vetted by rigorous peer review. As the political criticisms mounted, however, the Association backed off its defense of the study. APA's chief executive officer, psychologist Raymond Fowler, told Congress that the Rind et al. article "included opinions of the authors that are inconsistent with APA's stated and deeply held positions," "sexual activity between children and adults should never be considered or labeled harmless," and "it is the position of the Association that children cannot consent to sexual activities with adults."[125] The CEO added that the authors' conclusions "should have caused us to evaluate the article based on its potential for misinforming the public policy process. This is something we failed to do, but will do in the future."[126] He also promised to institute a process in which editors of APA journals would be required to "consider the social policy implications of articles on controversial topics."[127] Finally, and most significantly, Fowler said that the Association would seek to have the article (which had long since been published by APA) independently reviewed by a panel of the American Association for the Advancement of Science (AAAS).

Apparently APA's concessions were not sufficient to satisfy Congress. On July 12, 1999, the House of Representatives voted (355–0 with 13 abstentions) to pass a resolution in which "Congress...condemn[ed] and denounce[d] all suggestions in the article...that indicate that sexual relationships between adults and 'willing' children are less harmful than believed and might be positive for 'willing children'...and any suggestion that sexual relations between children and adults—regardless of the child's frame of mind—are anything but abusive [and] destructive..."[128] The Senate then unanimously passed the resolution.

One wonders what APA would have done had an independent review of the Rind et al. study found it somehow flawed. Fortunately for the Association, it never came to that. The AAAS Committee on Scientific Freedom, which had been asked to review the article, declined to do so, stating that they saw "no reason to second-guess the process of peer review used by the APA journal in its decision to publish," saw "no clear evidence of improper application of methodology or other questionable practices on the part of the article's authors" and "found it deeply disconcerting that so many of the comments made by those in the political arena and in the media indicate a lack of understanding of the analysis presented by the authors or misrepresented the article's findings."[129]

The APA's Council of Representatives then responded with its own resolution that psychologists "must be free to pursue their scientific investigations within the constraints of the ethical principles, scientific principles, and guidelines of the discipline"; that editors "must be free to publish...science in their journals even when findings are surprising, disappointing, or controversial"; that APA "will not condone any attempt to censor the reporting or discussion of science within its journals" and will not "retract a published paper [or] censure authors or editors for ethical scientific activities that yield potentially controversial findings."[130]

Beyond the Rind Meta-Analyses

The controversy over the effects of child sexual abuse that came to a head in the controversy over the meta-analyses of Rind and his colleagues did not end with the findings of the AAAS or the belated defense of academic freedom offered by the APA. Indeed, the controversy continues to this day. Much of this continued controversy, however, appears semantic, political, and probably altogether need-less. To begin with, better designed studies that have been published since the Rind controversy have, for the most part, continued to demonstrate that many victims of child sexual abuse are seriously harmed physically and psychologically. Although there continues to be no "smoking gun" evidence as to causation, and probably never will be, no serious observers take the position that child sexual abuse does not hold the potential for serious injury. Psychologist Susan Clancy, perhaps the most eloquent and persistent critic of the "trauma" theory of child sexual abuse, argues persuasively in her book, *The Trauma Myth: The Truth About The Sexual Abuse of Children and Its Aftermath*, that "sexual abuse is not invari-ably a traumatic experience for the victim"[131] However, even Clancy states flatly that the idea that "'no trauma' at the time of the abuse means 'no harm' for the victim later on in life…is a gross misconception."[132] As she adds, "Sexual abuse may not be a horror show for most victims when it happens, but it certainly can become so in later life. [V]ictims eventually understand the nature of what hap-pened to them and reconceptualize their previously ambiguous experiences for what they were—clearly sexual in nature."[133]

The bottom line is that, however controversial this subject remains and what-ever valid criticisms may continue to be leveled at the research done in this area to date, there can be no doubt that at least some victims of child sexual abuse are immediately injured by this abuse and that many others are placed at some degree of risk for future harm. There can also be no doubt that, regardless of debates over the reliability, validity, and meaning of incidence and prevalence data, too many children are being sexually victimized in the United States and elsewhere today. Instead of arguing over the finer details of these continuing and perhaps unresolv-able controversies, those interested in the health, welfare, and well-being of chil-dren would do better to invest their considerable energy and advocacy in helping to prevent child sexual abuse before it occurs rather than pointlessly debating what might or might not happen to victims when it does.

Prevention Strategies Aimed at Parents, Children, and the Community

As was observed in Chapter Two, child sexual abuse committed by strangers is relatively rare, at least as compared with that committed by persons known to victims. According to data detailed there, about 30 percent of sexually abused children are victimized by people they do not know. Furthermore, strangers tend to victimize older children. For example, according to data from the National Incident-Based Reporting System, strangers accounted for 3 percent of offenses against children younger than age 6 years, 5 percent of those against children aged 6–12 years, and 10 percent of those against juveniles 10–17 years of age.

Even though the chances are better than two-to-one that if a child is sexually abused the perpetrator will be someone known to him or her, the bulk of efforts to prevent child sexual abuse are aimed at what has been called "stranger danger." There are many differences in the nature and consequences of child sexual abuse that depend on whether the abuse is perpetrated by a stranger or a person known to the child. There are also often differences between prevention strategies proposed and/or implemented to protect children from sexual abuse by strangers and those aimed at preventing such abuse by family members and acquaintances. Overall, however, prevention techniques have much in common whether they are directed at stranger or family/acquaintance abuse.

This chapter—while noting the differences between efforts to prevent stranger abuse and those aimed at family/acquaintance abuse—deals more generally with strategies to prevent child sexual abuse in the home and the community. Because they are covered at length in later separate chapters, this chapter does not deal with several particular contexts in which child sexual abuse is common: institutions, including schools, daycare centers, juvenile correctional facilities, and voluntary youth-serving organizations; child prostitution and sex trafficking; online modalities that enable the sexual solicitation of children; and the creation, distribution, and possession of child pornography. Although there is often overlap among the categories to be examined here, this chapter deals separately with child sexual abuse prevention strategies aimed at parents, children, and the community. The chapter that follows examines child sexual abuse prevention strategies aimed at perpetrators and potential perpetrators.

PREVENTION STRATEGIES AIMED AT PARENTS

Parents are children's primary guardians and have the greatest responsibility for protecting them from child sexual abuse. For parents, as is the case with any constituency charged with protecting others, forewarned is forearmed. To effectively protect their children from sexual abuse, parents need, first and foremost, to know the nature and extent of the risk of such abuse. Thus, a major part of any strategy to prevent child sexual abuse must include effectively and accurately communicating the nature and extent of the risk in this context.

Such communication to parents is critical for a number of reasons. First, because it is so heavily emphasized in the media, there is the risk that parents may be left with a grossly exaggerated view of the risk of "stranger danger"; they may fail to adequately understand and prepare for the much greater risk of child sexual abuse in other venues, such as the home, schools, and youth-serving organizations where children spend most of their time. Parents may be overly concerned or worried about "stranger danger" and fail to see the much more common and often more serious threat of abuse posed by people known to would-be victims.

Also, parents and other members of the public who are ill-informed about the relative danger of child sexual abuse by strangers may unknowingly lend support to and/or rely too heavily upon legal initiatives that are clearly aimed at "stranger danger" but are ineffective or countereffective (e.g., as detailed later in this chapter, Megan's laws and related restrictions on the living arrangements and movements of convicted sex abusers). Additionally, some children and parents who are frequently confronted with exaggerated accounts of the risk of "stranger danger" may feel overwhelmed and either unnecessarily limit their (or their children's) lifestyles or adopt the attitude that this danger is so great and so pervasive that nothing can be done to effectively prevent victimization.

As Chapter Two established, realistic and reliable data on the nature and extent of "stranger danger" are available. The problem is how to get those data to parents, children, and others charged with the care of children. Given that most of these data are either gathered by the government or by studies funded by the government and are already available in free government publications, one might conclude that there is little left for government to do in this context. Although it is true that these data are "there for the taking," especially for anyone with access to the Internet, many people have no idea that these data are available, much less so easily accessible. Moreover, these data are generally not available in a summary or digest form that members of the public (or, for that matter, the media) can easily comprehend. To see the truth of that assertion, one need only look at Chapter Two of this volume, in which a conscientious effort was made by one skilled in statistical analysis and effective writing to present such data in a readily understandable fashion. The government needs to "translate" these data into public service messages or other popular media intelligible to the masses and to do so with a reliability and frequency that stand a chance of overcoming the powerful and often exaggerating messages on this topic emanating from the news and entertainment media and even some advocacy groups.

There is at least some evidence that educational efforts to date have had a positive effect in alerting parents and others to the extent and nature of "stranger danger." For example, a survey of 5,241 respondents, reported in 2010, found that 95 percent understood that "most sexually abused children are abused by someone they know" and 64 percent understood that "many sexually abused children are abused by other children or adolescents."[1] At the same time, however, other data indicate that "[t]he stereotype of the stranger sexual perpetrator still persists among some parents and guardians, indicative of a knowledge gap that [child sexual abuse] prevention efforts should address."[2]

Of course, knowledge of the extent of the threat of sexual abuse posed to children by strangers is only the beginning of educational efforts aimed at preventing such abuse. Among the goals of preventive programs designed to educate parents about child sexual abuse is making sure they know, among other things, that

1. Few child sexual abusers are pedophiles, previous sex offenders, or people whose appearance or behavior somehow emits clues that they may sexually offend against children.
2. Although the risk of "stranger danger" may be relatively small, it is ubiquitous and parents must exert age-appropriate vigilance whenever their children are in vulnerable situations (e.g., when children are without adult supervision in situations where contact with strangers is likely).
3. Child sexual abuse is not limited to instances of oral, anal, and vaginal intercourse, digital penetration, or penetration with objects, but includes a host of other acts, such as inappropriate touching of the child's genitals, buttocks, or breasts; requiring the child to touch those areas of the perpetrator; mutual masturbation; exposure of the child to the perpetrator's genitals or other private body parts; and exposure of the child to graphic sexual images or pornography.
4. Children are most vulnerable to sexual abuse when they are alone with an adult or older child; thus, parents need to minimize and, to the extent possible, monitor such occasions, such as by paying unexpected visits, making sure that these occasions are open to observation by others, planning what will go on during these occasions, talking to their children about what went on, and in some instances "find[ing] a way to tell the adults who care for [their] children that [they] and the child are educated about child sexual abuse."[3]

5. Grooming is often an essential part of the child sexual abuse process and is frequently accomplished by "abusers [who] become friendly with potential victims and their families, enjoying family activities, earning trust, and gaining time alone with children."[4]
6. Children need to be taught age-appropriate information about the wrongfulness of others touching their bodies and the possibility of abuse not only from strangers but also from adult friends, other children, and family members.
7. Parent-child communication is essential and children need to be taught "words that can help them discuss sex comfortably." [5]
8. Although there are no sure-fire physical or behavioral indicators that a child has been sexually abused, and many children show no overt evidence of such abuse, there are sometimes certain red flags, such as redness, swelling, or rashes in the genital area; sudden somatic complaints, such as chronic headaches or stomachaches; age-inappropriate sexual behavior and/or language; and marked behavioral swings, such as withdrawal or depression.[6]
9. When a child discloses sexual abuse, parents should not panic, but offer belief, support, reassurance, and appreciation; encourage talking but avoid asking leading questions; assure the child that he or she will be protected; and seek help from a professional trained to interview children about sexual abuse.

Parents also need to be made aware that one of the best antidotes to child sexual abuse is effective parenting. Common sense suggests that children are less likely to be sexually victimized if their parents spend large amounts of time with them, monitor their whereabouts and relationships, communicate openly and honestly with them, and provide them with appropriate nurturance and guidance. This is not to say that parents are to blame when their children are sexually abused by strangers, but rather that parents can be taught fairly straightforward parenting skills that may reduce, at least to some extent, the likelihood that their children will be sexually abused. Many schools, private agencies, and government programs already offer parent training, but increasing the availability of such training would likely have some preventive effect when it comes to the sexual abuse of children.

Unfortunately, although common sense may suggest that parent education will help prevent child sexual abuse, research to date does not support that hypothesis. In 2011, under a grant from the US Centers for Disease Control and Prevention, the Pennsylvania Coalition Against Rape and the National Sexual Violence Resource Center reviewed English language research on programs from 1987–2010 "intended to educate parents about primary, secondary, and tertiary [child sexual abuse (CSA)] prevention." These investigators concluded that:

[We] could not conclusively indicate that CSA prevention efforts increase parents' knowledge of CSA, given that current research on the topic is

insufficient or contradictory. Some evidence indicates that CSA prevention efforts motivate many parents to discuss CSA with their children, but
additional research is needed to replicate this finding. Finally, insufficient
research is available to indicate whether CSA prevention efforts geared
toward parents and caregivers result in lower rates of child sexual victimization. Future studies on all CSA prevention efforts targeting parents and
caregivers is needed to address these gaps in the research literature.[7]

These investigators further concluded that

Findings are mixed regarding the effectiveness of education programs in
motivating parents to engage in secondary prevention of CSA. Some programs demonstrated no impact on parents' awareness of abuse indicators,
nor did participants in those programs understand appropriate responses to
abuse disclosures.[8]

It is not clear why parent education approaches to the prevention of child sexual
abuse have not had more impact. However, three reasons may be offered as to
why these programs fail to demonstrate a more lasting impact. First, it may be
that such efforts to date have not been well designed or implemented. Second,
it may be that parents are more likely to take cues about child sexual abuse from
the popular news and entertainment media that dramatize and sensationalize the
issue than from community-based programs that tackle the issue in a straightforward but uninteresting manner. Third, it may be that some parents find the information provided by formal child sexual abuse training too personally threatening
to take seriously.

If these programs are poorly designed and implemented, the obstacle to parent
learning might be remedied by creating new programs that include input not only
from experts on child sexual abuse but those with expertise in communications,
educational psychology, and adult learning. Of course, more effective programs
of this sort are likely to cost more money. However, if government agencies were
willing to put less (or no) funding into clearly ineffective programs (e.g., the sorts
of sex offender registration and residency laws detailed in the next chapter of this
volume) greater resources could be devoted to effective parent training.

If parenting programs designed to prevent child sexual abuse are failing because
they cannot compete with the often more powerful and interesting (if not always
accurate) message about child sexual abuse being conveyed by the news and entertainment media, it may be time to make greater use of those media to help get the
appropriate message to parents. Some commentators have suggested the use of
public service announcements that, although very brief, might still reach some
parents. However, a better way to accomplish the goal of using the media to reach
parents with important and factual messages about child sexual abuse might be
having experts in public health, mental health, and the behavioral sciences offer to
collaborate with journalists and screenwriters. Working together, these collaborative teams could use newscasts, television shows, movies, and other presentations

to offer the necessary messages in ways more likely to catch the attention of, and sway the thinking of, parents whose children are at risk for child sexual abuse.

Finally, if the information that needs to be conveyed to parents is so personally threatening that they ignore it or deny that it has direct implications for them and their children, the information should be presented in less threatening ways. For example, as is detailed later in this chapter, it may be more useful not to target individuals in their roles as parents but rather in their roles as members of the community at large, all of whom have a major stake in preventing child sexual abuse.

PREVENTION STRATEGIES AIMED AT CHILDREN

Many efforts to prevent the sexual victimization of children have been directed toward children themselves. Such efforts include primary prevention programs that educate children to identify and resist sexual abuse, and secondary and tertiary prevention programs aimed at mitigating the effects of child sexual abuse that has already occurred and/or preventing further victimization of an already abused child.

Educating Children to Protect Themselves

One of the earliest and most common efforts to apply primary prevention principles to the sexual abuse of children was teaching children the difference between bad touch and good touch, how to resist bad touches, and to report bad touches to an adult. One such program is called Talking About Touching.[9] In this program, children are taught the difference between safe touches and unsafe touches. They are taught the Touching Rule, which says "A bigger person should not touch your private body parts except to keep you clean and healthy."[10] Children are also offered skills to "resist or avoid unsafe touches," informed that they "have a right to say how and by whom they are touched," and provided with "skills and vocabulary to help them avoid unwanted touches."[11]

Numerous other similar educational programs have been developed and implemented with millions of children, but not without controversy. Some critics have been troubled by the idea of giving children the responsibility for protecting themselves from sexual abuse. For example, as one group of authors has written, "It is not at all clear why children should be expected to be taught to protect themselves from sexual abuse. There certainly seems to be no similar expectation that children should be taught to protect themselves from physical or emotional abuse or neglect."[12] Others have claimed that children cannot comprehend or implement the content of these programs and that, even if they could, the approaches offered by these programs would not be effective. Still others have complained that these approaches had not been proven effective.

In a recent review of the literature on educational programs, such as "Talking About Touching," David Finkelhor referred to these latter critiques as conceptual and empirical. With regard to the "conceptual" critiques of these programs, Finkelhor concluded that the majority of research shows that "children at all ages do acquire the key concepts that are being taught."[13] He acknowledged that this "does not establish that children can necessarily implement" these concepts but concluded that "it is an argument against the broad claim made by critics that the concepts are categorically too complicated to be learned."[14] He added that even if all the concepts covered in these programs are not grasped by all children, they are still likely to be of benefit to some children. Moreover, he concluded that even if some of the concepts are difficult for some children to grasp, some such as "emphasis on the importance of telling an adult about an incident" are "noncontroversial and easy to understand and may be helpful for most children."[15]

Some critics have argued that there is no sound empirical evidence that these child education programs actually reduce the incidence of child sexual abuse. A review of the literature in this area suggests that this is a legitimate complaint. However, even if such programs have not been proven as primary prevention tools, they do likely have some, perhaps substantial, value in terms of secondary and tertiary prevention of child sexual abuse. As Finkelhor has observed, the research data are "virtually unanimous in showing that the programs promote disclosure," which may lead to "better outcomes" by ending or shortening the abuse, mobilizing resources, reducing isolation, identifying abusers, and reducing future offending.[16]

Finally, some critics have complained that child education programs in this context may have adverse psychological and behavioral consequences for some children, particularly that these programs may heighten children's anxiety and increase the chances that they will make false accusations of child sexual abuse. Overall, the research to date (although limited) does not support the notion that children exposed to educational programs regarding child sexual abuse become more anxious or worried. Moreover, limited research has not found children exposed to such programs are "more likely to misinterpret appropriate physical contact...and make false allegations" of sexual abuse.[17]

Of course, a great deal of education regarding sexual abuse can and should come to children from their parents. Although many parents do make an effort to educate their children to the dangers of child sexual abuse, some do not. For example, one recent survey of 289 parents and guardians of children in kindergarten through grade three, 21 percent of respondents indicated that they had not discussed child sexual abuse with their children.[18] Of that number, 41 percent explained that their children were "too young to understand sexual abuse; 36.1 percent said it had not occurred to them to discuss child sexual abuse with their children; and 23 percent reported that they did not know how to explain sexual abuse to their children."[19] To the extent that these data are representative of parents in general, they suggest that a substantial percentage of parents are not educating their children with regard to the dangers of child sexual abuse and that many of these parents might do so if they, themselves, were properly educated about the problem and how it can be effectively broached with young children.

Responding to the Initial Disclosure of Child Sexual Abuse

By the time a child discloses that he or she has been sexually abused, it is clearly too late for primary prevention strategies. However, proper handling of the disclosure may still have preventive effects, such as avoiding secondary victimization of the child; preventing further sexual abuse of the child; minimizing contamination that may interfere with the legal system's response to the disclosed abuse; and gathering information that will be useful to child protective agencies, prosecutors, and the courts.

Many (perhaps most) cases of child sexual abuse are not disclosed by the child victim. When a child does disclose that he or she has been sexually abused, numerous studies have found that the response of the person to whom the abuse is disclosed may make a difference in the child's response to the abuse and later psychological adjustment. For example, there is evidence that children whose disclosures of sexual abuse are met with supportive responses have more positive outcomes in terms of their eventual psychological adjustment. Furthermore, there is some evidence that children whose disclosures of child sexual abuse are not met with supportive responses may have poorer ultimate adjustments than children who did not disclose.[20]

How an adult responds to a child's initial disclosure of sexual abuse victimization no doubt will, and should, depend in part on the relationship of the adult to the child (e.g., whether the adult is a parent, teacher, health or mental health professional, police officer, child protective worker, and so forth). Although there has been little specific research on the subject, common sense, clinical wisdom, and research findings from related areas (e.g., developmental and cognitive psychology) have led to general agreement on certain aspects of a proper response to a child's disclosure of sexual abuse, regardless of the relationship between the child and the adult to whom the disclosure is made. For instance, it is generally agreed that the adult should remain calm, listen carefully to the child, believe the child, reassure the child, avoid interrogating the child, refrain from leading or suggestive questions, and eschew questions or statements that appear judgmental.

Many, but not all, professionals who may be confronted with initial disclosures of child sexual abuse are likely to be aware of this general consensus. Moreover, few parents or other nonprofessionals are likely to know that they should respond to disclosures in this manner. Thus, a key element in any regimen of secondary prevention of child sexual abuse should be educating adults regarding how to respond to such disclosures. Educational efforts of this sort could be presented to the general population through popular media and/or presented in narrower settings, such as schools, churches, and community organizations to more specifically targeted groups, such as parents of young children. Educational efforts aimed more specifically at professionals can and should be included in both their formal and continuing education.

Every American jurisdiction and many other nations have mandatory reporting laws that require designated professionals (e.g., those in the health, mental health, and educational professions) to report any reasonable suspicion of child abuse to law enforcement and/or child protective authorities.[21] Moreover, many jurisdictions require such mandated reporters to be trained in the parameters of these laws to obtain professional licensure. Thus, when a child's initial disclosure (or any other evidence, for that matter) leads a professional who is a mandated reporter to suspect that a child has been sexually abused, the professional is required by law to divulge what the child said about the alleged abuse. A significant implication of these mandated reporting laws is that a designated professional who receives a disclosure of child sexual abuse cannot and should not assure the child of confidentiality, even if the child asked that the disclosure be kept confidential or the disclosure was made in the course of what would otherwise be considered a confidential setting (e.g., where the professional is the child's counselor, psychotherapist, or other mental health professional). Although it is assumed that reporting a child's disclosure of sexual abuse to state authorities is invariably a benefit to the child, there is certainly no empirical evidence to support that assumption.

Investigating Allegations of Child Sexual Abuse

Reporting a child's disclosure of sexual abuse to law enforcement and/or child protective services will invariably lead to an investigation that will likely require further questioning of the child and his or her family members, often a physical examination of the child, and other experiences that, if not handled properly, may psychologically harm the child. These investigations are sometimes in the best interest of the alleged child victim (e.g., when a parent or family member is suspected of sexually abusing a child and an investigation is needed to determine whether the child needs to be separated and/or protected from the alleged abuser). Often, however, the essential purpose of the investigation is to find evidence that will allow the alleged abuser to be prosecuted. In such cases, although the investigation of the child's disclosure may not directly benefit the alleged child victim, it may help the criminal justice system prevent the alleged abuser from sexually offending against other children in the future.

Regardless of the purpose of the investigation into a child's disclosure, it has long been generally recognized that the investigative process holds significant potential for further harming a child who has already been traumatized by sexual abuse. Consider, for example, that even under the best of circumstances children who disclose sexual abuse are sometimes interviewed repeatedly about their disclosure and subjected to medical examinations, some of which can be quite invasive and even painful.

Recognizing that "the professional response to sexual abuse allegations could unduly exacerbate children's and caregivers' stress, particularly when multiple investigating agencies are involved,"[22] and that "[u]ntrained investigators may rely on suggestive questioning and make other interviewing errors"[23] that have the potential of impeding not only the investigation but also the prosecution of child sexual abuse, experts in the field of child abuse developed an innovative approach that combines investigation, prosecution, child protection, medical care, and mental health services within a single agency, known as a Children's Advocacy Center (CAC). Since 1985, over 700 CACs have been opened in the United States, at least one in every state.[24] Recently, one such center described the raison d'etre and operations of CACs as follows:

> Before the advent of Children's Advocacy Centers nationwide abused children were, unfortunately, retraumatized by the very system meant to serve them. Children were shuffled from one agency to another, and asked to repeat their stories to multiple professionals in cold, uninviting offices (such as police, sheriff, and District Attorney's offices). After the interviews, the agencies involved had great difficulty in collaborating on the cases, which oftentimes resulted in cases dropping out of the system.
>
> Today, when victims of abuse arrive at their respective Children's Advocacy Center, trained staff and volunteers warmly greet them in a child and family-friendly environment. These smallest victims of abuse are interviewed and videotaped only once and by a professional Forensic Interviewer on staff at the Advocacy Center—thereby minimizing the trauma they have already experienced.
>
> Forensic interviewers are trained to understand children's communication, talk with them clearly, and put them at ease, while still collecting sound investigative information. This one interview will serve the information needs of multiple agencies.
>
> Victim Advocates interview the family, gathering essential information regarding history, the child's behavior, how they became aware of the abuse, and any questions or concerns are addressed. The Victim Advocate also assesses the need for other services such as housing, food, utilities, a Protective Order and counseling.[25]

If CACs perform as intended, they have the potential to accomplish not only secondary and tertiary prevention but, in some instances, a kind of primary prevention of child sexual abuse (i.e., they will decrease the risk that child sexual abuse victims will be revictimized, they will help mitigate the psychological and/or physical harm already done to such victims, and they will assist in the prosecution and often the incapacitation of individuals who might otherwise continue to sexually abuse children).

Little research has been done to examine the efficacy of CACs, particularly in terms of their preventive value, and what research has been conducted has shown mixed results. For example, one study was published under the title: "Do Children's Advocacy Centers improve families' experiences of child sexual abuse investigations?"[25] In a quasi-experimental design, researchers compared data on child sexual abuse cases ($N = 229$) investigated through four long-standing CACs with data on similar cases investigated by agencies not using the CAC model. Following the investigation, nonoffending caregivers (mostly parents) were queried with 14 questions using a 4-point Likert-style scale and directed at "(1) satisfaction with the skill and responsiveness of investigators and (2) satisfaction with the forensic interview process and environment."[26] Children were presented with six questions using a similar Likert-style format: "how well they liked the places they were interviewed; how scared they felt during interviews; how well investigators explained what was happening to them; how well investigators seemed to understand kids; how they felt about the number of times they had to talk with investigators; and how they felt after talking with investigators."[27] Overall, caregivers who dealt with CACs "reported higher rates of satisfaction" than those who worked with other agencies, but "[n]o statistically significant differences were found between CAC and comparison cases" with regard to "whether the investigation changed how troubled their child was or how they felt about the number of interviews their child had during the investigation."[28] With the exception of one question regarding how much fear they experienced during interviews, children's responses did not significantly differ between the CAC context and other settings. "Significantly more children from CAC samples (35%, n = 90) described themselves as being not at all or not very scared compared to children from comparison samples (13%, n = 30) (p = .021)."[29]

Two other studies have examined the use of medical examinations and forensic interviews of children at CACs. One study found that children were much more likely to receive medical examinations at CACs versus other agencies and facilities (48 percent compared with 21 percent).[30] When a subset of the children's nonoffending caretakers were surveyed, there were no significant differences between those who dealt with CACs and those who were served by others in terms of satisfaction with the medical professional or the examination process. These findings are noteworthy because, as was pointed out in response to this study, "there are no national protocols for referrals or for exams at CACs, and...medical evaluations are often indicated despite the small possibility of evidence..."[31] In many cases (especially, for example, those in which there is no concern about penetration), the chance of any useful evidence coming from a medical examination of the child is slight and, even if found, such evidence is more likely to benefit the legal process than the child. Thus, given that a medical examination carries with it the possibility of additional psychological trauma to the child, the fact that CACs are more likely than other investigative agencies to use such examinations is not necessarily a clear positive.

In another study that examined forensic interviewing of children in CACs, researchers looked at three variables: (1) whether CACs offered a more child-friendly interview setting, (2) whether CACs demonstrated greater coordination among investigatory agencies, and (3) whether CACs reduced the number of interviews to which children were exposed.[32] Compared with other facilities and agencies, CACs were found to be more likely to conduct forensic interviews of the children in more child-friendly environments. In some locales, CACs were more likely than their counterparts to have investigative processes that reflected coordination both internally and externally, but in other jurisdictions there appeared to be no real difference between CACs and the agencies and facilities with which they were compared. Finally, this study considered the extent to which CACs and other investigators interviewed children. Regardless of the investigative setting, most children experienced only a single interview. However, the mean number of interviews children experienced was significantly greater ($P<.05$) in CACs (1.42) than in comparison facilities and agencies (1.29).[33]

This finding is especially noteworthy given that there is general agreement that when it comes to child interviews in this context, fewer is better than more, which is undoubtedly why a stated goal of CACs is that children be subjected to only one interview.[34]

Finally, a separate study examined the question that may be most related to primary prevention in the context of CACs: Do CACs contribute to the prosecution of child sexual abuse allegations? Data were gathered in two adjoining districts of a large city over an 11-year span. District One "experienced a significant increase in CAC participation in child sexual abuse cases" during the 11 years in question, whereas District Two's "use of CACs did not change substantially."[35] It was hypothesized that the growth in CAC use in the former district compared to that in the latter district would "correlate with a relative increase in the prosecution of child sexual abuse."[36] Based upon data from the District Attorney's Office, researchers concluded that although the rate of felony prosecutions for child sexual abuse was similar in both districts at the beginning of the 11-year span, by the end of that time the rate of such prosecutions was 69 percent higher in District One than District Two. Interestingly, however, "Despite these major shifts in felony prosecutions, the percentage of prosecutions ending in conviction (conviction rate) did not change appreciably between the two districts over time."[37]

As the authors of this study concluded, "the magnitude of association between CAC involvement and increased felony prosecutions is difficult to discount."[38] However, it is also "difficult to discount" the finding of no apparent association between CAC involvement in the investigation of child sexual abuse and conviction of the alleged offender. There are many reasons why the prosecution of an alleged sexual abuser might fail to result in conviction, some of which have little or nothing to do with the quality of the investigation of the child's disclosure. Still, this finding raises a serious question as to whether the CAC model is necessarily preferable to other investigatory approaches when it comes to obtaining convincing legal evidence of child sexual abuse.

Although the CAC model clearly has potential to play a significant role in the prevention of child sexual abuse, it has yet to be proven more effective in that regard than other less well-developed and less highly funded investigative approaches. Given how widely the CAC model has been adopted, it is truly surprising that more resources have not been devoted to researching its relative efficacy. Perhaps Faller and Palusci are correct in their explanation:

The lack of empirical support for child welfare innovations is fairly typical of how the child welfare system operates. Professionals, desperate to adopt better ways to help victims of child maltreatment, often implement interventions without a prior evaluation or an evaluation component. In other social and health policy domains, professionals do not implement untested interventions. For example, a new drug for the treatment of cancer would first be perfected in the laboratory, then used in animal research, then piloted with humans, then subjected to clinical trials, and finally used in double-blinded trials before widespread use with cancer victims. Not so with interventions in child welfare.[39]

Prosecuting Allegations of Child Sexual Abuse

In many cases, a child's disclosure or other evidence of child sexual abuse leads to legal proceedings against the alleged perpetrator. If the alleged perpetrator is not a parent or close family member, the proceedings almost always are criminal in nature. As is discussed in greater detail later in this chapter, a person criminally convicted of sexually abusing a child often faces extremely severe legal sanctions, some of which may be lifelong in nature. If a child has allegedly been abused by a parent or close relative, proceedings may occur in both criminal and family courts. Intrafamilial sexual abusers face not only criminal penalties but also other serious sanctions, such as removal from the home, loss of custody, and even termination of parental rights.

The legal system's response to allegations of child sexual abuse has multiple goals but at least one primary goal is to prevent further abuse. In some cases, that goal is served by a judicial finding of abuse and the removal of the offender from the home or the life of the child victim(s). In other cases a conviction for rape or sexual abuse paves the way for criminal sanctions that will likely prevent not only further victimization of the child complainant(s) but also other potential victims.

Although the capacity of the legal system to prevent child sexual abuse through family and criminal court sanctions should not be underestimated, those sanctions often come at a psychological cost to child victims. To secure a family court finding of sexual abuse and/or a criminal conviction for rape or sexual abuse, in many cases the state is required to present evidence to the court directly from the victimized child. Indeed, as one recent review has concluded: "The testimony of the alleged child victim is often the most important evidence in the prosecution of child sexual abuse. The child and the suspect are usually the only potential eyewitnesses, and physical evidence is often lacking."[40]

There has long been debate about whether requiring a child to testify in court against his or her alleged sexual abuser is beneficial or detrimental to the child's well-being. Without resolving that dispute, it does seem fair to conclude that in many cases, the benefit to the child victim from participating in court proceedings has at least the potential to be outweighed by the harm imposed by his or her extended involvement in the legal process. As early as 1986, the American Academy of Child and Adolescent Psychiatry concluded that child sexual abuse cases require special judicial treatment because

1. Young victims may not be able to understand trial procedures that have been designed for adults;

2. The atmosphere of the courtroom can be threatening, confusing, and frightening for children;
3. Additional emotional stress for sexually abused children can result from direct testimony in public;
4. Insensitive and repetitive cross-examination of abused children can be misperceived by them as further abuse;
5. Face-to-face confrontation by a child victim with the perpetrator may result in severe additional trauma...[41]

Recognizing that requiring a child to testify against an alleged sexual abuser may impose certain risks to the child's psychological well-being, most states have created special rules or procedures designed to avoid or at least minimize these risks. Unfortunately, as with many other child welfare interventions, there has been virtually no systematic empirical evaluation of the effects of these rules and procedures. Although these rules and procedures are presumed to help prevent further harm to already victimized children, and thus might be regarded as instances of secondary or tertiary prevention, their actual effects remain unknown. Perhaps more significantly, the implementation of these rules and procedures sometimes raises significant concerns about the constitutional rights of alleged sexual abusers.

CHILD WITNESS EDUCATION

Except for certain professionals and experts, most people are never called upon to testify in court. Thus, it is not uncommon for those who are required to testify to be given at least some training or orientation, usually from the attorney who will be questioning them on the witness stand. Children are even less likely than adults to ever testify but when they do they are likely to need greater preparation, not only to ensure their effectiveness but also to protect them from potential harm. Although there is little research on their efficacy, many efforts to educate children as witnesses, especially in child sexual abuse cases, are sensible, inexpensive, and unlikely to undermine the search for truth or the rights of the defendant.[42]

For example, it may be helpful to have the child visit the courtroom in which he or she will be testifying and to be told where he or she and others will be sitting and what role they will play in the proceedings. Children's questions about both the courtroom and the rules followed there can and should be answered in advance of their testimony. Answers should be honest but developmentally appropriate and as reassuring as possible. Children may also be given information that will help them cope with examination and cross-examination and enable them to be more effective witnesses. For example, a Pennsylvania program, "Preparing the Child Witness in Sexual Abuse Cases," suggests a number of concerns that professionals should address with child witnesses in advance of their testimony, including vocabulary, dealing with objections, coping with fatigue and confusion, requesting water and bathroom breaks, correcting mistakes, and handling feelings of intimidation and coercion.[43]

ALTERATIONS TO THE COURTROOM SETTING AND ROUTINE

Also largely untested in terms of their effects, but probably useful in some cases, are changes to the courtroom or courtroom routine that accommodate the developmental needs of child witnesses and perhaps make their testimony smoother and less traumatic. Many of these alterations represent both common sense and common decency. For example, there seems to be little downside and much potential upside to allowing as needed breaks for toileting, snacks, and rest, as long as such breaks are used for the child's benefit and not as strategic efforts to highlight or undermine the child's testimony.

Some other procedural alterations, however, have been more controversial and should be approached with caution if used at all. For example, under some state laws[44] and by US Supreme Court precedent,[45] children are allowed to testify outside the presence of the alleged abuser (the accused in a criminal trial or the respondent in a family court proceeding). The concern here is that children may be traumatized by having to testify about the alleged sexual abuse in front of the alleged abuser or that the abuser's presence may hinder the child's ability to testify effectively against him or her. In some jurisdictions, alleged victims are allowed to testify behind screens so that they may be seen by the judge, jury, and attorneys but not the defendant/respondent. In 41 states, alleged child victims may be allowed to testify from another room via closed circuit television.[46]

These practices not only raise concerns about the rights of criminal defendants to confront their accusers, but may do so unnecessarily. To prevent indiscriminate use of these procedural alterations, some states have required them to be allowed only after a judicial finding that the child who will testify is vulnerable to psychological harm if required to do so in the direct view of the alleged abuser.

For instance, in New York, child witnesses ages 14 and younger may testify in court via closed circuit television if the court finds them to be vulnerable. A child witness is to be declared vulnerable "when the court...determines by clear and convincing evidence that it is likely that [he or she] will suffer serious mental or emotional harm if required to testify at a criminal proceeding without the use of live, two-way closed-circuit television and that the use of such live, two-way closed-circuit television will diminish the likelihood or extent of, such harm."[47] Under the New York statute, "any physician, psychologist, nurse or social worker who has treated a child witness may testify...concerning the treatment of such child witness as such treatment relates to the issue [of vulnerability]."[48] In making its determination the court may consider the following factors, any one or more of which, if proven by clear and convincing evidence, is/are sufficient to support a finding that the child is vulnerable:

(a) The manner of the commission of the offense of which the defendant is accused was particularly heinous or was characterized by aggravating circumstances.

(b) The child witness is particularly young or otherwise particularly subject to psychological harm on account of a physical or mental condition which existed before the alleged commission of the offense.

(c) At the time of the alleged offense, the defendant occupied a position of authority with respect to the child witness.

(d) The offense or offenses charged were part of an ongoing course of conduct committed by the defendant against the child witness over an extended period of time.

(e) A deadly weapon or dangerous instrument was allegedly used during the commission of the crime.

(f) The defendant has inflicted serious physical injury upon the child witness.

(g) A threat, express or implied, of physical violence to the child witness or a third person if the child witness were to report the incident to any person or communicate information to or cooperate with a court, grand jury, prosecutor, police officer or peace officer concerning the incident has been made by or on behalf of the defendant.

(h) A threat, express or implied, of the incarceration of a parent or guardian of the child witness, the removal of the child witness from the family or the dissolution of the family of the child witness if the child witness were to report the incident to any person or communicate information to or cooperate with a court, grand jury, prosecutor, police officer or peace officer concerning the incident has been made by or on behalf of the defendant.

(i) A witness other than the child witness has received a threat of physical violence directed at such witness or to a third person by or on behalf of the defendant.

(j) The defendant, at the time of the inquiry, (i) is living in the same household with the child witness, (ii) has ready access to the child witness or (iii) is providing substantial financial support for the child witness.

(k) The child witness has previously been the victim of [a sexual offense] or incest. . .

(l) According to expert testimony, the child witness would be particularly susceptible to psychological harm if required to testify in open court or in the physical presence of the defendant.[49]

This sort of law seems to represent a reasonable compromise, if applied judiciously. Children who would likely suffer serious mental or emotional harm if required to face their alleged abusers while testifying in court are protected. The state is enabled to present often crucial evidence of sexual abuse that, in some cases, might not otherwise be presented. The defendant's right to confrontation, although limited, is still guaranteed by technology that allows the defendant and all others in the courtroom to see the child's live image while testifying and the child to see a live image of the jury and the defendant while testifying via closed-circuit television. Moreover, the defendant retains the right to a full cross-examination of the child witness and the court must instruct the jury to draw no inference from the prosecution's presentation of the child witness's testimony in this manner.

ALLOWING OTHERS TO TESTIFY FOR THE CHILD

Although the use of closed-circuit television for the testimony of alleged victims of child sexual abuse, especially in criminal trials, may seem to violate a defendant's constitutional right to confront his or her accuser, most courts including the US Supreme Court have not seen it that way.[50] Moreover, many state courts have gone much further than the use of closed-circuit television in these cases, frequently relaxing hearsay rules to essentially allow others to testify for the child.

For example, a child tells his mother, a doctor, a social worker, or a police officer that the defendant sexually abused him. Should the adult who heard the child's complaint then be allowed to testify about it in court? Ordinarily such testimony would be considered hearsay (an out of court statement made by one other than the testifying witness, being offered to prove the truth of the matter asserted in that statement) and would be inadmissible. However, courts have often allowed such testimony in child sexual abuse cases, thus sparing child victims the need at all to testify. Courts that have admitted such hearsay testimony have relied upon specific state laws and/or well-recognized exceptions to the hearsay rule.

As an example of the former, consider New York State case law providing that: "In a child protective proceeding, unsworn out-of-court statements of the victim may be received and, if properly corroborated, will support a finding of abuse or neglect; such out-of-court statements may be corroborated by '[any] other evidence tending to support' their reliability."[51] As examples of the latter, consider exceptions to the hearsay rule made for "excited utterances" and statements made for purposes of medical diagnosis or treatment.[52] Some courts have also admitted hearsay statements detailing an alleged child victim's out of court statements by invoking the so-called residual or catchall exception to the hearsay rule, an exception that permits hearsay testimony not covered by any specific exception, but which the court finds has circumstantial guarantees of trustworthiness.[53]

In recent years, however, US Supreme Court decisions regarding hearsay and the confrontation clause of the Constitution have raised doubts about the continued viability of these exceptions in criminal prosecutions. Until 2004, courts could constitutionally admit hearsay statements in criminal trials as long as they bore adequate indicia of reliability or fell within one of the firmly established exceptions to the hearsay rule. In 2004, however, the US Supreme Court overturned that rule, holding in *Crawford v. Washington* that courts must look not at the reliability of hearsay statements but rather at their nature.[54] Under *Crawford*, if such statements are found to be testimonial in nature, they may not be admitted in a criminal trial unless the person who made them is unavailable and the defendant had a prior opportunity to cross-examine him or her. The Court loosely defined a testimonial statement as one made "under circumstances which would lead an objective witness reasonably to believe that the statement would be available for use at a later trial."[55]

In interpreting the application of *Crawford* to cases involving the admissibility of hearsay statements made by children, a number of courts have held that the appropriate test for determining whether a statement is testimonial should consider not only the intent of the declarant (i.e., the child) but also the intent of the person(s) who elicited the child's statement.

For example, in *State v. Snowden*, the defendant was convicted of child sexual abuse based partly on the testimony of a social worker regarding statements made to her by the alleged child victims.[56] The trial court admitted this testimony, over the objection of the defense, under a state law providing a hearsay exception for statements of alleged child victims made to certain health or social work professionals, if the court determined that the hearsay statements possessed "particularized guarantees of trustworthiness."[57] In overruling the admissibility of the children's statements, an appeals court found that the interview conducted by the social worker was the "functional equivalent of a police interrogation."[58] That court also found that: "The children, as demonstrated through their responses, also actually were aware of the potential of their statements to be used at a later trial. Any therapeutic motive or effect of the interviews is irrelevant, in terms of proper Confrontation Clause analysis, to the overarching investigatory purpose of the interviews, and therefore testimonial nature, of the statements elicited."[59]

Cases such as this may have a significant impact not only in court but also in the investigations of child sexual abuse conducted by CACs. As law professor Deborah Paruch recently noted in a law review article ominously titled "Silencing the Victims in Child Sexual Abuse Prosecutions," "[C]hildren's statements made during forensic interviews in sexual abuse clinics or advocacy centers have been found to be testimonial. In fact, the majority of jurisdictions that have ruled on this issue have found children's statements, made under these conditions, to be testimonial."[60]

PREVENTION STRATEGIES AIMED AT THE COMMUNITY

Some strategies for preventing child sexual abuse must be aimed beyond parents and children and directed toward the community as a whole in order to have any chance of succeeding. There are multiple child sexual abuse prevention strategies that might be targeted at this broader constituency. The two that are considered here relate to reversing the growing tide of sexualization of children in American society and encouraging bystander intervention in cases of known or suspected child sexual abuse.

Limiting the Sexualization of Children

Child sexual abuse has many roots but surely at least some of them lie in the way society in general views children and their sexuality. Although existing social norms strongly discourage, if not forbid, adult sexual contact with children and adolescents, these norms are increasingly challenged by society's growing tendency to sexualize children and adolescents, especially girls. For example, in various media, minors are portrayed in ways that suggest that they are sexually

attractive or even seductive. Consider the increasingly common designer clothing advertisements featuring scantily dressed, provocatively posed young models or adult models in even more sexually provocative poses dressed to appear
as children; movies and even prime-time television programs in which teenagers and even some preteens are presented as sexually savvy, attractive, or even
overtly seductive; and preteen magazines, such as one featuring an article on "all
the essentials" girls that age need, including a telephone, trendy shoes, backpack,
journal, teddy, and a "lacy pink g-string."[61]

Moreover, advertisers and media are not the only culprits in today's sexualization of children and adolescents. Manufacturers produce and retailers market to
children such items as dolls dressed in sexually provocative outfits; thong under-
wear for preteens imprinted with words, such as "eye candy" and "wink wink";
and bikinis with push up bra tops for 7 year olds.[62]

Furthermore, parents enroll their children in so-called child beauty pageants, a
$5 billion industry in which some as young as 3 years old are made up and dressed
to appear like grown women and "trained to flirt and exploit their nascent sexuality in order to win."[63]

The use of children and adolescents in all of these ways might well be broadly
categorized as the sexual exploitation of children, which is bad enough. However,
the potential for harm may not stop there. As a Task Force of the American
Psychological Association (APA) noted in 2010:

> There is little or no research on the effects on adults of viewing sexualized
> images of girls or even sexualized images of adult women made up to look
> like girls (a common practice in magazine advertisements)…But there may
> be negative effects at a societal level in addition to possible negative effects
> to individual viewers; these include providing justification and a market for
> child pornography and the prostitution and sexual trafficking of children.
>
> One particularly pernicious effect of the constant exposure to sexualized
> images of girls is that individuals and society may be "trained" to perceive
> and label sexualized girls as "seductive"… Children are not legally able to give
> consent to sexual activity with an adult. When girls are dressed to resemble
> adult women, however, adults may project adult motives as well as an adult
> level of responsibility and agency on girls. Images of precocious sexuality
> in girls may serve to normalize abusive practices such as child abuse, child
> prostitution, and the sexual trafficking of children.
>
> Finally, the sexualization of girls may also contribute to the trafficking
> and prostitution of girls by helping to create a market for sex with chil-
> dren through the cultivation of new desires and experiences. If the ideal-
> ized female sexual partner is a 15- or 16-year-old girl, male consumers may
> demand pornography featuring such girls and the opportunity to pay for sex
> with them.[65]

Despite a dearth of empirical data on the effects of the apparently growing sexualization of children, particularly girls, it is difficult to disagree with the APA

Task Force's ominous speculations. Eventually greater empirical support for these speculations may emerge, but it is also difficult to disagree with the Task Force's implicit conclusion that intervention cannot wait for such support. The Task Force offered multiple recommendations for immediate implementation, including further research. Their recommendations were for interventions directed at professionals, policy makers, children, families, and society at large. The recommendations for society are ambitious and might best be characterized in the current context as prevention strategies aimed at the community. For example, the APA group recommended increasing public awareness and responsiveness to this issue through a "comprehensive, grassroots, communitywide effort" including "parents and other caregivers, educators, young people, community-based organizations, religious communities, the media, advertisers, marketing professionals, and manufacturers."[66]

More specifically, the Task Force recommended, *inter alia*, that APA "convene forums that will bring together members of the media and a panel of leading experts in the field to examine and discuss (a) the sexualization of girls in the United States, (b) the findings of this task force report, and (c) strategies to increase awareness about this issue and reduce negative images of girls in the media."[67] Additionally, the Task Force recommended that "APA work with Congress and relevant federal agencies and industry to reduce the use of sexualized images of girls in all forms of media and products."[68]

As part of its National Plan to Prevent the Sexual Abuse and Exploitation of Children, the National Coalition to Prevent Child Sexual Abuse and Exploitation has made similar kinds of recommendations for all individuals as follows:

> Encourage everyone to speak up against incidents or messages that normalize sexual harm, abuse, or exploitation.
>
> Speak against messages that portray children in ways that suggest they possess the same sexual interests as adults or are sexual objects for adults' use or abuse.
>
> Recognize that by identifying and speaking up against the hyper-sexualized treatment of children and other sexual harm to children, you help end the demand.
>
> Look for examples of clothes, toys, music, entertainment, and other media that contribute to the sexual objectification of children. When you find them, write letters to the editor, to company presidents, and to others who may have an impact on changing those products or messages. You can demand the change for children.
>
> Talk with others in all your spheres of influence (e.g., faith groups, professional organizations, civic organizations, family, community) about why so many adults see children as sexual objects and why so many adolescents and children see themselves similarly.
>
> When you are aware of businesses profiting from the sexual objectification, abuse, or exploitation of children, demand they stop before you give them your business...[69]

Whether the recommendations of the APA Task Force or the National Coalition will have the desired effect in reducing the sexualization, sexual abuse, and sexual exploitation of children remains to be seen, but for now there seems to be little reason not to advance and pursue these common sense, low-cost, low-risk strategies.

Encouraging Bystander Intervention

As the recent Penn State child sexual abuse scandal amply illustrated, in many instances where children are being sexually abused, others are aware of the abuse but do not take appropriate steps to stop it or even report it to proper authorities.[70] Perhaps worse yet, as that scandal also demonstrated, even when appropriate reports are made by those who know or suspect that child sexual abuse is occurring, these reports may be ignored.[71]

In the Penn State case, it appears that those who failed to take action to protect children who were being sexually abused by Jerry Sandusky, a former assistant football coach, had a variety of motives for inaction. However, one factor that may have played a prominent role is a variation on what social psychologists have long described as the bystander phenomenon:

> [O]nce we notice a possible emergency situation, we must make several decisions in order to help. We must decide that an emergency exists, that it is our personal responsibility to act, and that there is something we can do to help. To complicate matters, these decisions must be made under pressure; emergencies involve threat, ambiguity, urgency and stress. The presence of bystanders can influence this pressure-packed decision sequence at each step, tipping the scales toward inaction.[72]

In the context of child sexual abuse, this phenomenon may help explain why some who are suspicious or even aware of such abuse fail to report it: they believe that others know what they know and will take action. Additionally, those who are suspicious or even aware of child sexual abuse may fail to report because they may not be sure that what they suspect or know is in fact child sexual abuse. Moreover, they may be unaware of how and to whom their suspicions or knowledge should be reported and may be afraid to report for fear of being wrong, making the situation worse, or becoming involved in the often demanding machinations of the justice system.

Even those with good intentions may not report their knowledge or suspicions of child sexual abuse. For example, in the survey of 5,241 adults, reported in 2010 and mentioned earlier in this chapter, 91 percent of respondents "said that they would intervene in a child sexual abuse situation."[73] In the same survey, however, about 8 percent of the respondents knew of another adult who probably was or might have been sexually abusing a child in the preceding year. Among this group, 65 percent said they intervened in some way. Thirty-seven percent called the police or social services and 18 percent confronted the other adult, but 22 percent "stated that they did nothing."[74]

Among the reasons given by respondents for doing nothing were not understanding what behaviors should be of concern, fear of acting on suspicions that might ultimately prove mistaken, fear of making the situation worse, failure to perceive all options, and not knowing where to look for information or help.[75]

To counter these concerns with regard to the more general problem of sexual violence, numerous organizations and agencies have adopted what they call the bystander approach to preventing such abuse.[76] This approach—which is targeted at the community and the individual and emphasizes teaching people to recognize warning signs or indicators of sexual violence, giving them skills to intervene, and getting them to accept the responsibility for intervening—can and should be applied to the narrower but obviously related problem of child sexual abuse.

However, any effort to teach people about warning signs or indicators of child sexual abuse must be done with great care so as not to create overreactions and false-positive reports that could lead both children and adults to be harmed. This is particularly important because in the face of so many horrific cases in which bystanders knew about ongoing sexual abuse and did nothing (e.g., the Penn State, Boy Scouts, and Catholic Church sex scandals) there is a strong temptation to err too far on the side of caution. It should be kept in mind that in many if not most of these scandals, the bystanders in question were individuals in authority and people who knew or had every reason to know that children were being sexually abused. The situation is often much different when we, as a society, ask all individuals to take action when they suspect child sexual abuse.

As noted earlier in this chapter, every American jurisdiction requires certain categories of professionals to report reasonable suspicions of child abuse of any sort to state or local officials. These professionals commonly include physicians, nurses, licensed health and mental health professionals, teachers, childcare providers, law enforcement officers, and medical examiners. In the wake of the Penn State scandal, four states have applied these mandatory reporting laws to members of the faculty, administration, athletic staff, and in some instances even volunteers at institutions of higher learning. Moreover, in roughly 18 states, "*any person* who suspects child abuse or neglect is required to report."[77] Those states that require all persons to report child abuse, including child sexual abuse, have varying standards but, with one notable exception, all are quite similar if not essentially the same. Eight states (Idaho, Indiana, Kentucky, Maryland, Nebraska, Oklahoma, Texas, and Utah) require reports from all persons who have "cause to believe," "reason to believe," or "reasonable cause to believe" that a child is being abused or neglected.[78] In five states (Florida, New Mexico, New Hampshire, North Carolina, and Rhode Island), all those with "reasonable cause to suspect," "reasonable suspicion," or "reason to suspect" child abuse or neglect are required to report.[79] One state (Delaware) requires a report from anyone who "knows or in good faith suspects" child abuse or neglect.[80] Only one of these states, Tennessee, imposes a higher standard (i.e., anyone who has "knowledge" of child abuse or neglect is required to report).[81]

In all but one of the states that require individuals (other than designated professionals) to report suspicion or knowledge of child abuse, the penalty for willful failure to make a report is a misdemeanor. In Florida, failure to report is a felony.[82]

There is good reason to err on the side of child protection. There is also a clear need to motivate all citizens to report reasonable concerns about child sexual abuse. Unfortunately, however, there are few clearly reliable warning signs or indicators of child sexual abuse. Certainly, one who witnesses child sexual abuse or hears about it from a child victim or potential victim should report that information to the proper authorities (the police and/or child welfare agencies) regardless of whether they are required to do so by law. But where evidence is more equivocal, what do we want done? How far are we willing to go in erring on the side of caution?

Certainly no one wants to penalize citizens who make such reports in good faith, even if they prove to be wrong. To do so would undoubtedly deter many individuals from reporting. The laws in every American jurisdiction recognize this concern and provide some form of immunity from civil liability for those who, in good faith, report to authorities their suspicions of child abuse, whether or not they are required to make these reports. As the US Children's Bureau has explained concisely:

> The term "good faith" refers to the assumption that the reporter, to the best of his or her knowledge, had reason to believe that the child in question was being subjected to abuse or neglect. Even if the allegations made in the report cannot be fully substantiated, the reporter is still provided with immunity. There is a "presumption of good faith" in approximately 17 States, the District of Columbia, American Samoa, and Guam, which means that the good faith of the reporter is presumed unless it can be proven to the contrary.[83]

Given that these immunity laws are ubiquitous, at least in the United States, it seems reasonable to recommend that every state adopt a law requiring all persons who know of child abuse, including child sexual abuse, to report it to state authorities. The more difficult question is whether all states should follow the lead of those noted above and legally require all persons to report reasonable beliefs or suspicions of child abuse, including child sexual abuse. Unlike physical abuse, which often leaves bruises, cuts, welts, and other visible indicia of maltreatment, the objective manifestations of child sexual abuse, if any, are often, if not usually, impossible to see.

Psychologists, social workers, physicians, other health care professionals, and law enforcement officers frequently have a hard time assessing suspicions of child sexual abuse, even when a child makes a disclosure of such abuse. Is it reasonable to impose a duty to report suspicions of child sexual abuse on all laypersons, many of whom may not even be fully aware of what constitutes such abuse? Probably not, especially if the state is serious about branding as criminals and possibly even jailing those who fail to report reasonable suspicions. In all likelihood these laws were intended to serve, and do serve, hortatory and precatory rather than pre-scriptive functions. That is to say that these laws, which are rarely if ever enforced, are on the books to urge all citizens to take what is believed to be the right action (report reasonable suspicions of child abuse) but not to actually require them to do so.

There is, of course, some danger in having laws on the books that are not regu-larly enforced or not even meant to be enforced. In some cases, such laws may individually or collectively undermine respect for the law in general. However, in the case of mandatory child abuse reporting statutes, a rough cost-benefits analy-sis seems to favor these laws. They probably do little to undermine respect for the law in general. Moreover, although they may sometimes impose upon the government the economic burden of investigating complaints that prove to be unfounded, they help send an important message to the public about child abuse, may help counter the "bystander" phenomenon, and on occasion may actually inspire someone to report suspicions about a truly abusive situation that might otherwise have gone undetected.

Prevention Strategies Aimed at Perpetrators and Potential Perpetrators

In addition to prevention strategies aimed at parents, children, and the community, many programs to prevent child sexual abuse have targeted suspected, known, and potential perpetrators of such abuse. This chapter addresses some of these offender-directed strategies, including amending or abolishing statutes of limitation to make it easier to bring civil lawsuits and criminal charges against accused child sex abusers years or even decades after the alleged abuse; enhancing criminal penalties for those convicted of sexually abusing children; requiring convicted sex offenders to register and be subject to limitations on where they can live, work, and travel; and enabling the indefinite confinement of sex offenders even after they have served their entire criminal sentences.

All of these legal initiatives have a common justification. Each of them rests, in major part, on an assumption of deterrence. Proponents of these laws assert that imposing more punitive sanctions on those who sexually abuse children will deter other potential perpetrators from doing so. Most of these initiatives also rest upon a theory of incapacitation and control, the notion that an offender or would-be offender who is locked up or at least under some form of state control either cannot reoffend or at least will have a more difficult time doing so.

EXTENDING OR ABOLISHING STATUTES OF LIMITATION

Traditionally, nearly all crimes, with the frequent exception of murder, have been governed by statutes of limitation. These statutes usually provide that a crime must be prosecuted, if at all, within a given number of years from its perpetration. For example, in some jurisdictions, these statutes require prosecution of bank robbery no more than 5 years from the date of the robbery's occurrence. Similarly, most torts are also governed by statutes of limitation. For example, in many states a civil lawsuit alleging medical malpractice must be brought within 2 years of discovery of the alleged malpractice. In many states, where the plaintiff in a civil action was a child at the time of the alleged injury, the period limitations is tolled until the child reaches the age of majority, either 18 or 21 years, at which time the period of limitations begins to run. In other words, the "clock" does not begin running until the child is legally an adult. Additionally, in some jurisdictions, the statutory time limitation does not begin to run until a would-be plaintiff "discovers" (i.e., gains or regains conscious awareness of) the harm he or she has suffered at the hands of an alleged sexual abuser.

Sex offenses, including those committed against children, have long been governed by statutes of limitation in both criminal and civil cases. However, in recent years, many if not most jurisdictions have extended the time period in which an alleged child sexual abuser may be prosecuted or an alleged victim of child sexual abuse may sue an alleged perpetrator.[1] Some states (Alabama, Delaware, Florida, and Maine) have completely eliminated civil statutes of limitations in these cases.[2] Several states (California, Delaware, and Hawaii) have also passed legislation temporarily suspending their statutes of limitation in civil child sexual abuse cases to provide windows of time during which alleged victims, whose claims have already been time-barred, may be allowed to sue.[3] At least one state, California, attempted to provide such a window for criminal defendants who could not be prosecuted because their alleged sex offenses against minors were already barred by the statute of limitations. Under the California law, an alleged child sex abuser could be prosecuted even though the statutory time period had already expired, if the prosecution was commenced within a year of the alleged victim's report to police.[4] The US Supreme Court determined that this law was an unconstitutional violation of the *ex post facto* clause essentially because it retroactively changed the statute of limitations for some offenders.[5]

Traditionally, statutes of limitation have been justified on a number of policy grounds. Perhaps the most fundamental principle underlying these statutes is that it is unfair for a defendant to be required to defend himself or herself against stale complaints, given that with the passage of time often comes a loss of memory, key witnesses, and physical evidence. As one public defender agency explained: "[W]ithout a limitation period, evidence may be unable to be located, destroyed or may deteriorate. In addition, memories of witnesses fade and sometimes no longer exist. It may be difficult or impossible to locate witnesses who may have moved or have passed on. Without any finite period of time within which a prosecution can be brought, it may be impossible for an innocent person to fairly defend himself 30, 40, 50 or more years beyond the date of the offense."[6]

Another related but less pragmatic principle often cited in support of statutes of limitations is the offender's so-called right of repose: "The right of repose suggests that an individual should not have to live with the uncertainty of prosecution, and thus at the mercy of prosecutors, *ad infinitum*."[7] To put it another way, the right of repose is an "expectation that a defendant should not be required to defend against accusations after a plaintiff has consciously failed to come forward for many years."[8]

Despite these time-honored rationales, recently some commentators have called for the outright abolition of statutes of limitation, both civil and criminal, for any sex offense committed against a child. That would mean that any alleged sex offense against a minor could be the subject of a civil lawsuit and/or criminal prosecution at any time, no matter how long ago the alleged offense occurred. Proponents of abolishing statutes of limitation in this context have pointed, for example, to the injustice done in some of the major child sexual abuse scandals of the past half century (e.g., the widespread sexual abuse of children by Catholic priests), in which many victims were denied their day in court because the time limitations for bringing a lawsuit or a criminal prosecution had long ago elapsed.

More broadly, law professor Marci A. Hamilton has argued that "the single most important legal reform for all [child abuse] victims lies in eliminating [statutes of limitation]."[9] Professor Hamilton describes statutes of limitation as "a dam holding back the identities of predators from the public" and adds that: [t]he only way to enrich the databank of predator identities and to provide survivors with vindication and justice is to give those survivors more time, indeed, all the time they need, to prosecute and to file civil lawsuits."[10] Moreover, she asserts that abolishing statutes of limitation in cases of child sexual abuse will enhance the utility of some of the other putatively preventive tools, such as sex offender registration and civil confinement laws (both of which are discussed later in this chapter).

In theory, increasing time limits or abolishing statutes of limitation in child sexual abuse cases makes sense not only because it might lead to greater justice for abuse victims but because it might enhance the deterrent effect of the criminal and civil law in this context. Children often delay disclosure of such abuse and, in many cases, may be too young at the time of the abuse to realize its nature and implications. Moreover, in many cases, the negative consequences of such abuse may not become fully apparent for years.

To the extent that successful criminal prosecutions and/or civil lawsuits may be regarded as deterring child sexual abuse, increasing or eliminating the statutory period in which criminal prosecutions and civil actions may be brought for such abuse might be viewed as a form of prevention. Under laws extending time limits or eliminating statutes of limitations, a child sex abuser is arguably more likely to be punished, criminally and/or civilly, for his or her abusive conduct. Some would-be abusers might become aware of this and be less likely to offend; also, some offenders who may previously have escaped criminal punishment and confinement for child sex offenses due to short time limitations would be more likely to eventually be prosecuted and incarcerated, albeit in some instances many years after their crimes.

The rationales for having statutes of limitation in child sexual abuse cases have been roundly criticized. For example, as David Viens has observed:

> While it may generally be true that as time passes evidence becomes less reliable and the difficulty of defending against a charge increases, sufficient

protections for potential defendants exist in our legal system that militate against barring prosecution for child sexual abuse. Before filing charges against a defendant, the prosecutor must first be satisfied that there is probable cause, and once indicted, the rules of evidence, the allowance of zealous cross-examination, and the strict burden of proof in a criminal trial ensure that defendants receive a fair trial…The concept of repose "relies heavily on principles of self-reformation and rehabilitation," but as previously indicated, the typical child sexual abuser neither self-reforms nor rehabilitates. Further, it is widely accepted that "a policy of repose should be outweighed by the interests of justice." Thus, where a child sexual abuser takes "advantage of the tender years and perilous position of a fearful victim, it is the victim's lasting hurt, not the perpetrator's fictional reliance, that the law should count the higher."[11]

It is difficult to dispute that "a policy of repose should be outweighed by the interests of justice."[12] But is it always in the interests of justice to allow claims of child sexual abuse to be litigated civilly and/or criminally many years, if not decades after the abuse allegedly took place? Allowing such actions to be brought may provide some measure of solace if not justice for the plaintiff/complainant, but doing so also carries the potential for doing tremendous harm to the life and reputation of the defendant, even if he or she is found not liable or not guilty. Consider, for example, the recent case of Dale Kildee.

Dale Kildee served 36 years as a member of the US House of Representatives from Michigan. In 2011, as the 82-year-old congressman was about to retire from office, a distant cousin came forward with claims that Kildee had sexually abused him 50 years earlier. Kildee denied the cousin's claims and alleged that he was the victim of blackmail and a political scheme to make sure that his party lost the forthcoming election for his House seat.[13] The allegations generated tremendous local and national publicity and the alleged victim said in a television interview that the sexual abuse began when he was 15 years old and emerged only later in life as repressed memories. At the time these allegations emerged, Kildee could not be criminally prosecuted or sued because of the statute of limitations. Even with application of tolling provisions, his accuser would have had to bring a lawsuit against him within 1 year of the time he turned 18. In short, the accuser was decades too late to have his accusations heard in a court of law.

Some were critical of the Michigan law that they saw as protecting Kildee from facing his accuser in court. Others were critical of the law because it denied Kildee the chance to face his accuser, walk away with an exculpatory judgment, and clear his previously good name. Still others pointed out that in some states, both the accuser and accused would have gotten their day in court because of recent changes extending or abolishing the statute of limitations in child sexual abuse.

Imagine what the trial in such a case would have been like had these allegations arisen in a state in which a lawsuit could be brought for sexual abuse that allegedly occurred half a century earlier. Kildee would have been forced to retain counsel and defend himself. Although by law his accuser would have had the burden of proving that the sexual abuse occurred, the accuser's testimony would likely have been enough to take the case to a jury. Thus, in effect, Kildee would likely have been regarded as guilty until proven innocent. That is to say that he would probably need something more than his own testimony to rebut the awful charges against him. And what would that have been?

Could the former congressman have provided alibi witnesses for vague dates and times 50 years earlier? Could he have supplied datebooks or other evidence of his whereabouts around the time he is alleged to have sexually abused his younger relative? Perhaps, but it would have likely only been because of the public nature of his political work over many decades. More than likely, however, like most people, other than his own denials, he would have been left largely defenseless. If the jury found for the alleged victim, Kildee would have been immediately and indelibly branded a child sexual abuser. Even if he secured a verdict in his favor, there would likely always be some who doubted him and believed his accuser. In short, the best he could have hoped for, after a trial, would be a costly vindication in the eyes of some people.

Recent state actions to abolish statutes of limitations in cases of alleged sexual abuse represent, for the most part, an understandable but knee-jerk reaction to scandals, such as those involving the Catholic Church and other institutions in which children were sexually victimized for years and sometimes denied access to the courts years or decades later because of time constraints imposed by the law. Traditional statutes of limitation have served the justice system well for decades if not centuries before these changes were suggested or made. Children were afforded the added protection of tolling provisions that allowed them to wait until reaching adulthood to sue alleged perpetrators. Moreover, many states had discovery provisions that effectively tolled the period of limitations until an alleged victim of child sexual abuse gained or regained full awareness of what had been done to him or her.

Abolishing statutes of limitations may offer some victims an opportunity to pursue justice they might not otherwise have had. On the other hand, these changes to the law may often work to deny justice to individuals who are wrongly accused, either deliberately or accidentally, because of the vagaries and fallibility of human memory. They also work a hardship on the justice system because they require judges or jurors to make determinations about events that occurred not only in an earlier time, but in what was essentially another cultural milieu in which social norms and expectations about adults' dealings with children may not have been what they are today. Furthermore, not surprisingly, there is no evidence that abolishing or even expanding the time periods in which alleged child sexual abusers may be subjected to litigation (criminal or civil) has any incremental deterrent effect on potential child sexual abusers. Many acts of child sexual abuse are spontaneous and opportunistic, but even if a would-be perpetrator takes the time to calculate the odds of being held accountable for sexually abusing a child, it seems extremely unlikely that he or she will consider an issue as relatively arcane as the statute of limitations.

Abolishing criminal statutes of limitations in cases of alleged child sexual abuse might result in more child sex offenders being incarcerated and thus incapacitated in terms of their ability to reoffend while imprisoned. However, given the many barriers to conviction in current child sexual abuse prosecutions, one must wonder what the conviction rate would be in criminal prosecutions for child sexual abuse brought many years or even decades after the alleged crimes.

A more reasoned approach to this issue would involve efforts to empirically document the relative extent to which varying changes in the period of limitations has affected both civil and criminal litigation in child sexual abuse cases. Absent any reliable data or even estimates of this effect, centuries of legal tradition, not to mention concerns for fairness to defendants, should not be casually tossed aside in our zeal (however well founded) to prevent child sexual abuse and give its victims their day in court. Legislatures should not be swayed by the emotionally compelling arguments for abolishing statutes of limitations in this context but should cautiously consider expanding the prescribed time periods in a way that fairly takes into account the needs of alleged victims, alleged perpetrators, and society as a whole.

ENHANCING CRIMINAL PENALTIES FOR CONVICTED ABUSERS

In recent years, increased public and media concern about child sexual abuse has led many legislative bodies, courts, and parole authorities to drastically increase the prison sentences served by those convicted of committing such abuse. In many instances, child sexual abusers now face decades if not life in prison. As the National Conference of State Legislatures recently reported, over the past decade, at least 25 states have enacted laws that provide "mandatory 25 year minimum sentences for first time child sex crime offenders."[14] Until the US Supreme Court recently held the practice a violation of the Eighth Amendment ban on cruel and unusual punishment, some state laws allowed child rapists to be sentenced to death.[15]

A recent case in New York, a state that has not yet adopted such harsh penalties for child sex offenders, demonstrates that even without such extremely severe sentencing provisions, courts can and do still find ways to make child sexual offending the basis for a life sentence. In 2013 Nechemya Weberman, a New York rabbi, was found guilty of sexually abusing a child he was seeing for counseling. It was alleged that on numerous occasions over a 3-year period, when the girl was 12–15 years of age, Weberman fondled her breasts and vagina and forced her to perform oral sex. Convicted of 59 counts of sexual abuse, Weberman faced a maximum sentence of 117 years in prison, if the sentences he received were ordered to run consecutively instead of concurrently. In sentencing Weberman to 103 years of incarceration, the judge said: "The message should go out to all victims of sexual abuse that your cries will be heard and justice will be done."[16]

Among the common justifications for such severe sanctions is the widely held belief that these penalties deter would-be child sex offenders and thus serve a preventive function. In fact, however, as David Finkelhor has noted:

> No studies have tested whether sentencing practices have an effect on sex crime. Some studies of crime in general have linked higher incarceration rates with decreasing crime in general. The effect is thought to result more from incapacitation than from deterrence. It is not clear how much of the improvement is achieved through longer sentences and how much through increased apprehension and incarceration of criminals. Meta-analyses on the issue of sentence length suggest that length by itself bears no relationship to the likelihood to reoffend.[17]

Even if severe criminal penalties do not deter potential child sex offenders, they might be justified as a form of incapacitation or preventive detention. One can argue about the relative costs and benefits involved in the lengthy incarceration of child sex offenders but there can be little doubt that incapacitation is a highly effective form of prevention in that it ensures that a convicted child sex offender will not offend against other children, at least while he or she is incarcerated.

If society wants, and is willing to pay for, absolute safety from convicted child sex offenders, then clearly lengthy prison sentences (especially life imprisonment) for these offenders might seem sensible. Moreover, although the economic cost of incarcerating a child sex offender for 25 years to life is staggering, prison is cheaper than some alternatives. For instance, as is noted later in this chapter, the cost of confinement in prison is often much less than the cost of confinement of these offenders in treatment facilities under civil commitment laws. Also, many child sex offenders are subjected to costly measures, such as registration, global positioning satellite monitoring, and parole supervision, even after their release from prison. Thus, the cost of dealing with convicted child sex offenders, even outside of incarceration, is quite high.

The problem with incapacitation as a justification for extremely severe criminal penalties is that it flies in the face of what is known about recidivism rates among child sex offenders. Contrary to the beliefs of many, including legislators and public officials, the known recidivism rate for sexual offenders is remarkably low. In 2003, the US Department of Justice published a 3-year follow-up study of the recidivism of all 272,111 prisoners released from prison in 15 states in 1994 (Arizona, Maryland, North Carolina, California, Michigan, Ohio, Delaware, Minnesota, Oregon, Florida, New Jersey, Texas, Illinois, New York, and Virginia). Among these offenders, 3,115 had been convicted of rape, 6,576 of sexual assault, 4,295 of child molestation, and 443 of statutory rape.[18]

During the 3 years after their release, only 1.3 percent of released nonsex offenders (3,328 of 262,420) were arrested for a sex offense. Although sex offenders were four times more likely than released nonsex offenders to be rearrested for a sex crime in that 3-year period, their rate of rearrest for a sex offense was just 5.3 percent (517 out of 9,691), a rate much lower than often assumed. During that same 3-year period, 5 percent of convicted rapists (155 out of 3,115), 3.3 percent of child molesters (141 out of 4295), 5.5 percent of sexual assaulters (362 out of 6576), and 2.5 percent of statutory rapists (11 out of 443) were arrested for new sex offenses.

Other data support the Justice Department's report on sex offender recidivism. For example, among 232 male sex offenders released by the Alaska Department of Corrections in 2001, just 3.4 percent were arrested for a sex offense in the next 3 years.[19] An Illinois study found that, within 1, 3, and 5 years after their release from custody, less than 4 percent of convicted child molesters, and only about 7 percent of convicted rapists, were rearrested for a sex offense.[20] An Idaho study, published in 2009, found that among a randomly selected sample of 447 child sex offenders, with "exposure to recidivism in time periods ranging from 2 to 15 years," only 41 (9.2 percent) were again convicted of another sex crime.[21]

A 2004 study, limited to released sex offenders in Canada and the American states of California and Washington, reported sexual recidivism rates much greater than those reported generally in the United States. This study examined a diverse sample of 4,724 sex offenders released from federal, state, or provincial prisons or from a maximum security psychiatric facility. In most but not all instances, both charges and convictions for sexual offenses were used as recidivism criteria.[22]

Use of a statistical technique known as "survival analysis" resulted in estimates of recidivism rates for 5, 10, and 15 years postrelease. Offenders who died or were reincarcerated were removed from the data pool, so that only those who were at risk of reoffending were considered at any given time period. "The overall recidivism rates (14% after 5 years, 20% after 10 years and 24% after 15 years) were similar for rapists (14%, 21% and 24%) and the combined group of child molesters (13%, 18%, and 23%)."[23]

Although these estimates greatly exceed the sexual recidivism rates found in American studies, it is interesting to note how they were interpreted by the Canadian researchers:

> Most sexual offenders do not re-offend sexually over time. This may be the most important finding of this study as this finding is contrary to some strongly held beliefs. After 15 years, 73% of sexual offenders had not been charged with, or convicted of, another sexual offence. The sample was sufficiently large that very strong contradictory evidence is necessary to substantially change these recidivism estimates.[24]

None of the studies just described are fully accurate assessments of sexual recidivism since neither convictions, charges or even arrests are precise proxies for crimes committed because many sexual offenses are never reported and, among those that are reported, not all result in an arrest, charge or conviction. Still, the best available data suggest that sexual recidivism rates for released sex offenders, including child sex offenders, are rather low, especially in the United States.

Thus, although preventive strategies that rely upon severe criminal sanctions, justified by incapacitation, may stop some child sexual abusers from reoffending, the number so affected is likely to be relatively small. In sentencing child sex offenders to extremely lengthy prison terms, society will thus be paying huge sums of money to prevent what is not likely to have occurred without such lengthy confinement. To put it most bluntly, resources that could be better deployed in preventing the sexual abuse and exploitation of children will often be wasted in efforts to prevent recidivism that probably would not have occurred in any event.

In addition to general deterrence and incapacitation, denunciation and retribution are important and commonly accepted justifications for criminal punishment in American society. Denunciation and retribution no doubt have some psychological and symbolic value to both society and victims of crime and may arguably be worth the economic costs they entail. But does either of these justifications contribute to the prevention of child sexual abuse and exploitation? It could be argued that they are an important part of the overall goal of general deterrence. However, there are also strong arguments that these extraordinarily severe criminal sanctions not only reflect but help fuel the extreme stigmatization, if not demonization, of child sex offenders in current society, which in turn may increase rather than decrease the likelihood that a convicted child sex offender will reoffend if and when he or she is released from confinement.

Finally, proportionality, the notion that the punishment should fit the crime, should also be considered in determining the severity of criminal punishment for convicted child sex offenders. It is sometimes argued that penalties for child sex offenses are too severe because they may exceed penalties for murder. The Weberman case just mentioned is a prime example. In New York State the maximum sentence for most murders is 25 years to life in prison. In extraordinary cases, such as torture killings or mass murder, the maximum penalty is life without parole. Weberman committed an abominable series of sex offenses against a teenage girl, but did not murder her or anyone else. He certainly did not commit mass murder. Yet, his sentence (effectively life in prison without parole) is the same as that which could have been imposed upon someone who committed mass murder or killed a single person by means of torture.

Outside the death penalty context, the US Supreme Court has essentially held that there is no requirement of proportionality in criminal sentencing.[25] Thus, short of imposing the death penalty, states and the federal government are free to impose upon convicted child sex offenders whatever length of incarceration they see fit. However, if lawmakers are truly concerned about preventing child sexual abuse and exploitation, they may want to more carefully and rationally consider the criminal punishments they prescribe for such crimes. As already noted, to the extent that extreme criminal penalties contribute to the stigmatization if not demonization of child sex offenders, they may prove to be counterproductive, at least in those cases in which the offender is eventually released from prison, increasing rather than decrease the likelihood of reoffending. Beyond that, however, there is also the concern that if penalties for some less serious child sex offenses become too harsh and are perceived by the public as grossly disproportionate, judges and juries may become less willing to convict defendants charged with committing them, even when the evidence of guilt is strong.

Criminologists often point out that the deterrent function of such punishment stems not only from its severity, but also from the probability of arrest and conviction. Indeed, "[m]any existing studies allow us to draw the inference that the magnitude of the effect of the certainty of punishment, particularly the probability of arrest, is greater than that of the effect of the severity of punishment."[26] Although there are no data demonstrating this in the narrow context of child sexual abuse, it may well be the case. David Finkelhor has observed:

> The most elemental thing the criminal justice system can do about a crime is to increase its detection and disclosure and the likelihood that the offender will be arrested and prosecuted. Disclosure can terminate abusive relationships, which are frequently ongoing in child sexual abuse, and prevent future ones. The offenders who are caught, even if they are not incapacitated, are deterred through embarrassment, humiliation, and increased vigilance by members of their social network. Other potential offenders are deterred by the circulation of news that offenders get caught.[27]

If Finkelhor is correct, then equal or even greater deterrence of child sexual abuse may be achieved by limiting periods of extremely expensive incarceration and using the money thereby saved to promote greater victim disclosure, improve investigations, and increase the timeliness and efficacy of prosecutions.

SEX OFFENDER REGISTRATION, NOTIFICATION, AND RESTRICTION LAWS

Today, nearly 750,000 Americans are registered sex offenders, a 23 percent increase from 6 years earlier.[28] Registered sex offenders are required by law, both state and federal, to regularly provide law enforcement officials with their names, photographs, addresses, and other identifying information, some or all of which is made readily available to anyone with access to the Internet. Many of these offenders also face a variety of legally imposed restrictions on where they can live, work, and travel.

Sex Offender Registration and Notification

Although sex offender registries date back to at least the 1930s, they did not become a national phenomenon until the past two decades or so. The first modern sex offender registration law was enacted in the state of Washington in 1990.[29] The Washington statute was the first in the nation to authorize law enforcement authorities to notify community residents when certain released sex offenders moved into their neighborhoods.[30]

Under Washington's Community Protection Act, sex offenders were to be registered and classified as Level I, II, or III. Registry information regarding

Level I offenders, those deemed at low risk of reoffending, was to be shared with law enforcement agencies and, upon request, could be disclosed to any victim or witness to the offense and to any individual who lived near where the offender resided, expected to reside, or was regularly found. Registry information about Level II offenders, those believed to present a moderate risk of reoffending, could be disclosed to public and private schools; child care centers; day care providers; businesses and organizations primarily serving children; women or vulnerable adults; neighbors of the offender; and community groups located near the residence where the offender resided, expected to reside, or was regularly found. Registry information regarding Level III offenders, those determined to be at a high risk of reoffending, was to be disclosed to the public at large.

Over the next 16 years or more, legislators in every state as well as those in Congress enacted laws requiring sex offender registration, notification, and restriction. Today most of these laws are known as Megan's Laws because they were modeled, at least in part, after the original Megan's Law. The original Megan's Law was passed in New Jersey in 1994 after an incident earlier that year in which 7-year-old Megan Kanka was lured into the home of a neighbor, Jesse Timmendequas, who raped and strangled her. Unknown to Megan's parents, Timmendequas, who lived across the street, had earlier been convicted for aggravated assault and attempted sexual assault of another child and had been imprisoned for 6 years.[31]

In the immediate aftermath of Megan Kanka's murder, more than 400,000 New Jersey residents signed a petition demanding a law that would, among other things, require the state to register sex offenders and notify the public of their presence in the community.[32] In less than 90 days, and without holding a single public hearing, the New Jersey legislature responded favorably by enacting the original Megan's Law.[33]

The constitutionality of New Jersey's Megan's Law was challenged almost immediately. The state's Supreme Court held that the registration and notification requirements specified by the Act were constitutional:

> The Registration and Notification Laws are not retributive laws, but laws designed to give people a chance to protect themselves and their children. They do not represent the slightest departure from our State's or our country's fundamental belief that criminals, convicted and punished, have paid their debt to society and are not to be punished further. They represent only the conclusion that society has the right to know of their presence not in order to punish them, but in order to protect itself. . .
>
> The choice the Legislature made was difficult, for at stake was the continued apparently normal lifestyle of previously-convicted sex offenders, some of whom were doing no harm and very well might never do any harm, as weighed against the potential molestation, rape, or murder by others of women and children because they simply did not know of the presence of such a person and therefore did not take the common-sense

steps that might prevent such an occurrence. The Legislature chose to risk unfairness to the previously-convicted offenders rather than unfairness to the children and women who might suffer because of their ignorance, but attempted to restrict the damage that notification of the public might do to the lives of rehabilitated offenders by trying to identify those most likely to reoffend and limiting the extent of notification based on that conclusion.[34]

Support for a national Megan's Law arose quickly after enactment of the New Jersey law. In 1996, after only brief debate, Congress enacted a federal version of the statute, requiring all states to establish some form of community notification. Members of Congress supporting the law argued that it was necessary because: "A study of imprisoned child sex offenders found that 74 percent had a previous conviction for another child sex offense"[35]; "There is a ninety percent likelihood of recidivism for sexual crimes against children"[36]; and "[W]e know that more than 40 percent of convicted sex offenders will repeat their crimes."[37] The bill passed in the House of Representatives by a vote of 418-0 and in the Senate by unanimous consent.

The federal version of Megan's Law required that each state "shall release relevant information that is necessary to protect the public."[38] Subsequent federal guidelines, developed under the new law, provided that: "Information must be released to members of the public as necessary to protect the public from registered offenders."[39] Following enactment of the federal Megan's Law, every state that had not already done so enacted some form of public notification regarding sex offenders. By the end of 1996, every state, the District of Columbia, and the federal government had enacted some variation of Megan's Law. In a series of cases that followed, the US Supreme Court affirmed the constitutionality of the law's key provisions.[40]

In 1996, less than 5 months after the federal version of Megan's Law was signed into law, Congress amended it, passing the Pam Lyncher Sexual Offender Tracking and Identification Act of 1996, which mandated that recidivist sex offenders and those convicted of "aggravated" sexual violence register for life.[41] In 2006, 10 years after enacting the federal Megan's Law, Congress passed the Adam Walsh Child Protection and Safety Act, named in honor of a 6-year-old boy who was abducted and murdered in Florida.[42] The Adam Walsh Act included the Sex Offender Registration and Notification Act (SORNA), which created a national sex offender registry, required every American state and territory to establish and maintain an online registry of sex offenders, and mandated that every jurisdiction upload its registry to a federal website accessible to the public by 2009.[43] SORNA also applies retrospectively to all sex offenders regardless of when they committed their offenses, were convicted, or were released; requires all registered offenders to update their required information in person; and expands registry data to include updated photographs, social security numbers, fingerprints, palmprints, DNA samples, and motor vehicle license numbers and descriptions.

Additionally, SORNA requires certain juvenile sex offenders to register and creates a three-tiered risk assessment scheme for all sex offenders based upon the severity of the offense rather than any individual risk determinations. Under the Act, depending upon the crime(s) for which they were convicted, sex offenders are assigned to one of three levels or tiers. Level one offenders, those whose offense(s) are among the least serious, must register for at least 15 years and update their registration annually. Level two offenders are required to register for 25 years and verify their registrations semiannually. Level three offenders, whose offense(s) are among the most serious, must register for the duration of their lives and update their registrations every 3 months. The Act provides no means by which a registrant may challenge the required duration of his or her registration.

Although to date not all states have fully complied with the requirements of SORNA, the existing state and territorial sex offender registries are readily accessible from a single online source, the Dru Sjodin National Sex Offender Public Website, named in honor of a 22-year-old North Dakota college student who was kidnapped, sexually assaulted, and murdered in 2003.[44]

Visitors to this website may search for a registered sex offender by name; state, territory, or Indian nation; county; town; and/or zip code. The information available on the website about any given offender depends on the state, but all listings contain offenders' names; aliases, if any; photographs; dates of birth; and physical descriptions. All contain some description of the offender's sex crime(s), some of which are nothing more than the name given the offense in the state's penal law or a vague reference, such as "sex offense, second degree." Most listings contain offenders' addresses and vehicle information including make, model, color, and license plate number. Some also contain links to an online map pinpointing the exact location of the offender's address. Other data sometimes available include the name and location of any school the offender is attending; current supervision status; employment address; and scars, marks, and tattoos. A few websites even allow visitors to sign up to receive e-mailed updates when there is a change in the offender's reported address or to submit information to law enforcement authorities regarding the whereabouts of an offender.

According to the US Department of Justice, "Since its launch in the summer of 2005, there have been more than 17 million [website] user sessions, with 2.3 billion hits. Today, [the website] remains extremely active, averaging 2.3 million hits per day and 14,000 daily users."[45]

Sex Offender Residency and Travel Restrictions

In addition to requiring sex offenders to register and have their information made readily available to the public, many jurisdictions have also imposed residency and travel restrictions. At least 30 states have enacted residency restrictions prohibiting sex offenders from living within a specified distance of schools, day-care centers, parks, or other places where children congregate. The required distance a registered sex offender must live from these places ranges from 500–2500 feet.

Additionally, several hundred municipalities have passed similar local ordinances. In fact, some cities, towns, and villages have effectively banned registered sex offenders from living anywhere within their limits.

At the state level, for example, in Alabama and Iowa, convicted sex offenders may not reside or work within 2,000 feet of schools or childcare facilities; Arkansas has the same rule but limits it to the most serious sex offenders; Oklahoma maintains the same distance requirement but limits it to schools. Other states, including Florida, Kentucky, Indiana, Louisiana, Missouri, Michigan, Tennessee, and West Virginia have similar laws but impose a distance limit of 1,000 feet. Some of these states also include playgrounds, ball fields, school buses, bus stops, or any other places where minors congregate. Georgia law provides that a registered sex offender may not reside, work, or loiter within 1,000 feet of any school, childcare facility, school bus stop, or place where minors congregate. Still other states, such as Illinois and South Dakota, apply a 500-foot buffer zone.

Even in states that have placed statewide residency restrictions on registered sex offenders, some municipalities have enacted even more stringent restrictions. For example, in Florida, which has a statewide ban on registered sex offenders living within 1,000 feet of schools, day-care centers, parks, and other places that attract children, more than 60 municipalities have their own residency restriction ordinances, which include parks, playgrounds, churches, and libraries, among other places where minors might congregate.

In Georgia, one municipality has banned sex offenders from residing within 2,500 feet of a school.[46] In Texas, where the Parole Board determines how close a sex offender may live or even go near to a "child safety zone," several municipalities have enacted buffer zones of between 1,000 and 2,000 feet; at least one has criminalized knowingly renting a sex offender a place to live within a restricted zone.[47] In California, parts of one county have restricted registered sex offenders from being within 300 feet of libraries.[48]

In addition to residency restrictions, some states and municipalities have enacted employment restrictions, under which registered sex offenders are not allowed to work at and/or within a certain physical proximity to a school, day-care center, park, or other place where children might congregate.[49] These laws are generally in addition to others that prohibit convicted sex offenders from being employed in teaching, childcare, or other occupations that serve children. Such laws are not limited by the nature of the work or limited to work done at a school, day-care center, park, or other place where children may congregate. Thus, for example, a salesperson could not make a sales call within the prohibited zone, and a deliveryman could not deliver a package in such an area. At least nine states have such laws.[50]

In 2008, California voters overwhelmingly approved a public ballot initiative, Proposition 83, barring all registered sex offenders from living within 2,000 foot of a school or park and requiring that all paroled felony sex offenders wear a global positioning satellite tracking device for the rest of their lives.[51] With passage of Proposition 83, California became one of at least two dozen states that require global positioning satellite monitoring of paroled sex offenders.[52]

Common Sense versus Empirical Data

It is clear from their legislative histories and the court decisions affirming their constitutionality that sex offender registration and notification laws and their accompanying restrictions on residency and employment were intended to prevent sexual offending, particularly sex offenses against children, by reducing the likelihood that a previously convicted sex offender will reoffend. Although courts have acknowledged the heavy burden these laws place on convicted offenders who already have been appropriately punished for their crimes, they have almost unanimously upheld these laws in large measure because they believe that reducing sex offense recidivism is a salutary goal and that common sense dictates that these laws are helping, or at least will help, achieve that goal. For example, as the New Jersey Supreme Court said in upholding the original Megan's Law, if people in a community are made aware of the sex offenders among them, they can take "common-sense steps" to protect themselves and their children.[53] As the US Court of Appeals for the Eighth Circuit concluded in upholding Iowa's residency restriction law, legislators are simply using "common sense" when they enact such statutes or ordinances.[54]

It is difficult to argue with common sense but whether these laws have the preventive effect legislatures and courts believe they do is an empirical question. Although no research has yet directly answered that question, numerous studies have provided empirical data that may be more useful than mere reliance upon common sense.

At least 18 published and unpublished studies have attempted to assess the efficacy of sex offender registration and notification laws in reducing recidivism among convicted sex offenders or the commission of sex offenses more generally. In 2009, a team of researchers at the Washington State Institute for Public Policy conducted a meta-analysis of some of these studies with the goal of answering this question: "Does sex offender registration and notification affect measured crime outcomes?"[55] Data used in these studies were gathered from 16 states: California, Delaware, Florida, Illinois, Maryland, Michigan, Minnesota, New Jersey, New York, North Carolina, Ohio, Oregon, South Carolina, Texas, Virginia, and Washington.

The two studies directed at the general deterrence effect of registration and notification laws were insufficient for a meta-analysis, but provided interesting results. The first relied upon data from the National Incident-Based Reporting System.[56] As was noted in Chapter Two of this volume, National Incident-Based Reporting System is a federal crime reporting system that is replacing the well-known FBI Uniform Crime Reports. National Incident-Based Reporting System is "an incident-based reporting system for crimes known to the police. For each crime incident coming to the attention of law enforcement, a variety of data are collected about the incident. These data include the nature and types of specific offenses in the incident, characteristics of the victim(s) and offender(s), types and value of property stolen and recovered, and characteristics of persons arrested in connection with a crime incident."[57] In 2008, Prescott and Rockoff examined the effects of sex offender registration and notification laws in 15 states and were the first and only researchers to date to separately examine the effects of registration and notification. Their data suggest that although the average registration law results in a statistically significant 10 percent reduction in overall sex offense rates, that positive effect is more than overcome by the negative effects of notification laws. As they explain:

> We find evidence that registration reduces the frequency of sex offenses by providing law enforcement with information on local sex offenders... We also find evidence that community notification deters crime, but in a way unanticipated by legislators. Our results correspond with a model in which community notification deters first-time sex offenses, but increases recidivism by registered offenders due to a change in the relative utility of legal and illegal behavior. This finding is consistent with work by criminologists suggesting that notification may increase recidivism by imposing social and financial costs on registered sex offenders and making non-criminal activity relatively less attractive. We regard this latter finding as potentially important, given that the purpose of community notification is to reduce recidivism.[58]

The second study related to general deterrence was reported in 2006 by Shao and Li, who used FBI Uniform Crime Reports data from all states from 1970–2002 to explore the effect of registration laws on reported rapes.[59] They found a statistically significant 2 percent reduction in reported rapes associated with sex offender registration laws.

Reviewing these two studies, the Washington researchers suggested that although these studies do provide "some indication" that sex offender registration laws may lower the rates of certain sex crimes, efforts to generalize should be undertaken with caution, given the extremely limited number of studies.[60]

The other seven studies that were included in the Washington meta-analysis dealing with the possible deterrent effects of sex offender registration and notification laws provide a more robust finding. The individual results of these studies showed no clear pattern. One study found increased rates of recidivism, two found decreases in recidivism, and four found no statistically significant differences in recidivism. For the Washington research team, the results were clear: "For this group of studies, we performed a meta-analysis and found no statistically significant difference in recidivism rates for either sex offenses or total offenses."[61] It is also worth noting that even those studies that were considered but not included in the Washington meta-analysis because they lacked sufficient methodological rigor yielded results that were predominantly consistent with the finding of the meta-analysis.

One of these latter studies seems especially pertinent, even though it was not included in the Washington meta-analysis. In a study conducted under the auspices of the Research & Evaluation Unit of the Office of Policy and Planning in the New Jersey Department of Corrections and sponsored by the National Institute of Justice, researchers compared the rearrest rates of registered sex offenders with those of sex offenders not required to register before implementation of the original Megan's Law.[62] They used a 6-year follow-up and conducted a time-series analysis. Although this was excluded from the Washington meta-analysis because offenders in the registration group had fewer prior sex offenses than those in the nonregistration group and the research team did not use multivariate analysis to control for between-group differences, the study's results and conclusions are striking:

> Megan's Law has no effect on community tenure (i.e., time to first re-arrest).
> Megan's Law showed no demonstrable effect in reducing sexual re-offenses.
> Megan's Law has no effect on the type of sexual re-offense or first time sexual offense (still largely child molestation/incest).
> Megan's Law has no effect on reducing the number of victims involved in sexual offenses.[63]

In addition to studies examining the intended effects of sex offender registration and notification laws, some researchers have examined what might be called the unintended consequences of these laws. For example, Levenson and Cotter undertook an "exploratory study" of a nonrandom sample of 135 sex offenders from two outpatient sex offender counseling centers in Fort Lauderdale, Florida.[64] All subjects in this study were on probation for sex offenses, all were in sex offender treatment, and all volunteered to complete a survey developed by Levenson and Cotter. Ninety-seven percent of these subjects identified themselves as child molesters.

At the time of this study, Florida prohibited sex offenders from living within 1,000 feet of a school, park, playground, day-care center, or other place where children regularly congregate. In response to questions about the effects of these restrictions, 22 percent of the offenders reported having had to move out of a home they owned; 28 percent reported having had to move from an apartment they had rented; 25 percent reported having been unable to return to their homes when released from prison; 44 percent reported being unable to live with supportive family members; 57 percent reported having trouble finding housing; 48 percent reported having suffered financially; and 60 percent reported that they had suffered emotionally. Additionally, most of these offenders reported that the residency restrictions would have no impact on their future offending behavior. Many reported feeling that if they wanted to reoffend, the residency restriction would not stop them; many also reported that they "have always been careful not to reoffend in close proximity to their homes, so geographical restrictions provided little deterrence."[65]

The effects of sex offender residency restrictions have been examined by a number of other recent studies. Chajewski and Mercado tried to determine the effects various sex offender residency restrictions (1,000 feet versus 2,500 feet from schools) would have in three New Jersey settings: a rural town, a suburban county, and a city.[66] They found that if a 1,000-foot residency restriction were enacted in a rural town with a population of approximately 17,402, 31.25 percent of the sex offenders living there would have to relocate, and that a 2,500 foot residency restriction would require all sex offenders to move away. They also found that in a large mostly suburban county with a population of approximately 982,561, a 1,000 foot residency restriction would require 37.50 percent of the county's registered sex offenders to find alternative housing, and that a 2,500 foot restriction would require 91.07 percent of registered sex offenders to relocate. Finally, they found that enactment of a 1,000-foot restriction in a city with a population of about 273,546 would put almost two-thirds (64.80 percent) of registered sex offenders in violation, and that with a 2,500-foot restriction almost all (98.47 percent) such offenders would be in violation of the residency restriction.

Significantly, Chajewski and Mercado also found that "nearly all sex offenders and community members lived within 2,500 feet of the schools, suggesting that these are not deterministic choices made uniquely by sex offenders to live in these locations, but rather are dependent upon urban planning."[67] Additionally, they cautioned that they had "examined the distances around registered schools and daycare centers with school components only, and did not consider parks, playgrounds, shopping centers, bus stops, or other areas where children gather that have been included in some statutes and local ordinances."[68] As a result, they observed that "this analysis should be considered exceptionally conservative in that these findings would likely be amplified were the analyses to have included these additional areas."[69]

Earlier, Zandbergen and Hart described using similar methodology to quantify the impact of residency restrictions on registered sex offenders in Orange County, Florida.[70] They found that housing options for registered sex offenders, prohibited from living within 1,000 feet of places where children congregate, "were limited to only 5 percent of potentially available parcels…mostly in low-density rural areas."[71] They also found that "[i]ncreasing the buffer zone from 1,000 to 2,500 feet had only a minor impact on housing options."[72] Zandbergen and Hart concluded that "These findings support the argument that residency restrictions for sex offenders contribute significantly to their social and economic isolation [and to the risk of] larger numbers of sex offenders being homeless and transient."[73]

A federal appeals court, although concluding that Megan's Laws are not punitive in the legal sense, nevertheless summarized many of the "indirect effects" of these laws:

People interact with others based on the information they have about them. Knowing that someone is a convicted sex offender and has been evaluated as a continuing risk is likely to affect how most people treat that person.

There can be no doubt that the indirect effects of Tier 2 and Tier 3 notification on the registrants involved and their families are harsh. The record documents that registrants and their families have experienced profound humiliation and isolation as a result of the reaction of those notified. Employment and employment opportunities have been jeopardized or lost. Housing and housing opportunities have suffered a similar fate. Family and other personal relationships have been destroyed or severely strained.

Retribution has been visited by private, unlawful violence and threats and, while such incidents of "vigilante justice" are not common, they happen with sufficient frequency and publicity that registrants justifiably live in fear of them. It also must be noted that these indirect effects are not short-lived...[74]

The "vigilante justice" to which the court referred was illustrated in more than 100 affidavits gathered and presented by New Jersey public defenders representing registrants challenging the law.[76] For example,

Registrants [spoke] of having glass bottles thrown through their windows; being "jumped from behind" and physically assaulted while the assailants yelled "You like little children, right?"; having garbage thrown on the lawn; people repeatedly ringing the doorbell and pounding on the sides of the house late at night; being struck from behind by a crowbar after being yelled at by the assailant that "People like you who are under Megan's Law should be kept in jail. They should never let you out. People like you should die. When you leave tonight, I am gonna kill you"...[76]

In addition to receiving threats, some convicted offenders reportedly have been killed by vigilantes who located them by using addresses and/or other information provided on government sex offender registries.[77]

Lawmakers have apparently realized that sex offender registration and notification laws could facilitate vigilantism. Many states passed laws prohibiting the use of sex offender registry information for purposes of harassing, discriminating against, or assaulting sex offenders, and several have given sex offender registrants a civil cause of action against persons who misuse registry information.

The direct and indirect economic costs of sex offender registration, notification, and restriction laws have been enormous. Although Congress allocated $47 million to cover startup costs associated with the federal sex offender registry under the Adam Walsh Act, the costs of implementing SORNA were otherwise left almost completely to the states.[78] Estimated startup costs for SORNA implementation ranged from about $850,000 in Wyoming to nearly $60 million in California. Overall, states spent an estimated $488 million on these startup costs, which do not reflect the money spent annually to maintain the registries. For example, the estimated cost of maintaining Megan's Law in New Jersey for one recent year was $5.1 million.[79]

In addition to direct economic costs, sex offender registration and notification laws also exact indirect economic costs. Most notably, economic research indicates that these laws have a negative effect on the value of real property located near the residence of a registered sex offender. A study that examined approximately 3,200 home transactions in an Ohio county over a 1-year period found that, on average, houses located within one-tenth of a mile of a sexual offender sold for 17.4 percent less than similar houses located farther away; houses located between one- and two-tenths of a mile from an offender sold for 10.2 percent less; and houses located between two- and three-tenths of a mile from an offender sold for 9.3 percent less. As the authors of this study explained, speaking of public notification of the presence of a registered sex offender, "Once that information is made available to the public, we have found that it has an effect on the price of houses. If you have a person who committed a sex offense next door to you, or even a block away, or two-tenths of a mile away, you pay a price."[80]

More recently, another multiyear study of home assessments and sales in a North Carolina county found "extremely localized" but "economically and statistically significant negative effects" of the location of sex offenders' residences on the value of nearby real estate: "Houses within a one-tenth mile area around the home of a sex offender fall by 4 percent on average (about $5,500)... [But] the effect varies with distance... [H]ouses next to an offender sell for about 12 percent less while those a tenth of a mile away or more show no decline."[81]

Beyond Common Sense

Not only do sex offender registration, notification, and restriction laws cost untold millions if not billions of dollars to enforce each year, they have not reduced the number of sex offenses in the United States or even that among previously convicted sex offenders who have been the direct targets of these laws. Worse yet, by virtue of their punitive nature, these laws may not only fail to reduce recidivism among convicted sex offenders but may, in some instances, actually increase the likelihood that convicted sex offenders will recidivate. As a recent report by Human Rights Watch cautioned:

> Current registration, community notification, and residency restriction laws may be counterproductive, impeding rather than promoting public safety. For example, the proliferation of people required to register even though their crimes were not serious makes it harder for law enforcement to determine which sex offenders warrant careful monitoring. Unfettered online access to registry information facilitates—if not encourages—neighbors, employers, colleagues, and others to shun and ostracize former offenders—diminishing the likelihood of their successful reintegration into communities. Residency restrictions push former offenders away from the supervision, treatment, stability, and supportive networks they may need to build and maintain successful, law abiding lives.[82]

Yet another significant problem with sex offender registration, notification, and restriction laws is that they may create among the public a false sense of security that leads some, especially parents and caretakers of children, to be less mindful of the dangers of sexual victimization. For example, one who peruses an online sex offender registry may be relieved to learn that there are no registered sex offenders living in his or her zip code or, if there are, that their names, photographs, addresses, and other identifying information are immediately visible. Even those who never view a registry website may take false comfort in the belief that although they are not aware of the names, addresses, and other identifying features of nearby convicted sex offenders, the existence of the registry and website means that some people are aware, and their awareness makes everyone at least somewhat safer.

Similarly, knowing that by law convicted sex offenders are not allowed to live within 2,500, 1,000, or even 500 feet of a school, day-care center, playground, park, or other place where children congregate, parents and caretakers may conclude that children are thus safer and less in need of care and supervision when they are in these "child safety zones." Unfortunately, the facts do not support any such conclusion.

Sex offender registration, notification, and community restriction laws arose out of an understandable visceral response to a small number of outrageous sex crimes, coupled with false beliefs about the rate of recidivism among convicted sex offenders. These laws have been passed with little or no concern for either cost or the likelihood that they will, in fact, reduce either sex offender recidivism or the number of child sex offenses in general. Indeed, some of these laws have been passed with no public input and little if any debate. These laws have been upheld by courts in deference to the common sense conclusions of legislatures that these laws would actually reduce the number of sex crimes. The consensus of empirical research, however, is that these sex offender registration and notification laws have no statistically significant effect on sex offender recidivism and thus fail to provide the protection upon which they are premised and which they promise the public.

CIVIL COMMITMENT OF SEX OFFENDERS

In addition to attempting to prevent child sexual abuse and exploitation by enhancing criminal penalties for those convicted of such conduct, 20 states and the federal government have also enacted so-called sexually violent predator (SVP) laws.[83] These statutes vary from state to state, but nearly all of them (including the federal law) follow in large measure the model first adopted in the state of Washington in 1990. Sex offenders who are about to be released from prison, having served their entire terms of incarceration or having otherwise reached their maximum release dates, are screened by state employees who review their files and decide whether or not they should be considered for SVP status. Those found to warrant further consideration are referred for additional scrutiny that often includes a formal psychological or psychiatric evaluation. The results of that evaluation are used, in conjunction with the offender's overall history and record, to determine whether he or she is to be petitioned (i.e., ordered into court to face the charge that he or she is a sexually violent predator).

Offenders found by the courts not to be SVPs are generally released from custody altogether or on some form of parole. Depending on the state, those who are determined to be SVPs (generally those found to have a mentally abnormality that predisposes them to reoffend if not confined) are indefinitely committed to a secure prison-like sex offender treatment center or conditionally released to the community under strict and intensive supervision that generally amounts to a form of "super-parole." In only one state, Texas, is the latter disposition mandatory.[84]

All states with SVP statutes offer some form of treatment to those adjudicated as SVPs. Indeed, they are required to offer such treatment by a US Supreme Court decision holding that confinement under an VP law is not punitive if it includes some form of treatment.[85] The form such treatment takes varies from state to state. In all states, periodic judicial review of the offender's status as a sexually violent predator is required, and those found no longer to be SVPs must be released. It is generally expected, however, that to reach that point an offender must have successfully completed all stages of his or her prescribed treatment plan, a regimen that generally takes many years. Although some SVPs have been ordered released, either outright or on some form of strict and intensive community supervision, in most states most offenders deemed SVPs have been confined more or less permanently.[86] Moreover, many SVPs who have been released have later had their releases revoked and been returned to civil confinement.[87]

The low percentage of committed offenders who are released from SVP civil commitment appears to be largely the result of three factors: (1) the popular image, shaped by the application of certain psychiatric diagnoses, that such offenders are permanently mentally abnormal; (2) the popular but erroneous view, reinforced by the application of static, statistically generated predictions of risk, that these offenders are and always will be at a high risk of reoffending; and (3) unresolved questions about the efficacy of current treatment modalities for sex offenders and the practical concern that many committed SVPs are not receiving any treatment.

Mental Abnormality

Although no statute or court decision demands it, a finding that a sex offender qualifies for SVP civil commitment requires, as a practical matter, a formal diagnosis by a qualified mental health professional. Moreover, although the statutes do not require it, that diagnosis must generally be one recognized in the field of mental health (i.e., specified in the American Psychiatric Association's *Diagnostic and Statistical Manual of Mental Disorders, Fourth Edition* [*DSM-IV*]).[88] Thus, the *DSM-IV* has, de facto, become part of every SVP law.

Conscientious reliance upon the *DSM-IV* for this purpose, however, has created numerous problems for experts and the courts because many candidates for SVP status do not meet the criteria for a DSM diagnosis. This is not surprising because the DSM was developed for clinical purposes and not for the classification of criminal conduct.[89]

Necessity, of course, is the mother of invention, so the lack of meaningful DSM diagnoses for most candidates for SVP commitment has caused many mental health experts to make creative use of the DSM: in some instances relying upon diagnoses that may or may not be accurate but are so common among sex offenders as to have little value separating ordinary offenders from those who cannot control their sexual impulses, stretching diagnoses to fit facts that otherwise would not support them, and simply making up diagnoses that are not in the *DSM*.

ANTISOCIAL PERSONALITY DISORDER

Antisocial personality disorder (ASPD) is defined in the *DSM-IV* largely on the basis of criminal or antisocial behavior:

A. There is a pervasive pattern of disregard for and violation of the rights of others occurring since age 15 years, as indicated by three (or more) of the following:
    (1) failure to conform to social norms with respect to lawful behaviors as indicated by repeatedly performing acts that are grounds for arrest
    (2) deceitfulness, as indicated by repeated lying, use of aliases, or conning others for personal profit or pleasure
    (3) impulsivity or failure to plan ahead
    (4) irritability and aggressiveness, as indicated by repeated physical fights or assaults
    (5) reckless disregard for safety of self or others
    (6) consistent irresponsibility, as indicated by repeated failure to sustain consistent work behavior or honor financial obligations
    (7) lack of remorse, as indicated by being indifferent to or rationalizing having hurt, mistreated, or stolen from another
B. The individual is at least age 18 years.
C. There is evidence of Conduct Disorder with onset before age 15 years.
D. The occurrence of antisocial behavior is not exclusively during the course of Schizophrenia or a Manic Episode.[90]

ASPD is the most common diagnosis applied to sex offenders considered for SVP commitment.[91] That is not surprising given that so many prison inmates would qualify for this diagnosis. Some authorities have estimated that 50–70 percent, or even as many as 80 percent, of male prison inmates in the United States meet the DSM criteria for ASPD.[92]

There is great debate among mental health professionals in general over whether ASPD is a mental disorder or merely a description of behaviors associated with persistent criminality. There is, however, widespread agreement if not consensus that whatever ASPD is, it is not likely to respond to any currently available treatment.

Among mental health experts who specialize in the evaluation and treatment of sex offenders, this debate has been sharpened to the question of whether this diagnosis is sufficient, by itself, to support a clinical conclusion that an individual is a sexually violent predator. Although all acknowledge that some courts appear to have answered this question in the affirmative, others note that: "As most professionals know, research is mixed regarding the relationship between ASPD and/or psychopathy and sexual recidivism. While ASPD is a very good predictor of future general and violent recidivism, it has not proved to be a consistent predictor of future sexual re-offending."[93]

Even the Association for the Treatment of Sexual Abusers, a national organization of individuals who assess and treat sex offenders and that has an obvious tangible stake in SVP laws has taken the position that "The presence of an antisocial personality disorder in and of itself is not sufficient to meet the criteria for sexual predator laws."[94]

PEDOPHILIA

One diagnosis that is recognized by the DSM and relevant to the question of whether a sex offender is likely to reoffend is pedophilia. The *DSM-IV* describes the diagnostic criteria for pedophilia as follows:

A. Over a period of at least 6 months, recurrent, intense sexually arousing fantasies, sexual urges, or behaviors involving sexual activity with a prepubescent child or children (generally age 13 years or younger).
B. The person has acted on these urges, or the sexual urges or fantasies cause marked distress or interpersonal difficulty.
C. The person is at least age 16 years and at least 5 years older than the child or children in Criterion A.
Note: Do not include an individual in late adolescence involved in an ongoing sexual relationship with a 12- or 13-year-old.[95]

Unfortunately, this diagnosis, which clearly applies only to sexual attraction to prepubescent children, has been applied "indiscriminately to individuals who offend against children (anyone under the age of consent) whether or not they meet the rather specific diagnostic criteria."[96]

For example, to some evaluators, the age, sexual maturity, and duration requirements for this diagnosis seem to matter little. Consider *Commonwealth v. Connolly*, a 2009 Massachusetts SVP proceeding in which four psychologists testified.[97] The first found no evidence of pedophilia because the respondent's victim was older than age 13 and the sexual conduct took place over a 2-month period. A second doctor testified that "in her opinion the respondent did not meet the criteria for Mental Abnormality...based...on the fact that the only offense occurred in the context of a relationship with an adolescent who he had known for less than three months, the age of the victim was thirteen; that the victim was pubescent; and he was able to ejaculate. She opined pedophilia is defined as sexual attraction to prepubescent children, and that as such the respondent did not meet criteria for that diagnosis."[98] A third psychologist testified that the respondent's "presentation was not consistent with an identifiable mental disorder as recorded in the Diagnostic and Statistical Manual"[99] and added that his "behavior was consistent with a condition described as Hebephilia,"[100] a so-called diagnosis (discussed later) related to sexual attraction to older, pubescent teenagers. The fourth psychologist, although not of the opinion that the respondent was a "sexually dangerous person" as SVPs are referred to in Massachusetts, "concluded that he met the clinical diagnostic criteria for pedophilia..."[101]

Many victims of sexual abuse, although young, are pubescent. Indeed, under statutory rape laws in some states, a minor as old as 17 years, 11 months and 31 days who willingly engages in sex with an adult is considered a sex crime victim. In every state, anyone (child, adolescent, or adult) who is forced to have sexual contact against his or her will is a sex crime victim.

In a rather transparent effort to ensure that all otherwise eligible sex offenders (including those whose preferred sexual targets are pubescent teenagers rather than children) may be subject to a diagnosis for SVP commitment purposes, some mental health professionals have attempted to create the diagnosis of hebephilia. Hebephilia describes the sexual attraction of an adult to a pubescent (i.e., sexually mature) person who is under the age of consent. Hebephilia is not, however, a recognized diagnosis. Indeed it was specifically rejected as such by the authors of the *DSM-IV*.[102]

The fact that hebephilia was specifically excluded from the *DSM-IV* has not stopped some SVP evaluators from claiming that this is a recognized diagnosis. Nor has it stopped some mental health professionals from unsuccessfully lobbying the American Psychiatric Association to include hebephilia in the forthcoming *DSM-V*.[103] Although some courts have accepted as valid the purported diagnosis of hebephilia, others have not. As one federal court recently held: "Significantly, the American Psychiatric Association considered and rejected hebephilia as a diagnostic category for a mental disorder. Moreover, there is no expert testimony in this record that psychiatric experts generally accept this definition of hebephilia as a mental disorder."[104]

PARAPHILIA NOT OTHERWISE SPECIFIED

According to the *DSM-IV*, "[t]he essential features of a Paraphilia are recurrent, intense sexually arousing fantasies, sexual urges, or behaviors generally involving (1) nonhuman objects, (2) suffering or humiliation of oneself or one's partner, or (3) children or other nonconsenting persons that occur over a period of at least 6 months."[105] *DSM-IV* lists eight specific paraphilias: exhibitionism (deviant arousal to "public exposure of one's genitals to an unsuspecting stranger"); fetishism (deviant arousal involving the use of nonliving objects); frotteurism (deviant arousal "involving touching and rubbing against a non-consenting person"); pedophilia (deviant arousal "involving sexual activity with a prepubescent child or children"); masochism (deviant arousal "involving the act [real not simulated] of being humiliated, beaten, bound, or otherwise made to suffer"); sadism (deviant arousal "involving acts [real, not simulated] in which the psychological or physical suffering [including humiliation] of the victim is sexually exciting"); transvestic fetishism (deviant arousal involving "cross-dressing"); and voyeurism (deviant arousal to "observing an unsuspecting person who is naked, in the process of disrobing, or engaging in sexual activity").[106]

The *DSM-IV* also includes a diagnostic category called "Paraphilia Not Otherwise Specified." According to the diagnostic manual, "This category is included for coding Paraphilias that do not meet the criteria for any of the specific categories. Examples include, but are not limited to, telephone scatologia (obscene phone calls), necrophilia (corpses), partialism (exclusive focus on part of body), zoophilia (animals), coprophilia (feces), klismaphilia (enemas), and urophilia (urine)."[107]

As noted above, some sex offenders who are the subject of SVP civil commitment proceedings are diagnosed with the paraphilia known as pedophilia. Exhibitionism, frotteurism, sadism, and voyeurism are also paraphilias that have been used to satisfy or partially satisfy the mental abnormality requirement for SVP civil commitment.

From the perspective of the government, a major problem in many cases is that the individual recommended for SVP civil confinement does not have a mental disorder or personality disorder, including one or more of the paraphilias recognized in *DSM-IV* or by most mental health professionals. For example, many opportunistic child sex offenders, while criminals and perverted in the lay sense of that term, are not mentally ill, personality disordered, sexually sadistic, or even pedophilic as those terms are defined by the *DSM-IV*. In many cases this obvious problem has been addressed through the attempted use of the residual diagnosis of "Paraphilia Not Otherwise Specified." For example, in *U.S. v. Shields*, a 2009 federal case, although the court rejected the government's claim that hebephilia was a mental disorder, "[t]he government argue[d] that, in some circumstances, hebephilia falls within a category within the *DSM-IV*: Paraphilia Not Otherwise Specified (Paraphilia-NOS)."[108] The court held that the government had failed to establish "how the psychiatric community determines what may properly be included within the Paraphilia NOS category."[109]

Predicting Recidivism

SVP laws require proof not only that a sex offender has a mental abnormality but also that he or she is likely to sexually reoffend if not civilly committed. In other words, these laws require courts to predict recidivism. Even offenders who are mentally abnormal are not to be committed unless, as a result of their abnormality, they are also likely to engage in future sex offenses.

As was noted earlier in this chapter, contrary to common belief, the known recidivism rate for sexual offenders is remarkably low. Psychologists and other social scientists have long recognized that predicting any kind of future behavior is fraught with difficulty and uncertainty, but especially so when the behavior one is trying to predict has a low base-rate. Given that an overwhelming majority (probably somewhere between 73 and 94 percent) of released sex offenders do not appear to commit new sex crimes, trying to predict whether a given offender will do so or not is a profoundly difficult, perhaps impossible, task.

Nevertheless, that is exactly the task that legislators and judges have prescribed for the SVP civil commitment process. In response to this demand, psychologists and others have attempted predictions of recidivism in one or both of two ways: clinical judgment and statistical inference. Unfortunately, as is widely recognized, clinical predictions of future dangerousness, including sexual recidivism, are notoriously subjective, prone to bias, and frequently wrong. Given the unimpressive track record of such clinical predictions, coupled with the high stakes in the SVP civil commitment context, some social scientists have attempted to develop statistical methods to predict the likelihood that a given sexual offender will recidivate sexually.

Although often referred to as actuarials, actuarial risk assessment instruments, or actuarial risk tools, in reality these methods are simple paper checklists of a relatively small number of factors research has found to be associated with sex offender recidivism in large groups of known recidivists. Numerous such checklists have been devised and used in the SVP context over the past couple of decades. Some courts have been willing to allow the predictions made based upon the checklists to be used as a predicate for civilly confining convicted sex offenders who have completed their criminal sentences, but others have refused to do so. For example, in rejecting the most commonly used and widely studied of these checklists, the Static-99[110]—which is used by some SVP evaluators to assign a recidivism risk level to a particular sex offender (low, moderate-low, moderate-high, or high)—a New York court held that:

> [T]he STATIC-99 has no predictive value for an individual. The STATIC-99 does not and cannot measure an individual's risk of reoffending. Rather, it ranks an individual with a group sharing certain characteristics. In other words, the STATIC-99 score only indicates that a respondent has characteristics which correlate with a group of individuals whose rate of recidivism is "x" percent. The offender's risk may be higher or lower than the probabilities estimated in the STATIC-99, depending on other risk factors not measured by the STATIC-99.
>
> The hearing testimony revealed that there are other drawbacks and inadequacies in the STATIC-99. It is only moderately accurate for the use intended...One law journal opined that in predicting whether an individual is more likely than not to recidivate consistent with the group's percentage rate of recidivism, "the STATIC-99 cannot do much better than a coin flip."
>
> Moreover, "static" tests based exclusively on historical factors do not take into account dynamic (changing) factors in determining risk. The goal of actuarial risk assessment is to achieve an objective criteria for measuring risk, but there exists no accepted mechanism to take into account individual and dynamic factors before reaching a conclusion. For example...Jeffrey Dahmer, who was convicted of various sexual offenses and in fact consumed the body parts of his victims, would score only a 2 on the STATIC-99 (low risk), because the more deviant aspects of his crimes are not "risk factors" listed in the STATIC-99, and thus are not reflected by his score...On the other hand, an offender who scored "high risk," but who suffered a stroke and is now paralyzed, would not present a heightened risk of reoffending...

Nor does the STATIC-99 delineate recidivism rates by the type of offense committed. No mechanism exists to distinguish pedophiles and other persons with recognized deviancies from other sex offenders. For example, incest offenders recidivate at a significantly lower rate than offenders who target victims outside of the family. Child molesters who target male victims recidivate at a significantly higher rate than those targeting only female victims. As explained in one scholarly journal, "The current research of actuarial measures is highly reductionist, in collapsing most sex offenders into a single category. This profound disregard for the heterogeneity of sexual offenders may lead to serious errors in prediction. Even the most basic typologies (e.g., rapists and child molesters) are neglected. For example, child molesters are often motivated by sexual aspects of offending...in contrast, rapists are often motivated by anger and commit nonsexual offenses. Lumping together all paraphilias and sex offenses confounds any attempt at meaningful interpretation. Unquestionably, more focused methods are needed that take into account both clinical conditions (e.g., paraphilias) and offense types." [111]

Finally, regardless of whether experts and courts are confused about or ignorant of the limitations of the Static-99 and other similar actuarial tools, these checklists are problematic because of the substantial likelihood that the "scores" they provide will erroneously categorize individual offenders.

Forensic psychologist Stephen Hart and his colleagues used a well-established statistical method to "evaluate the 'margins of error' at the group and individual level for risk estimates made using ARAIs" (actuarial risk assessment instruments), particularly the Static-99.[112] These researchers found that "at the individual level, they were so high as to render risk estimates virtually meaningless."[113] They also reported that their analysis raised serious concern about the margin of error of these checklists, even at the group level: "[S]ome professionals argue that it is appropriate to use ARAIs to make relative risk estimates concerning individuals (e.g. 'Jones has a higher risk for violence than does Smith'). However, our findings indicate that the margin of error in group findings is substantial, leading to overlap among ARAI score categories. This means that it is perhaps difficult to state with a high degree of certainty that one individual's risk for future violence is higher than that of other individuals."[114] As a result of their findings, Hart et al. concluded that: "The ARAIs cannot be used to estimate an individual's risk for future violence with any reasonable degree of certainty and should be used with great caution or not at all."[115]

Sex Offender Treatment

Although the US Supreme Court upheld the constitutionality of SVP civil commitment laws in *Kansas v. Hendricks*, it did so by a five to four vote. Justice Anthony Kennedy, who provided the fifth and decisive vote, wrote a separate concurring opinion that emphasized the requirement that committed sex offenders receive meaningful treatment, and appeared to hinge the constitutionality of the law on that factor: "A law enacted after commission of the offense and which punishes the offense by extending the term of confinement is a textbook example of an *ex post-facto* law. If the object or purpose of the Kansas law had been to provide treatment but the treatment provisions were adopted as a sham or mere pretext, there would have been an indication of the forbidden purpose to punish."[116]

Is sex offender treatment provided for those committed and confined under SVP laws effective? The answer to that question appears to be: "We really do not know." In 2009, Levenson and Prescott succinctly summarized studies of contemporary sex offender treatment as follows:

Early studies of sex offender treatment stirred skepticism about the benefits of rehabilitation, but more recently, some researchers have reported significant treatment effects. On the other hand, a 12-year follow-up of treated and untreated Canadian sexual offenders found no significant differences in recidivism between the groups. Outcome research from the Sex Offender Treatment and Evaluation Project (SOTEP; a methodologically rigorous long-term investigation conducted in an inpatient program in California) revealed that offenders who received treatment generally reoffended at similar rates as those who did not receive treatment. Of importance, however, is that SOTEP results indicated that offenders who successfully achieved treatment goals (as opposed to simply receiving treatment) sexually reoffended less often than those who did not seem to "get it". Debates persist regarding whether sex offender treatment is effective in preventing future sex crimes.[117]

It has often been observed that well-designed and implemented sex offender treatment outcome studies are difficult to find. As Howard Barbaree, one of the leading authorities in the field of sex offender treatment, has pointed out:

Numerous recidivism studies have been reported but the interpretation of the findings remains controversial. The usual recidivism study has been conducted in the following way: A sample of men who have received treatment in a program, either institutional or community-based, have been studied some months or years after the completion of treatment. The recidivism in this group, defined as rearrests or reconvictions for sexual or nonsexual violent crime, has been compared with the recidivism among men in a sample of convenience who did not receive treatment but were found to be equivalent in other important respects.[118]

As Hanson, Broom, and Stephenson further explain:

The central problem concerns potential differences between the treatment and comparison groups. The standard method for minimizing differences is to randomly assign offenders to treatment and no-treatment groups; such designs, however, are difficult to implement and sustain in criminal justice settings…When long follow-up periods are required, there is ample opportunity for the research design to be corrupted (e.g., "untreated" offenders receive treatment, administrative support collapses). Consequently, most sex offender treatment outcome studies were not initially designed as such; instead, they have taken advantage of "natural experiments."[119]

Added to these inherent problems in sex offender outcome research is the difficulty of establishing statistically significant effects when relying upon sex offender recidivism, a low-base rate phenomenon, as the criterion for success. As Prentky and Schwartz have put it:

> When the proportion of non-treated sex offenders who re-offend is relatively small (for example, around 15%) the proportion of treated sex offenders who re-offend must be very small (around 8-10%) for there to be a statistically significant difference. At the present time, given current methods of treatment and conditions of treatment (typically in prison), reducing re-offense rates among treated sex offenders to 8-10% is rarely accomplished. The result is a mixed, and often confusing, message. Treatment often reduces re-offense rates but not enough to be statistically significant. This same "mixed message" has been trumpeted both by treatment advocates and treatment opponents to support their "causes."[120]

Some researchers have attempted to produce more optimistic results by conducting meta-analyses that combine the results of multiple outcome studies, most of which used small samples with no random assignment and many of which were unpublished and thus not subject to peer review.

Two of the largest and best known of these meta-analyses were reported in 2002 and 2005. In the 2002 meta-analysis, Karl Hanson and his colleagues summarized data from 43 studies that included 9,454 sex offenders and reported that "Averaged across all studies, the sexual offence recidivism rate was lower for the treatment groups (12.3%) than the comparison groups (16.8%, 38 studies, unweighted average)."[121] The Hanson study also reported "a similar pattern" for "general recidivism" in a group comprised of 30 studies (i.e., a 27.9 percent rate for treated offenders and a 39.2 percent rate for comparison offenders).[122] Harris and Rice, however, reviewed the same studies as Hanson et al. and reached a very different conclusion:

> Upon close inspection, we conclude that such designs involve noncomparable groups and are too weak to be used to draw inferences about treatment effectiveness. In almost every case, the evidence was contaminated by the fact that comparison groups included higher-risk offenders who would have refused or quit treatment had it been offered to them. We conclude that the effectiveness of psychological treatment for sex offenders remains to be demonstrated.[123]

In the 2005 meta-analysis, Losel and Schmucker examined 69 studies comprised of 80 separate comparisons of 22,181 treated and nontreated sex offenders[124] and reported that:

> The 74 comparisons reporting data on sexual recidivism revealed an average recidivism rate of 12% for treated groups and 24% for comparison groups (unweighted average). This is a 50% reduction. However, when we calculated the recidivism rates for treated and comparison participants taking the respective sizes of TG [treatment groups] and CG [comparison groups] in the 74 comparisons into account (i.e., when we calculated an n-weighted average for treated and comparison groups), the difference in recidivism rates vanished completely (11% each for treated and comparison participants).[125]

However, Losel and Schmucker also reported that the mean rates of recidivism were 11.1 percent for the treated offenders and 17.5 for offenders in the comparison groups. They noted that this effect was larger than that found in the Hanson et al. 2002 meta-analysis of psychological treatment and stated that "Most probably this is due to our inclusion of both psychological and medical models of treatment. The average effect of physical treatment is much larger than that of psychosocial programs. The main source for this difference is a very strong effect of surgical castration..."[126]

More recently, in 2012, Dennis and colleagues published a systematic review and meta-analysis of randomized controlled trials of sex offender treatment, studies in which sex offenders were randomly assigned to psychological sex offender treatment, probation, or other psychological therapy. They examined 10 such studies and concluded that "Currently RCT [randomized controlled trial] evidence does not support that psychological interventions reduce the risk of sexual reoffending."[127] Based upon that conclusion, Dennis et al. questioned the ethics of requiring sex offenders to participate in treatment purportedly to reduce the likelihood that they will reoffend:

> [M]any countries have enacted legislation whereby incarcerated sex offenders have to participate in a sex offender programme to reduce the likelihood of further re-offending, if they are to be considered for release. If, however, the programme itself is of unknown efficacy, is it legitimate to detain such individuals? The results of this and similar reviews ought, at the very least, cause practitioners to pause and consider whether such practice is ethical.[128]

A final concern with regard to sex offender treatment for those offenders civilly committed under SVP laws is that, whether such treatment works or not, many committed offenders are not receiving it. Many civilly committed sex offenders go untreated because their mental and physical infirmities preclude their participation. One national survey found that 12 percent of those committed under SVP laws suffered from severe, debilitating mental illnesses, such as schizophrenia and bipolar disorder.[129] But most of those who remain untreated do so because almost all sex offender treatment regimens require full disclosure of all past sex offenses, often enforced by polygraph testing, and many offenders fear the legal repercussions of such disclosure. For example, 80 percent of SVPs in California, 75 percent in Wisconsin, and 70 percent in Florida refuse treatment, mostly on the basis of legal advice and/or concern that disclosing past offenses may hurt their chances of release or lead to additional charges against them.[130]

Furthermore, civilly committed sex offenders who do participate in sex offender treatment get very little of it. One media report concluded that civilly committed sex offenders "spend an average of less than 10 hours a week" in treatment.[131] According to the New York Times, many spend the rest of their time taking health and social improvement classes (e.g., Athlete's Foot, Lactose Intolerance, Male Pattern Baldness, Flatulence, and Proper Table Manners) as well as music and art classes.[132]

The Cost of Civil Confinement

Because 20 states and the federal government each operate a separate system for dealing with SVP cases, and because so many different state and federal agencies deal with cases, it is difficult to determine exactly how much confinement of sex offenders costs taxpayers. In 2008, it was estimated that states were spending spent over $450 million a year simply providing secure confinement and treatment and that states were spending an average of more than $94,000 per offender simply providing secure confinement, care and treatment.[133] The comparable annual cost of confining these individuals to prisons at that time averaged about $26,000.[134]

More recently the Associated Press found that the 20 states with SVP laws would spend $500 million a year to confine and treat civilly committed offenders. Associated Press also reported that the annual costs per offender were $175,000 in New York, $173,000 in California, and $96,000 on average among the 20 states.[135]

These data, of course, were not fully accurate because they did not include costs paid by many states to build new facilities (or renovate old ones) to securely confine SVPs. For example, in 2006, California spent $388 million to construct a secure state hospital intended to house up to 1,500 civilly committed SVPs;[136] Virginia constructed a similar facility for 60 SVPs at a cost of $62 million.[137] Minnesota recently spent $45 million on a building to provide secure care for SVPs and embarked upon construction of another such building at a cost estimated to be in the range of $45–89 million.[138] New York spent $30 million to turn a building (formerly used to house civilly committed psychiatric patients) into a secure place of confinement for individuals committed under its SVP law.[139]

These data also do not account for costs of items other than confinement, care, and treatment. As a matter of law, alleged SVPs have the right to a probable cause hearing and a full jury trial before being civilly committed. They also have the right to have their commitments reconsidered by a court every year or two. And they have the right to state-funded counsel and experts at all stages of SVP litigation, including annual or biennial retention proceedings.

Other costs of SVP laws are real but cannot be quantified or valued in dollars and cents. The first is a cost borne by society as whole; the second is one that primarily affects the mental health professions, their practitioners, and their patients.

The courts, including the US Supreme Court by the narrowest of margins, have constitutionally authorized SVP civil commitment based on reasoning that is at best highly debatable, at worst disingenuous. They have justified a massive intrusion on individual liberty interests by holding that SVP commitment (being confined indefinitely in a prison-like setting until one is no longer sexually dangerous) is not punitive, even though it is clearly based not only on crimes the individual has committed, but crimes for which he or she has already been punished. They have then concluded that SVP statutes, which are retroactive by design, do not violate the Constitution's ban on *ex post facto* lawmaking because they are not punitive. The courts have abandoned generations of legal precedent that protects individuals from having their liberty interests curtailed solely on the basis of predictions of future criminality and explained this result by giving constitutional recognition to "mental abnormality," a term with no generally accepted meaning in either law or the behavioral sciences. Finally, the courts have made this infringement of liberty contingent on the state's obligation to provide committed individuals with sex offender treatment, a concept that is both amorphous and unproven. In so doing, they have, in the eyes of some, diminished the liberty interests of all and debased the Constitution.

According to the American Psychiatric Association, in creating and upholding SVP laws, legislators and the courts have mounted "a serious assault on the integrity of psychiatry...bending civil commitment to serve essentially non-medical purposes [and] undermin[ing] the legitimacy of the medical model of commitment."[140] Moreover, as was noted earlier in this chapter, SVP laws have led to abuses of diagnoses and diagnostic criteria by some mental health professionals in efforts to meet the "mental abnormality" requirement imposed by these laws. In the long run, when mental health professionals bend the standards of their own professions, however noble they may believe their cause to be, they undermine public trust in their work, their own integrity, and that of their professions.

The benefits of SVP laws are similarly difficult to specify with any precision. If SVP laws do, in fact, reduce sexual recidivism, they have many benefits, tangible and intangible. As Donato and Shanahan have observed, "obvious" tangible benefits would include reduced "expenditures on police, social welfare services (possibly including foster care), and medical services such as specialist care by child protection units, doctors, psychologists, psychiatrists, and counselors, as well as offender-related costs such as incarceration and court costs, to name but a few." [141]

Reducing sex offender recidivism would also result in numerous "obvious" intangible but vitally important benefits which "include, but are not necessarily limited to [preventing] physical injury and illness, emotional and psychological pain and trauma, fear, anxiety and depression, and other psychiatric disorders" as well as "the potential for intergenerational costs when victims themselves become perpetrators, thus continuing the cycle of sexual abuse."[142]

The fact that the tangible and intangible benefits that may accrue from a reduction in sex offender recidivism cannot be readily quantified, if calculated at all, does not detract from their reality, value, or significance. There can be little doubt that virtually every sex offense causes substantial economic losses for both the victim and society. There also can be no doubt that every such act results in physical and/or psychological harm, often devastating and permanent injury, to the victim, indeed harm that, in some instances, may spread as victims become victimizers.

What is in doubt, however, is whether SVP laws reduce recidivism. It is possible that the mere presence of SVP laws has some as yet undocumented marginal deterrent effect on sex offender recidivism. And, of course, the confinement of committed SVPs definitely limits their ability to reoffend while they are in secure, prison-like facilities. However, the only aspect of SVP laws that has been specifically purported to reduce recidivism and subjected to significant empirical scrutiny is sex offender treatment.

As has already been suggested, if not established, the research on sex offender treatment and recidivism is inadequate to answer the question of whether the former reduces the latter. As noted earlier, while some meta-analyses purport to find significant positive treatment effects, most studies underlying these analyses suffer from serious methodological flaws. Even if the meta-analyses are to be taken at face value, the most they can fairly say is that, in general, sex offender treatment may have some positive, albeit marginal, effect on recidivism.

However, most, if not all, of these outcome studies dealt with sex offenders who *agreed to be treated*. No doubt some cooperated to secure an extratherapeutic benefit, such as a reduced sentence or an enhanced chance for early release. However, it does not appear that any of them were offenders indefinitely committed to treatment against their will under SVP statutes. Thus, there simply are no data that would answer the question of whether sex offender treatment mandated under current SVP laws reduces recidivism.

Given the huge costs, tangible and intangible, of implementing SVP statutes, the data on sex offender recidivism reviewed earlier in this chapter, and the lack of evidence that they prevent future sexual offending, these statutes make little sense as a means of preventing child sexual abuse. Similar to the severe criminal sanctions discussed earlier, SVP laws might be justified as a form of incapacitation: they may stop some child sex offenders from reoffending (at least while they are civilly confined). In all likelihood, however, these extremely costly laws are attempting to prevent offenses that are not likely to have occurred even without postincarceration civil confinement.

Worse yet, from a prevention perspective, the presence and implementation of these laws may have negative effects. To the extent that the public believes that these widely publicized laws are functioning effectively as intended (i.e., to indefinitely lock up the worst sex criminals after they have served their prison sentences) parents and others who care for children may be lulled into a false sense of security and be less cautious when it comes to protecting youngsters from sexual abuse. As with extraordinarily long and costly prison sentences, resources that could be better used in preventing child sexual abuse and exploitation will often be wasted in efforts to prevent recidivism that probably never would have occurred.

Internet-Related Sexual Abuse and Exploitation of Children

It is difficult to overestimate the role of the Internet in modern society. Virtually every area of life involves some interaction with e-mail, texting, instant messaging, or the World Wide Web through a host of devices including personal computers, laptops, tablets, and smartphones. Today, whether directly or indirectly, virtually everyone is dependent to some extent on the Internet. For the most part, the Internet has been a positive social force, enhancing communication, commerce, and human relations. However, in a few areas, including the sexual abuse and exploitation of children, the Internet has enabled significant harm.

This chapter examines some of the ways in which the Internet has been used as a tool to sexually abuse and exploit minors and considers the efficacy of current efforts to prevent or curtail such use of its components. The primary ways in which the Internet is used in this negative fashion are to distribute images (photographs and videos) of child sexual abuse, commonly referred to as child pornography; and to solicit sex from minors.

CHILD PORNOGRAPHY

In recent decades, possession of images of child sexual abuse has been made an extremely serious crime, almost always punishable by lengthy sentences, in some cases prison terms that amount to life without parole. In some instances, those convicted of possessing child pornography have received criminal sentences well in excess of those meted out to offenders who have actually sexually abused or even raped children. For example, in one Arizona case, a 52-year-old first-time offender who possessed thousands of child pornography images was convicted and sentenced to 200 years in prison without the possibility of parole or even pardon by the Governor.[1] His sentence was upheld by the state's highest court and affirmed when the US Supreme Court refused to hear his claim that the sentence was cruel and unusual and violated the Eighth Amendment.

This case is extreme, but thousands of other men have been convicted of possessing child pornography and sentenced to terms of imprisonment that are measured in decades rather than years. Indeed, the presumptive sentences in such cases have become so severe that many judges, particularly those on the federal bench, have begun refusing to sentence those convicted of possession of child pornography to the lengthy prison terms called for under the Federal Sentencing Guidelines. Sentences imposed upon many convicted possessors of child pornography remain severe if not draconian, but often not nearly as harsh as they could be under existing law.

Current Child Pornography Law

It has long been a federal crime to knowingly possess, manufacture, distribute, or access (with intent to view) child pornography. Production and commercial distribution of child pornography was criminalized by federal law in 1977. Possession of child pornography was made a federal crime in 1991. Moreover, all 50 states and the District of Columbia have now enacted laws criminalizing the possession, manufacture, and distribution of child pornography. As a result, a person who knowingly possesses child pornography may be subject to federal and/or state charges and lengthy incarceration. Under federal law, one convicted of possession of child pornography can expect not only a stiff prison sentence but "shall forfeit [to the government] any interest" in virtually any personal or real property related to the offense.[2] For the most part, the forfeiture features of these laws have been used to seize computers, printers, CDs, and related items, but in numerous cases defendants convicted of possessing child pornography have been ordered to turn their homes over to the federal government.[3]

In addition to imprisonment and forfeiture, federal law requires every convicted child pornography offender to make restitution to all of his victims (i.e., every child victimized in the making of each child pornography image he possessed). Federal law provides that courts are required to order restitution in the "full amount of a victim's losses"[4] stemming from any offense involving "sexual exploitation and other abuse of children,"[5] which includes possession of child pornography.

Although state laws vary in scope, most share aspects of the more commonly used federal law against possessing child pornography. The federal law is applicable in nearly every case because it applies to images that in any way affect interstate or foreign commerce or have been transported (by whatever means) across state lines. Given that virtually all child pornographic images are today transmitted via the Internet or were created and/or stored at some point on media that travelled in interstate or foreign commerce, the federal law reaches nearly all child pornography offenders.

The legal definition of child pornography is broad. As the US Department of Justice has summarized it:

Child pornography is defined by law as the visual depiction of a person under the age of 18 engaged in sexually explicit conduct. This means that any image of a child engaged in sexually explicit conduct is illegal contraband. Notably, the legal definition of sexually explicit conduct does not require that an image depict a child engaging in sexual activity. A picture of a naked child may constitute illegal child pornography if it is sufficiently sexually suggestive. In addition, for purposes of the child pornography statutes, federal law considers a person under the age of 18 to be a child. It is irrelevant that the age of consent for sexual activity in a given state might be lower than 18. A visual depiction for purposes of the federal child pornography laws includes a photograph or videotape, including undeveloped film or videotape, as well as data stored electronically which can be converted into a visual image. For example, images of children engaged in sexually explicit conduct stored on a computer disk are considered visual depictions.[6]

The criminalization of the possession of child pornography in the United States is expansive not only in terms of its definitional aspects and reach of jurisdiction, but even more so in the nature of the criminal sentences imposed under these state and federal laws. Individuals convicted of possessing child pornography, especially those prosecuted in the federal courts, face almost certain lengthy prison sentences. By statute, one convicted of knowingly possessing (or attempting or conspiring to possess) child pornography or knowingly accessing child pornography with intent to view it (or attempting or conspiring to do so) shall be fined, imprisoned not more than 10 years, or both.[7] However, if one so convicted has a prior conviction for "aggravated sexual abuse, sexual abuse, or abusive sexual conduct involving a minor or ward, or the production, possession, receipt, mailing, sale, distribution, shipment, or transportation of child pornography," he shall be fined and imprisoned for no less than 10 years and no more than 20 years.[8]

Federal law also prescribes a minimum sentence of 5 years and a maximum of 20 years imprisonment for any person who "through the mails, or using any means or facility of interstate or foreign commerce or affecting interstate or foreign commerce by any means, including by computer" knowingly receives, mails, transports, ships, distributes, reproduces for distribution, advertises, promotes, presents, distributes, or solicits, sells, or possesses (with the intent to sell) any child pornography.[9] The penalties are the same for attempting or conspiring to commit any of these acts. However, if one so convicted has a prior conviction for "aggravated sexual abuse, sexual abuse, or abusive sexual conduct involving a minor or ward, or the production, possession, receipt, mailing, sale, distribution, shipment, or transportation of child pornography," he shall be fined and imprisoned for no less than 15 years and no more than 40 years.[10] It should be noted that among these acts prohibited by federal law, and carrying a minimum sentence of 5 years in prison, is the *receipt* of child pornography. There has been some legal confusion over the difference between receipt of child pornography and possession of child pornography, which has no minimum sentence. Those found in possession of child pornography have sometimes been charged with possession, sometimes with receipt, and sometimes with both offenses for the same images. It has been argued by some defendants that they cannot be charged with both offenses for the same images because "as a practical matter, for anyone to knowingly possess something, he or she must necessarily have received it."[11]

By charging "receipt" in addition to or instead of "possession," a prosecutor is able to virtually ensure that one found in possession of child pornography will be subject to a minimum sentence of 5 years in prison. As one United States Attorney testified before the US Sentencing Commission in 2009, "[I]nstead of charging a child pornographer with only possession, which carries no mandatory minimum, we encourage [Assistant United States Attorneys] to work with their investigative agents to establish grounds for a charge of 'receipt' too because that offense has a mandatory minimum."[12]

Additionally, federal law prescribes minimum and maximum sentences of 5–20 years in prison for a first offender and 15–40 years for a repeat offender who "knowingly distributes, offers, sends, or provides to a minor any visual depiction, including any photograph, film, video, picture, or computer generated image or picture, whether made or produced by electronic, mechanical, or other means, where such visual depiction is, or appears to be, of a minor engaging in sexually explicit conduct."[13]

Finally, federal law prescribes a fine and sentence of no more than 15 years for anyone who knowingly produces with intent to distribute or does distribute "child pornography that is an adapted or modified depiction of an identifiable minor."[14]

In addition to federal child pornography laws, each state has its own sentencing structure for possession of child pornography. Forty-nine states criminally punish simple possession of child pornography; the sole exception is Nebraska, which criminalizes only possession of child pornography with intent to distribute. Most but not all states prescribe criminal penalties much less severe than those meted out in federal court. Twenty-two of the 49 states that punish simple possession of child pornography prescribe mandatory minimum sentences.

Possessors of child pornography convicted in all federal courts and many state courts also face not only lengthy prison terms but the possibility of indefinite, even lifetime, civil confinement to prison-like institutions under the sexually violent predator laws described in the previous chapter.

Actual sentences handed down in federal child pornography prosecutions depend not only on the nature of the conviction and the defendant's prior convictions, if any, for child pornography or other child-related sex crimes, but also on the presence of so-called enhancements specified under the US Sentencing Guidelines, a point system driven by such factors as the number of child pornography images possessed, the ages of the children depicted, whether or not a computer was used to obtain or store the depictions, and whether the material portrays sadism, masochism, or other violence.[15] Since 2005, under the US Supreme Court decision in *United States v. Booker*, federal judges are no longer required to strictly adhere to the Sentencing Guidelines.[16] That decision has had far-reaching implications for the sentencing of child pornography offenders who have possessed or traded but not produced images of child sexual abuse. As the US Sentencing Commission concluded in 2013, "[Since] 2005, there has been a steadily decreasing rate of sentences imposed within the applicable guidelines ranges in non-production cases. That rate decreased from 83.2 percent in fiscal year 2004...to 32.7 percent in fiscal year 2011."[17]

Judicial Reaction to the Increasingly Harsh Penalties Prescribed for Possession of Child Pornography

It is hardly surprising that the number of nonproduction child pornography cases sentenced within the federal guidelines dropped so precipitously, given what some federal judges were saying about the sentences that were being imposed under those guidelines. For example, federal Court of Appeals Judge Gilbert Merritt wrote in a stinging dissent, "[O]ur federal legal system has lost its bearings on the subject of computer-based child pornography. Our 'social revulsion' against these 'misfits' downloading these images is perhaps somewhat more rational than the thousands of witchcraft trials and burnings conducted in Europe and here from the Thirteenth to the Eighteenth Centuries, but it borders on the same thing."[18]

In another child pornography possession case, US District Court Judge William C. Griesbach rejected the sentencing guidelines range, which called for imprisonment between 97 and 212 months, and instead sentenced the convicted defendant to 60 months in prison, the minimum sentence allowed by federal law.[19] In so doing, Judge Griesbach wrote in 2008:

> [The defendant], like many who have accessed child pornography via their computer, seems not to have initially appreciated the magnitude of the offense he was committing or the risk that he would be caught. The manner in which computer technology and high speed internet access have made such material readily available in the presumed privacy of the home has removed several substantial impediments to seeking out such material that previously existed. No longer must a person travel to the seedy side of town, walk into a dirty book store, make a request for the sordid material to another person from whom one's identity could not be readily concealed, and pay for it. The easy availability of the material at no cost with the click of a mouse, while at the same time preserving one's anonymity, leaves little but one's natural aversion to depictions of the abuse and degradation of children to stand in the way of obtaining it. And as the popular culture has become more and more saturated with a debased concept of human sexuality, this natural aversion in many people seems to have grown weaker.
>
> A further factor seems to be the lack of appreciation of the harm that simply viewing such material does to children. In some respects, the internet seems analogous to a huge file cabinet containing an almost limitless number

of documents and other forms of information. Under this view, accessing child pornography can be rationalized as simply pulling out a drawer and simply looking at photos that someone else took in the past. As long as the individual who accesses the pornography is not himself abusing children to produce it, selling it in order to profit from it, or paying for it so as to stimulate demand for it, he can tell himself that he has done no harm to the children depicted. This line of reasoning, of course, is directly contrary to Congress' finding...that "[e]very instance of viewing images of child pornography represents a renewed violation of the privacy of the victims and a repetition of their abuse." And it also ignores the fact that further demand for such material is fueled by those who seek it out and share it with others. But these harms are indirect and abstract, and thus often unappreciated or easily ignored. This is apparently why people who express shock at the idea that they would ever intentionally harm a child can engage in such behavior.

While these changes in technology and the culture, and the lack of appreciation of the harm done to children do not excuse the behavior, they do suggest an explanation for why people such as [the defendant] with no previous history of criminal or abusive conduct seem to be committing such crimes with increasing frequency. They also suggest that with the realization that such conduct is not anonymous, that it carries substantial penalties, and that even simply viewing it does substantial harm to children, first-time offenders such as [the defendant] are unlikely to repeat...[20]

Judge Griesbach added that:

[T]he fact that a person was stimulated by digital depictions of child pornography does not mean that he has or will in the future seek to assault a child. [The defendant], like all human beings, has free will, and neither a psychologist, nor a judge, can predict what a person will choose to do in the future. A court should exercise caution to avoid imposing a sentence for a crime some fear a defendant could commit in the future, instead of for the crime he actually committed and for which he is before the court.[21]

In addition to their written opinions and sentencing memoranda in specific cases, numerous federal judges also testified when in 2009 the US Sentencing Commission held several public hearings on the criminal punishment of possession of child pornography. For example, US District Judge Robin J. Cauthron testified that:

The Guideline sentences for child pornography cases are often too harsh where the defendant's crime is solely possession unaccompanied by an indication of "acting out" behavior on the part of the defendant. It is too often the case that a defendant appears to be a social misfit looking at dirty pictures in the privacy of his own home without any real prospect of touching or otherwise acting out as to any person. As foul as child pornography is, I am unpersuaded by the suggestion that a direct link has been proven between viewing child porn and molesting children.[22]

Chief US District Court Judge Gerald Rosen testified as to the "unfairness of treating one person sitting in his basement receiving videos over the Internet the same as a commercial purveyor of child pornography."[23] He added that "In some cases, a person who has watched one video gets a maximum sentence that may be higher than someone sentenced for raping a child repeatedly over many years."[24]

More recently, when federal trial judges were surveyed in 2010, 69 percent of those who responded said penalty ranges for receipt of child pornography were too high; 70 percent said penalty ranges for possession offenses were too high.[25]

Child Pornography Possession Laws and Primary Prevention of Child Sexual Abuse

Although there are no reliable data as to its prevalence in the world today, child pornography is often estimated to be a global scourge of major proportions. Some claim that as many as 1 million new images of child sexual abuse are made available on the Internet every week, while others estimate that the total number of such images available on the Internet is between 500,000 and 1 million.[26] The truth is that no one knows how many child pornography images are available and at what rate this number is increasing. As criminologists Richard Wortley and Stephen Smallbone have explained: "Child pornography may be uploaded to the Internet on websites or exchanged via e-mail, instant messages, newsgroups, bulletin boards, chat rooms...peer-to-peer (P2P) networks [and] hidden levels of the Internet."[27]

One such "hidden level" of the Internet where child pornography is believed to flourish is the so-called Dark Web, (sometimes also referred to as the Deep Web) a generic term used to describe websites not indexed by Google or any other major search engine.[28] To access these websites, users must first download a free program that essentially functions as a web browser for the Dark Web and allows users to surf the web anonymously by masking their IP addresses.[29] Many Dark Web sites include blogs dealing with child pornography; explicit images of sexual assaults on minors; and materials dealing with stalking, kidnapping, abusing, and even killing children. Little has been publicly reported about the contents of the Dark Web, but in 2011 a loosely organized band of hackers calling themselves Anonymous made their way into a child pornography website dubbed Lolita City and available only through the Dark Web. Anonymous subsequently exposed the login details for nearly 1500 users, sabotaged the website, and ultimately managed to shut it down.[30]

There is limited information regarding the children who are victimized and portrayed in child pornography. Available data suggest that most but far from all are females, that they range in age from infancy to adolescence, and that about half are younger than age 12.[31] There is also limited information regarding the content of child pornographic images, perhaps because it is regarded as a crime to even view child pornography unless one is authorized to do so. Federal authorities have provided extremely graphic verbal accounts of such images. Suffice it to say that some of these images are beyond disgusting and include, for example, the oral, anal, and vaginal rape of children, some as young as infants; digital penetration; penetration with dildos; and the use of ropes, restraints, dog collars, and other sadomasochistic paraphernalia.[32]

Given what is known about the relationships between child abuse victims and their abusers (see Chapter 2), it is not surprising that "most identified victims of child pornography production offenses are abused by a family member or acquaintance."[33]

Those who manufacture images of child sexual abuse have engaged in the sexual abuse of children or have at least been accomplices to such abuse. These individuals are clearly child sexual abusers; they can and should be punished for both child sexual abuse and manufacturing child pornography. They harm their victims both directly and indirectly as they sexually abuse them and then make images of that abuse available to others (usually via the Internet), thus perpetuating the harm to the child long after the initial abuse has occurred. This is true whether they manufacture such images for economic gain, to give away, or to use in trade with others to add to their own collections of child pornography. Severe penalties for those who produce child pornography are warranted under every major theory of criminal punishment, including denunciation, retribution, incapacitation, and deterrence. To the extent that such penalties deter the production and dissemination of child pornography, they surely have a hand in preventing child sexual abuse.

Some producers of child pornography may create these images solely for their own private use, but such cases seem relatively rare. Although there has been and likely continues to be child pornography produced solely for commercial use (i.e., sale) most images of child sexual abuse that change hands today are given away or traded for other such images. Probably the most common way this is accomplished is by the use of Internet peer-to-peer file-sharing networks. These networks are often used to trade music, videos, pictures, and so forth. They allow users to search the computers of others who are logged into the network and to locate and download files from those computers without cost. It appears that the lion's share of child pornography images is today disseminated in this fashion.[34]

Except for the limited number of individuals who produce child pornography exclusively for their private use, virtually all those who create images of child sexual abuse distribute such images to others in some fashion. Thus the threat of severe punishment for such distribution may deter not only the sale, trade, or giving of child pornography, but probably also its production. Even if severe sanctions for those who distribute child pornography do not deter production or distribution, these sanctions can be justified under theories of denunciation and retribution.

The more difficult question is whether there is preventive value in imposing harshly punitive criminal sanctions upon individuals who possess but neither produce nor distribute child pornography. According to a study conducted by the US Sentencing Commission, in fiscal year 2011, more than one-third of child pornography offenders (34.6 percent) had not distributed images of child sexual abuse to others.[35] Imposing lengthy prison sentences for simple possession of child sexual abuse images has been justified for a variety of reasons. First, it has been contended that simply by seeking out and possessing such images, offenders have created or at least contributed to a market for child pornography. Second, it has been maintained that many if not most individuals who possess child pornography are also hands-on offenders—people who have or, unless incarcerated, likely will engage in the direct sexual abuse of children. Third, it has been argued that, in some cases, child sexual abusers use child pornography to help groom their victims for abuse.

The Market Argument

With regard to the market justification, as the US Sentencing Commission noted in 2013, "as a result of changes in the child pornography 'market' since the early 1990s, non-commercial child pornography distribution has overtaken commercial pornography distribution, and most offenders thus pay nothing to receive child pornography."[36] Moreover, as the Commission also pointed out:

> In recent decades, criminal punishments for the production, distribution, receipt, and possession of child pornography in part have been based on the belief that such punishments will help "destroy" (or at least significantly reduce) the "market" for child pornography. Critics have contended that recent changes in Internet technology have undercut the ability of the criminal laws to affect the "market."
>
> To date, social science research has not addressed whether, or to what extent, criminal punishments have affected the commercial or non-commercial "markets" in child pornography since the advent of the Internet and P2P file sharing. In view of the exponential growth in child pornography in recent years and the worldwide scope of such offending, such research may be impossible to undertake.
>
> ***
>
> Although paying customers of child pornography still exist today, in recent years the non-commercial market for child pornography has "exploded" and the commercial market has assumed a much smaller portion of the overall market. As non-commercial distribution has eclipsed commercial distribution, the typical offender today receives images without providing financial support to the commercial child pornography industry...
>
> The Commission's analysis of fiscal year 2010 federal child pornography cases...reveals that the typical...offender received and/or distributed child pornography and/or distributed child pornography using a P2P file-sharing program and not for financial gain. Most offenders used open P2P file-sharing programs that did not require the offenders to trade images in order to receive new images or videos from another.[37]

***

The clearest example of a child pornography market appears to exist online where individuals trade with one another in a non-commercial manner in child pornography communities. In fiscal year 2010, the non-commercial pornography market appeared most active in the approximately 25 percent of cases in which offenders engaged in "personal" distribution to another individual. These individuals engaged in behaviors including bartering images in Internet chat-rooms, trading via closed P2P programs such as Gigatribe, and participating in hierarchical child pornography communities."[38]

In 2012, advocates speaking on behalf of both victims and offenders agreed the Internet has all but done away with what once may have been a thriving commercial market for images of child sexual abuse. Ernie Allen, then President and CEO of National Center for Missing and Exploited Children, testified: "I believe that the problem of commercial child pornography has shrunk dramatically. However, the noncommercial distribution of child pornography has exploded... There are millions of child pornography images being traded online by individuals who view them for sexual gratification. Offenders can access them for free on all platforms of the Internet, including the World Wide Web, peer-to-peer file-sharing, programs and Internet Relay Chat."[39]

Speaking on behalf of federal public defenders, who provide legal counsel and defense to many child pornography offenders, Deirdre D. von Dornum told the Federal Sentencing Commission that the market for child pornography is worldwide and "cannot be significantly impacted" by severely punishing those in the United States who possess this contraband.[40] She added that: "Child pornography thrives in cyberspace independent of an organized market place... Because child pornography is free, widely available and easy to produce, it is not subject to the normal laws of supply and demand. To possess or distribute child pornography, all one really needs is access to the Internet. One does not have to pay or barter anything for the images, and need not conduct business with the producer."[41]

In support of her arguments that "the demand for child pornography images does not appear to fuel the production of child pornography," and "it is unlikely that harsh punishment of an end user will do anything to destroy the market for child pornography," von Dornum pointed to recent research:

One of the few studies of child pornography production found no evidence to support a common assumption that possession of child pornography results in more production. In a national study of arrests for child pornography production at two different points in time (2000-2001 and 2006), researchers found no evidence that child pornography production is increasing or that child pornography producers were targeting younger victims or violent abuse. Perhaps most significantly, the data "suggest that online distribution often was not a motivation for CP production." Instead, "a substantial number of CP producers appear to be creating images for their own use and not for distribution or trading"...

Also relevant here is the U.N. Report, which remarked on the dearth of empirical evidence supporting the theory that "children are being victimized for the sole purpose of making marketable child pornography." While noting the need for more research, it concluded that "in most cases, the images are generated as a result of the abuse, rather than the abuse being perpetrated for the purpose of selling images."[42]

Perhaps the current state of affairs with regard to the worldwide "market" for child pornography has been best summarized by the Second World Congress on Commercial Sexual Exploitation of Children: "[O]nce an image has been digitised and is in the public domain these days it will inevitably find its way on to the Internet where it could be picked up and used both in a commercial and a non-commercial setting. The distinction between commercial and non-commercial child pornography thus ceases to have any real significance in this context."[43]

THE HANDS-ON ARGUMENT

Severe criminal punishment for those who possess but do not manufacture or distribute child pornography is sometimes justified on the grounds that those who possess images of child sexual abuse are frequently if not usually hands-on child sex offenders and that possession of child pornography fuels the child sexual abuse they commit. Are many or most child possessors of child pornography past, current, or potential child sex abusers? Does possession of child pornography increase the likelihood of sexual offending against children? Several empirical studies have addressed these and related questions.

Canadian researchers Seto and Eke followed for 3 years the subsequent criminal histories of 201 child pornography offenders identified through a search of the Ontario Sex Offender database.[44] One hundred and twelve of these offenders had been charged with a criminal offense before their child pornography convictions: 45 percent had committed prior nonviolent offenses, 30 percent had prior violent offenses, 24 percent had prior contact sexual offenses, and 15 percent had prior child pornography offenses.

Thirty-four (17 percent) of these offenders reoffended during the follow-up period, 30 in the community and four while still incarcerated. Of those who reoffended while incarcerated, two were charged with new child pornography offenses, one with a nonsexual violent offense, and one with a contact sexual offense against a fellow inmate. Of the remaining reoffenders, 11 (6 percent of the follow-up sample) committed a violent offense; 9 (4 percent of the sample) committed sexual contact offenses; and 11 (6 percent of the sample) were again charged with a child pornography offense. Just "one of the offenders with only child pornography offenses committed a contact sexual offense in the follow-up period."[45]

Seto and Eke concluded that: "More of this group of offenders might subsequently commit a sexual offense as the duration of the follow-up period increases, but our finding does contradict the assumption that all child pornography offenders are at a very high risk to commit contact sexual offenses involving children."[46]

In a study of British child pornography possessors, Webb and colleagues compared a convenience sample of 90 such men with 120 who had sexually abused children younger than 16. Twenty (22 percent) of the child pornography offenders had previous convictions: 15 for "general offenses"; seven for "sexual offenses" (mostly possession or production of child pornography); and three for "violent offenses."[47] None of the contact child sex offenders had a prior child pornography conviction. Webb et al. collected follow-up data for an average of 18 months on 190 of these subjects, all of whom were on probation in the community: 117 child sexual abuse offenders and 73 child pornography offenders. They considered "failure" to include being charged with or convicted of a sexual offense; being convicted of a general criminal offense; being returned to court or custody for "inappropriate behavior"; engaging in "high-risk behaviors (for example, increased internet usage, or heavy drinking which was previously associated with internet sexual offending)"; and being the subject of "child protection investigations in relation to new allegations or concerns regardless of the outcome."[48]

During the follow-up period, child sexual abuse offenders had significantly more failures (29 percent) than did child pornography offenders (4 percent). Only one child pornography offender was convicted for a general offense and just two were convicted for further Internet sexual offenses. None of the child pornography offenders otherwise breached the conditions of their presence in the community or were recalled to court.

In a Swiss study, Endrass and colleagues examined the subsequent criminal charges over a 6-year period of 231 men charged with possession of child pornography during a special police Internet operation.[49] Among this sample, 11 (4.8 percent) had a prior conviction for a sexual and/or violent offense; two (1 percent) for a "hands-on" child sex offense; eight (3.3 percent) for a "hands-off" sex offense; and one for a nonsexual violent offense. "[A]pplying a broad definition of recidivism, which included ongoing investigations, charges and convictions," Endrass et al. found that seven men (three percent) "recidivated with a violent and/or sex offense," nine (3.9 percent) "with a hands-off sex offense" and just two (0.8 percent) "with a hands-on sex offense."[50] Endrass and his colleagues concluded that: "Consuming child pornography alone is not a risk factor for committing hands-on sex offenses—at least not for those subjects who had never committed a hands-on sex offense. The majority of the investigated consumers had no previous convictions for hands-on sex offenses. For those offenders, the prognosis for hands-on sex offenses, as well as for recidivism with child pornography, is favorable."[51]

Riegel took another approach to the question of whether possessors of child pornography are or will become "hands-on" child sex offenders.[52] Focusing on a particular subtype of child pornography possessors, he asked: "Does viewing erotic pictures of boys exacerbate the tendency for pedosexually inclined males to seek out boys for sexual purposes?"[53] He developed a 101-item Internet survey that drew anonymous responses from 290 men (ages 18–60) from North America, Europe, Australia, New Zealand, and the United Kingdom who self-identified as "Boy-Attracted Pedosexual Males."[54] Among this cohort, 228 (78.6 percent)

reported no involvement with law enforcement with regard to accusations of sexual contact with boys, but 18 (6.2 percent) reported they had been incarcerated
for such conduct.

Altogether, 33.5 percent reported viewing child pornography on the Internet
"quite regularly," 25.5 percent "frequently," 17.9 percent "occasionally," 10.7 percent
"sporadically," 7.2 percent "rarely," and 5.2 percent "never."[55] The child pornography these men reported viewing included images of nudity, disrobing, subjuga-
tion, masturbation, fellatio, and/or anal intercourse; some images involved boys
alone, others boy with boys, and yet others boys with men. The reported mean
length of use of such images was over 3 years.

Asked if viewing of these images "was useful as a substitute for actual sexual
contact with boys, in that their urges and drives were redirected and given an out-
let that affected no other person," 83.8 percent said "frequently" to "invariably."[56]
Asked whether the use of such images "increased their tendency to seek out boys
for the sole purpose of sexual activity," 84.5 percent said "rarely" or "never."[57]

Based upon these data, and subject to numerous limitations, Riegel concluded
that there is a correlation between possessing child pornography but "very little
support" for the social perception that such possession "is a substantive causative
factor in actual or potential sexual contacts and activities" with underage males.[58]

More recently, two related groups of researchers have conducted separate
meta-analyses of existing data regarding online sex offenders and their offenses.
These meta-analyses examined data dealing with a combination of child pornography offenders and offenders who had used the Internet to solicit sex from minors
(so-called luring offenders, whose offenses are described later in this chapter).

Comparing online offenders with offline offenders, Babchishin and colleagues
relied upon data from 27 studies reported from 2000–2009.[59] They found that
online offenders showed more victim empathy; more sexual deviancy; fewer cognitive distortions; slightly less emotional identification with children; and less
of a tendency to engage in "impression management" (i.e., present themselves
in an unduly positive light).[60] They also reported that while the data in their
meta-analysis was insufficient to compare the two groups of offenders in terms
of prior criminal involvement, such involvement was "low among the online sexual offenders."[61] "[O]nly 12% of the online offenders" in the studies analyzed had
prior records of nonsexual crimes.[62] "Criminal involvement is substantially less
than in samples of child molesters."[63]

Babchishin et al. concluded that that although research in this field is "too new
to conclude whether online offenders are truly distinct from offline offenders,"[64]
"[m]any of the observed differences can be explained by assuming that online
offenders, compared to offline offenders, have greater self-control and more psychological barriers to acting on their deviant interests."[65]

The other recent meta-analysis, conducted by Seto, Hanson, and Babchishin
and reported in 2010, included 24 studies involving 4,697 online offenders.[66]
Studies relying upon official records indicated that 12.3 percent of these offenders
had prior sexual offenses, mostly against children. Studies relying upon self-report
data indicated that 55.1 percent of offenders "disclosed prior sexual contacts with

children."[67] Significantly, however, the Seto et al. meta-analysis also examined the rate of sexual recidivism for online offenders. Follow-up periods in the studies analyzed ranged from 1.5–6 years (with most less than 4 years) and recidivism included a high of 10.3 percent in one study, 8 percent in another, less than 6 percent in five other studies, and zero in two studies. Based upon their meta-analysis, Seto and colleagues report that: "The fixed effect estimate for sexual recidivism was 3.9% and the random effects estimate was 2.8%. The observed rates for other types of recidivism were similarly low (0.7% to 3.4%)."[68]

Seto and colleagues cautioned that because most online sex offenders are charged with child pornography offenses as opposed to luring offenses, these results appear more specifically applicable to the former than the latter offenders. In conclusion, however, they note that "Although there is considerable overlap between online and offline offending, our results suggest there is a distinct group of online offenders whose only sexual crimes involve illegal (most often child) pornography or, less frequently, illegal solicitation of minors using the internet."[69]

Most recently, in 2012, Lee and colleagues set out to answer the question: "What is the likelihood that an individual convicted of child pornography offenses has a prior history of a hands-on sexual offense involving a child or has a high probability of committing such an offense?"[70] They studied a sample of 349 offenders confined for sex offenses. In all, they found that 113 had committed only an Internet sexual offense and had no record or self-report of hands-on sex offending, 176 were "child molesters" who reported no Internet sex offenses, and 60 were "child molesters" who reported having committed an Internet sex offense.[71]

After conducting numerous statistical and factor analyses, based on questionnaires filled out by offenders in the sample, Lee et al. concluded, inter alia, that:

> CP [child pornography] offenders appear to comprise a subgroup of sex offenders characterized by taxonomic heterogeneity. [T]hose apprehended with CP have a sexual interest, if not a sexual preference, for children, and, given prevailing DSM [Diagnostic and Statistical Manual of Mental Disorders] criteria, are frequently diagnosable as pedophiles...Paradoxically, this group of pedophiles, as noted, is at low risk to commit hands-on sexual assaults of children.[72]

The Grooming Argument

Grooming is a term used to describe efforts by child sex abusers to ingratiate themselves with potential victims, gain their trust, lower their inhibitions, make them more receptive to abuse, and make it less likely that they will later disclose abuse. There is anecdotal evidence that some child sex abusers use pornography, including child pornography, as part of the grooming process. In particular, it is believed that some would-be offenders use child pornographic images to introduce the notion of adult-child sex to potential victims and "normalize" such conduct.

Undoubtedly some child sexual abusers do use child pornography in this fashion, but what little systematic data there are on the subject seem to indicate the number of such offenders is relatively small. For example, in the study reported by Riegel and mentioned previously, 290 child pornography possessors attracted primarily to boys were asked if they had shared child pornography with a boy; 76.6 percent said "never," 7.2 percent "once," 10 percent "rarely," and 6.2 percent "occasional[ly]."[73]

In any event, as noted previously, it appears that pornography possessors are generally at low risk of committing "hands-on" offenses against children. Thus, it seems unlikely that child pornography is frequently used as a tool for grooming victims of child sexual abuse.

Also, exposing minors to pornography of any sort is a crime, in and of itself, in virtually all American jurisdictions. In almost every state, presenting pornography to a minor constitutes the crime of endangering the welfare of a child, generally defined as knowingly acting in a manner likely to be injurious to the physical, mental, or moral welfare of a child. In some jurisdictions, exhibiting child pornography to a minor violates specific criminal statutes prohibiting such conduct. For example, under federal law, it is a crime punishable by 5–20 years in prison to knowingly distribute, offer, send, or provide child pornographic images to a minor. Under the federal statute, such images include those depicting a minor, or even what appears to be a minor, engaging in explicit sexual conduct.[74] Under Virginia law, it is a felony for anyone 18 or older to display "child pornography or a grooming video or materials to a child under 13 years of age with the intent to entice, solicit, or encourage the child to engage in sexual activity."[75] Under that statute "'Grooming video or materials' means a cartoon, animation, image, or series of images depicting a child engaged in the fondling of the sexual or genital parts of another or the fondling of his sexual or genital parts by another, masturbation, sexual intercourse, cunnilingus, fellatio, analingus, anal intercourse, or object sexual penetration."[76]

Neither the market, hands-on, nor grooming arguments offer much justification for the severe sanctions currently imposed on those who possess but do not manufacture or distribute child pornography. Although these sanctions may be justified on the grounds of denunciation and retribution (although some may even doubt that), they certainly do not seem to hold much promise for the primary prevention of child sexual abuse.

Child Pornography Possession Laws and Secondary Prevention of Child Sexual Abuse

Although extremely harsh criminal penalties for possession of child sexual abuse images do not appear to have been effective in reducing the problem of child pornography, it is possible that other tools might be able to do so. Child pornography harms children in at least two significant ways. First, children are sexually abused in the making of these images. Second, their abuse is memorialized in digital photographs or videos, leaving a permanent record of that abuse that is often distributed throughout the world via the Internet. Effective prevention measures need to be directed toward both of these harms.

Rescuing the Victims of Child Pornography

With regard to the former harm, the sexual abuse children experience in the making of these images, one obvious means of prevention lies in removing children from situations in which they are being abused for the production of child pornography. Efforts to rescue children from those who are sexually abusing them and then distributing images of their abuse have been successful in many cases. The primary tool for such efforts is the Child Victim Identification Program (CVIP), a federal law enforcement initiative. CVIP involves, among other activities, collecting and cataloging all child pornography images that have come to the attention of law enforcement agencies. Analysts carefully comb these images for any evidence that might identify the location of the abuse or the identity of the victim or the perpetrator (e.g., newspapers, calendars, envelopes, or unusual items). As Michelle Collins, who oversees this work, has explained, "Such unique identifiers may not be recognizable to CVIP staff members, but it is highly probable somebody may recognize them."[77]

Collins cites, for example, a recent case in which CVIP analysts examined a number of images that depicted the sexual abuse of six prepubescent girls. The abuse appeared to be taking place in a private home. Enhancing the images, analysts were able to see an envelope containing the name of a storage facility (which was then traced to the Minneapolis area) and portions of a child's uniform on which the letters "MINNEA" could be seen. The analysts were also able to determine the type of digital camera used to create the images and the approximate dates on which they were created. This information was passed on to federal agents in Minneapolis, who successfully identified all of the children in less than 1 week.

Another example of the use of such technology and analysis is what federal law enforcement officials have dubbed "the Sunflower case."[78] In November 2011, Danish law enforcement agents alerted US officials about posts on an online pedophile bulletin board that included images of an 11-year-old girl, whom the poster said he intended to rape. Visible in one image was a yellow road sign bearing a sunflower graphic unique to the State of Kansas. Law enforcement agents drove across Kansas highways trying to locate the sign depicted in the photograph. In less than 2 weeks, they located not only the sign in question but were able to make an arrest and rescue the girl before she was again victimized.

These cases were probably cited because of their impressive results, but they are far from the only such cases in which federal agents have used a combination of computer technology and determined detective work to rescue victims of child pornography. For instance, in late 2012, agents of the US Immigration and Customs Enforcement Agency marked the 1-year anniversary of "the Sunflower case" with what they called Operation Sunflower. Using photograph forensics, Immigration and Customs Enforcement Agency agents identified 123 victims of child pornography. The result was a 19-state raid in which 245 alleged producers of child pornography were arrested and "44 children were directly rescued from their abusers and 79 were identified as either being exploited by others outside of their home or are now adults who were victimized as children."[79]

Use of Internet Screening Technology

One obvious way to limit the spread of child pornography images, and thus lessen the harm done to child pornography victims, is to use screening technology to block transmission of these images via the Internet. As noted previously, the federal government has amassed a huge database of child pornography images. Included in the database are the hash values of these images. Every digital file has such a value, a unique alphanumeric representation of the data contained therein, which has been described as a fingerprint or digital DNA.

By proving Internet service providers (ISPs) with the hash values of known child pornography images, those entities may screen files being transferred online in order to determine whether they likely contain child pornography. If they do, their transmission can be blocked. Beyond that, in most cases, it is possible to determine the IP address from which the suspect files have been requested and sent. In recent years, under heavy pressure from government officials, a number of ISPs have begun to screen files being transmitted via bandwidth they control.

Numerous concerns have been raised about this practice: (1) problems securing the cooperation of ISPs, (2) privacy rights of Internet users, (3) issues related to jurisdiction because a great deal of child pornography is transmitted to and from nations other than the United States, and (4) worries that limiting online access to child pornography might inadvertently lead to more sexual abuse of children.[80]

For the most part, ISPs are private businesses under no legal obligation to screen Internet content transmitted via their bandwidth. In the United States, ISPs are legally required to report known illegal activity involving the use of their services but are not required to actively monitor their services for illegal use. Nor are they responsible for the content featured on websites using their services. Nevertheless, some ISPs have voluntarily cooperated with hash value screening. A recent publication of the US Department of Justice explained the issue further and was cautiously optimistic about gaining voluntary cooperation from ISPs in the fight against child pornography:

ISPs have a central role to play in combating Internet child pornography. The more responsibility ISPs take in tackling the availability of child pornography images on the Internet, the more resources police can devote to addressing the production side of the problem. However, there are two competing commercial forces acting on ISPs with respect to self regulation. On the one hand, if an ISP restricts access to child pornography on its server, it may lose out financially to other ISPs who do not. Therefore, it will always be possible for offenders to find ISPs who will store or provide access to child pornography sites. On the other hand, ISPs also have their commercial reputation to protect, and it is often in their best interests to cooperate with law enforcement agencies. Most major ISPs have shown a commitment to tackling the problem of child pornography. By establishing working relationships with ISPs, and publicizing those ISPs who take self regulation seriously, police may be able to encourage greater levels of self regulation.[81]

With regard to privacy concerns, the US Supreme Court has long held that child pornography enjoys no First Amendment protection. The extent to which ISPs can lawfully screen for child pornography using hash values remains an open question, but it seems likely that courts would allow such screening, particularly if it is not used to identify specific individuals whose rights to privacy might otherwise be violated.

The jurisdictional issue is certainly real. Even if US law mandated ISPs to cooperate with hash value screening, which so far it does not, there would be no guarantee that other nations would follow suit or that foreign ISPs would voluntarily cooperate. However, 121 nations have signed an international treaty that bans the sale and production of child pornography. In the preamble to that ban, signatory nations specifically agreed upon the need for "closer cooperation and partnership between Governments and the Internet industry," which obviously includes ISPs.[82]

Finally, one federal law enforcement official has cautioned that filtering "could work too well" and that "[i]f child pornography became too hard to find...it might create demand for new images and cause more children to be abused."[83] This concern about hash value screening working too well is difficult to answer in the absence of data. However, imagine the results if such screening were applied universally and with full efficacy. In that case, all or virtually all child pornography images known to law enforcement would be blocked from transfer via the Internet. Because almost all child pornography images are now transferred via the Internet, access to the vast bulk of such images would be curtailed. Those interested in skirting this system could do so by producing new images of child sexual abuse, but only temporarily because once an image became known to law enforcement, its transfer would be blocked. There is also the possibility of editing or tampering with images to change their hash values, but even current law enforcement technology seems capable of dealing with that possibility.

It is too early to tell what impact hash value screening may have as a measure to prevent child sexual abuse but it seems clear that this technology has the potential to make it extremely difficult to use the Internet to transmit images of child sexual abuse.

SHUTTING DOWN CHILD PORNOGRAPHY WEBSITES

Another strategy that has been considered important is shutting down Internet websites that sell, trade, or otherwise distribute child pornography. As was mentioned previously in this chapter, recently a band of hackers was able to break into and shut down a child pornography website on the so-called Dark Web. If these amateurs were able to shut down such a website, then surely government and ISPs have the capacity to do the same thing. The fact is that they are already doing so and that, as was mentioned previously, websites offering child pornography "are often shut down as soon as they are discovered."[84] As a Justice Department publication recently noted:

A number of ISP associations have drafted formal codes of practice that explicitly bind members to not knowingly accept illegal content on their sites, and to removing such sites when they become aware of their existence. Service agreement contracts with clients will often set out expected stan-dards that apply to site content. Large ISPs may have active cyber patrols that search for illegal sites.[85]

Although shutting down websites that feature images of child sexual abuse is part of the arsenal against child pornography, and thus has a role in the preven-tion of child sexual abuse, for a couple of reasons that role is relatively small. First, most child pornography is exchanged via peer-to-peer file sharing, not through websites. Second, many websites featuring images of child sexual abuse are run from servers in Eastern Europe where they are beyond the reach of American law.

This concern about jurisdiction, although real, has been overcome to some extent through the consent and cooperation of other sovereign nations. However, some countries have no laws against child pornography and they and others might not be willing to cooperate with the United States in shutting down child pornog-raphy websites run from servers located within their borders. In such instances, US law enforcement could infiltrate and shut down foreign child pornography websites (just as the hacking group Anonymous has done) and then deal with any international fallout that arises after the fact. It seems unlikely that many foreign nations would rise to protect the rights of their citizens to distribute images of child sexual abuse free from interference from the US government. Some nations might well complain more generally about such intrusions upon their sovereign rights. If they did, international law provides a forum in which such disputes could be adjudicated. In that case, it is possible that the United States might be found to be in violation of international law, condemned by some in the world community, and even sanctioned.

The Problem of Sexting

Sexting involves the electronic transmission of sexual images (usually nude, par-tially nude, and/or sexually provocative photographs) via text messaging or other online methods. Although this practice is not limited to any age group or means of digital transmission, the term is most often associated with adolescents who use their cell phones to take such photographs of themselves and send them to peers. The term has also come to encompass the further distribution of these images by those who initially received them. Sexting is considered by some, primarily pros-ecutors, to be the equivalent of the distribution of child pornography.

EXTENT OF THE PROBLEM

In recent years, numerous national surveys have attempted to determine how prevalent sexting is among American youth. In 2008, the National Campaign to Prevent Teen and Unplanned Pregnancy conducted an online survey of a sample of 653 teenagers ages 13–19 and 627 young adults ages 20–26.[86] Among the teen-agers surveyed, 20 percent (18 percent of the boys and 22 percent of the girls) had transmitted nude or seminude photographs or videos of themselves to others via the Internet or cell phone text messaging. Among girls in the 13–16 age range, 11 percent had done so. Most of these images were sent to boyfriends or girl-friends. Among teenagers who sent such images, 66 percent of girls and 60 per-cent of boys said they did so for fun or to flirt. However, 12 percent of the girls reported that they felt pressured to send nude or seminude images of themselves. Also, 15 percent of teenagers who sent such images directed them to persons they knew only from online contact.

In 2009, the Associated Press and MTV surveyed a nationally representative sample of 1,247 young people ages 14–24.[87] Among respondents in the 14–17 age range, 24 percent reported that they had been involved in sending, receiving, or forwarding naked images. Also in 2009, Cox Communications and the National Center for Missing & Exploited Children surveyed 655 youngsters ages 13–18.[88] Nineteen percent of the respondents said they had sent, received, or forwarded nude or partially nude photographs via cell phone. Eighty-one percent of these "sexters" were under the age of 18. Sixty percent of those who sent "sexts" sent them to girlfriends or boyfriends, but 11 percent sent them to people they did not know. In another 2009 survey, the Pew Research Center surveyed a nationally representative sample of 800 youths who were 12–17 years old and owned a cell phone.[89] Fifteen percent of these youngsters reported that they had received, on their cell phones, text message including sexually suggestive nude or nearly nude images of someone they knew. Four percent of the youths surveyed said they had texted such images of themselves to others.

In a similar survey conducted in the United Kingdom by researchers for the University of Plymouth in 2009, 535 students ages 13–18 were questioned about sharing personal images and videos.[90] Forty percent of these youths reported sex-ting ("sharing explicit images electronically") and 27 percent said that in their experience sexting occurred regularly or "all of the time."[91]

After reviewing these surveys and other estimates, Lounsbury and colleagues concluded that media reports about sexting may have exaggerated the true extent of the problem. They found flaws in all of these surveys and suggested that until more reliable data are available, scholars and journalists should "simply say: 'there are no consistent and reliable findings at this time to estimate the true prevalence of the problem.'"[92]

THE HARM OF SEXTING

Little if any systematic research has examined the harm caused by sexting. Some have argued that sexting is normative adolescent behavior that is the predictable if not inevitable result of the "convergence of technology with adolescents' devel-opmental need to experiment with their sexual identity and explore their sexual relationships."[93] Because youngsters have generally voluntarily created and dis-seminated nude or partially nude images of themselves, the argument continues, they are not victims in the sense that youngsters depicted in child pornography are.

There can be no doubt that being sexually abused and having that abuse photo-graphed and made widely available on the Internet generally results in far greater harm than does sexting. However, anecdotal evidence suggests that sexting may have serious psychological consequences for the young person who sends out nude or partially nude photographs or videos of himself or herself. Although the most common sexting scenario appears to be one in which a youth sends such photographs or videos only to a boyfriend or girlfriend, cell phone technology is so ubiquitous and simple that in a matter of minutes, these images can be transmitted to dozens, even hundreds, of others. In many cases, that is precisely what has happened. Often, for whatever reason, the recipient of a sext will share that image with one of more others who then proceed to do the same until the image has made its way to many of the initial sender's peers and other unintended recipients.

At the least, the result is often embarrassment for the youngsters depicted in the sexted images. However, in numerous cases, these adolescents have not only been embarrassed but have become the subject of ostracism, harassment, and bullying. In extreme cases, the responses of peers have led to serious emotional problems and even suicide.[94]

PREVENTING SEXTING

In purported efforts to prevent sexting, numerous law enforcement agencies and prosecutors have turned to child pornography laws, alleging that those who engage in any aspect of sexting (sending, receiving, forwarding) have committed a serious criminal offense. The apparent theory behind these prosecutions is deterrence; it is believed that by criminally punishing youngsters who engage in sexting, others will become less inclined to involve themselves in this phenomenon.

Some of these prosecutions have been derailed by the courts, which have sometimes found ways to exclude sexting from state child pornography laws (e.g., by deciding that the images involved did not meet the legal definition of child pornography). However, there have been a small number of reported criminal convictions. In one case, for example, an 18-year-old Florida youth, Philip Alpert, had been sent nude photographs by his 16-year-old girlfriend while they were a couple.[95] When they broke up, Alpert forwarded the photographs of the girl to nearly 100 of her friends and relatives. Charged with 72 counts of lewd and lascivious battery, possession of child pornography, and distribution of child pornography, Alpert pleaded guilty and was sentenced to 5 years' probation. However, under Florida's version of Megan's Law, Alpert was required to register as a sex offender for 25 years. As a result, he is subject to residency and work limitations and a Florida Department Law Enforcement Sex Offender/Predator Flyer posted online shows his photograph and identifying information (including date of birth; hair and eye color; height; weight; address; and automobile year, make, color, and license plate number). The posting also contains a link to a map that shows the precise location of his residence.[96]

In Iowa, 18-year-old Jorge Canal, Jr. was asked by a 14-year-old girl for a photograph of his genitals.[97] Canal complied, using his cell phone to text her a shot of his erect penis and another of his face. When the girl's parents found the photographs on her phone, police charged Canal with distributing child pornography. After being convicted by a jury, Canal was sentenced to 1 year of probation, fined $250, and required to register as a sex offender. A state appeals court upheld his conviction.

The response to the criminal prosecution of sexting as child pornography offenses has varied widely. At one end of the spectrum have been prosecutors who have embraced such prosecution and promised more. For example, in 2013, Robert Kinzer, an Assistant District Attorney in Massachusetts warned that: "When you send that text message, you have disseminated child pornography...We do not have any exceptions in our law for kids who are really in love, for girls who wanted to do it and for guys who promised they wouldn't share it, or for two kids who are dating..."[98]

At the other end of the spectrum are calls to treat sexting not as a crime, and certainly not as child pornography, but rather as a social problem best addressed by parents and educators. As a recent report from the National Institute of Justice concluded:

> Given the large number of youths participating in sexting, and the general belief that their behaviors are more foolish than criminal, law enforcement and prosecution should not be the first response. More logically, parents and educators should be the first to respond to sexting. Since sexting among adults is legal, and the vast majority of sexting activity appears to be performed by young people, it makes sense to place monitoring and punishment in the hands of those most likely to encounter youth sexting.[99]

There is a strong argument against bringing harsh criminal laws to bear upon youngsters when their misconduct causes little harm and is the result of a combination of immaturity, developmentally typical adolescent sexuality, and the ready availability of technology that almost invites sexting. Moreover, in many instances, there is little reason to believe that the criminal law is likely to be a significant deterrent to such misconduct.

However, sexting is not always the relatively harmless and victimless adolescent phenomenon some seem to believe it to be. In certain instances, sexting clearly constitutes what can only be regarded as a form of child sexual exploitation, has serious consequences for victims, and should be treated as criminal. It is clear from some of the survey research mentioned previously that some teenagers feel pressured into sending out nude or seminude images of themselves. Whether that pressure comes from peers, boyfriends, girlfriends, or persons met online, it should be discouraged as much as possible. General peer pressure may be difficult to deter, but criminalizing pressure from a specific individual in this context may help protect vulnerable youngsters from being pressured into acting in ways they later regret.

Even in cases in which there is no perceived pressure to produce sexting images, some youngsters who do so are later placed in jeopardy by the acts of others who have access to those images. The case of Phillip Alpert just mentioned is a clear example. The teenage girl who sent him the nude photographs of herself likely did so under the assumption—if not the implicit or explicit agreement—that they would go no further. When Alpert forwarded these photographs to hundreds of others, he may not have been guilty of transmitting child pornography (as that crime is ordinarily envisioned) but he was certainly guilty of imposing a potentially serious harm on the girl. Being required to register as a sex offender for 25 years seems much too harsh a penalty for such conduct, and much greater punishment than is necessary to deter this sort of conduct. However, to allow such callous disregard for the privacy and psychological well-being of another to go without any criminal sanction is to disregard the potential for grave harm and to forego any possibility of deterrence.

Perhaps the optimal way of preventing the potential harms associated with texting is through a combination of educational, criminal justice, and remedial interventions. Efforts are underway in most states, and should continue, to educate juveniles about the dangers of sexting. Many states have tried, most without success, to create laws dealing with sexting as a less serious offense than the production, transmission, or possession of child pornography.[100] Legislatures should redouble their efforts to develop criminal sanctions for sexting that fit the crime—primarily misdemeanors punishable by fines and community service or, in particularly egregious cases, relatively brief periods of juvenile detention. Finally, whatever sanctions are imposed, they should be accompanied by efforts specifically designed to prevent reoffense.

INTERNET SEXUAL SOLICITATION

The Internet offers many opportunities for sexually abusing and exploiting children. Many sex offenders use the World Wide Web, chatrooms, instant messaging, and other features of the Internet to locate and then exploit vulnerable youngsters, either online or in-person. In some instances, the abuse is limited to exposing victims to sexually explicit chats, e-mail, instant messages, or other forms of written communication. In some cases, offenders send sexually explicit images (including adult and/or child pornography) to their targets and/or solicit sexually explicit photographs of their targets. Offenders sometimes use webcams to expose themselves to their targets in real time and/or seek sexual exposure from targets. A small number of offenders also use the online contacts they make with children and adolescents to attempt to arrange in-person meetings. A small number of attempts are successful and culminate in actual sexual contact between the perpetrator and victim. In many cases, the offender's effort to meet a young victim in person fails because the intended target, believed by the offender to be a child or adolescent, is in fact an adult posing as a youth as part of a law enforcement or vigilante sting operation.

Nature and Extent of the Problem

Several studies have shed light on the nature and extent to which minors are sexually abused or exploited via the Internet. The Youth Internet Safety Survey I, conducted in 1999–2000, involved interviewing "a nationally representative sample of 1,501 youth aged 10 to 17, who used the Internet regularly."[101] Nineteen percent of these youngsters reported having "received a sexual solicitation or approach over the Internet in the past year," while approximately three percent reported receiving an "aggressive sexual solicitation" via the Internet during that same time period.[102] Sexual solicitations and approaches were defined as "Requests to engage in sexual activities or sexual talk or give personal sexual information that were unwanted or, whether wanted or not, made by an adult."[103] Aggressive sexual solicitations were defined as "Sexual solicitations involving offline contact with the perpetrator through regular mail, by telephone, or in person or attempts or requests for offline contact."[104]

The Survey found that "More than three quarters of targeted youth (77%) were age 14 or older… Only 22% were ages 10 to 13."[105] In 65 percent of the reported incidents, "the youth met the person who solicited them in a chat room; in 24% of episodes the meeting occurred through Instant Messages."[106] The study found further that "[i]n 10% of incidents, the perpetrators asked to meet the youth somewhere, in 6% the youth received regular mail, in 2% a telephone call, in 1% money or gifts. In one instance, the youth received a travel ticket."[107] Most of the offenders were reported to be youths or young adults and only two of the reported incidents resulted in relationships that that "may have had sexual aspects."[108]

The National Juvenile Online Victimization Study, conducted in 2000–2001, surveyed 2,574 enforcement agencies and found that arrests for Internet-related sex offenses against children constituted a "small fraction" of overall arrests for child sex offenses.[109] Among Internet-related sex offenses leading to arrest, 36 percent were for possession, distribution, and/or trade of child pornography; 39 percent involved crimes with identified victims, including production of child pornography; and 25 percent involved solicitations made to undercover law-enforcement officers posing as minors.[110] In approximately half of the arrests involving crimes against identified victims, the offender used the Internet to initiate a relationship with the victims. Nearly all (99 percent) of the victims of "Internet-initiated sex crimes" were 13–17 years old and none were younger than 12 years. Nearly half (48 percent) were 13 or 14 years old.[111]

In the more recent Youth Internet Safety Survey II, conducted in 2005, researchers interviewed a sample of 1,500 American youths between the ages of 10 and 17. As opposed to the earlier Safety Survey, when 19 percent of respondents reported having been sexually solicited online, only 13 percent reported having had such an experience within the preceding year. Again, the vast majority of targets of online sexual solicitation were older juveniles: 81 percent were 14 or older while "[n]o 10 year olds and only 3% of 11 year olds were solicited."[112]

Unlike the earlier survey, in which 24 percent of the solicitors were said to be 18 or older, respondents in this study reported that 28 percent of solicitors were 18 or older. As in the earlier Survey, researchers learned that few targets of online sexual solicitations met their solicitors in person and even fewer had actual sexual contact with adults who solicited them.

Legal Response to Online Solicitation

Online solicitations of minors for sex violate the criminal law, regardless of whether they culminate in any in-person contact. Offenders who have noncon-sensual sexual contact with minors are subject to prosecution for rape, sodomy, and/or sexual abuse, depending on the nature of the contact. Adults who engage in consensual sexual contact with minors, regardless of how they met them, are generally subject to prosecution for statutory rape. In 2008, it was estimated that "25% of the sex crimes committed against minors and reported to the police involve[d] statutory rape" and that "Internet-initiated sex crimes would have accounted for approximately 7% of all statutory rapes."[113]

Statutory rape is generally a strict liability offense, meaning that any mistake, even a reasonable one, regarding the victim's age is usually not a defense. Criminal sanctions for statutory rape range from as little as 6 months in jail to as much as life in prison.

Until recently, in most jurisdictions, adults who unwittingly solicited sex online from undercover police operatives, thinking that they were communicating with a minor, could be punished, at worst, for attempted statutory rape. In recent years, however, both state and federal governments have criminalized online solicitation of sex from minors.

Federal law in this regard is straightforward and harsh: "Whoever, using the mail or any facility or means of interstate or foreign commerce, or within the special maritime and territorial jurisdiction of the United States knowingly per-suades, induces, entices, or coerces any individual who has not attained the age of 18 years, to engage in prostitution or any sexual activity for which any person can be charged with a criminal offense, or attempts to do so, shall be fined under this title and imprisoned not less than 10 years or for life."[114]

Courts have held that a defendant may be convicted of enticement of a minor not only for communicating with an actual child but also for attempting to do so, as in so-called Internet sting cases where the defendant has communicated with an adult law enforcement decoy, believing the officer to be a minor.[115] The federal courts have routinely rejected defenses of impossibility and entrapment raised by defendants who never communicated with a minor but were caught in an online sting operation. It should be noted that not all of these sting operations have been conducted by law enforcement agents.[116] Private vigilante groups and some commercial media outlets have run their own sting operations and used them to publicly expose offenders to the public. Some of the individuals caught in these private sting operations have been prosecuted, but others have not.[117]

Are Extremely Harsh Criminal Penalties for Internet Solicitation Necessary to Prevent Child Sexual Abuse?

Some data, although limited, suggest that online offenders, including child pornography offenders and those who use the Internet to solicit sex from minors, may constitute a distinct group of offenders unlikely to commit other sexual crimes. Recent meta-analyses have found a number of distinct differences between online and offline offenders. For example, online offenders have been found to have substantially less prior criminal involvement than child molesters[118] and "recidivism rates [that] appear to be quite low."[119] Online offenders also appear to show more victim empathy, more sexual deviancy, fewer cognitive distortions, slightly less emotional identification with children, and less of a tendency to engage in "impression management" than offline offenders.[120] Moreover, they may have "greater self-control and less impulsivity than offline offenders" as well as "more psychological barriers to acting on their deviant interests."[121]

Of course, once an offender soliciting sex from a minor online succeeds in meeting the youth and having any sort of sexual encounter, that offender is no longer merely an online offender. There are few if any data to suggest that such an offender is different from other offenders who have unlawful sexual relations with minors. However, Wolak et al. make the point that these luring offenders and their offenses "more often fit a model of statutory rape—adult offenders who meet, develop relationships with, and openly seduce underage teenagers—than a model of forcible sexual assault or pedophilic child molesting."[122]

Mitchell, Wolak, and Finkelhor, have also sought to determine whether suspects caught in law enforcement Internet sting operations "pose a significant threat to youth."[123] In so doing, they examined a subsample of cases from the National Juvenile Online Victimization Survey, a federally sponsored study of Internet sex crimes against minors.

These researchers reported that, based upon the National Juvenile Online Victimization data they reviewed, 13 percent of the offenders arrested in sting operations had previously committed sex crimes against victims they had identified online. They also reported that there were many differences between offenders caught in stings and those who had offended against actual juveniles. Sting offenders were significantly older, more affluent, more likely to be employed, more likely to be living with a minor at the time of the offense, less likely to have demonstrated deviant or violent behavior in the past, and less likely to have been previously arrested for a sexual or nonsexual offense.

The best available data, derived from the federally funded Youth Internet Safety Surveys and National Online Juvenile Victimization Study, suggest that online sexual offenses constitute an extremely small percentage of all sex crimes against juveniles. These data suggest that while 13 percent of American youths might be expected to be sexually solicited online in a given year, less than a third of those will be asked to meet the adult solicitor, less than a third of those asked will in fact meet the solicitor, and those who do will be mainly older teenagers who are often meeting solicitors who are in their early 20s. These data also suggest, however, that when a youngster who has been sexually solicited online meets the solicitor, sexual contact will occur in most cases.

The federal data are troubling because it appears that a substantial percentage of American children are being approached sexually online and thus being put at risk for at least some degree of emotional harm. However, these data also suggest that in those relatively rare cases in which these youngsters are victimized by hands-on sexual abuse, it is primarily in the form of what would otherwise be referred to as statutory rape: voluntary sexual contact that is by law deemed nonconsensual because of the age and immaturity of one of the parties.

This is not to say that statutory rape is a victimless crime or an offense that does no harm to juveniles. Statutory rape is a crime in every American jurisdiction in part because of the near universal belief that even willingly engaging in sex with an adult is potentially detrimental to the interests of a minor. Adults, even young adults, who are found to have had voluntary sexual relations with minors are routinely punished, albeit generally not too severely, by the criminal law. Yet, in federal courts today, adults who commit the same offenses with youngsters contacted via the Internet, are severely punished (i.e., generally sentenced to at least 10 years in prison). Moreover, even those who use the Internet in unsuccessful attempts to have sex with minors (or adults pretending to be minors) receive similarly harsh federal sentences.

What is there about statutory rape or attempted statutory rape using the Internet that makes these offenses so much worse than "ordinary" statutory rape or attempted statutory rape that compels the federal government to make the punishments imposed for the former set of crimes so much greater than those imposed for the latter?

The most obvious answer seems to be that online offenders trolling the Internet for underage sex partners probably have a much greater chance of succeeding in that quest than do offenders who rely upon other means to meet potential victims. Offenders using the Internet have almost instant access to hundreds, even thousands of potential victims, and can make their initial approaches anonymously, with only a relatively small investment of time and energy, and with little likelihood of being apprehended by authorities. If one youngster rebuffs their online advances, they can immediately and with just a few keystrokes move on to another. However, more typical statutory rape offenders must make their initial advances in person, risk face-to-face rejection if not immediate arrest, and generally have to either quickly seduce their victims or invest a good deal of time developing a relationship that may or may not culminate in sexual relations.

Also, online offenders pollute the Internet and make it less safe and desirable for use by children and adolescents. Even if they never succeed at having sex with a minor approached online, or indeed never intend to do so but simply wish to act out their fantasies in a form of "cybersex," these offenders risk emotionally harming all youths they sexually solicit. And because of the ubiquitous nature of the Internet, the number of youngsters at risk for such harm is astronomical.

There can be little if any doubt that the government has a strong and legitimate interest in protecting minors from exposure to the possible emotional harm

anything, they may overestimate the extent to which students are sexually abused (as that term is more generally used) by educators. Of course, there is probably no reason to believe that sexual abuse by educators is any less underreported than any other form of child sexual abuse. Thus, the actual data Shakeshaft relied upon may well underreport sexual abuse in the schools.

In any event, the AAUW data and those from other less extensive studies make it clear that sexual abuse in schools, perpetrated by both peers and educational personnel, is a serious problem. Although most of the research in this area has examined public schools, it is clear that religious and private schools are not immune from the problem. As is detailed later in the section of this chapter on clergy abuse, much of the recently exposed sexual abuse of children by clerics, especially Catholic priests, took place in parochial schools and church-related educational facilities. In recent years, even some of America's most elite private schools have been exposed as institutions in which educators frequently have used their positions of trust and authority to obtain sexual gratification from students. Recently, for example, the *New York Times* exposed 16 years of sexual abuse of male students by teachers at the renowned Horace Mann School, one the nation's most prestigious and oldest (founded 1887) preparatory schools, which has a $346 million endowment, an 18-acre New York City campus, and tuition in excess of $40,000 a year.[8]

Preventing Sexual Abuse in Schools

Over the past several decades, schools have played a key role in the prevention of child sexual abuse, such as alerting students to the dangers of such abuse, teaching them ways to avoid it, and telling them how to report it if it happens. Ironically, however, while these efforts were being made part of the curriculum in many schools, children in many of those very same schools were being sexually abused not only by their peers but by teachers, coaches, counselors, administrators, tutors, and even bus drivers, lunchroom, personnel, and parent volunteers.

Although many approaches to preventing child sexual abuse in general are clearly applicable to preventing such abuse in schools, there are also many school-specific prevention tactics worth implementing.

UNDERSTANDING AND COMMUNICATING THE NATURE OF THE RISK

Here, as in most areas of public health concern, a crucial aspect of prevention is to understand the nature of the risk and to communicate that understanding to those who need to know. Who is at risk of being sexually abused at school, by whom, and under what circumstances?

All students may be said to be at risk of sexual abuse in schools. However, although students, parents, educators, and school support personnel need to be trained to keep that in mind, research has provided at least some guidance as to relative risk. These same groups should be made aware that female students, students of color, and students with disabilities have been found to be more vulnerable to child sexual abuse in the school setting. One report, for example, based upon a database of more than 50,000 students, indicated that students with disabilities were three times more likely than students without disabilities to be sexually abused. Moreover, the same report concluded that "Students with behavior disorders were more than five times as likely as non-disabled students to be sexually abused, with mentally retarded students more than three times as likely."[9]

Students, parents, and school personnel also need to be alerted to what constitutes child sexual abuse. For example, although the list used in the AAUW study described previously goes well beyond what both the public and the law generally define as child sexual abuse, all of these behaviors are inappropriate in a school setting and should be routinely reported and investigated.

All of a school's constituencies also need to understand who is at risk of perpetrating sexual abuse in the schools. First, all involved in schools must realize that although the greatest threat comes from students themselves, school personnel also perpetrate a great deal of sexual abuse in the schools. Given the dominant role that teachers play in the school setting in terms of their contacts with and immediate authority over students, it is no surprise that among school personnel, teachers appear to pose the greatest risk of sexual abuse to students, followed closely by coaches, substitute teachers, bus drivers, and teacher's aides. Although studies of disciplinary proceedings have found that 80–96 percent of educators who sexually abused children were male, at least two studies that asked students about sexual abuse by educators (including the AAUW study) found that more than 42 percent of educators who committed sexual offenses against students were female.[10]

While none of these data make it much easier to categorize educational personnel likely to sexually offend against student as opposed to those unlikely to offend, they represent important information for all constituencies in the schools who, without such data, might be tempted to consider certain school personnel as beyond reproach when it comes to posing a sexual risk to students. Indeed, as Shakeshaft implies, all involved in the schools should also realize that being a good, popular, and/or trusted teacher does not decrease, and might even increase, the risk posed by that individual:

> In elementary schools, the abuser is often one of the people that students most like and that parents most trust. The abusers of children younger than seventh grade have different patterns than those who abuse older children. The educators who target elementary school children are often professionally accomplished and even celebrated... Many educators who abuse work at being recognized as good professionals in order to be able to sexually abuse children. For them, being a good educator is the path to children, especially those who abuse elementary and younger middle school students. At the late middle and high school level, educator abusers may or may not be outstanding practitioners. At this level, the initial acts are somewhat less premeditated and planned and more often opportunistic, a result of bad judgment or a misplaced sense of privilege.[11]

Finally, students, parents and teachers need to be educated with regard to grooming as a precursor to sexual abuse of students by educators. Grooming involves a set of behaviors in which many perpetrators engage over a period of time to target and engage potential victims; assess their vulnerabilities; gain their trust; and ingratiate themselves with them and/or others (such as parents) who may control access to them. In the school setting, grooming by educators may include activities that potential victims and their parents' value, such as attention above and beyond what is normally provided to students, individual contacts with children outside the school setting, and efforts to develop friendships or other social relationships with their parents. Students, parents, and school personnel also need to be made aware that sexual harassment and/or lesser forms of inappropriate sexual conduct by educators (e.g., making sexual comments, jokes, gestures, looks, or showing, giving, or leaving sexual pictures, photographs, illustrations, messages, or notes) may also be grooming tactics.[12]

HARDENING TARGETS

Threat assessment and prevention professionals often speak of target hardening, by which they mean taking steps to modify the environment to reduce opportunities for the commission of offenses in specific contexts.[13] Schools and their students are generally regarded as "soft" targets because schools are usually large, open structures with multiple rooms and other enclosed, hidden, semihidden, or secluded places.

As a result of a brief but dramatic epidemic of school shootings, many schools have taken obvious steps to harden themselves as targets of weapon violence by, for example, banning backpacks, using metal detectors, and limiting building access. The threat of child sexual abuse in schools, however, is unlikely to be reduced much by such measures, except perhaps to the extent that they may make it more difficult for potential outside predators to find their way into school buildings without detection. That risk, however, is exceedingly small. The threat of child sexual abuse in this context comes largely from within (i.e., from students and school personnel).

Target hardening in schools involves structural and procedural changes that deter such abuse by making it more difficult for perpetrators to sexually abuse students without being detected. Some of these structural changes are relatively obvious, although still not without controversy: for example, video monitoring danger spots (private, secluded, and/or out of the way places where sexual abuse might occur without witnesses); removing doors and other physical barriers that provide visual privacy; making greater use of windows or half-walls that provide greater transparency; and enhancing lighting in dark or dimly lit areas.

Procedural changes that may help schools become harder targets involve managing the flow of people within the building (i.e., setting and enforcing standards as to who may be where at what times and under what circumstances). One example that has been endorsed by a number of educators involves "avoid[ing] or limit[ing] private behavior, such as closed door meetings with students or after-hours activities involving only one student."[14] Other examples include instituting or strengthening enforcement of check in–check out procedures to keep better track of where any student or school employee is at any given time; using roving hall monitors or security officers to routinely patrol private spaces in which sexual abuse might be expected to occur (e.g., lavatories, storerooms, boiler rooms, basements, janitorial closets, and elevators); and the required wearing of photograph identification name tags by all students and school personnel while on school property, in school vehicles, or involved in off-campus school-sponsored activities.

Clearly, there is only so much that a school can be reasonably expected to do to harden itself as a target without compromising its paramount educational mission and/or vastly exceeding its budget. Also, even turning schools into well-patrolled fortresses would not protect all students from sexual abuse, because there have been documented cases in which children have been fondled or otherwise sexually abused even in open, well lit, and full classrooms. Still, schools owe it to their students to take all reasonable steps to maintain a level of safety and order conducive to the educational process.

To the extent that steps to prevent child sexual abuse in the schools entail extra financial expenditures, school officials would do well to consider the financial burden created for schools when child sexual abuse occurs on their premises. In recent decades, public, private, and parochial schools have been forced to pay hundreds of millions of dollars in judgments or settlements in lawsuits brought on behalf of sexually abused students. For example, in one 5-year period alone, the New York City School District paid nearly $19 million to settle claims of students allegedly sexually abused by school personnel.[15] Some but not all of those judgments and settlements have been paid by insurance companies.[16]

Developing and Enforcing School Policies to Minimize Risk

Most if not all states require fingerprint and criminal background checks on all applicants for jobs working with children in public schools. In many jurisdictions, however, private (particularly religious) schools are exempt from these laws. Fingerprint and criminal background checks undoubtedly do screen out some individuals who might otherwise have been given jobs in the schools and sexually abused students. However, because most sex offenders are first-time offenders, these mechanisms seem unlikely to exclude the bulk of potential sex abusers from employment in schools. Moreover, to the extent that students, parents, and school officials rely upon these mechanisms as valid exclusionary measures that protect students from sexual abuse by school employees, they may be lulled into a false sense of security. Of course, these mechanisms have no effect upon peer-to-peer sexual abuse in the schools.

Beyond trying to screen out individuals whose criminal records suggest that they pose a sexual risk to students, schools need to develop and enforce ongoing polices that require all suspicions of child sexual abuse to be immediately reported and investigated without delay. In most states teachers and school administrators and officials are designated by law as mandated reporters and in some states all school personnel are so designated; mandated reporters have a legal duty to report to child welfare authorities any reasonable suspicion of child abuse or neglect of any sort. To insure the broadest range of reports of suspected child sexual abuse in schools, mandatory reporting laws should be expanded to include all school employees and should be supplemented by school policies applicable to every school employee, whether teacher, principal, counselor, coach, janitor, bus driver, or cafeteria worker. Moreover, all school personnel, whether mandated reporters or not, should be trained and required to report *any and all* suspicions or reported suspicions of child sexual abuse, whether apparently reasonable or not; this is not an area in which schools can afford to have their employees be overly cautious in deciding which suspicions to report; even rumors and "gut level" concerns about the possibility of a student being sexually abused should be reported immediately and without concern for the consequences to any school employee, including the reporter. Naturally, however, there should be clear, upfront assurances that reports that turn out to be false or unsubstantiated (unless made by the reporter in bad faith) will have no employment implications whatsoever for the reporter.

Child sexual abuse is, of course, also a crime but often allegations of sexual misconduct in the schools are not reported to the police. Although schools need to have their own internal policies and procedures for immediately dealing with such allegations, they are generally not equipped to carry out the kind of comprehensive investigations conducted by law enforcement agencies and required in most such situations. Thus, suspicions of child sexual abuse in the school setting should be reported not only to child welfare authorities (as required by mandatory child abuse reporting laws) but also to the police. Indeed, to avoid duplicate investigations (which may expose victims to the potential psychological harm entailed in multiple interviews), in most cases investigation of allegations of child sexual abuse in the schools is best left to law enforcement personnel who are specially trained to conduct them. Of course, school policies should require all school personnel to cooperate fully with such investigations conducted by law enforcement officers.

CHILD SEXUAL ABUSE IN JUVENILE CORRECTIONAL FACILITIES

Recently, the Bureau of Justice Statistics (BJS) of the US Department of Justice reported on a nationwide survey of the sexual abuse of children being held in America's juvenile correctional facilities.[17] Between June 2008 and April 2009, BJS surveyed 166 state-owned or operated facilities and 29 locally or privately operated juvenile correctional facilities, in which adjudicated youth were held for at least 90 days. In an October 2010 report, titled "Report of Sexual Victimization in Juvenile Correctional Facilities," the federal government's Review Panel on Prison Rape concluded that:

In a society that values the dignity of each individual, any incident of sexual victimization of a youth in custody is unacceptable. From this perspective, the Panel reviewed the BJS Juvenile Report and noted that violent sexual assault in juvenile facilities is relatively rare and that facility staff members, for the most part, do not victimize juvenile offenders. The Panel commends juvenile justice administrators who have, as a whole, worked hard toward eliminating sexual victimization in their facilities.[18]

Astonishingly, in the very next paragraph, the Panel summarized the findings of the national survey as follows:

The BJS Juvenile Report found that of the estimated 26,551 adjudicated youth held in state facilities or large non-state facilities in 2008-09, about 12.1% (3,220) reported experiencing sexual violence. About 2.6% of these reported incidents involved other youths, whereas about 10.3% involved facility staff members. For the reported youth-on-youth incidents, 2.0% involved nonconsensual acts; for the reported staff-on-youth incidents, 4.3% involved force and 6.4% did not involve force. Facilities that housed only female youth offenders had the highest rates of youth-on-youth victimization (11.0%), whereas facilities that housed only male youth offenders had the highest rates of staff sexual misconduct (11.3%).[19]

Based upon these data, it is literally true that staff members in juvenile correctional facilities "for the most part, do not victimize juvenile offenders."[20] But if, as these data indicate, more than 10 percent of juveniles incarcerated in these facilities are being sexually abused by staff members, it is hard to understand why the Panel would commend administrators of these facilities on their efforts to eliminate child sexual abuse in these institutions. It is even harder to understand how the Panel concluded that "violent sexual assault in juvenile facilities is relatively rare."[21] "Relatively rare" as compared with what? Certainly not compared with violent sexual assault in adult prisons and jails. In a report published in August 2010 based on data gathered around the same time as those in the juvenile corrections survey just described, US Justice Department's BJS reported that:

Today's BJS report, "Sexual Victimization in Prisons and Jails Reported by Inmates, 2008-09," is based on a nationwide survey of inmates in federal and state prisons and in county jails. According to the BJS, 4.4 percent of prison inmates and 3.1 percent of jail inmates reported having experienced one or more incidents of sexual victimization by other inmates and/or staff at their current facility in the preceding 12 months. While some suffered a single assault, others were raped repeatedly: on average, victims were abused three to five times over the course of the year. The survey did not include minors held in these facilities, but in a similar BJS report released in January 2010, more than 12 percent of youth in juvenile detention reported sexual abuse, or one in eight.[22]

Perhaps the only plausible rationale for the Panel's rosy assertion is the finding that a handful of juvenile detention facilities accounted for well more than their fair share of the sexual abuse of incarcerated children, thus driving up the overall numbers. For example, the Report found that 36.2 percent of the youth at the Pendleton Juvenile Correctional Facility in Indiana reported being sexually victimized at the facility, with more than 18 percent reporting "staff sexual misconduct with force" and 16.8 percent reporting "staff sexual misconduct without force."[23] Similarly, 26 percent of juvenile inmates at the Woodland Hills Youth Development Center in Tennessee reported incidents of sexual victimization, all perpetrated by staff members.[24] A total of 32.4 percent of the juvenile inmates at the Corsicana Residential Treatment Center in Texas reported sexual victimization (13.9 percent by another youth and 23.7 percent by a staff member).[25]

In the same study, however, the Ft. Bellefontaine Campus of the Missouri's Division of Youth Services, a large juvenile detention center, had "no reported incidents of sexual victimization during the reporting period,"[26] and at the Rhode Island Training School, a similar secure youth detention facility, "there was a single reported juvenile-on-juvenile sexual encounter...but a thorough investigation concluded that the charge was unfounded."[27]

Who Are the Victims?

According to the "Report of Sexual Victimization in Juvenile Correctional Facilities,"

> [M]ales were more likely than females to experience sexual activity with staff; females were more likely than males to report forced sexual activity with other youth; black youth were more likely than white youth to experience sexual victimization by facility staff; youth with a sexual orientation other than heterosexual were significantly more likely to experience sexual victimization than heterosexual youth; youth who had a prior history of sexual assault were twice as likely to report sexual victimization than youth with no history of sexual assault; and among youth who reported being victims of sexual assault at another facility, two-thirds reported being sexually victimized at the facility that currently housed them.[28]

Who Are the Perpetrators?

According to the 2010 BJS report, roughly 80 percent of those children who were sexually abused in juvenile correctional facilities were victimized by staff members while the other 20 percent or so were victimized by another youth in the facility. The gender breakdown among perpetrators is surprising, given what is known about perpetrator gender in virtually every other context in which children are sexually abused by adults: "Approximately 95% of all youth reporting staff sexual misconduct said they had been victimized by female staff [who constituted only] 42 percent of the staff in state juvenile facilities."[29]

What is the Nature of the Abuse?

According to the 2010 BJS report, among the 2.6 percent of youths sexually abused by peers in juvenile correctional facilities, more than 76 percent had been involved in nonconsensual "contact between the penis and the vagina or the penis and the anus; contact between the mouth and the penis, vagina, or anus; penetration of the anal or vaginal opening of another person by a hand, finger, or other object; and rubbing of another person's penis or vagina by a hand."[30] The remaining cases of nonconsensual peer-on-peer sex abuse involved "kissing on the lips or other part of the body, looking at private body parts, showing something sexual like pictures or a movie, and engaging in some other sexual contact that did not involve touching."[31]

With regard to sexual abuse of youths by staff members in juvenile correctional facilities, the BJS report emphasized that: "Reports of staff sexual misconduct with youth were classified separately depending on whether the misconduct involved any force, threat, pressure, or offers of special favors or privileges. An estimated 4.3% of youth (1,150 nationwide) reported that they had sex or other sexual contact with facility staff as a result of force. An estimated 6.4% (1,710) of youth said they had sexual contact with facility staff without any force, threat, or other explicit form of coercion."[32]

The report further indicated, however, that in both categories of staff-perpetrated sexual abuse (those involving force and those involving no force) more than 90 percent of the abuse involved "contact between the penis and the vagina or the penis and the anus; contact between the mouth and the penis, vagina, or anus; penetration of the anal or vaginal opening of another person by a hand, finger, or other object; and rubbing of another person's penis or vagina by a hand."[33]

In both categories of staff-inflicted abuse (with force and without force) the remaining cases included "kissing on the lips or other part of the body, looking at private body parts, showing something sexual like pictures or a movie, and engaging in some other sexual contact that did not involve touching."[34]

Child Sexual Abuse in Adult Prisons

In every American state, youths 18 or older are regarded as adults for criminal law purposes. In 10 states (Georgia, Illinois, Louisiana, Massachusetts, Michigan, Missouri, New Hampshire, South Carolina, Texas, and Wisconsin), that age is 17. In three states (Connecticut, New York, and North Carolina), it is 16. Moreover, all 50 states have laws allowing children even younger than 16 who are convicted of very serious crimes to be prosecuted and punished as adult criminals.[35] As a result of these laws, on any given day, there are more than 100,000 juveniles younger than 18 in adult prisons and jails in the United States.[36]

Recent efforts by the US government to measure the incidence of rape in adult prisons have deliberately ignored many of these youths by limiting the studies to incarcerated offenders over the age of 18. Thus, there are no recent, reliable data regarding the sexual abuse of youth younger than 18 who are incarcerated in prison rather than juvenile correctional facilities. However, recent federal data do indicate that while "[r]ates of inmate-on-inmate sexual victimization were unrelated to age among state and federal prisoners…[i]n both prisons and jails, rates of reported staff sexual misconduct were lower among inmates in the oldest age categories (ages 45 to 54 and ages 55 or older) compared to inmates ages 20 to 24."[37] The same data also indicate that prison inmates aged 18–19 had the highest likelihood of any age group of being sexually abused by prison staff. It should be noted, however, that while the percentage of 18- and 19-year-old prison inmates reporting staff sexual abuse was 3.9 percent in 2008–2009, that is less than half the reported incidence of staff-on-inmate sexual abuse reported in juvenile correctional facilities during the same time period.

Preventing Child Sexual Abuse in Juvenile Correctional Facilities

Preventing child sexual abuse in juvenile correctional facilities is an especially difficult task, given the closed and authoritarian nature of most of these facilities, total institutions in which delinquent, troubled, neglected, and/or previously abused children "are expected to follow all orders issued by the adults in charge, submit to strip searches by adults, and depend on those in authority to meet basic needs and protect them from potential perpetrators."[38] Any successful effort at preventing child sexual abuse in this context will clearly have to take into consideration these and other unique circumstances that exist in juvenile correctional facilities.

Limiting Exposure of Youth to Juvenile Correctional Facilities

Perhaps the most fundamental way of preventing child sexual abuse in juvenile correctional facilities is to limit the exposure of youngsters to these facilities. The risk of being sexually abused, although serious, is only one of the many dangers children face when they are locked up around the clock in total institutions that are largely out of public sight, often understaffed, and frequently overcrowded. These institutions are commonly inhabited by adolescents who have been abused, have limited capacities for self-regulation and impulse control, and are undergoing the hormonal and other physical changes normally associated with human development at their age. In short, even the best of these facilities may be, by their very nature, breeding grounds for child sexual abuse.

Children committed to juvenile correctional facilities range from those who have committed no crimes (i.e., status offenders who are truant, runaways, or otherwise refuse to obey adult authority) to those who have committed serious crimes of personal violence (rape, robbery, assault, and even homicide). Under the Juvenile Delinquency Prevention Act of 2002, states are prohibited from housing status offenders in secure detention facilities, but "many jurisdictions take advantage of exceptions to this rule and confine youths with minor infractions in facilities for serious offenders."[39] As a result, on one recent annual "census day" there were approximately 4,800 status offenders being housed in juvenile correctional facilities nationwide.[40]

Although there remains great debate about the purposes served by institution-alizing any children in these facilities, there can be little doubt that many young-sters who are committed to these facilities do not need to be there for purposes of public protection. For many of these youths, the goal of rehabilitation would more effectively, efficiently, and economically be met by community interventions that do not involve incarceration. Thus, one simple way to prevent at least some children from being sexually abused in these institutions is to make sure that they are never committed to such places.

Moreover, even for youths deemed to require such institutionalization for incapacitative or rehabilitative reasons, it appears that the less time they spend in these facilities, the lower their risk of being sexually abused. One of the key find-ings of the BJS survey described above was that "Facilities in which youth were held an average of less than 5 months had the lowest rates of sexual victimiza-tion (7.4%), compared to facilities in which youth were held for longer periods (12.7% in facilities with an average of 5 to 6 months and 14.2% in facilities with an average of 7 to 12 months)."[41] Clearly, some juvenile delinquents, such as those adjudicated for crimes of violence and regarded as dangerous may require lengthy periods of confinement for reasons of public safety. However, most other juvenile delinquents, even those who have committed serious property offenses deemed to call for incarceration most likely do not require lengthy periods of confinement. Moreover, for whatever period of time incarceration is deemed necessary, there is little if any excuse for housing nonviolent, nondangerous juvenile offenders with their violent and/or dangerous counterparts.

CREATING SMALLER INSTITUTIONS

Other key findings of the BJS survey with implications for prevention related to the size of the juvenile correctional facilities studied and their ratios of staff to inmates. To begin with, those institutions with no or extremely few cases of child sexual abuse were small facilities, whereas those with the highest number of such cases were large. Contrasting two of the institutions mentioned previously, Ft. Bellefontaine Campus in Missouri and Pendleton Juvenile Correctional Facility in Indiana, the Justice Department's Review Panel on Prison Rape noted that:

> The Panel recognizes that some juvenile justice systems in the country may acknowledge Ft. Bellefontaine's positive record but dismiss it as a replicable model because it serves only twenty four residents. In contrast, Pendleton has well over two hundred. Juvenile justice systems dealing with bud-get constraints and existing large physical plants may view emulating Ft. Bellefontaine's approach to juvenile corrections as impractical. According to Missouri DYS, the size of Ft. Bellefontaine is a deliberate organizational deci-sion; no facility in the Missouri system has more than fifty beds. Although the Panel is aware of the financial, political, and institutional pressures that may prevent states from following Missouri's example, many of the administra-tors of juvenile correctional facilities who presented testimony at the Panel's hearings recognized the importance of placing youths in small facilities close

to their homes. Consistent with the views of the administrators who testified at the Panel hearings, the Panel encourages state juvenile correctional systems to consider adopting the strategic goal, perhaps as part of a long-term plan, of placing youth offenders in smaller facilities.[42]

Interestingly, if not surprisingly, the Justice Department panel also reported that the three juvenile corrections institutions surveyed with the highest rates of child sexual abuse had staff-to-inmate ratios that were, for the most part, not significantly different from those of the two surveyed facilities that had no cases of child sexual abuse during the period studied. The staff-to-inmate ratios were as follows: Pendleton Juvenile Correctional Facility, 1:3; Corsicana Residential Treatment Center, 1:6.6; Woodland Hills Youth Development Center, 1:5; Ft. Bellefontaine Campus, 1:6; and Rhode Island Training School, 1:8.[43]

IMPROVING SCREENING AND PLACEMENT
As the National Prison Rape Elimination Commission has observed, there is little evidence-based information available that would help juvenile facilities identify potential victims of child sexual abuse. There is, however, some reason to believe that among youngsters who are most at risk for sexual abuse in these facilities are those who have previously been abused; suffer from developmental disabilities or psychological disorders; or are gay, lesbian, bisexual, or transgendered. In its report, the Commission recommended careful screening of youths entering juvenile correctional facilities for these and any other vulnerabilities they may present. The Commission further recommended that "[b]ecause addressing certain personal issues can be traumatic for youth... questioning about sexual orientation, gender identity, prior sexual victimization, history of engaging in sexual abuse, and mental and physical health should be conducted solely by medical and mental health practitioners."[44]

The Commission also recommended an in-depth screening process that would include not only interviews of incoming inmates but reviews of their court, casework, and institutional records. Indeed, "[t]he Commission's standard on the placement of youth in juvenile facilities mandates that staff use all information about the risk of sexual abuse to determine safe housing, bed, program, education, and work assignments. Any information that may indicate heightened vulnerability to sexual abuse... must be taken into consideration in determining appropriate placements."[45]

The Commission further emphasized that screening is an ongoing process that should continue throughout a youngster's incarceration: "Because vulnerability factors, the mix of potential predators and victims, and other characteristics change over time, staff must reassess residents periodically and adjust placements when necessary to keep all residents safe from sexual abuse. If an incident of sexual abuse occurs and is discovered, staff must reassess placement decisions for the victim and, if the abuse was perpetrated by another resident, for the perpetrator as well."[46]

Finally, with regard to placement, the Commission took a strong stand against commingling juvenile and adult offenders in the same institution: "Although the

Juvenile Justice and Delinquency Prevention Act of 2002 prohibits the incarceration of juveniles with adults except in very limited circumstances, this protection
does not apply to youth who are prosecuted as adults.... Because of the extreme
risk of sexual victimization for youth in adult facilities, the Commission urges that
individuals below the age of 18 be held separately from the general population."⁴⁷

EDUCATION, TRAINING, AND ENCOURAGING REPORTING

Clearly, as in every context in which child sexual abuse occurs, prevention of such
abuse in juvenile correctional facilities partially depends upon educating potential victims, perpetrators, and witnesses. Given the closed, authoritarian nature
of most juvenile correctional institutions, it is not difficult to imagine that some,
perhaps many, incarcerated youths do not perceive what they experience as sexual
abuse or, if they do, do not report it. Thus, juveniles incarcerated in these facilities
need to be taught what constitutes sexual abuse and what they should do if they
experience or witness it. Rudimentary as that approach may sound, it is undoubtedly easier said than done.

Given the diverse nature of the inmate population of juvenile correctional
facilities (sometimes ranging in age from 6–20 years and presenting a wide diver-
sity of cultural, ethnic, socioeconomic, and educational backgrounds) clearly a
broad range of targeted educational efforts are required. Educational materials
and presentations for youth will have little value, however, if they do not use
age-appropriate language and concrete examples, especially when discussing
how to report abuse. Given the range of ages in many facilities, a one-size-fits-all
approach will not work. As the National Prison Rape Elimination Commission
has suggested, "Presentations, materials, and follow-up contacts should be struc-
tured to match the emotional, cognitive, and sexual development of particular
age groupings of children and teens and must reach youth who speak limited or
no English, have limited reading skills, are visually impaired, or are deaf."⁴⁸

Of course, particularly in this context, education cannot be limited simply to
the population of potential victims. If the numbers reviewed previously are anywhere near accurate, many staff members in juvenile correctional facilities either
do not understand what constitutes sexual abuse or they are quite willing to inflict
such abuse on the children they are employed to care for, protect, and rehabilitate.
Either way, given these data as well as the nature of these facilities, there can be no
excuse for not adequately training staff with regard to child sexual abuse, including that inflicted by staff as well as juveniles.

It would seem to go without saying but, as the Commission noted, juvenile correctional facilities must establish and announce to both staff and inmates a zero
tolerance policy for sexual abuse. Beyond that, however, as the Panel on Prison Rape
observed, staff members must be trained regarding "the importance of maintaining professional boundaries in youth correctional settings."⁴⁹ Specifically they need
to be taught to "identify early indicators, called 'red flags' or 'slippery slopes,' that
should put staff members on notice that either they or one of their colleagues may
be in danger of crossing a professional boundary that could lead to an inappropriate
relationship with a youth," including, for example, "bringing presents to a youth,

sharing personal information with a youth, treating a youth more favorably in comparison to others, and spending time with a youth beyond regular duty hours."[50]

The Panel noted that "when female staff members are experiencing difficulties in their personal lives (e.g., divorce or other loss), they may be especially vulnerable to developing inappropriate relationships with male youth offenders."[51] Moreover, the Panel added: "[T]he consensus among the juvenile corrections administrators who appeared at the Panel hearings, which the Panel also endorses, is that providing effective training to staff, especially female staff, on recognizing behavior that risks crossing a professional boundary would strengthen prevention of staff-on-juvenile sexual misconduct."[52]

Anecdotal evidence suggests that staff training should be extensive. Consider, for example, the staff training required at the Ft. Bellefontaine Campus of the Missouri's Division of Youth Services and at the Rhode Island Training School, two juvenile correctional facilities with extraordinary records regarding sexual abuse of their juvenile inmates. At Ft. Bellefontaine: "Within the first two years of employment, all...staff must complete at least 180 hours in adolescent care with forty hours of on-the-job coaching. After the initial training, each staff person receives annually forty hours of professional development training."[53] Before being hired at Rhode Island Training School, "the applicant must complete six weeks of training, with forty hours each week...Every week, staff members attend a training session offering professional development."[54]

Most professionals who work in juvenile correctional facilities are mandated reporters, required by law to report any reasonable suspicion of child abuse, including sexual abuse. Others who work in these facilities are generally under a similar requirement imposed by institutional policies. Beyond laws and policies, however, juvenile correctional facilities need to inculcate in their staff a moral obligation to report suspicions of abuse, including child sexual abuse. These facilities must also develop procedures that make reporting such suspicions as easy and painless as possible. Employees should be given multiple ways in which to exercise their duty to report, including the option of reporting anonymously. Anonymous reports of sexual abuse in these institutions may not carry the same weight as those made openly, but where a child's safety and mental health are at stake, any report is better than no report.

Staff members also need to be taught to overcome what might be called the 100 percent positive syndrome. In critiquing his own institution, the previous superintendent at the Pendleton Juvenile Correctional Facility Pendleton (where more than 18 percent of incarcerated youth reported "staff sexual misconduct with force" and 16.8 percent reported "staff sexual misconduct without force") suggested that "employees may discount what they are observing because they have a relationship with the coworker and they know that the ramifications of falsely accusing a colleague are grave."[55] In his own words,

> I think that in most cases people work so closely with one another that they believe in that person, and they don't believe that that other person would get off into a situation like that or do anything that would harm a kid, and they

know that those are serious allegations to raise against another fellow staff member, and if you're going to raise that type of allegation, you need to be 100 percent sure that that's what's taking place.[56]

Clearly, neither society nor juvenile correctional facilities want to encourage false allegations of child sexual abuse, but neither can they afford to wait until a staff member is absolutely certain that abuse has occurred before making a report that triggers an investigation. In that regard, employees of these facilities should be held to the same standard as mandated reporters in most jurisdictions: not certainty, not even reasonable certainty, but reasonable suspicion of abuse.

Children incarcerated in juvenile correctional institutions are under no legal obligation to report abuse they suffer or witness. These facilities may have policies requiring children to report abuse they experience or witness, but such policies are almost impossible to enforce in this context. Many youngsters do not report sexual abuse in juvenile correctional facilities because they fear reprisal, not being believed, and/or the stigma of being regarded by some as a "snitch." Juvenile correctional institutions need to overcome these concerns by clearly stating expectations; giving juvenile inmates multiple ways of confidential reporting (including anonymously); guaranteeing protection to those who report abuse; and providing supportive treatment to alleged and established victims.

Children in these institutions also need to see that reports of abuse are acted upon swiftly and fairly and that there are visible consequences for the abuser. As the National Prison Rape Elimination Commission concluded: "No culture of safety and of zero tolerance for sexual abuse can exist when perpetrators operate with impunity, without fear of serious consequences for their behavior, and are free to retaliate against or further victimize their accusers or others. If perpetrators are not held accountable, victims and witnesses of abuse will view reporting as futile and remain silent. Punishing perpetrators also has a deterrent effect, cautioning those who might be inclined to engage in abuse to think twice. And it is, of course, what justice requires."[57]

Other ways that have been suggested and/or tried in efforts to encourage reporting sexual abuse in juvenile correctional facilities include involving families in the care and treatment of their incarcerated children and inviting them to raise any concerns they have regarding the way their children are being treated at any time; providing children with personal or legal advocates, inside and/or outside the facility, in whom they can confide concerns about the institution; and providing swift and thorough investigations of all reports.

CHANGING THE CULTURE

The juvenile justice system began under what was referred to as the "rehabilitative ideal," the notion that children and adolescents are not adults and when they commit crimes they should be treated, not punished. Less than a century after its founding, the juvenile justice system in America took a radical turn toward criminalizing delinquency, treating juvenile offenders as adults, and replacing rehabilitation with punishment as the underlying rationale for juvenile correctional facilities. Many in the field of juvenile corrections believe that the wave of child sexual abuse in these facilities that has developed in recent decades is, at least in part, a result of this criminalizing and punitive trend. As the Justice Department's Review Panel on Prison Rape reported in 2010:

> Every administrative leader of a juvenile correctional system who testified before the Panel stressed the importance of institutional culture. They recognized that in the world of juvenile corrections, there is a spectrum of competing models, with the therapeutic-rehabilitation model on one end and the punitive-correction model on the other. Among the institutions that the Panel selected to study, Ft. Bellefontaine presents an example of the therapeutic approach, whereas Pendleton presents, at least until the recent past, an example of the punitive approach. Regardless of how they may characterize their own institutions, all of the administrators who presented testimony to the Panel said that they valued a therapeutic culture, and they were either already committed to one or were taking steps to achieve one. All of the administrative leaders who testified also underscored the significance of differentiating juvenile correctional systems from their adult counterparts. Youth who are in custody are still in development, and institutions that serve young people well have programs and staff that take youth development into account.... The consensus among the leaders of juvenile correctional institutions, a consensus that the Panel supports, is that in creating safe institutions that are free of sexual abuse, juvenile correctional systems should promote a therapeutic culture, promoting programming that focuses on rehabilitation and engages families in planning for a youth offender's successful transition back to the community.[58]

CHANGING THE FACILITY'S PROCEDURES AND STRUCTURES

At least one study of institutional child sexual abuse has found that most adults who sexually abuse children in institutional settings act alone. In this study, which was not limited to residential settings, 92 percent of adult abusers acted on their own, but 100 percent of those who sexually abused children in residential settings acted by themselves.[59] To the extent that these findings may be generalized to include most juvenile correctional facilities, they lead to the inescapable conclusion that, outside of collusion or conspiracy by staff, child sexual abuse in this context virtually requires that the perpetrator have an opportunity to be alone with the victim. Thus, a way to significantly limit the sexual abuse of children in juvenile correctional facilities is to require that staff never be alone with a child or children.

Given the kind of around-the-clock service provided by staff in these institutions, it may be difficult to mandate such a policy across the board. It seems likely that there will sometimes, perhaps often, be instances in which a staff member must be alone with one or more children. Thus, perhaps a more reasonable alternative is to not only discourage staff from being alone with children whenever possible, but also use various forms of surveillance in cases where staff members do need to be alone with children.

One feasible alternative is to construct all areas in which staff are alone with children (e.g., interview and counseling rooms) with large windows that allow these areas to be readily and easily seen by other staff and children. Another alternative, which is widely used in many juvenile correctional facilities, is the generous placement of video cameras throughout the institution, but especially in secluded spots, areas that are not heavily trafficked, and any areas in which staff are allowed to be alone with children. For example, in response to the BJS study of child sexual abuse, including data on the Corsicana Residential Treatment Center, officials there installed nearly 900 video cameras.[60] A third alternative relates to the time period any child is allowed to go without being observed by a staff member. For example, when confronted with the data on child sexual abuse at the Pendleton Juvenile Correctional Facility, officials determined that most such abuse took place during the evening shift. In response, they changed their "eyes on" requirement, mandating that staff on that shift observe children at least once every 5 minutes rather than 15 minutes, as was the previous rule.[61]

Although these construction and monitoring recommendations may be regarded as intrusive and will certainly diminish the privacy experienced by both staff and children in these facilities, they will not only protect children from sexual abuse but also protect staff from false accusations of such abuse.

PERIODIC CONDUCT OF RISK AUDITS

Smallbone, Marshall, and Wortley have recommended that institutions, including but not limited to juvenile correctional facilities, supplement individual screening of employees and volunteers with "risk assessments... performed on the institutional setting itself."[62] In some ways, the BJS survey described previously represents a kind of institutional risk assessment, at least for the facilities it included. However, these authors are suggesting a much broader and detailed form of self-study. They point to a strategy under development by the New South Wales Commission for Children and Young People. In addition to developing a screening tool for those who apply for positions working with children, the Commission developed two instruments: one aimed at assessing the risk of abuse posed by the organization, and the other the risk posed by specific positions in the organization. An organization is rated with regard to formal job descriptions that specify appropriate and inappropriate staff conduct toward children, the presence of a risk management coordinator, a formal plan for minimizing risk, making staff aware of that plan, regularly reviewing the plan, and so forth. Specific positions are rated with regard to whether they involve working alone with children, working with children outside the regular workplace, or working with particularly vulnerable children; whether they involve close physical or emotional contact with children; whether training and supervision are provided regarding identification and response to risky staff conduct; and so forth. As Smallbone et al. concluded: "in developing these instruments, the Commission recognizes that risks for children in institutions do not reside solely within the individual."[63]

SEXUAL ABUSE BY CHILD-CARE PROVIDERS

In the 1980s and 1990s, the United States witnessed what at first blush appeared to be an epidemic of mass sexual abuse in child day-care centers. From coast to coast, owners and workers in such centers were accused of the grossest forms of child sexual abuse imaginable, much of it allegedly committed as part of bizarre, orgiastic, satanic rituals that purportedly included both animal and human sacrifice. Most of these cases were given extensive, if not national, media coverage.

Probably the most widely publicized of these cases involved allegations in 1984 against seven adults associated with the McMartin Daycare Center in Manhattan Beach, California. One parent, Judy Johnson, complained to police that her two-and-a-half-year-old son (who had attended the McMartin Center on 10 occasions) had been molested by Ray Buckey, a child-care aide and the son of the center's owner. As law professor Douglas Linder has explained, Johnson's allegations "became increasingly bizarre" and would eventually be recognized as "the delusions of a paranoid schizophrenic."[64] However, her accusations of ritualistic child sexual abuse triggered an investigation in which a social worker interviewed some 400 children who had attended the McMartin center. Using unorthodox interview methods, the social worker and her associates "relied heavily on leading questions and subtle pressure to persuade children to join the chorus of accusers."[65] Ultimately they diagnosed 384 of these preschoolers and former preschoolers as having been sexually abused by adults at the day-care center.[66]

These often bizarre allegations led to a preliminary hearing that lasted more than a year and cost taxpayers more than $4 million. The hearing was followed by an initial trial in which Ray Buckey and his mother Peggy Buckey faced a total of 65 charges (charges against the five other defendants were all dropped by a District Attorney, who labeled the evidence against them as "incredibly weak").[67] After a trial that took more than 30 months, and deliberations that went on for two-and-a-half months, the jury acquitted the defendants on 52 charges but deadlocked on 13 charges against Ray Buckey. The state retried Ray Buckey on eight counts. After hearing 3 months of evidence, the jury again deadlocked, although they had voted in favor of acquittal on six counts.

The state, having already spent $15 million on the trials (not including the $4 million spent on the preliminary hearing) declined to retry Buckey, who had been jailed for 5 years awaiting trial and verdict. Meanwhile, one of the initial prosecutors on the case told interviewers that he doubted the defendants' guilt. Furthermore, he and another prosecutor had withheld information that would have helped from the defendants' case and damaged the credibility of the initial complainant, Judy Johnson. Johnson, the prosecutor said, had claimed that Ray Buckey "flew in the air,"[68] that Peggy Buckey had drilled holes in the alleged victim's armpits, and that the alleged victim had also been sodomized by an AWOL marine and a public school official.

As Professor Linder observed, the McMartin trial led day-care workers across the country to avoid physical contact with children for fear of being accused of sexual abuse, forced many day-care centers to close, and led to an epidemic of sex abuse charges against day-care providers across the country, many of which proved to be false.[69]

Although the McMartin prosecution, and the many other unfounded day-care child sexual abuse allegations it helped spawn around the country, cast a dark shadow on day-care centers everywhere that remains to some extent to this day, in fact day-care centers are generally quite safe places for children.

The Incidence of Child Sexual Abuse in Day-Care Centers

Very little systematic study of child sexual abuse in day-care centers has ever been undertaken, but one major study was conducted in the late 1980s by David Finkelhor and colleagues.[70] Finkelhor et al. reviewed the official data regarding substantiated cases of sexual abuse occurring in licensed day-care centers over a 3-year period. The study was limited to centers serving more than six children. Finkelhor et al. found evidence of child sexual abuse in 270 day-care facilities, yielding 1,639 victims younger than the age of 6 years, and 382 perpetrators.

Finkelhor et al. reported that roughly a quarter of the cases involved abusers who were owners or directors of the centers, half of whom were reported to have acted alone in perpetrating the abuse. Another quarter of the abusers were male relatives of an owner, director, or employee of the center, and 36 percent of the cases involved such an abuser. About 30 percent of the abusers were teachers or child-care professionals, among whom nearly two-thirds were reported to have acted in concert with another in perpetrating sexual abuse. Another 15 percent of the abusers were nonprofessional caregivers and 20 percent of the cases involved perpetrators who were center employees not directly involved in child care, mainly bus drivers and janitors. A small proportion of the reported abuse, less than 6 percent, involved perpetrators who were nonemployees or others having no affiliation with the center. Overall, 36 percent of the abusers were female and 64 percent male. Roughly 73 percent of female offenders reportedly acted in concert with other abusers, whereas only 14 percent of male abusers reportedly did so. Only 8 percent of the abusers had any prior criminal record of child abuse.

Although Finkelhor considered these data "disturbing," he emphasized that they must be viewed in context and that they are not "an indication of some special risk to children in day care."[71] For example, based on these numbers, he and his colleagues estimated that 5.5 out of every 10,000 children enrolled in day care were sexually abused each year. However, they also estimated that 8.9 out of every 10,000 preschool children were sexually abused at home each year.

Although some critics argued that this study was incomplete and may have underestimated the number of children sexually abused in day-care centers,[72] Finkelhor noted that the comparison data regarding the number of children sexually abused in their own homes was also likely an underestimate, and probably more so than the data on those children sexually abused in day-care centers because victims and witnesses of such abuse were more likely to report it when it was perpetrated by people other than family members.

Moreover, the study was lauded by the Child Welfare League of America, whose Executive Director concurred that day-care centers are "generally safe places for children," and the National Association for the Education of Young Children, whose spokesperson saw its findings as indicating that "sexual abuse is not a systemic problem of child-care centers."[73]

At the time of the Finkelhor et al. study, there were an estimated 4 million American children in licensed day-care facilities serving more than six children.[74] Applying the estimated figure of 5.5 sexually abused children per 10,000 enrolled in such day-care centers results in an estimate that at the time of this study, the annual number of victims of child sexual abuse in licensed day-care facilities serving more than six children was 2,200. Finkelhor et al. arrived at a similar estimate of 2,500.[75]

More recently, the Office on Child Abuse and Neglect of the US Department of Health and Human Services, relying upon data gathered from 39 states in 2006, reported that less than 1 percent of all child maltreatment during that year was reported to have occurred in child-care settings. In all, 5,321 child day-care providers were found to be perpetrators of any sort of abuse or neglect. Of that number, 21.9 percent involved sexual abuse.[76] Even more recently, the NCANDS report "Child Maltreatment" estimated that during federal fiscal year 2010, the number of unique child abuse victims was 695,000 nationally, 3,685 (0.4 percent) of whom were abused by a day-care provider.[77] The percentage of these cases that involved sexual abuse is not known, but there is every reason to believe that it was substantially less than 100 percent.

Clearly the Finkelhor et al. estimates from 1988 cannot be directly compared with the data and estimates provided by the Office on Child Abuse and Neglect for 2006 or those published by NCANDS for 2010 because the data on which they are based were gathered in different ways. However, it is striking to note that all three studies essentially led to the same conclusion reached by Finkelhor et al. more than a quarter of a century ago: "Day care is not an inherently high-risk locale for children, despite frightening stories in the media."[78]

Preventing Child Sexual Abuse in Day-Care Centers

Although children in day-care centers are not at a high risk of being sexually abused, they are among the youngest and most vulnerable potential targets of such abuse. Moreover, to the extent that they are placed at risk in this context, it is because of the critical role that day care plays in the modern American economy. Nearly 65 percent of American children younger than age 6 years require child care because their parents are working; roughly one-third of these children are cared for in day-care centers; and more than a million people earn their living as child-care workers in day-care centers.[79] Parents who must place their children in day-care centers in order to earn a living and support themselves and their children want and need to believe that their children will be safe in these facilities; they would be reluctant to place their children in such care if they believed otherwise. Thus, it is no exaggeration to say that, in a very real sense, the American economy depends upon ongoing efforts to prevent child abuse, including sexual abuse, in its child day-care facilities.

Efforts to prevent sexual abuse of children in day care are not new. They date back at least to the early 1980s when the allegations in such cases as the McMartin prosecution were sensationalized by the mass media. Over the years, however, these efforts have become more organized, systematic, and logical. Although there remains a paucity of empirical evidence to suggest that they are effective, many of these efforts appear to be sensible and defensible both for the safety of children in day care and for protection of the adults who care for them in that setting and may be at risk of being falsely accused of sexual abuse.

UNDERSTANDING AND COMMUNICATING THE NATURE OF THE RISK

As just noted, child day care plays a critical role in the economy as well as the daily lives of many American working families. Although many parents pay others to watch their children during certain hours of the day, they often have misgivings or feelings of guilt or regret about doing so. No one wants to make it more difficult for parents who use day care to do so, or to see a repeat of the day-care sexual abuse hysteria that swept the country in 1980s. However, a crucial step in any effort to prevent child sexual abuse in day-care centers is making sure that parents and all others with a stake or interest in day care are made aware of the risk of child sexual abuse in this context, limited though it may be.

Most day-care providers (some estimate as many as 97 percent) are women.[80] As the Finkelhor et al. study made clear, "in day care, women make up a third of all abusers and half of the abusers among caregivers."[81] Because, as they noted, parents and others see sexual abuse by females as "so improbable," they need to "be educated to view females as potential sex abusers" in this context.[82]

USING PARENTS AS MONITORS FOR BOTH SAFETY AND DETERRENCE

Parents also need to be made aware that they are among the most potent forces available in making child sexual abuse less likely to happen in day-care centers. Absent staff collusion, those bent upon perpetrating sexual abuse in child day-care centers need, above all else, a relatively high degree of privacy and the reasonable assumption that they will not be unexpectedly observed committing such abuse. As is detailed later, day-care center policies should be directed to these concerns. However, parents can assist by making frequent, unannounced, and irregularly timed visits to centers providing day care for their children.

Finkelhor et al. reported that, in their study of sexual abuse in day-care centers, "Limits on parental access was a significant risk factor."[83] For example, they found that "programs that limited parental access were more likely to have multiple-perpetrator sexual abuse."[84] As Karageorge and Kendall noted in their 2008 US Department of Health and Human Resources report on "The Role of Professional Child Care Providers in Preventing and Responding to Child Abuse and Neglect": "Most early childhood education programs encourage parents to make unannounced visits at any time during daily operations."[85] Parents of children in day care need to have, and to exercise the option for, such unannounced visits, both to monitor the safety of their own children and to provide a possible deterrent against abuse of all children in the center's care.

Of course, staff also need to monitor the behavior of parents when they visit the day-care center. As Finkelhor et al. also observed, "[T]here may also be some risks associated with parental involvement. Parents can be perpetrators."[86]

Requiring Day-Care Centers to be Licensed
Only one of America's states (Idaho) does not license child day-care facilities and only three states (Idaho, Louisiana, and New Jersey) do not license family child-care homes, which are essentially smaller and less formal day-care operations conducted in homes rather than centers.[87] More than 90 percent of day-care centers (107,000 of 117,000) and more than 95 percent of family child-care homes (199,000 of 209,000) are state-licensed.[88] State licensing laws vary across jurisdictions, but all "provide a baseline of protection for the health and safety of children in out-of-home care."[89] Licensure laws determine, among other requirements, staff qualifications; staff-to-child ratios; necessary physical facilities; uniform health and safety standards; and hiring practices (including, for example, criminal record and/or fingerprint checks, which are discussed later in this chapter). These laws also provide for some level of periodic inspection, most commonly on an annual basis but sometimes including unannounced inspections. Finally, most such laws provide that day-care providers who violate conditions mandated by their licensure may be sanctioned and even required to close.

Virtually all of these laws exempt at least some day-care programs from the licensing requirements, which explains why not all such programs are licensed. For example, 27 states exempt "facilities that provide service where parents are on the premises and accessible (e.g., shopping malls, resorts, and/or health clubs)"; 26 exempt "facilities with small numbers of children"; 24 exempt "facilities operating part-day or for a small number of hours per day/week"; 12 exempt "facilities operated by religious organizations"; and 10 exempt "facilities operated by local, state, or federal government agencies."[90] The breadth of these exceptions, coupled with the finding that the number of unlicensed day-care centers is increasing and many licensed centers are switching to unlicensed status, has led some child welfare advocates to argue for the abolition of all exemptions and thus the requirement that all child-care providers be licensed by the state.

Certain aspects of day-care licensing laws probably have a positive effect on efforts to prevent the sexual abuse of children in child-care settings. To the extent that these laws are beneficial in these efforts in licensed facilities, it would probably be helpful to such efforts to require that all child-care centers be licensed. For example, licensing ordinarily carries with it staffing ratios, staff qualifications, hiring requirements, periodic inspections, and required training, all of which might help create a child-care environment in which there is less likelihood of sexual abuse. However, the relationship between these and other aspects of current day-care licensing laws and the prevention of child sexual abuse is speculative at best and will remain so until empirical research demonstrates otherwise.

Perhaps the most that can be said at this point is that there are many good reasons for requiring the licensure of child day-care facilities and few if any reasons to believe that licensing laws would have a negative impact on the incidence of child sexual abuse in this context. The only salient reason why licensing might negatively impact the incidence of child sexual abuse in day-care centers is if it creates the illusion that these facilities are safer than they really are and that causes staff members and parents to be less careful in monitoring for abuse.

CRIMINAL RECORD AND FINGERPRINT CHECKS

Child welfare experts and authorities have recommended numerous ways in which day-care centers can and should alter their policies and procedures in order to minimize the risk of abuse, including sexual abuse, to children in these settings. For example, many have recommended that day-care centers be required to conduct detailed background checks on all applicants for employment. The idea is that checking the backgrounds of would-be child-care workers and other day-care personnel will enable centers to screen out those who have records of child abuse or neglect, sexual offending, or committing criminal offenses that would make them risky choices to work with young children. All 50 states require some kind of criminal background check on those who apply to work in licensed day-care facilities[91] but only 11 states require day-care centers to conduct a full background check including state and federal fingerprint databases, criminal records, child abuse and neglect registries, and sex offender registries.[92] Thirty-two states use fingerprints to conduct a check of FBI records and 30 use fingerprints to conduct checks of state criminal records.[93] Of course, not all day-care centers are licensed; some are exempt from licensing laws and others operate informally outside the law. As Child Care Aware of America has pointed out, "Background checks are of limited value unless they are based on fingerprints. A simple background check using a name search is simply not as effective as a background check using a fingerprint match. Using only a name check can allow an individual to circumvent a criminal records check and be approved to provide child care where a fingerprint check would have revealed a criminal record."[94]

Numerous investigations have found instances of sex offenders working in child day-care programs who could have been screened out of such employment had they been subjected to criminal background and/or fingerprint searches. For example, following one brief investigation, the US General Accounting Office (GAO) reported in 2011 that:

> The cases GAO examined show examples of individuals convicted of serious sexual offenses who gained access to child care facilities as maintenance workers, spouses or friends of providers, a cafeteria worker, and a cook. At least seven of these cases involve offenders who previously targeted children,

and in three of the cases, the offenders used their access to children at the facilities to offend again. Among the cases, GAO found instances of providers who (1) knowingly hired offenders and (2) did not perform preemployment criminal-history checks. GAO also found examples of facilities operating without licenses, and facilities that employed offenders while receiving federal funds.[95]

Among the cases described by the GAO, four were highlighted. In a Missouri case, state officials investigating allegations of child abuse discovered "a maintenance worker previously convicted of attempted child molestation working at an unlicensed facility."[96] The facility was not licensed and falsely claimed to be operating as a school rather than a child-care center. In Kentucky, an investigation determined that the "owner of a licensed child-care facility hired a cook to work in her cafeteria in January 2008 because she wanted to help him, even though she knew that he had been convicted for sexually abusing a woman."[97] In Washington, D.C., a sex offender's parents hired him as a janitor in a licensed day-care center that received $1 million or more in federal funding, "even though he had been convicted for attempting to sexually abuse a young girl."[98] In New York, an organization that operated several licensed day-care facilities and received more than $750,000 in federal assistance failed to conduct a criminal history check on a man hired as a janitor who had a conviction for sexually abusing a child.[99]

There are, however, numerous concerns about the value of background checks in the child day-care context. First, in many states there are no background check requirements in the case of small, unlicensed day-care centers. Second, background checks that do not rely upon fingerprints may miss many offenders who use aliases or have changed their names. Third, even the most comprehensive criminal background checks fail to exclude many potential child sexual abusers because many if not most such abusers have no formal record of criminal acting out, child abuse, or sexual offending at the time they are hired.

Finally, there is significant concern about the cost of such searches relative to their likely benefit. In the 1980s, the US Department of Health and Human Services estimated that:

A total of 680,000 current employees in licensed child care plus a 47% annual turnover/growth in staff = 1 million employees to be screened. The cost of 1 million state fingerprint checks (@ $13) and FBI checks (@ $12) = $25 million. If 5% of those screened have criminal records, and perhaps 2% of those with criminal records are sex abusers, then the checks might uncover 1000 previous abusers. (This is a rate of.1%, higher than the hit rate from the Florida and New York experiments.) The cost of finding these 1000 potential abusers ($25 million) would be the equivalent of $25,000 per abuser.[100]

It is now estimated that there are more than 900,000 Americans directly employed in licensed child care.[101] Moreover, the cost of fingerprint checks today is estimated to be in the $18–$24 range.[102] The FBI records check now costs $18.

Thus, assuming that the HHS estimates are reasonably accurate, the equation stated above would now read:

> A total of more than 900,000 current employees in licensed child care plus a 47% annual turnover/growth in staff = 1.32 million employees to be screened. The cost of 1.32 million state fingerprint checks (@ $18) and FBI checks (@ $18) = $47 million. If 5% of those screened have criminal records, and perhaps 2% of those with criminal records are sex abusers, then the checks might uncover 1320 previous abusers. The cost of finding these 1320 potential abusers ($47 million) would be the equivalent of roughly $37,000 per abuser.

Is $37,000 too much to spend to stop one potential abuser from being hired to work in child day care? That is a difficult if not impossible question to answer. Because the recidivism rate for sex offenders is relatively low, the likelihood that a given sex offender who was employed in day care because he or she was not subjected to fingerprinting and a criminal background check is probably quite low. However, that likelihood might be much higher than would otherwise appear, given that the individual in question is not only a sex offender but a sex offender who is seeking employment in child care. Also, of course, many sex offenders have more than a single victim. In the study by Finkelhor et al. of substantiated cases of sexual abuse in day care, 50 percent of the cases involved two or more victims, 36 percent three or more victims, and 10 percent 12 or more victims.[103] Thus, the estimated cost of preventing child sexual abuse in day care via fingerprinting and criminal records searches might be substantially reduced if looked at in terms of the number of victims rather than offenders.

In addition to raising concerns about the cost-effectiveness of pre-employment criminal background and fingerprint checks in this context, some commentators have noted that criminal background and fingerprint checks result in a great number of false-positives (those who have offended in the past but are unlikely to do so again) and false-negatives (those who have no recorded history of sexual offending but will go on to commit such offenses in the day-care setting, if hired). To these concerns might be added the worry that parents as well as day-care providers may be lulled into a false sense of security by the use of pre-employment criminal background and/or fingerprint checks.

Although these points are well taken, as a practical matter, it seems highly unlikely that in the current or foreseeable political environment state and federal legislators and regulators will be willing to allow licensed child-care providers to forego these checks, despite their high cost and limited efficacy.

INSTITUTING "NEVER ALONE" RULES, INCREASING STAFF, AND/OR USING VIDEO MONITORING

As noted previously, absent staff collusion, child sexual abuse is highly unlikely to occur in child day-care centers absent a degree of privacy that gives would-be perpetrators the reasonable assumption that they will not be observed when committing such abuse. Careful monitoring of staff interaction with children seems likely to provide some measure of deterrence and the more staff a facility has, the easier it is to rely upon mutual monitoring. But monitoring, however careful, is not surveillance and may leave gaps in which staff members are alone with children and thus may feel better able to commit acts of sexual abuse without detection. Although costly in terms of staffing, and perhaps impossible in some smaller facilities, such as family home care, ideally no staff member should *ever* be alone with any child. Such a rule not only protects children but helps protect staff from false allegations of child sexual abuse. Where possible, the use of relatively inexpensive video cameras (both visible and hidden) may supplement in-person monitoring and surveillance and add an even greater deterrent.

Structural Changes to the Physical Layout of Day-Care Centers

In their study of child sexual abuse in day-care centers, Finkelhor et al. found that "in almost two-thirds of all cases, abuse occurred in the bathroom."[104] As a result, they suggested the need for clearly articulated rules about toileting and other activities in the bathroom, giving children information about what is and is not appropriate bathroom conduct, and using "lower partitions, entrances that cannot be closed, and enclosures" that would "permit more supervision of bathroom activity."[105]

Additionally, many of the structural changes that were mentioned previously in this chapter with regard to schools could and should be adapted to day-care centers as well (e.g., removing doors and other physical barriers that provide visual privacy, making greater use of windows or half-walls that provide greater transparency, and enhancing lighting in dark or dimly lit areas). Of course, these changes would, in some cases, be costly and in other cases impossible (e.g., small family home day-care situations). Still, where economically and practically feasible, they should be implemented to protect children from all manner of abuse and neglect and to provide greater protection to staff against false allegations of sexual abuse.

Preventing Coercion and Intimidation

In the cases they studied, Finkelhor et al. noted that day-care sexual abusers often threatened their child victims in order to keep them quiet about the abuse. They reported that perpetrators of sexual abuse in this context threatened to harm the children and their parents and claimed to have "supernatural powers to carry out these threats."[106] It may be asking too much of young children to expect them to learn to protect themselves from being sexually abused by adults, especially those in positions of authority and trust. However, as Finkelhor et al. suggest, it may be helpful to "devise messages to give even young children that will make them less vulnerable to this kind of intimidation."[107] For example, children should be informed with age-appropriate language and concepts that they need to tell others about any such threats and that such threats are not realistic and should not be feared. As Finkelhor et al. also noted, this particular strategy may not only prevent some cases of day-care sexual abuse from occurring, but also serve to reduce the psychological trauma inflicted upon children who are sexually abused in day care by limiting the fear and powerlessness they feel as a result of the abuse.[108]

SEXUAL ABUSE COMMITTED BY MEMBERS OF THE CLERGY

For more than a decade, the public has been made aware of another form of institutional child sexual abuse, that committed by members of the clergy, largely but not exclusively by Catholic priests. Although the problem of clergy child sexual abuse dates back half a century or more in the United States and elsewhere, and church leaders were aware of it for much of that time, it was not until after the turn of the twenty-first century that the news media began to make clear the shocking extent to which such abuse had been occurring. Since at least as far back as 2002, American media accounts have been rife with reports of hundreds of priests, deacons, and other clergymen sexually abusing children in churches, parochial schools, orphanages, and other religious institutions in which members of the clergy had frequent contact with children. These media accounts, as well as reports from state attorneys general and grand juries, have made the public all too aware not only that this sort of abuse occurred but that church officials often knew about it, frequently turned a blind eye to it, and allowed it to continue by transferring known and suspected child sex abusers from one location to another within the church organization instead of removing them from the clergy.

Incidence and Details of Child Sexual Abuse by Catholic Priests

Although certainly not the only religion whose clergy have sexually abused children and whose church hierarchy has covered up such abuse and allowed it to flourish for decades, the Roman Catholic Church appears to be by far the most culpable religious group in that regard. Catholic priests also appear to be the most well-documented and thoroughly studied group of clergy who have perpetrated child sexual abuse. For example, in 2011 researchers at the John Jay College of Criminal Justice reported the results of a study commissioned by the US Conference of Catholic Bishops (USCCB). The report, entitled "The Causes and Context of Sexual Abuse of Minors by Catholic Priests in the United States, 1950-2010" and based upon a review of records provided by the denomination, concluded that 4,392 of the 109,694 priests who served in ministry from 1950 through 2002 had substantiated allegations of at least one instance of child sexual abuse made against them.[109]

The John Jay researchers reported further that 56 percent of these "priest-abusers" had a single victim and that 3.5 percent of these abusers "were responsible for abusing 26 percent of victims who had come forward by 2002."[110] Moreover, they indicated that 81 percent of victims were male and most were adolescents, not children: 6 percent were younger than age 7, 16 percent were 8–10 years old, 51 percent were 11–14, and 27 percent were 15–17.[111]

The John Jay research group also reported that priest-abusers were accused of committing a gamut of sexual offenses "ranging from touching outside the clothes to penetration" and that nearly all of these abusers allegedly "committed more than one type of abusive act and involved the youths in explicit sexual activity."[112] They added that "The most common place for the abuse to occur was in the home of the priest (41 percent), though it also occurred with frequency in the church (16 percent), in the victim's home (12 percent), in a vacation house (10 percent), in school (10 percent), or in a car (10 percent)."[113]

Perhaps most significantly, in terms of assessing the risk of child sexual abuse by Catholic priests today, the John Jay team reported that "The annual number of incidents of sexual abuse by priests during the study period increased steadily to a peak in the late 1970s and early 1980s and then declined sharply after 1985."[114] According to data provided to the researchers by the USCCB, this downward trend in allegations of child sexual abuse made against Catholic priests basically continued though 2009, the last year covered in the report. For example, these data indicate that "The total number of new allegations of abuse...has declined from 898, reported in 2004, to 398, reported in 2009."[115]

There is some doubt about the completeness of the John Jay findings. For example, one of the authors was asked about the study's reliance in part upon self-reported data from Catholic bishops who were, themselves, under investigation. Margaret Leland Smith, who did the data analysis for the study, responded that the research "was not an audit process" and emphasized that the same historical pattern was found "in diocese after diocese and region after region across the country."[116] She added that the study focused on substantiated allegations of child sexual abuse by priests and said: "[O]ne can make an inference that there may have been other allegations that the dioceses did not submit because they did not find them substantiated. I have no evidence one way or the other on that."[117]

To the extent that the John Jay findings are reasonably valid and reliable, it appears that over a nearly 60-year period, about 4 percent of Catholic priests serving in ministry in the United States were accused of sexually abusing one or more children and that most such abuse took place decades ago. Still, it is apparent even from the John Jay data that child sexual abuse committed by members of the clergy is not a problem that has been eradicated, even within the Catholic Church. Moreover, there continue to be many reported cases in which children are abused not only by clergy from other religions but also by lay church members and volunteers placed in positions of authority over, or responsibility for, children and adolescents.

Preventing Child Sexual Abuse by Clergy and Other Church Personnel and Volunteers

Efforts to prevent the sexual abuse of children by nonclergy church personnel and volunteers should, for the most part, consist of many if not all of the strategies already detailed in this chapter for preventing child sexual abuse in schools and child-care facilities. In this regard, there is little reason to treat church-based schools and day-care centers any differently than those that have no religious affiliation or sponsorship. Although churches may be exempt under the First Amendment from some forms of government regulation that would apply to other youth facilities, such as schools, day-care centers, recreational facilities, and other programs that provide services to children, there is nothing to keep churches from initiating these sorts of preventive efforts of their own accord.

Churches interested in preventing child sexual abuse on their premises should clearly consider taking affirmative and aggressive steps to understand the nature of the threat of child sexual abuse within their walls and communicate that understanding to children and their parents. They should also modify the physical environments where children congregate for educational, recreational, and child care purposes (e.g., minimizing enclosed, hidden, semi-hidden, and secluded places; using video monitoring where appropriate; removing barriers to visibility; making greater use of windows and half-walls; and increasing lighting). Additionally, churches should also institute and enforce "never alone" rules that prohibit adult staff or volunteers from private one-on-one contacts with any child. Moreover, even if they are not required to do so by law, they should consider the value of fingerprint and criminal records checks for those staff and volunteers hired or chosen to work with children of any age. Finally, where possible and likely to be of value, they should develop and implement screening procedures for those seeking to work with children, whether as employees or volunteers. Of course, the same caveats that were raised previously in this chapter about these methods of prevention also apply to churches; there is no guarantee that all or even any of them will be effective. They are, however, likely to have at least some deterrent effect.

The more difficult, if not unique, problem facing churches in preventing child sexual abuse deals not with lay employees or volunteer church members, but with the clergy. Priest, ministers, rabbis, imams, and other ordained members of the clergy occupy special positions in churches, synagogues, temples, and other places of worship. In many religions, it is an article of faith that these members of the clergy are endowed with sacred or even prophetic authority, have been granted divine powers well beyond those of any lay person in the congregation, and are to be trusted without question. Although these perceived clerical attributes may be fundamental to carrying out the religious purposes of these institutions, they also create situations in which clergy members may abuse their extraordinary power and get away with doing so. More specifically, the special and powerful role of the clergy in religious organizations sometimes makes it possible for them to sexually abuse children with impunity. Clearly, only a very small percentage of clergy in any denomination engage in such conduct, but when they do it has an especially corrosive effect not only on victims and their families but on the religious institutions these perpetrators have been serving.

CHANGING THE CULTURE
Most major religious denominations are steeped in culture that has its roots in hundreds if not thousands of years of tradition. Although major changes in

church tradition are unlikely, at least in the short run, many if not most major religious denominations have recently taken affirmative steps to change the culture of their institutions in an effort to prevent child sexual abuse by their clergy. Perhaps the most prominent of these efforts is the Charter for the Protection of Children and Young People promulgated by the USCCB in 2002 and revised in 2011.[118] This document, spurred by the revelations of child sexual abuse by Catholic priests, commits the Church to creating a safe environment for children and young people, making prompt and effective responses to allegations of child sexual abuse, cooperating with law enforcement, disciplining abusers, providing accountability, and undertaking healing of and reconciliation with victims and survivors.

Similarly, many Protestant churches (including Episcopal, Presbyterian, Lutheran, Baptist, and others) and Jewish synagogues have recognized the dangers of child sexual abuse by members of the clergy and taken steps not only to alert members of their congregations but to fundamentally alter the way both clergy and congregants think about this issue.[119]

After the USCCB issued its Charter for the Protection of Children and Young People, the group also proposed and adopted an accreditation program for all dioceses. This program holds religious communities within the Church to 25 standards of excellence. One of these standards requires each religious community to "educate its members regarding the prevalence, identification, and prevention of child sexual abuse of minors, giving special attention to topics that are of unique relevance to religious."[120] Monica Applewhite, a social worker who has developed sexual abuse prevention and response programs for the Catholic and Episcopal Churches as well as many other religious organizations, and Paul Macke, a Jesuit priest and pastoral counselor, have described how one Catholic religious community, the Society of Jesus, responded to this standard: "The first round of education focused on the sexual abuse of minors, the effects of abuse, characteristics of perpetrators, the warning signs that another religious could be crossing boundaries, and what to do if abuse is suspected."[121]

The Charter for the Protection of Children and Young People also directs Catholic dioceses to "provide education and training for children, youth, parents, ministers, educators, volunteers and others about ways to make and maintain a safe environment for children and young people."[122] Since then, the Catholic Church, among other religious communities, has invested much time, effort, and money in educational programs designed to help prevent child sexual abuse. As of 2010, more than 5 million children and 2 million adults had received child sexual abuse education from the Church, at a cost of more than $170 million to the Catholic Church of the United States.[123]

To date, there is no way to tell whether these denominational educational efforts have been effective in preventing child sexual abuse in churches and church-related settings, but there is also no reason to believe that they have not. The unanswered question appears to be not whether these efforts have helped but to what extent. That is a question that, if it can be answered at all, requires substantial empirical research.

ZERO TOLERANCE POLICIES

Another way in which the response of churches, especially the Catholic Church, has changed in the past decade or so is the implementation and enforcement of zero tolerance policies. While a number of denominations have made it clear that sexual contact between clergy and church members, whatever their age, will not be tolerated under any circumstances, the Catholic Church, to its credit, has taken zero tolerance further than most others. Early on, a draft of the USCCB's Charter for the Protection of Children and Young People contained an exception that would have allowed a priest who had committed only one act of child sexual abuse and had not been diagnosed as a pedophile to avoid being removed from the ministry. This provision was not included in the final draft of the Charter.[124]

Instead the Charter provides that a priest or deacon who admits to, or is found to have committed, "even a single act of sexual abuse" is to "be offered therapeutic professional assistance both for the purpose of prevention and also for his own healing and well-being," but he is also to be "permanently removed from ministry."[125] This zero tolerance or "one strike and you're out" policy was initially controversial among church leaders. However, as one group of commentators has observed, it was "no longer a realistic option" for the church to do otherwise.[126]

Lacking empirical data, it is impossible to determine whether and, if so, to what extent, this zero tolerance policy has helped prevent child sexual abuse by priests and deacons. It may have done so but it also may have given parishioners, particularly parents, a false sense of security about the rectitude of their clergy and the safety of their children. Others have complained that this policy is too harsh and does not "model forgiveness."[127] As one commentator, who is both a priest and a clinical psychologist involved in the treatment of sex offenders, has put it:

> Now that we know that 98 percent of the clerical sex offenders are not pedophiles after all, is it time to reconsider the *Charter's* zero-tolerance policy? Most solid psychologically based research points to the mental health benefits of forgiveness. Can we figure out a way to be forgiving as well as accountable and protective of our children?[128]

The answers to these questions are, of course, unknown. Forgiveness may well be beneficial to the mental health of those who grant it, but if history is any guide, it seems likely that the Catholic Church made the right move when it adopted its zero tolerance policy and that other religious organizations would do well to take the same approach. Returning known child sexual abusers to ministry would almost certainly increase the risk to at least some children and probably increase the discomfort of many others. Moreover, it would require informing parishioners of the offender's history (thus likely undermining the efficacy of his ministry) and probably necessitate expensive and intrusive monitoring procedures.

PSYCHOLOGICAL SCREENING

Today, the Roman Catholic Church and many other religious groups routinely require the psychological screening of candidates for the ministry. Indeed, many denominations, including the Catholic Church, psychologically screen individuals before they are even allowed to begin the process of education and training that will ultimately lead to ordination. Typically these screenings involve clinical interviews by psychologists or other mental health professionals, often coupled with objective psychological testing. The rationale for this type of screening is that, if a candidate has a mental disorder, personality disorder, or a history that suggests the potential for either, that is likely to be exposed by a clinical interview and/or psychological testing.

Depending upon the quality of the assessment and the sensitivity of the testing procedures used that may be the case. To the extent that such screening identifies individuals who may not be psychologically fit for ministry, undoubtedly some potential child sex abusers will be hindered if not prevented from becoming members of the clergy. However, to date there are no known clear psychological markers that identify current or potential child sexual abusers or validly predict who will sexually abuse a child. Moreover, simply because a candidate for the ministry does not appear to suffer from a mental illness or personality disorder and does not manifest any significant behavioral does not mean that candidate will not become a child sexual abuser once admitted to the clergy.

It has also been noted that the process of conducting effective psychological screenings of candidates for the clergy, particularly in the Catholic Church, may be hindered by the Church's own rules. Specifically, some churches refuse to ordain homosexuals. The Catholic Church presents perhaps the clearest example of how that policy makes effective psychological screening of clergy aspirants difficult, in some cases impossible.

Despite the church's ban on homosexuals in the priesthood, it is reliably estimated that 25–45 percent of today's Catholic priests are homosexuals.[129] Thus it is clear that the church's own ban on homosexuals in the ministry is not stopping homosexuals from becoming ordained. The clear consensus of research is that homosexuality is not associated with the sexual abuse of children or adolescents; is not a mental illness; and does not present any greater propensity to mental illness, personality disorder, or behavior dysfunction than heterosexuality. Thomas G. Plante, a psychologist who has conducted more than 600 psychological screening evaluations for the Catholic Church and others, has concisely explained the problem:

> Psychologists conducting screening evaluations are, therefore, in a bind as to how to evaluate applicants' psychosexual development and functioning if stating that their sexual orientation is homosexual will disqualify applicants for the priesthood. Thus, a "don't ask, don't tell" policy seems to be functioning at the present time. This creates trouble in that a vigorous and complete evaluation of an applicant's psychosexual functioning, maturity and development is often stymied. Even if an evaluation of an applicant's sexual history and experiences is conducted, it may not appear in a written report due to concerns that homosexual orientation might prevent the applicant from being considered for ordination in the Catholic Church.[130]

Sex Offender Treatment

As noted previously in this chapter, the Catholic Church and some others now enforce a zero tolerance policy in which clergy determined to have committed child sexual abuse are removed and permanently barred from the ministry. As noted previously in this volume, sex offender treatment is, at best, controversial. Some child sex abusers who undergo so-called sex offender treatment may cease acting out sexually against children, but there is no way to attribute such change to psychological treatment alone, or even in part. Also, there is no reason to believe that clergy child sex abusers are any more or less amenable to sex offender treatment than other child sex abusers who are not members of the clergy. Thus, even if churches are willing to take the risk and give a second chance to one of their clergy who is a known child sex abuser, there is little reason to expect that psychological treatment will have a significant preventive effect.

CHILD SEXUAL ABUSE IN YOUTH-SERVING ORGANIZATIONS

In 2012, Jerry Sandusky, a former assistant football coach at Penn State University, was convicted of sexually abusing 10 boys, all from deprived backgrounds, over a 15-year period. Sandusky gained access to these boys and others by using his connection to the university's football team and its facilities as well as his own organization, the Second Mile. The Second Mile, which Sandusky founded and supported largely on the basis of his connection to Penn State football, was a nonprofit agency purportedly designed to provide services to underprivileged, at-risk youth.

As the case against Sandusky developed, many observers were shocked to learn not only of the abuse but that top university officials knew of some of the abuse, turned a blind eye to it, and allowed Sandusky to continue to use his university connections and access to university facilities to continue abusing young boys for years.

For all the media attention the Sandusky cover-up generated, it was far from the first time a major youth-serving institution had been implicated in not only sexually abusing children, but covering up that abuse. The Roman Catholic Church has already been mentioned in that regard. Evidence dating back many decades indicates that Cardinals, Bishops, and others in the church hierarchy were long aware of priests who sexually abused children but either took no action, ordered these priests to treatment, and/or simply transferred them to other places of ministry, where they were free to (and often did) continue sexually abusing children.

The sexual abuse of children in, and the cover-up of that abuse by, youth service organizations is hardly limited to the Catholic Church, Penn State, and the Second Mile. Perhaps the most egregious example, aside from the Catholic Church, is the organization known as the Boy Scouts of America. The Boy Scouts is one of the oldest, largest, and most respected if not revered youth-serving organizations in the nation. Incorporated in 1910, the Scouts have approximately 2.7 million youth members and more than a million adult volunteers.[131]

Recent litigation has led to the release of thousands of files kept by the Boy Scouts. Release of these files, which document sexual abuse of Boy Scouts by adult volunteers going back as far as 1911, was resisted by the Boy Scouts' attorneys across the nation as they defended the organization against multiple lawsuits brought by men who were sexually victimized as boys by scoutmasters and other adults affiliated with the Scouts. Many of these files have been made available online by the *Los Angeles Times*.[132]

The Boy Scouts of America hired a prominent social worker, Janet Warren, to review these files and prepare a report.[133] Warren, who was paid $475 per hour for her review,[134] also testified as an expert witness on behalf of the Boy Scouts in a lawsuit brought by a former Scout who was found to have been sexually abused by a Scout leader.[135] In that case, the jury determined that the Boy Scouts were at fault and awarded the child sexual abuse victim $18.5 million in damages.[136]

In a 2012 statement published after her report, Warren indicated that she had reviewed more than 1,200 so-called Ineligible Volunteer (IV) files that were kept by the Scouts over the years regarding adults in the organization who had reportedly sexually abused children.[137] The files she reviewed spanned the period from 1960–1995.[138]

In the statement summarizing her findings, Warren emphasized several points. First, she observed that the abuse chronicled in these files happened years earlier and involved a "small number of men."[139] Second, she concluded that youngsters were safer from sexual abuse in the Boy Scouts than in "society at large."[140] Third, she reported that the documents she reviewed were not "'secret files' of hidden abuse" and that most contained evidence that the abuse detailed in them had in some way been made public.[141] Finally, she stated that although some known sex offenders had been allowed to return as adult volunteers in Scouting, often because they had received psychiatric treatment, the number of such cases was "extraordinarily rare."[142]

Reporters from the *Los Angeles Times*, who reviewed many of the same files, had a rather different view of them. Looking at 1,600 of these files from 1970–1991, the *Times* concluded that "Over two decades, the Boy Scouts of America failed to report hundreds of alleged child molesters to police and often hid the allegations from parents and the public…Scouting officials frequently urged admitted offenders to quietly resign—and helped many cover their tracks."[143]

According to the *Times*' study, in most cases, the Scouts learned of abuse allegations after they had already been reported to the police. However, the study also found that in more than 500 cases, the Scouts learned of alleged abuse from Boy Scouts, parents, staff, or anonymous tips; in about 80 percent of those cases, there is no evidence that the Scouts reported the allegations to law enforcement authorities.[144] Indeed, according to the *Times*, "In more than 100 of the cases, officials actively sought to conceal the alleged abuse or allowed the suspects to hide it."[145]

The *Times* reported that many files it reviewed contained a form letter in which alleged child sexual abusers in the organization were told, "We are making no accusations and will not release this information to anyone, so our action in no way will affect your standing in the community."[146]

The *Times* analysis of the Boy Scout IV files revealed numerous egregious cases that aptly illustrate what their reports called "a culture in which even known molesters were shown extraordinary deference."[147] For example, they point to one Los Angeles Boy Scout leader who was found with hundreds of photographs of naked Scouts, many of whom were depicted receiving enemas from the leader. After Scout officials worked with law enforcement and child protection agencies to avoid embarrassment to the Scouts, the records revealed that their efforts were summarized as follows: "We recognize that this unfortunate situation was no reflection on the Boy Scouts of America whose integrity and reputation must be maintained."[148]

Although the Boy Scouts have received the most public attention of any youth-serving organization (other than the Catholic Church) for child sexual abuse within its ranks, many children have been sexually victimized by adult volunteers and leaders in countless other such organizations ranging from small groups, such as Sandusky's Second Mile and local football, baseball, and soccer leagues, to much larger national organizations including, for example, Big Brothers/Big Sisters, Boys and Girls Clubs of America, and the Young Men's Christian Association.

Unlike the Boy Scouts of America, however, most other youth-serving organizations have not so meticulously catalogued the sexual abuse of children known to have occurred under their auspices. Thus, there are no reliable data regarding how often children are sexually victimized in these organizations. As Warren noted regarding the Boy Scouts, the overall rate of child sexual abuse in these organizations is likely low, in most cases probably lower than the rate in society at large. However, any rate higher than zero means that children are being sexually abused in voluntary participation contexts specifically designed to serve them, programs in which they and their parents are asked to place full trust in the adult staff and volunteers, some small number of whom will betray that trust if presented with situations that allow them to do so.

Given the voluntary nature of these organizations, as opposed to schools and juvenile correctional facilities, no children are required to be involved in their activities. If these organizations prove incapable of preventing child sexual abuse in their ranks, parents and society will lose trust in them, their membership will dwindle, and some will likely become defunct. Thus, it is critical that all of these organizations recognize the risk of child sexual abuse in their activities and take affirmative, effective steps to reduce if not eradicate that risk.

Preventing Sexual Abuse in Child-Service Organizations

Many of the strategies for preventing child sexual abuse that have already been discussed in this chapter can be directly applied to voluntary youth-serving organizations. Indeed, when the US Centers for Disease Control and Prevention

(CDC) was tasked with developing such strategies in this context, they identified six "key components of child sexual abuse prevention for [such] organizations":

1. Screening and selecting employees and volunteers
2. Guidelines on interactions between individuals
3. Monitoring behavior
4. Ensuring safe environments
5. Responding to inappropriate behavior, breaches in policy, and allegations and suspicions of child sexual abuse
6. Training about child sexual abuse prevention.[149]

Some examples of such strategies can be found in the Boy Scouts new Youth Protection Policies. These policies require anyone who witnesses or suspects child abuse or neglect of any child to report it.[150] The Policies prohibit "one-on-one contact" between adults and scouts and require "two-deep [adult] leadership...on all outings" as well as "[s]eparate accommodations for adults and Scouts."[151] The Policies also set rules for privacy, secrecy, and attire.[152]

Although these common sense policies were developed by and for a specific youth-serving organization, the Boy Scouts of America, most of them also have a broader application and are certainly worth considering in a wide variety of youth-serving organizations.

UNDERSTANDING AND COMMUNICATING THE NATURE OF THE RISK

Notably absent from the CDC's recommendations for preventing child sexual abuse in youth-serving organizations is understanding and communicating the nature of the risk. For decades, some of these groups have been aware of sexual abuse of children in the course of their activities but have gone to great lengths to hide or minimize the significance of the risk of such abuse, largely to protect the reputation of the organizations and, by implication, the livelihoods of the paid executives who run these organizations.

For example, as has already been noted, the Boy Scouts of America failed to report to law enforcement officials most cases of alleged sexual abuse known to them. Moreover, it appears that in a substantial portion of these cases, they took affirmative steps to "conceal the alleged abuse or allowed the suspects to hide it."[153] As a result, thousands, perhaps millions, of parents were left with the false impression that child sexual abuse was not a problem (or at least not a significant one) for the Boy Scouts. Worse yet, perhaps, when evidence of widespread sexual abuse in the Boy Scouts began to emerge in lawsuits brought against the organization by victims of such abuse, the organization not only vigorously contested these legal actions but fought hard to keep their damning IV files from being made public. Furthermore, when it became clear that a court would order the release of these files, the Boy Scouts commissioned their own review of the files by a social worker who concluded that "youth were safer in Scouting than in society at large."[154]

Failure to accept, understand, and communicate the nature of the risk of child sexual abuse in a youth-serving organization was also amply and tragically illustrated by the recent Penn State scandal. Not only did former assistant football coach Jerry Sandusky use university facilities and the lure of Penn State's famous football program to groom and sexually abuse young boys but it appears that he did so under the suspicion, if not the knowledge, of various university officials, who seemed more concerned about maintaining the university's reputation than acknowledging the ongoing child sexual abuse and thereby alerting parents, children, and others to the risk Sandusky posed. Moreover, as in the case of the Boy Scout sex abuse scandal, it appears that even as the details of the Sandusky's abuse were becoming public, some university officials continued to attempt to minimize the damage to the institution. Ultimately, the National Collegiate Athletic Association fined Penn State $60 million, banned the school's football team from postseason play for 4 years, and vacated the team's victories dating back to 1998. Moreover, the former President of Penn State was indicted by a grand jury on eight counts of perjury, obstruction, and endangering welfare of children; two other former Penn State officials, a Vice President and the Athletic Director, were charged with perjury, obstruction of justice, conspiracy, endangering the welfare of children, and failure to report a crime.

To their credit (albeit in response to demands from the courts, the media, and the public) both the Boy Scouts and Penn State have finally acknowledged the problem and have taken clear steps to prevent further sexual abuse of children in their programs and facilities. This belated acknowledgement, understanding, and communication of the risk of child sexual abuse is definitely the first step required in any effort to prevent child sexual abuse in these and other youth-serving institutions in the future.

Screening and Selecting Employees and Volunteers

In addition to strategies that have already been mentioned in this chapter regarding the screening and selection of individuals allowed to work with children (e.g., fingerprint and background checks), the CDC emphasized the importance of both a written application and personal interview.

With regard to the written application, the CDC suggested that such applications:

- Ask about previous work and volunteer experiences.
- Ask questions pertinent to child sexual abuse screening.
- Provide a permission form for contacting personal references and performing a criminal background check. . .
- Ask open-ended questions that encourage broad answers. . .
- Use disclosure statements to ask applicants about previous criminal histories of sexual offenses, violence against youth, and other criminal offenses. . .
- Clarify that you are interested in learning about an applicant's past perpetration of child sexual abuse rather than a history of victimization.[155]

Written applications have been used for decades in public and private schools and other government-regulated youth-serving organizations and agencies.

There is no evidence that using a written application for would-be volunteers and employees of youth-serving organizations will eliminate or even reduce the risk of child sexual abuse within those groups.

The problem seems to be that there are no questions that reliably identify potential child sexual abusers and differentiate them from applicants who would not pose a risk to children. Consider, for example, the relatively new application used by the Boy Scouts of America.[156] That application asks the applicant's name, address, telephone numbers, date of birth, ethnic background, gender, social security number, occupation, employer, e-mail address, and whether the applicant is an Eagle Scout. The application also asks for the applicant's Scouting history, previous experience working with youth, previous residences for the past 5 years, current affiliations with other community organizations, and the name and telephone numbers of three references. Finally, the applicant is asked: "Do you use illegal drugs?" "Have you ever been convicted of a criminal offense?" "Have you ever been charged with, or investigated or arrested for child neglect or abuse?" "Has your driver's license ever been suspended or revoked?" "Other than the above, is there any fact or circumstance involving you or your background that would call into question your being entrusted with the supervision, guidance, and care of young people?"[157]

The Boy Scouts have acknowledged that "While no current screening techniques exist that can identify every potential child abuser, we can help reduce the risk of accepting a child abuser by learning all we can about an applicant for a leadership position—including his or her experience working with children and why he or she wants to be a Scout leader."[158] Despite a lack of empirical evidence to support that assertion, there is good reason to believe that it may be true. To begin with, the written application, with its pointed questions, makes it clear to applicants that the organization is serious about screening out those who would put children at risk. Undoubtedly some potential child sex abusers will lie on this application and make their way through the screening process, but the formality of the application itself may deter some would-be abusers from even applying for fear that they will be exposed, labeled as potential abusers, and embarrassed by their exclusion.

Much the same might be said about personal interviews with candidates for employment or volunteer positions in this context. The CDC recommended "[a]sking open-ended questions that encourage discussion" and "[c]larify[ing] and expand[ing] upon the applicant's answers to questions from the written application."[159] Among the questions and rationales for these questions suggested by the CDC are:

> What type of supervisory situation do you prefer?
> If applicants are very independent, they may not fit in an organization whose policies and procedures require close supervision.
> What age/sex of youth do you want to work with? How would you feel about working with a different age/sex? If an applicant seems fixated on one age/sex, be wary. However, it may be that the applicant has experience or

is gifted with working with certain age groups. Asking follow-up questions about why an applicant has a strong preference can help you determine if there is cause for concern.

Is there anyone who might suggest that you should not work with youth? Why or why not?

Why do you want the job?

What would you do in a particular situation? Set up scenarios that involve potential concerns, boundary issues, or youth protection policies and interactions to gauge the applicant's response. Be concerned if applicants disregard the organization's policies and procedures or handle a situation poorly.

What makes you a good candidate for working with youth?

What would your friends or colleagues say about how you interact with youth?

What other hobbies or activities do you enjoy? Determine if applicants have mature, adult relationships—not just relationships with youth.[160]

Requiring personal interviews with applicants for paid and volunteer positions working with youth may have a deterrent effect similar to that hypothesized for requiring written applications. However, there is no evidence that these or any other particular questions are likely to have any more than marginal efficacy, if that, in efforts to weed out those who would pose a risk of sexual abuse to youth served by the organization. Even if screening interviews were to be conducted by mental health professionals with expertise in psychological assessment and the prediction of sexual dangerousness, currently available research suggests that the results might not be much better.

Because most applicants (even those who do pose risk of child sexual abuse) will not have criminal records and written applications and personal interviews have only limited value in this context, the CDC has recommended carefully checking references for all applicants. The CDC has further recommended that such checks be done verbally and not simply via written communication because "[c]onversations can elicit much more information than written responses."[161] Finally, the CDC also recommended that, for obvious reasons, references should not be limited to family members and friends of the applicant. Here, as with written applications and personal interviews, there is no guarantee that verbal reference checks will identify potential child sexual abusers, but such checks do seem likely to add to the screening process a dimension that is not tapped by simply posing questions to the applicant in writing and in person.

TRAINING VOLUNTEERS, EMPLOYEES, AND YOUTH

Although many, perhaps most youth-serving organizations by now are alert to the need to train employees about child sexual abuse and its prevention, many have been slower in recognizing the need to offer training to volunteers and the youth they serve. The CDC has succinctly summarized the "critical content" for training employees and volunteers as well as the youth they serve.[162] Caregivers, whether employees or volunteers, need to "understand child sexual abuse and their role in preventing it…in the context of explaining healthy sexual development (e.g., what is appropriate and when)."[163] As the CDC has urged, in training all adults working in their programs, youth-serving organizations should

> Define child sexual abuse, including the continuum of appropriate, inappropriate, and harmful behaviors.
> Challenge commonly held myths about child sexual abuse, such as the myth that most offenders are strangers and are easily identifiable.
> Describe warning signs for sexually offending behaviors and victimization (i.e., what to watch for).
> Discuss how to talk to their children about sexuality and child sexual abuse as well as how to talk to other adults about child sexual abuse both before and after any suspicion of sexual abuse has been raised. . .
> Explain caregivers' responsibility to act if they witness or hear about inappropriate or harmful behaviors.
> Describe where to go for help within your organization, such as who the point person for child sexual abuse is inside your organization.
> Provide resources for seeking help outside your organization, such as child sexual abuse prevention organizations. . .
> Describe what your organization does, such as its mission and role.
> Define what activities are appropriate and inappropriate in your organization, such as whether your organization sponsors overnight trips, mentoring, or one-on-one coaching.
> Delineate responsibilities of the caregiver and your organization. For example, define who is responsible for transporting youth.
> Encourage caregivers to attend sessions and programs whenever they can to make sure that youth are being protected and that policies are being followed.[164]

The CDC has also emphasized the need for these organizations to train the youth they serve. Noting the importance of keeping in mind the age and developmental levels of children involved, the CDC has urged youth-serving organizations to provide youth with "general information about child sexual abuse, including what constitutes appropriate, inappropriate, and harmful behavior from adults and other youth"; an understanding of "the importance of reporting sexual abuse"; and knowledge of "to whom they should report what they believe is inappropriate or harmful behavior."[165] The CDC also urged youth-serving organizations to "[e]mpower youth to intervene or tell someone when they see inappropriate or harmful interactions between adults and youth or between youth"; "[e]ncourage youth to tell a trusted adult about inappropriate or harmful things that have happened to themselves or their friends"; [e]ncourage them to adopt healthy strategies to protect themselves, such as checking with a caregiver/adult before doing activities, going places with friends instead of alone, and identifying trusted adults"; and "[t]each [them] to recognize appropriate behavior and to avoid exploitive or inappropriate behavior toward others."[166]

Along the lines of the "critical content" for training advocated by the CDC, the Boy Scouts of America have recently developed a Youth Protection Training Program, which includes training about child sexual abuse. The course may be taken online by anyone but is required of all registered Scouting volunteers. Indeed, registered volunteers must take the course every 2 years or they will not be allowed to reregister.

The course, which takes roughly one half-hour to complete, is comprised of an interactive online video that includes a virtual reading of the Boy Scouts' Youth Protection Policies, emphasizing at times those policies most relevant to the prevention of child sexual abuse.[167] Periodically, throughout the video, the viewer is asked to respond to multiple choice questions, which essentially test whether the viewer has been paying attention to what was just said in the video. Upon completion of the video, the viewer is presented with two wallet cards and a certificate bearing his name and certifying that he has completed the Youth Protection Training course.

Although this is undoubtedly a step in the right direction, and is probably more training than many youth-serving organizations provide, the Youth Protection Training course is extremely brief and superficial. To be fair, the video does refer the viewer to other Boy Scout publications that may help provide a broader education regarding child sexual abuse and its prevention, but there is no requirement that volunteers read or even familiarize themselves with any of these publications. Requiring would-be volunteers to view this video has the benefit of highlighting the importance of preventing child sexual abuse in the Scouts and other youth-serving organizations but because of its brevity and superficiality it seems unlikely to have much if any more value than would accrue from simply requiring that would-be volunteers read the organization's Youth Protection Policies. At the same time, given that this video is widely touted as mandatory Youth Protection Training for all would-be volunteers, it may create the impression among parents and the community that Scout leaders are better trained in understanding and preventing child sexual abuse than they actually are.

CHANGING INSTITUTIONAL CULTURE AND LEADERSHIP

Both the Boy Scout and Penn State scandals were enabled by organizational cultures in which leadership appeared more concerned with the reputation of the institution than with protecting the children they served. Sadly, this mentality is understandable in many youth-serving organizations for a number of reasons. To begin with, these organizations depend upon their reputations in order to function. Parents who do not believe their children are safe while in the care of such an organization will soon refuse to allow their children to participate in the activities of that organization. Because most of these organizations rely upon philanthropy for financial support, their ability to maintain their programs may be severely compromised by the reputational damage that comes with reports of child sexual abuse within the organization. Also, because most of those who work with children in these organizations are volunteers who do not rely upon this activity for their livelihoods, many will not want to be associated with organizations that carry the stigma of child sexual abuse and will refuse to volunteer or volunteer elsewhere. Moreover, many volunteers may be deterred from serving organizations in which child sexual abuse is reported for fear that they may put themselves at risk for false reports of such abuse. Furthermore, paid employees of these organizations, which often include the top leadership, obviously have a substantial stake in maintaining the reputation of the organization for which they work. As the Penn State scandal demonstrated, those who lead organizations often have deep personal, noneconomic, investments in the reputations of the organizations they serve.

Although a number of these concerns may be addressed by training of the sort already described in this chapter, youth-serving organizations are unlikely to significantly improve the ways in which they go about trying to prevent child sexual abuse unless the leadership of those organizations firmly commits them to placing the welfare of children above all other concerns. For example, in the aftermath of the Penn State scandal, a team of independent investigators, led by former FBI Director Louis Freeh, castigated the University's leadership for "an over-emphasis on 'The Penn State Way' as an approach to decision-making, a resistance to seeking outside perspectives, and an excessive focus on athletics."[168] Instead, Freeh and his colleagues recommended that the University's leaders "create a values- and ethics-centered community where everyone is engaged in placing the needs of children above the needs of adults [and] an environment where everyone who sees or suspects child abuse will feel empowered to report the abuse."[169]

Speaking more generally of the role of institutional culture and leadership in preventing child sexual abuse in youth-serving organizations, the CDC has urged that leaders of such groups recognize that:

> Child sexual abuse prevention efforts enhance your organization's mission to nurture and protect youth.
> The well-being of youth (including their freedom from child sexual abuse) is part of your organizational mission.
> Policies to protect youth also protect your organization and the employees/volunteers who work there.
> Organizations that are proactive about child sexual abuse prevention show corporate responsibility.[170]

Today, many if not most youth-serving organizations are beginning to follow such advice.

The institutional culture in many such organizations appears to be changing for the better and there is a growing recognition that children are vulnerable to sexual abuse in these organizations and must be protected from that abuse even if doing so means bad publicity and a loss of reputation. Sadly, what often seems to be motivating this change in institutional culture is not a newly found concern for children but rather the self-serving economic and personal calculus that arises from multimillion dollar legal judgments, court orders requiring the public release of embarrassing organizational records of sexual abuse, fines, other sanctions, and in some cases even criminal prosecution.

Prostitution of Minors

The prostitution of minors is a common but frequently overlooked form of child sexual abuse. Often unfortunately referred to as child prostitution, this phenomenon involves minors who trade sex for cash, food, shelter, or protection. Some percentage of youths who engage in the sex trade appear to do so on their own out of a desire to increase their access to money or other valuable goods or simply to survive on the streets, but most so-called child prostitutes are managed or "pimped" by adults or older juveniles who force them into acts of prostitution, take most if not all of the proceeds from those acts, and generally control these youngsters' lives.

The prostitution of minors is often not regarded as a form of child sexual abuse because the children involved are seen as committing a crime (i.e., prostitution) and thus somehow blameworthy. Indeed, when child prostitution is discovered by the authorities, prostituted children are often arrested or detained as juvenile delinquents. Moreover, adults who patronize prostituted youths are frequently regarded merely as customers or "johns" and, if arrested at all, are charged with minor offenses, such as soliciting or patronizing a prostitute. In short, what would otherwise be at a minimum the offense of statutory rape is routinely treated as a minor crime because of the commercial context in which the adult-child sex occurs.

The prostitution of minors is a worldwide phenomenon that occurs in most countries, including the United States. Such prostitution can be and most often is a local arrangement in which children are coerced into providing sexual services to others for money or survival (mainly food, shelter, and/or protection). However, the prostitution of minors is also frequently part of much larger national or even international arrangements known as child sex trafficking and child sex tourism. Child sex traffickers induce children to leave their homes and then move those children into prostitution in another part of the country or a different nation altogether. Sex trafficking often involves some kind of organized crime structure in which children are literally bought and sold into sexual slavery or indenture. Child sex tourism is the term used to describe arrangements whereby "tourists" seeking sex with children travel to largely urban areas in their own nations or (more often) other countries in which such sex is cheap, plentiful, and unlikely to result in arrest or other sanctions. Children prostituted to sex tourists include both local youths and those who have been trafficked.

SCOPE OF THE PROBLEM

There are no reliable empirical data regarding how many children are prostituted generally, trafficked for purposes of prostitution, or sexually abused by so-called sex tourists. This should come as no surprise given the unlawful and often hidden nature of these phenomena. Given what is known about these offenses, it seems fair to say that most of them do not come to the attention of the authorities and that, even when they do, they are often misclassified. For example, it is widely acknowledged that children are trafficked for many purposes, including all sorts of cheap or free labor. Thus, even when traffickers are "caught in the act" in the early stages of the process, it is frequently impossible to say whether they were engaged in sex trafficking. Also, many trafficked children refuse to report their plight or cooperate with government authorities for fear of arrest, deportation, or reprisal from the individuals or syndicates who trafficked them. Indeed, there are many reports of children being arrested as prostitutes, posing as adults, and sometimes even presenting forged documents identifying them as young adults. Finally, authorities in many countries simply turn a blind eye to the prostitution of minors, juvenile sex trafficking, and child sex tourism because all of these activities benefit these nations economically.

The lack of data, however, has not kept many sources from estimating the extent of these crimes. Sadly, some of these "estimates" seem to have no reliable basis in fact and may undermine the credibility not only of those who make them but other more credible sources in the fight to eradicate the prostitution and sex trafficking of children. Consider, for example, these oft-cited estimates. (1) At any given moment there are between 100,000 and 300,000 children being prostituted in the United States.[1] (2) In one recent 6-month period, the number of minors being prostituted rose "exponentially" in three states: "Michigan: a 39.2 percent increase; New York: a 20.7 percent increase; and Minnesota: a staggering 64.7 percent increase."[2] (3) More than a million children are sexually trafficked around the world every year.[3] (4) A total of 50,000 women and children are trafficked into the United States each year, half for sexual purposes, from Latin America, the former Soviet states, and Southeast Asia alone.[4] (5) Internationally, at least a million children are forced into prostitution every year and the true number could be as high as 10 million.[5] (6) Internationally, child sex tourism involves the prostitution of 2 million children annually.[6]

The origins of the first two estimates—100,00–300,000 American children being prostituted and exponential increases in their numbers in three states in just 6 months—are instructive and provide vivid examples of why all of these estimates must be considered with great caution.

100,000–300,000 American Children Prostituted?

Consider first the estimated number of American children being prostituted at any given time. The 100,000–300,000 figure has been repeatedly testified to before Congress and repeatedly reported in dozens of media sources.[7] The source of that estimate is Ernie Allen, former President and CEO of the federally funded National Center for Missing & Exploited Children, whose mission is "to serve as the nation's clearinghouse on issues related to missing and sexually exploited children."[8] As Allen testified before a Congressional committee in 2010:

> The National Center for Missing & Exploited Children (NCMEC) estimates that at least 100,000 American children are the victims of commercial sexual trafficking and prostitution each year. How did we arrive at that number? The offenders don't file tax returns and few of these cases actually make it into the justice system.
>
> The primary basis for our estimate is the research of Dr. Richard Estes and Dr. Neil Alan Weiner at the University of Pennsylvania, funded by the U.S. Department of Justice through its National Institute of Justice. Dr. Estes and Dr. Weiner estimated that 293,000 US children are "at risk" of commercial child exploitation each year. However, they provided much greater detail and analysis.
>
> Dr. Estes estimated that the number of 10-17 year olds involved in commercial sexual exploitation in the US each year likely exceeds 250,000, with 60% of these victims being runaway, thrownaway or homeless youth. Commercial sexual exploitation is broader in scope than just child prostitution, but there is little doubt that the commercial sexual exploitation of runaway, thrownaway and homeless youth is overwhelmingly prostitution. 60% of 250,000 is 150,000.
>
> The researchers also estimated that one third of street-level prostitutes in the U.S. are less than 18 while half of off-street prostitutes are less than 18. With the explosion in the sale of kids for sex online, it is clear that more kids are at risk.
>
> Some runaway groups have estimated that as many as 1/3 of teen runaways/thrownaways will become involved in prostitution within 48 hours of leaving home. The Justice Department's National Incidence Study of Missing, Abducted, Runaway and Thrownaway Children (NISMART II) estimated that there are nearly 1.7 million runaway/thrownaway episodes each year, of which just 357,600 are reported to police. Of that total, 1.6 million are 12–17 years old, and 1.3 million are gone from 24 hours to 6 months. So, eliminating those gone for less than 24 hours and taking half of the balance (the boy/girl ratio of runaways is 50/50), we arrive at 650,000 girls. Taking 1/3 of that number would lead us to infer that roughly 200,000 plus runaway/thrownaway girls are lured into prostitution each year.
>
> Thus, while 100,000 is clearly a very conservative number, NCMEC continues to use that estimate because we believe it is empirically sound and

completely defensible. In a larger sense, we believe it reasonable to estimate a range of 100,000–300,000 per year with comfort and confidence.[9]

Between January 1999 and March 2001, Estes and Weiner sought to identify "those subgroups of children that are at the greatest risk of being sexually exploited" by meeting with and surveying governmental and nongovernment agencies that served sexually exploited children in 28 American, Canadian, and Mexican cities; interviewing law enforcement and human service decision-makers; and conducting focus groups.[10] They also interviewed small numbers of sexually exploited children, child sex traffickers, and adults who bought sex from children.[11]

Estes and Weiner readily acknowledged that their study was beset by numerous methodological problems, exacerbated by the "complex, multidimensional nature" of child sexual exploitation as well as "high degree of secrecy associated with sex crimes against children."[12] Estes and Weiner further candidly noted that their findings were not a direct calculation of the number of American children at risk for being prostituted and certainly not a calculation or even an estimate of the number of American children who were being prostituted or otherwise subjected to commercial sexual exploitation, but an estimate of "the number of children 'at risk' of commercial sexual exploitation."[13] They added that: "A different type of study from ours—one that uses a different methodology and a higher investment of resources—is needed to carry out a national prevalence and incidence survey that could produce an actual headcount of the number of identifiable commercially sexually exploited children."[14]

Not surprisingly, academic criticism of Estes and Weiner's conclusions has been blunt and harsh. David Finkelhor, renowned sociologist, professor, Director of the Crimes Against Children Research Center, and the generally acknowledged dean of data when it comes to child sexual abuse of any sort, said of the Estes and Weiner study, "As far as I'm concerned [it] has no scientific credibility to it. That figure was in a report that was never really subjected to any kind of peer review. It wasn't published in any scientific journal... Initially [Estes and Weiner] claimed that [100,000–300,000] was the number of children [engaged in prostitution]. It took quite a bit of pressure to get them to add the qualifier [at risk]."[15] Stephen Doig, a Pulitzer prize-winning journalist and journalism professor who specializes in analyzing quantitative data, said the "study cannot be relied upon as authoritative," adding that "Many of the numbers and assumptions in these charts are based on earlier, smaller-scale studies done by other researchers, studies which have their own methodological limitations. I won't call it 'garbage in, garbage out.' But combining various approximations and guesstimates done under a variety of conditions doesn't magically produce a solid number. The resulting number is no better than the fuzziest part of the equation."[16] Jay Albanese, a criminologist and professor who served as Chief of the International Center at the National Institute of Justice, the research arm of the US Department of Justice (USDOJ), from 2002–2006 and authored the USDOJ publication, "Commercial Sexual Exploitation of Children: What Do We Know and What Do We Do About It" in 2007, said most bluntly of all: "There's tons of estimates on human trafficking. They're all crap... It's all guesswork, speculation... The numbers are inherently unbelievable."[17]

Despite the great skepticism expressed about the Estes and Weiner study, a decade later, multiple national news media outlets were still touting Ernie Allen's interpretation of its findings. For example, in 2011, *USA Today* used the occasion of the Super Bowl to quote Allen, telling readers that 100,000–300,000 American children are subjected to commercial sexual exploitation annually.[18] Three months later, the usually circumspect *New York Times* restated that estimate without any attribution.[19]

Around the same time, actor Ashton Kutcher spoke to a CNN talk show host and repeated in a widely televised public service announcement that there were "between 100,000 and 300,000 child sex slaves in the United States today."[20] The national weekly, *The Village Voice* then undertook its own investigation of the truth of Kutcher's remarks. Reporters examined police records dealing with juvenile prostitution in America's 37 largest cities and found that a total of only 8,263 arrests had been made for child prostitution in the preceding decade, roughly 827 arrests per year. Comparing those figures with the 100,000–300,000 estimate widely used by others, the reporter labeled the latter numbers "propaganda."[21]

There is virtually no question that arrests of juveniles for prostitution markedly underestimate the extent to which minors are subjected to prostitution. As noted previously in this chapter, many prostituted children refuse to report their victimization, fearing exposure to criminal charges, and many who are arrested may pose as and be processed criminally as adults. Also, juveniles who are prostituted are unlikely to be arrested in jurisdictions in which prostitution more generally is not a high priority for law enforcement. For these and other reasons, we cannot be content to rely upon arrest reports as a proxy for the prostitution of children. Still, as David Finkelhor has observed, "You have to say, 'We don't know.' Estimates have been made, but none of them have a real scientific basis to them... All you can say is, 'This is the number the police know about, and we think there are more than that, but we don't know how many more.'"[22]

Exponential Increases in Just 6 Months?

In 2010, the Women's Funding Network announced that: "An independent tracking study released today by the Women's Funding Network shows that over the past six months, the number of underage girls trafficked online has risen exponentially in three diverse states. Michigan: a 39.2 percent increase; New York: a 20.7 percent increase; and Minnesota: a staggering 64.7 percent increase."[23] According to an August 2010 press release:

> The May tracking study is designed to count adolescent girls using scientific probability methods when they are encountered through two sources: ads on Internet classifieds websites and escort services. These are two of the main sources by which johns find girls. The May results are part of a multi-year

quarterly tracking study that began in February 2010. For the counts, researchers called, tracked and calculated all escort service listings, in addition to methodically evaluating placed ads featuring young girls on popular Internet sites being used by johns looking for commercial sex with adolescent girls.[24]

The full report of the study revealed that the number of adolescent girls involved in prostitution in Michigan, Minnesota, and New York was calculated periodically by examining online classified advertisements for sex services that featured photographs purporting to be those of the "young" female prostitutes whose services were offered in the advertisements.[25] Advertisements on various websites in each venue were monitored by the researchers who made determinations of the age of the prostitutes by viewing the photographs attached to their advertisements. These determinations were, however, discounted statistically because in an earlier part of the study done by the same company, 100 randomly selected adults were shown photographs of young women, asked to state the age of the women pictured, and were able to correctly determine whether a pictured female was under 18 just 38 percent of the time. To account (and apparently correct) for this limitation, the company multiplied the periodic counts of young women believed to be younger than 18 by .38 to determine how many of the advertised females were, in fact, less than 18 years of age.

Although the methodology used in this study is far from clear, at least based on the 24-page self-published report of its authors, it seems clear that it is woefully inadequate to support the conclusion that the number of adolescent girls being prostituted rose dramatically, if at all, in any of the cities examined. To begin with, this aspect of the study was limited to classified advertisements containing photographs and there is no way to know whether these advertisements with photographs were representative of all advertisements offering sexual services by underage females. More significantly, there is obviously no way to know whether the photographs accompanying the advertisements studied were, in fact, those of the females whose services were touted in the text of the advertisements. Applying the .38 correction based upon the assumed error rate of 38 percent in identifying the minor status of those pictured in the classified photographs cannot be justified, given the method by which that rate was established.

Not surprisingly, the reaction of researchers, scholars, and others to this study was fiercely negative. One sociologist, Eric Grodsky of the University of Minnesota, concluded that "You couldn't get this kind of thing into a peer-reviewed journal. There are just too many unanswered questions about their methodology."[26] Ric Curtis, Professor and Chair of the Anthropology Department at the John Jay College of Criminal Justice in New York, said, "I wouldn't trust those numbers. This new study seems pretty bogus."[27] David Finkelhor noted that, given the study's methodology, the purported increases observed "could just be noise" or "random fluctuations."[28] In his view, "The trend analysis is simply a function of the number of images on these sites. It's not necessarily an indication that there's an increase in the number of juveniles involved."[29]

The two examples described in detail here, as well as numerous others, represent serious overestimates of the extent to which American children are being prostituted. They seem to be the result of overzealous but perhaps good faith efforts on the part of advocacy groups to call greater attention to the problem. They may also represent more self-serving efforts to advance particular political agendas and increase the funding for such organizations, some of which have budgets (privately and/or publically financed) in the millions and dozens if not hundreds of employees whose jobs depend upon success in lobbying efforts, grantsmanship, and other fund raising.

Although the problem of prostituted children in America is in all likelihood much less serious than many advocates have tried to make it out to be, there is certainly no denying that this phenomenon exists; that many American children are being prostituted; or that prostitution has horrible, potentially devastating, consequences for these children (a number of which are cataloged later in this chapter).

More Than 1 Million Women and Children Sexually Trafficked Annually; 25,000 into the United States from Latin America, the Former Soviet States, and Southeast Asia Alone?

For years, the United Nations Educational, Scientific and Cultural Organization (UNESCO) has been developing a database to compile and compare various published statistics on the trafficking of human beings worldwide. UNESCO's Trafficking Statistics Project succinctly summarized the problem with such statistics:

When it comes to statistics, trafficking of girls and women is one of several highly emotive issues which seem to overwhelm critical faculties. Numbers take on a life of their own, gaining acceptance through repetition, often with little inquiry into their derivations. Journalists, bowing to the pressures of editors, demand numbers, any number. Organizations feel compelled to supply them, lending false precisions and spurious authority to many reports.[30]

The estimate that more than a million children are trafficked for sexual purposes annually throughout the world flies in the face of other statistics collected on the subject by UNESCO. For instance, the Federal Bureau of Investigation (FBI) reports 700,000 women and children trafficked annually worldwide for all purposes; the United Nations Children's Fund (UNICEF) estimates 1.75 million; the International Organization on Migration says 400,000; and the UN estimates that 1 million men, women, and children are trafficked annually for all purposes worldwide.[31]

The most widely cited and exhaustive statistics on human trafficking come from the annual reports of the US State Department on trafficking in persons. According to recent State Department reports, 600,000–800,000 people are trafficked across international borders annually, 14,500–17,500 of whom are trafficked into the United States.[32] These estimates not only belie the estimate that more than a million women and children are trafficked for sexual purposes annually throughout the world, but also the assertion that 25,000 women and children are trafficked into the United States annually from Latin America, the former Soviet states, and Southeast Asia alone.[33]

The point, however, is not that any nation or organization has cornered the market on accurate data on human trafficking in general or sex trafficking in particular, but that even the best numbers (whatever one believes them to be) are educated guesses and that even the most conservative of these estimates put the number of women and children who are sexually trafficked in the United States and abroad at intolerable levels that demand action.

Internationally 1–10 Million Children are Forced into Prostitution Every Year?

Just as there are no reliable statistics on the prostitution of children in the United States, so too there are no reliable data on the extent of the problem worldwide. There is, however, good reason to believe that the incidence of child prostitution is much greater in developing countries than it is in the United States or other Western nations. In 2006, one of the most reliable sources of data on the subject, the UNICEF estimated that "one million children—mainly girls but also a significant number of boys—enter the multi-billion dollar commercial sex trade globally every year."[34] In 2010, Siddharth Kara, author of the acclaimed book, *Sex Trafficking: Inside the Business of Modern Slavery*, estimated that "the total number of individuals [including children] for commercial sexual exploitation is between five hundred thousand and six hundred thousand out of a total number of annual trafficking victims of 1.5 to 1.8 million [including those trafficked for sexual and non-sexual purposes]."[35] By 2012, UNICEF had raised that estimate to 2 million children trafficked annually for sexual purposes. As UNICEF explained:

> Surveys indicate that 30 to 35 percent of all sex workers in the Mekong subregion are between 12 and 17 years of age. The Thai Government estimates that there are 12,000 to 18,000 child prostitutes in Thailand. There has been a 20 per cent increase in the number of child prostitutes in Thailand over the past three years. About 60 percent of 71,281 registered prostitutes in Indonesia, where the sex industry is found in two thirds of the country, are between 15 to 20 years of age. In Taiwan, between 40,000 and 60,000 children are sex workers. In China, the estimates of child sex workers range from 200,000 to 500,000…Studies show as many as one third of sex workers in Cambodia are children under 18 years of age.[36]

Those numbers pertain only to East Asia. According to a survey by "India Today" magazine there are between 400,000 and 500,000 child prostitutes in India,[37] but

India's federal police have reported that they believe that roughly 1.2 million of that nation's children are involved in prostitution.[38] Although the Brazilian Interprofessional Association for the Protection of Children and Adolescents estimates that 2 million children 10–15 years old have been forced into prostitution in Brazil,[39] that nation's own Federal Police estimate the number of prostituted children to be 250,000.[40] In Russia, the Ministry of Interior estimates that as many as 17,000 children are involved in prostitution but End Child Prostitution, Child Pornography and Trafficking of Children for Sexual Purposes (ECPAT), a global network of organizations and individuals working to eliminate child prostitution, child pornography, and the trafficking of children for sexual purposes, reports that in Moscow alone that number may be 20,000–30,000.[41] ECPAT also reports that about 40,000 children are involved in prostitution in Venezuela,[42] and approximately 25,000 in the Dominican Republic.[43]

In Africa, the commercial sexual exploitation of children is believed to be rampant in many countries, but solid data or even estimates are difficult to find. However, recent reports from South Africa and Kenya are informative. The Police Child Protection Unit in Johannesburg has reported that about 28,000 children are engaged in prostitution there.[44] Also, a study conducted in Diepsloot, a severely impoverished neighborhood in the north of Johannesburg, found that 40 percent of girls 15 and younger were involved in prostitution, mostly what has been characterized as "survival sexual exploitation."[45] In Kenya, which has an overall population of about 40 million, a joint report issued by the national government and UNICEF has concluded that 10,000–15,000 children are involved in prostitution in areas along that nation's coast.[46]

Even in the progressive and relatively affluent Northern European nation of Norway, a recent study of almost the entire total population of 14–17 year olds in Oslo schools ($N = 10,828$) found that 1.4 percent had sold sex at least once.[47] In striking contrast with almost every other estimate or survey of child prostitution, regardless of country, Oslo boys who sold sex outnumbered girls who did so by a 3:1 ratio.[48]

Two Million Children Involved in Child Sex Tourism Annually?

Is it possible that as many as 2 million children are prostituted internationally each year as part of the child sex tourism business? Looking solely at the supply side, it is conceivable but highly unlikely. If one accepts the 2012 UNICEF estimate that 2 million children are prostituted annually across the world, nearly every one of those children would have to serve at least one sex tourist to make this estimate of the number of children involved in sex tourism accurate. Of course, if the actual number of children prostituted each year is higher than the UNICEF estimate, this estimate of the number of children involved in sex tourism has a better chance of being accurate. The numbers of children exploited by child sex tourism will undoubtedly depend upon how broadly child sex tourism is defined. As ECPAT has observed, "Child sex tourists can be domestic travelers or they can be international tourists."[49] If the definition of this phenomenon is not limited to sex tourists who cross international boundaries to buy sex with children, then many more children will be considered to be victims of child sex tourism.

Overall, however, given all available international data and estimates regarding the prostitution of children, it seems more likely that the recent estimate of the US State Department (namely that about a million children are prostituted annually in child sex tourism) is closer to being accurate. However, in the final analysis, it is impossible to disagree with ECPAT's assertion that "[c]hild sex tourism is a developing phenomenon" and "[I]t is difficult to obtain accurate figures for CST, either regarding the number of child victims or the number of child sex tourists. There are many factors that make obtaining accurate data a challenge. Firstly, since child sex tourism is an illegal activity, it is mostly hidden or involves organized criminal groups. Secondly, it is a topic that is still regarded as a taboo subject: in many parts of the world, key stakeholders deny the existence of the issue or downplay it, fearing that highlighting it will produce a negative image of the destination and hinder tourism development."[50]

Thus, in the final analysis, the question of how many children are involved annually in the child sex tourism trade may best be answered by simply acknowledging that although we do not have precise numbers, we do know that the number is large and intolerable by any measure.

NATURE OF THE PROBLEM

The prostitution of children, wherever it occurs and regardless of whether it involves trafficking or tourism, has many common features, including but not limited to the following: (1) prostituted children engage in sex with others, usually adult men in exchange for money, tangible goods, shelter, and/or protection; (2) most of these children do not voluntarily agree to their prostitution but rather are recruited into or coerced to remain in the sex trade by adults; (3) the prostitution of children is a multibillion dollar global industry, whose beneficiaries include pimps, traffickers, mobsters, and legitimate business people whose services are used to foster the child sex trade; and (4) children who are prostituted are, ipso facto, sexually abused and at risk for all of the frequent negative consequences of child sexual abuse as well as others peculiar to the child sex trade.

Prostitution of Children as an Economic Exchange

At its most basic level, the prostitution of children involves an economic exchange: sexual use of the child's body is traded for something of value. Ordinarily, that something of value is money. Although, as is detailed later in this chapter, prostituted children benefit little if at all economically from this exchange, there can be little doubt that the primary driving force in the prostitution of children is economic. Without economic incentives, pimps, traffickers, and others whose services make the prostitution of children possible would have no motive to prostitute children.

Similarly, if all children had their basic economic needs met, few would be at risk for being prostituted. Certainly, some small proportion of children who are prostituted put themselves at risk of prostitution needlessly, as in cases in which some suburban, middle class American children purportedly prostitute themselves to get money to afford expensive clothes and jewelry (what some have dubbed "designer sex").[51] However, the one factor that is almost invariably present in the lives of children who end up being prostituted is economic deprivation (i.e., poverty). Many prostituted children, not only abroad but also in the United States, are drawn directly or indirectly to prostitution in a misguided effort to better their economic situations or, in many instances, simply to survive (i.e., obtain adequate food and shelter). Poverty, of course, is also linked in many cases to child abuse and other family dysfunction that seems to contribute more indirectly to placing children at risk for being prostituted. For example, many prostituted children, especially in the United States, have fled abusive and/or dysfunctional families only to find themselves easy prey for pimps and child sex traffickers who falsely promise them not only necessities and protection but luxuries and love.

Recruitment and Coercion

A recent analysis by the USDOJ succinctly summarized the process by which many if not most American girls are recruited and coerced into prostitution:

> Pimps scout bus stations, arcades, and malls, focusing on girls who appear to be runaways without money or job skills. Pimps, or their procurers, befriend the children by showing affection and buying them meals, clothes, jewelry, or video games in exchange for sex. Eventually, pimps use the children's emotional and financial dependency to coerce them into selling sex for money that is turned over to the pimp. In time, the relationship becomes less emotional and more "contractual" as the pimp sets a minimum on the child's earnings.[52]

After a girl is prostituted on a regular basis, her pimp controls her life by the threat or use of physical force (including beatings, sexual abuse, and rape) as well as psychological abuse (including alienation from family and others; efforts to undermine self-esteem; and control over the child's access to food, clothing, and shelter). Under the guise of protection and even love, pimps assume virtual control over all nearly all aspects of the prostituted child's life. Many pimps also provide the children they prostitute with drugs. After the prostituted child becomes addicted to a drug, such as crack cocaine, the pimp uses the drug as a means of controlling the child and enforcing his or her cooperation with prostitution. In extreme, but not uncommon cases, some prostituted children are virtually imprisoned by pimps. Some of these children are also literally sold to other pimps and then told that they must not only earn their daily keep through prostitution but "pay back" the amount the new pimp paid to purchase them.

In any event, every effort is made by pimps to exercise ownership over "their" children and ensure their continued cooperation in prostitution. In perhaps the most extreme example of the exercise of such power over prostituted children, some pimps have even begun using tattoos to physically brand the children whose lives they control.

Although there is evidence that "third-party exploiter cases" represent most prostituted children in the United States, there are also data to support the existence of at least two other typologies of prostituted children: "solo cases" and "child sexual abuse with payment cases."[53] In a recent study, Kimberly Mitchell and colleagues concluded that whereas 57 percent of prostituted children (or "juveniles involved in prostitution" as they prefer to call these youngsters) operate under the control of pimps or other third-party exploiters, 31 percent of these children appear to be engaging in prostitution on their own and 12 percent are children being sexually abused by family members or acquaintances and being paid for their cooperation.[54]

Mitchell and colleagues classified juveniles involved in prostitution by third-party exploiters as being either prostituted by smalltime pimps (59 percent) or organized sex dealers (41 percent), including criminal gangs and others working in conjunction with massage parlors, motels, and/or online escort services.[55] Acknowledging that many juveniles involved in prostitution who fall into the solo category are cases of "stereotypical runaway survival sex," Mitchell and colleagues divide the solo category into two separate subtypes: prostituted children who are "on the street" (i.e., "homeless, drug addicted, or cut off from family resources") and those who, at least according to one report, are living at home and engaging in prostitution "as a form of adventure or even status."[56] Not surprisingly, these researchers report that they "cannot provide a reliable statistical breakdown of the size of the on-the-street versus the home-based solo juvenile involved in prostitution."[57]

Mitchell et al. add that money was exchanged for sex in 98 percent of the cases they studied. The number of "clients" (their term for men who purchase sex from children) to which these children were prostituted in an average week ranged from 1–40 and the most common sex acts included vaginal intercourse (83 percent); oral sex (87 percent); anal sex (23 percent); and group sex (17 percent).[58]

As bad as life is for American children who are prostituted, the lives of their counterparts in other less affluent and developed nations appear to be much worse. Most of these youngsters turn to prostitution wittingly or unwittingly in efforts to escape from crushing poverty and the almost complete lack of economic opportunity imposed by the circumstances of the nations in which they have grown up. Many of these children are recruited by local operatives with promises of the opportunity for a more prosperous life in another more affluent country. They are then trafficked to other nations and forced into prostitution and find themselves in situations from which they cannot realistically escape. The compelling testimony of Steven R. Galster, then-Executive Director of the Global Survivor

Network, before the US Congress details who these trafficked youngsters are, how they are recruited, and how they are retained as virtual sex slaves:

We found 4 types of women and girls involved in the sex trade, many were victims of sexual slavery, some were not: [1] Those who had been completely duped and coerced into being sex workers. These women/girls expected to perform some other line of work. [2] Those who were told half-truths by their recruiters about their employment. For example, they may have been told they would have to dance and strip for clients, but not that they would be expected to perform extra services (like having some form of sex with the client), and/or that the sums of money they were promised were completely fictitious. In most cases, these women experienced little to no freedom of movement outside of work because they had been put in debt bondage circumstances and were not allowed to keep their own passport. [3] Those who were adequately informed of the type of work they would be performing, did not want to do it, saw no viable economic alternative, and therefore knowingly relinquished control to their trafficker who exploited their economic and legal situation for financial gain, while maintaining the women in debt bondage situations. [4] There were those women who were adequately informed of the type of work they would be performing, were not uncomfortable performing it, and were in control of their finances and had relatively good freedom of movement. Under the definition of trafficking…this type of woman would not have been trafficked, unless, one could easily argue, she was under the age of 18.

Recruitment Practices were nearly uniform for women in the first 3 categories: Those who were completely duped and/or coerced had responded to public ads or word of mouth offers to work abroad as waitresses, au pairs, entertainers, and the like. Behind the newspaper ads, or word of mouth offers, is usually a small to medium size company, which is often not legally registered, run by as few as 2 people who, through their local and international contacts, arrange visas and transport from the country of origin to the country of destination. Those who were adequately informed of the work they would perform (while uncomfortable with being a sex worker, but seeing no viable economic alternative), often found the work opportunity through a friend who was also going abroad to be a sex worker, or had already been abroad in this capacity.

Once having transported the woman to her destination of work, the traffickers take away her passport and keep it. The traffickers also keep control over her earnings, paying her whatever and whenever they want…Peonage is often exercised gradually…control over their freedom of movement and control over their own money and bodies was taken by traffickers and pimps gradually. The fact that the women and girls had been duped and/or coerced into performing services they did not want to perform, or work longer hours under bad conditions for little to no money, did not occur to them for several weeks or more, by which time they are stuck and too tired and afraid to fight their boss(es). They become fixated on the need to repay their debt and make some profit for themselves—and often their families back home...

[A]ll the women and girls we met who had been trafficked...feared taking their case to local police because...they feared the police as much as they feared their trafficker and/or pimp. They did not trust either, but they still felt they had to hide behind their trafficker for fear, ironically, of being turned in by him—or her...[They] realized they could be deported for working illegally as an alien, and as a prostitute. Deportation, while seemingly an option for escape, would actually lead to retribution by the trafficking network, which would at the very least call in the sizeable debt incurred by the victim who agreed to the contract mentioned earlier. Even worse, by going to the police, the woman puts her life in danger. There have been cases where these women have been threatened, beaten, and even killed by traffickers.[59]

A Multibillion Dollar Industry?

Although hard data are difficult to come by, it is generally acknowledged that the prostitution of children worldwide generates billions of dollars in income for both criminals and legitimate businesses.

In the recent study mentioned previously, Mitchell et al. found that the average price paid by an individual client for sexual services from a child involved in prostitution ranges from "less than U.S. $50 (28%) to more than U.S. $150 (18%)."[60] Given this price range, pimps prostituting just one or two children can earn hundreds if not thousands of dollars a week. Those with larger "stables" of prostituted children can obviously earn a great deal more. As the USDOJ reported in 2010:

Some criminals have turned away from illicit activities such as drug dealing and robbery toward child sex trafficking, from which they can generate potentially several thousand dollars per day, as a single child can generate as much as $1,000 on a weekend night. Simply, it is cheaper for a criminal to prostitute a child (which involves supplying the child with her primary needs of food, clothes, and shelter) than to commit other crimes such as drug dealing (which require a large capital investment up front to acquire the contraband). In fact, the profitability of child prostitutes to the pimp has increased as Internet advertising and web-enabled cell phones have aided pimps in reaching a larger client base; they can schedule more sexual encounters per child.[61]

Pimps are not the only criminals who benefit economically from the child sex trade. Many international child sex trafficking operations require the services of a long chain of operatives, including those who recruit children, those who arrange their transport, those who transport them to other nations, and those who ultimately sell them to pimps and others in the destination countries. Along the way others, such as corrupt civil servants who issue false passports, visas, and other documents, also share in the wealth created by the prostitution of children. Because some prostituted children end up as victims of child pornography when their sexual interactions are photographed and videotaped for sale commercially, child pornographers also benefit from the prostitution of children.

Although his "conservative numbers" deal with children and adults (mainly women) trafficked for sexual exploitation, Kara reported that:

> The sale of trafficked sex slaves to brothel owners and pimps generated revenues of $1.0 billion in 2007, or a global average sale price of $1,895 per slave. After costs, these sales generated approximately $600 million in profits. Second, the commercial exploitation of trafficked sex slaves generated $51.3 billion in revenues in 2007, the result of millions of men purchasing sex from slaves. After costs, the slaves' exploiters cleared $35.7 billion in profits, or a global average of $29,210 per slave.[62]

Legitimate or quasi-legitimate businesses are also beneficiaries of the spoils resulting from the prostitution of children around the world. For example, travel agents who arrange itineraries for child sex tourists, local hotel owners who provide accommodations for them, and even the airline companies that fly them around the world all take a bite from the poisonous but lucrative apple of child prostitution. So, too, do companies that offer classified advertising, either online or in print media, and publish (for profit) advertisements for sexual services, at least some (if not many) of which promote the prostitution of children.

Negative Consequences for Prostituted Children

There can be no question that children who are prostituted are victims of sexual abuse. Some prostituted children are subjected to unwanted sexual acts dozens or even hundreds of times, sometimes with as many different individuals. Does the fact that money changes hands to allow that abuse to occur make it any less abusive or any less likely to have adverse consequences for the child?

Although there have been few efforts to systematically study the consequences of being prostituted as a child, there is little if any reason to believe that the adverse consequences of such experience would be any less serious than those apparently suffered by many victims of other forms of child sexual abuse (see Chapter 2 of this volume). Indeed, given the repetitive nature of the abuse suffered by prostituted children, there are many reasons to believe that the negative consequences for these children may be even more severe than those suffered by other child sex abuse victims.

Clearly, as has been observed elsewhere, the frequency of sexual acts and the number of individuals with whom prostituted children have sex place these youngsters at serious risk of contracting sexually transmitted diseases (including HIV infection) and becoming pregnant, which poses its own health risks, even to minors who (unlike many prostituted youth) are in good health and receive appropriate medical and prenatal care. Prostituted children also often suffer mal-nutrition as well as physical injuries associated with physical and sexual abuse.

Additionally, these exploited youngsters are routinely found to suffer from a host of psychological symptoms and disorders. Given that many sexually exploited children have come from dysfunctional families and were psycholog-ically troubled before they were prostituted, it is sometimes difficult to say for sure what psychological symptoms and disorders are the direct consequence of commercial sexual exploitation and the awful lifestyle with which it is associated. However, one recent study of American girls who have been domestically traf-ficked for sexual exploitation found that many suffer from:

Mental health problems, including PTSD and somatic complaints (head-aches, chronic pain) resulting from the trauma. . .
Alcohol and other drug use, as well as addiction. . .
Extreme anxiety and fear;
Changed relationships with others (including the inability to trust);
Self-destructive behaviors (including suicide attempts);
Changed feelings or beliefs about oneself (including profound shame and guilt);
Changed perception of the perpetrator (including establishing a traumatic bond); and
Despair and hopelessness.[63]

PREVENTING CHILD PROSTITUTION

Like other forms of child sexual abuse, the prostitution of children is difficult to prevent because so much of it occurs in private but also because it is often an extremely profitable business whose stakeholders go to great lengths to pro-tect their economic interests. The prostitution of children is also difficult to pre-vent in large part because many, often including law enforcement, regard it more as a nuisance crime than one of the most insidious forms of child sexual abuse. Indeed, even prostituted children often do not regard themselves as victims of sexual abuse.

Defining Child Prostitution as Child Sexual Abuse

Perhaps the most fundamental way child prostitution can be prevented is prop-erly recognizing (and educating others to recognize) that, whatever else it may be, this phenomenon is a form of child sexual abuse. Strides have been made in that direction in recent years as some advocates have pointed out that the term "child prostitution" is misleading and stigmatizing because it implies that children bought and sold for sex are either not victims or are willfully engaged in their own victimization. Some experts still cling to the notion that prostituted children are not always victims and that referring to them in this manner implies that they are. For example, as recently as 2010, Mitchell and colleagues, one of whom is the renowned sociologist, David Finkelhor, have written:

> [W]e do not find value in some other current efforts to rename the problem. For example, there have been proposals to talk about this population as "prostituted juveniles," and while this does have the virtue of emphasizing the victimization element in many of these youth's situations, not all these youth are necessarily prostituted by someone else, which is the clear implication of the phrase... Among the terminology available, we favor ' "juveniles involved in prostitution" as an adequate general term that contains a minimum of assumptions about the youth in this population.[64]

Do some prostituted children voluntarily engage in the sex trade? If so, does that mean they are not victims of child sexual abuse? Compare laws governing what is known as statutory rape: an adult having sex with a minor who, although not objecting to the activity, is (for good reasons) not considered capable of giving consent to it. Every American jurisdiction has such laws on the books; generally these laws are predicated on the belief that juveniles under a certain age (which varies from state to state) are not mature enough to make an informed decision to have sex with an adult. Statutory rape is not only considered a form of criminal rape, and sometimes punished rather harshly, but it is a strict liability offense, meaning that an honest or even reasonable belief that the minor was above the age of consent is no defense.

There is limited anecdotal evidence that some children do engage in prostitution on their own (i.e., they are prostituted but not at the behest of another, such as a trafficker or pimp). However, to claim that this places them outside the realm of sexual abuse victimization generally ignores both facts and common sense. First, it appears that most prostituted children are controlled by traffickers or pimps. Also, a small but substantial percentage of prostituted children seem to be youngsters who are being subjected to sexual abuse by family members or acquaintances and being financially rewarded for their cooperation and/or silence. No one would seriously question that youths in these two categories are victims of child sexual abuse.

Even prostituted children who sell sex to adults on a solo basis, indeed even that sketchy minority who purportedly sell themselves sexually "as a form of adventure or even status,"[65] are invariably victims of sexual abuse. First of all, they are most often children who have been reduced by their economic, family, and social circumstances to the point at which prostitution may be their only means of survival. Beyond their motives for engaging in sex for money, none of these youngsters are regarded as legally or psychologically capable of consenting to sex; all are being taken advantage of by adults, primarily men, seeking "no strings attached" sex with young females, most of whom are not sufficiently mature to deal with the psychological fallout from such intimate acts and all are thereby placed at risk for serious physical and/or psychological harm.

Changing the Legal Response to the Prostitution of Children

It has taken a long time to successfully argue that children are the victims rather than the perpetrators of so-called child prostitution, and (as noted previously) some are not yet fully convinced of that. Once that argument prevails, however, it is relatively easy to justify a legal response that places criminal responsibility for the prostitution of children were it belongs: on child sex traffickers, pimps, and the adults who have sex with children.

STATE PROSTITUTION AND STATUTORY RAPE STATUTES

In 2010 the USDOJ noted that "Clients of child victims of prostitution are, in fact, child sex offenders; however, this form of child sexual exploitation often goes unpunished. In fact, the exploited child victim of prostitution is much more likely to be arrested for prostitution offenses than is the offender. For example, a 2005 study for Congress showed that in Boston, 11 female prostitutes (adult and child) were arrested for each male client arrest; in Chicago, the ratio was 9 to 1; and, in New York City, the ratio was 6 to 1."[66]

The USDOJ attributed some of these disproportionate arrest ratios to child victims representing themselves to police as adults and/or presenting false identification indicating that they are at or above the legal age of consent. It is clear, however, that this explanation does not fully account for prostituted children being much more likely than their clients to be arrested. Another plausible explanation is that law enforcement personnel are more concerned about stopping prostitution than stopping the prostitution of children. The true identity and age of a prostituted child who comes to the attention of the police can usually be ascertained but it may take time and effort. It is easier to simply charge the prostituted child with prostitution and hand her over to the criminal and/or juvenile justice systems to sort out the details.

That means, of course, that when men who buy sex with children are discovered, they are most likely to be charged, if at all, with the very minor offense of patronizing or soliciting the services of a prostitute. In New York State, for example, patronizing a prostitute is a class A misdemeanor, the maximum penalty for which is 1 year in jail, a sentence rarely imposed.[67]

New York law, and laws in other jurisdictions, also now provide for harsher penalties for those convicted of having sex for a fee with minors. In New York, for example, paying for sex with a person less than 14 is a class E felony punishable by up to 4 years in prison,[68] and paying for sex with a person younger than 11 is a class D felony punishable by up to 7 years in prison.[69]

Also, in New York, as in other states, there are offenses known as statutory rape. Under New York law, for example, an adult who has sex with a person younger than 17 may be convicted of third-degree rape, a class E felony punishable by up to 4 years in prison[70]; if convicted of having sex with a person younger than 15, he or she may be convicted of second-degree rape, a class D felony punishable by up to 7 years in prison[71]; and if convicted of having sex with a person younger than 11, he or she may be convicted of first-degree rape, a class B felony punishable by up to 25 years in prison.[72] To convict a defendant of statutory rape, all the state needs to provide is that the sexual conduct occurred between the adult and the minor. As noted previously in this chapter, it is no defense to this crime that the adult who had sex with a minor honestly or even reasonably believed that the minor was above the age of consent. Interestingly and tellingly, however, under New York law "In any prosecution for patronizing a prostitute in the first or second degrees [i.e., having sex for a fee with a child under 14 or under 11, respectively], it is a defense that the defendant did not have reasonable grounds to believe that the person was less than the specified age."[73]

In addition to statutory rape and enhanced patronizing charges for those who buy sex with children, most states also have statutes that criminally sanction the promotion of prostitution. In New York, for example, anyone who "advances or profits from prostitution" is subject to prosecution for promoting prostitution in the fourth degree, a class A misdemeanor.[74] Advancing or profiting from prostitution of a person younger than 19 is a class D felony[75]; advancing or profiting from prostitution of a person younger than 16 is a class C felony punishable by up to 15 years in prison[76]; and advancing or profiting from prostitution of a person less than 11 is a class B felony.[77]

Furthermore, most states have statutes that criminally punish both endangering the welfare of a child and unlawfully dealing with a child. In New York, for example, one who "knowingly acts in a manner likely to be injurious to the physical, mental or moral welfare of a child less than seventeen years or directs or authorizes such child to engage in an occupation involving a substantial risk of danger to his or her life or health" is guilty of a class A misdemeanor[78]; one who "knowingly permits a child less than eighteen to enter or remain in or upon a place, premises or establishment where [prostitution] is maintained or conducted" is guilty of unlawfully dealing with a child in the first degree, also a class A misdemeanor.[79]

All of these laws could apply not only to pimps but to others, such as adult prostitutes who recruit and/or help manage children who are prostituted. New York and many other states also have statutes criminalizing promoting or compelling prostitution (either as a principal actor or an accomplice); sex trafficking; and even permitting prostitution to occur on one's premises.

One of the obvious purposes of criminal punishment is to deter criminal conduct, so-called general deterrence. Although the criminal law may not provide as much general deterrence as some believe, there is no reason to believe that any deterrent effect the law does have will be any less in this context than others. Adults who buy and sell sex with children or have any other involvement in the prostitution of children are guilty of multiple state crimes and should be arrested, charged, prosecuted, and, if convicted, incarcerated accordingly. For example, adults who buy sex with children should be prosecuted not only for patronizing a prostitute but for statutory rape (which, as noted previously, is a strict liability offense and allows no defense of mistake of age) and endangering the welfare of a child. Pimps and others who prostitute children should be prosecuted not only for promotion of prostitution, but also endangering the welfare of a child, unlawfully dealing with a child, and being an accomplice to statutory rape.

Imposing these legal sanctions that are already on the books in virtually every state will at the very least significantly increase the risk of commercially exploiting children and may ultimately reduce both the supply and demand for sexually exploited children.

FEDERAL PROSTITUTION, TRAFFICKING, AND TOURISM STATUTES

Several federal criminal statutes are also available for use against those who buy or sell sex with children, who traffic children for sexual purposes, or who travel outside the United States to engage in sexual acts with children.

To begin with, federal law provides that "[w]hoever knowingly transports any individual in interstate or foreign commerce, or in any Territory or Possession of the United States, with intent that such individual engage in prostitution, or in any sexual activity for which any person can be charged with a criminal offense, or attempts to do so, shall be fined under this title or imprisoned not more than 10 years, or both"[80]; and "[w]hoever knowingly persuades, induces, entices, or coerces any individual to travel in interstate or foreign commerce, or in any Territory or Possession of the United States, to engage in prostitution, or in any sexual activity for which any person can be charged with a criminal offense, or attempts to do so, shall be fined under this title or imprisoned not more than 20 years, or both."[81] These statutes obviously can and should be used to prosecute not only international child sex traffickers, but local traffickers who transport children across state lines for purposes of prostitution. They may and should also be used to prosecute those who entice or coerce (often by means of Internet communications) children to cross state or international boundaries for purposes of prostitution.

Federal laws also provide for criminal punishment of those who, through interstate or foreign commerce, knowingly recruit, entice, harbor, transport, obtain, or provide by any means a person younger than 18 to be used in a commercial sex act. The same stature also provides criminal sanctions for those who benefit, financially or by receiving anything of value, from participation in any such venture. The statute further provides that (1) "if the offense was effected by force, fraud, or coercion or if the person recruited, enticed, harbored, transported, provided, or obtained had not attained the age of 14 years at the time of such offense, [the perpetrator shall be punished] by a fine...and imprisonment for any term of years not less than 15 or for life" and (2) "if the offense was not so effected, and the person recruited, enticed, harbored, transported, provided, or obtained had attained the age of 14 years but had not attained the age of 18 years at the time of such offense, [the perpetrator shall be punished] by a fine...and imprisonment for not less than 10 years or for life."[82]

These provisions have potentially far-reaching impact and could be used to prosecute not only traffickers and their investors, associates, and abettors, but also pimps, brothel owners, and even the end-of-the-line consumer who purchases sex with a child he or she knows has been transported in interstate or foreign commerce.

Finally, to help curb so-called child sex tourism, the Protect Act of 2003 provides that "[a] person who travels in interstate commerce or travels into the

United States, or a United States citizen or an alien admitted for permanent residence in the United States who travels in foreign commerce, for the purpose of engaging in any illicit sexual conduct with another person shall be fined under this title or imprisoned not more than 30 years, or both."[83] Under this law, the United States may exercise extraterritorial jurisdiction over certain sex offenses against children. That means that the United States may prosecute criminal sexual conduct that takes place beyond US borders even if such conduct was legal in the country where it occurred. As the USDOJ has explained: "For example, if an individual traveled to a country that had legalized prostitution, and while they were there they paid a child for sex, that individual could still be convicted under this statute."[84] A related law criminalizes being a "child sex tour operator" (i.e., "facilitating the travel of U.S. Citizens or legal permanent residents, knowing that they are traveling for the purpose of engaging in illegal sex with a minor").[85] The penalty under that statute is also up to 30 years in prison. The constitutionality of these laws has been affirmed by the courts.

Although it is probably too early to assess the efficacy of these various federal statutes in the prevention of child sexual abuse and exploitation, the number of arrests made under these laws has been impressive. For example, in 2003, the Department of Homeland Security launched Operation Predator, a law enforcement program targeting adults who sexually exploit children in violation of these federal laws, whether in the United States or elsewhere. In 2012, the US Immigration and Customs Enforcement announced that arrests for these offenses since 2003 have surpassed the 10,000 mark, including the arrests of 99 sex tourism offenders, all of whom have been convicted.[86] Given estimates of the number of adults who are actually committing these offenses, some might wonder if these arrests represent just the proverbial drop in the bucket. Perhaps so, but they represent an important start on the road to eradicating child sexual exploitation. Also, even if the numbers of arrests and convictions are small compared with the real scope of the problem, these arrests may do more than simply take these particular child sex exploiters off the street. They may well have a much broader deterrent effect and actually contribute to the primary prevention of child sexual exploitation by interstate and international prostitution of children, trafficking in child sex slaves, and child sex tourism.

INTERNATIONAL LEGAL EFFORTS

In 2003, the General Assembly of the UN adopted a resolution supplementing the UN's Convention against Transnational Organized Crime: the United Nations Protocol to Prevent, Suppress and Punish Trafficking in Persons, especially Women and Children.[87] As the European Union has noted,

> The Protocol to Prevent, Suppress and Punish Trafficking in Persons, especially Women and Children is the first global legally binding instrument with an agreed definition of trafficking in persons. The Protocol contains provisions on a range of issues, including criminalisation, assistance to and protection for victims, the status of victims in the receiving states, repatriation

of victims, preventive measures, actions to discourage the demand, exchange of information and training, and measures to strengthen the effectiveness of border controls. The protocol stipulates that state parties must adopt or strengthen legislative or other measures to discourage the demand that fosters all forms of exploitation of persons, especially women and children that leads to trafficking.[88]

Moreover, as the UN has observed, "The intention ... is to facilitate convergence in national approaches with regard to the establishment of domestic criminal offences that would support efficient international cooperation in investigating and prosecuting trafficking in persons cases. An additional objective of the Protocol is to protect and assist the victims of trafficking in persons with full respect for their human rights."[89] According to the Protocol:

"Trafficking in persons" shall mean the recruitment, transportation, transfer, harbouring or receipt of persons, by means of the threat or use of force or other forms of coercion, of abduction, of fraud, of deception, of the abuse of power or of a position of vulnerability or of the giving or receiving of payments or benefits to achieve the consent of a person having control over another person, for the purpose of exploitation. Exploitation shall include, at a minimum, the exploitation or the prostitution of others or other forms of sexual exploitation, forced labour or services, slavery or practices similar to slavery, servitude or the removal of organs.[90]

By May 2013, the UN Trafficking Protocol had been signed by 154 countries.[91] Since the Protocol was passed, the number of countries with antitrafficking legislation has more than doubled and most of the signatory nations have developed national plans and established special anti–human trafficking police units.[92] As the UN has essentially acknowledged, it is too early to gauge the effect of the Protocol, in part because different countries still use different definitions and methods of data collection:

There is also a need to encourage Member States to collect more and better information on the state of human trafficking in their countries. Some countries could cite the number of victims or offenders, for example, but had no data on the gender, age or citizenship of these people. Domestic crimes that are tantamount to trafficking are not being tallied in national totals. By setting the accounting agenda, it is possible that lagging states could be encouraged to meet their obligations to pass appropriate laws and in thinking about the human trafficking problem strategically.[93]

Despite the lack of hard and comparable data, the UN Trafficking Protocol should be regarded as an important weapon in the fight to prevent the global sexual trafficking of children. The Protocol has clearly affected the way in which governments worldwide view this problem. Even if their recent laws against trafficking prove to have only symbolic or hortatory value, the Protocol will have achieved an important goal.

In addition to antitrafficking legislation, at least four countries including the United States now have extraterritorial jurisdiction laws that allow the prosecution of their citizens for engaging in child sex tourism crime abroad.[94] Many now also have criminalized organizing or publicizing trips for purposes of buying sex with or otherwise sexually abusing children; conviction carries lengthy prison sentences and often includes large monetary fines.[95]

Private Sector Initiatives

In 1999, the World Tourism Organization ECPAT and Nordic Tour Operators created a global Code of Conduct to Protect Children from Sexual Exploitation in Travel and Tourism.[96] The Code has been signed by almost 1,000 travel industry members worldwide, each of which has committed to abide by six criteria:

1. To establish an ethical policy regarding commercial sexual exploitation of children.
2. To train the personnel in the country of origin and travel destinations.
3. To introduce a clause in contracts with suppliers, stating a common repudiation of commercial sexual exploitation of children.
4. To provide information to travelers by means of catalogues, brochures, in-flight films, ticket-slips, home pages, etc.
5. To provide information to local "key persons" at the destinations.
6. To report annually.[97]

ECPAT has suggested that those in the travel and tourism industry take even further steps to help prevent child sex tourism:

Commit in person and as a sector to its progressive eradication

Develop an overall plan of action to promote for sustainability (environment, conservation of tradition and culture, protection of children and so on), that is more effective than ad hoc single actions

Tour Operators and Travel Agents should speak up against child sex tourism in one voice

Become signatory to the existing Code, or come up with an alternative

Inform tourists on child sex tourism, additionally to the general travel information

Firmly transmit to clients and suppliers a total rejection of sexual exploitation of children

Observe the law and inform tourists about this

Train tourism personnel

Terminate contracts with accommodations if these allow sexual exploitation of minors at their premises

Withdraw all services towards persons identified as child sex tourists

Impose fines or take away membership of national associations of tour operators and travel agents to travel organizations that allow child sex tourism

Put in place reporting and monitoring mechanisms

Allow no access for children to premises unless accompanied by family

Contribute financially to research and awareness efforts by NGOs and local groups[98]

It is impossible to say how many individual and corporate agents in the private travel and tourism business have followed ECPAT's advice, but these suggestions are sensible and, if followed by enough of those in the travel and tourism industry worldwide, seem bound to help reduce the scourge that is child sex tourism.

Outside the travel and tourism industry, other private sector actors have also contributed efforts that may help reduce the prostitution of children. One of the major contributors in that regard may well be the popular online classified advertising website known as Craigslist. As noted previously in this chapter, some allege that pimps use online classified advertisements to prostitute children. Two of the largest and most profitable classified advertising websites are Craigslist and Backpage (which was previously owned by the publishers of the Village Voice, a national weekly online newspaper, which has been highly critical of some recent claims about the extent of child prostitution in the United States). A number of studies, observers, and advocacy groups maintain that classified advertising web-sites, such as Craigslist and Backpage, have been widely used to sell the sexual services of children.[99] For example, CNN reported that the FBI found more than 2,800 advertisements for child prostitution posted in the erotic services section of Craigslist, which covered every state and a number of foreign countries.[100]

In 2009, under pressure from politicians and law enforcement officials, Craigslist decided to remove the erotic services section from its website and replace it with an adult services category in which every advertisement would be prescreened. Furthermore, advertisers would be required to pay a $10 fee, which Craigslist would contribute to charity.[101]

Years later, Craigslist competitor Backpage allegedly still runs classified adver-tisements offering children for prostitution.[102] Backpage has responded that they are doing all they can to police sexually related classified advertisements and reject advertisements that might involve the prostitution of children.[103] Backpage has also claimed that they are fully cooperative with law enforcement in helping to investigate those who place suspect advertisements.[104]

Backpage's efforts have not been acceptable to many of the website's most vocal critics. In 2012, a bipartisan group of US Senators introduced a "Sense of the Senate resolution" calling on the owners of Backpage to eliminate the adult ser-vices section of their website.[105]

Senator John Cornyn of Texas stated that "The so-called 'Adult Entertainment' section is nothing more than a front for pimps and child sex traffickers. This is absolutely sickening, and should be stopped with all the tools available to us."[106] Senator Richard Blumenthal of Connecticut added that: "Unconscionably, Backpage is enabling prostitution and human trafficking through the adult section of the website, supporting an avenue for abuse and violence against women and children. Backpage must shutdown the adult section immediately ending its involvement in such repugnant and destructive practices."[107]

Echoing the Senators' demands, the National Association of Attorneys General sent a letter (signed by Attorneys General from 46 states) to Backpage's parent company urging it to remove the adult section.[108] That letter was followed up by another from 600 members of the clergy urging the same course of action.[109] Beyond that, more than 266,000 people signed a petition on the website "change. org" calling for an end to Backpage's adult services section.[110] Finally, more than 30 corporations, including American Airlines and Best Buy, have removed their advertisements from websites and newspapers published by Village Voice.[111]

Backpage refused to back down and vigorously asserted its First Amendment rights as well as the Communications Decency Act of 1996, which absolves Internet service providers from liability for concerning materials posted on their websites by other parties.[112] Defenders of Backpage have pointed out that, in fact, the website's adult advertising may be a boon to law enforcement seeking to identify and punish those who prostitute children.[113] Backpage reportedly has 123 moderators who examine advertisements before they are published and try to spot those that may involve the prostitution of children.[114] Furthermore, because those who post on the Backpage adult services section are required to provide their credit card numbers, in most cases authorities will have little if any difficulty identifying those who place the suspect advertisements and are likely involved in prostituting children.[115]

It should also be noted that although Craigslist has shut down its adult services section, it seems clear that pimps and prostitutes continue to use the website's classified advertisements to sell sex. According to a 2012 Bloomberg News account, classified advertisements for prostitution still show up in the casual encounters and therapeutic massage sections of Craigslist.[116] Moreover, according to the AIM Group, a national marketing consulting group, after Craigslist dropped its adult services section, advertisements for prostitution moved to other websites, such as Backpage.[117]

There are numerous anecdotal reports of pimps using Craigslist, Backpage, and other online classified sites to advertise the prostitution of children, but there are no reliable empirical data that demonstrate the effect, if any, that classified advertising for prostitution has on the market for prostituted children. Given the legal, and possibly constitutional, barriers to an outright ban on sexual service advertisements, such as those posted on these websites, the most reasonable course of action at this time may be for law enforcement to work closely with Craigslist, Backpage, and other such sites to monitor advertisements that are offered for posting, determine who is posting suspect advertisements, and then investigate whether these individuals are, in fact, involved in the prostitution of children.

Educational Initiatives

Educational initiatives should be at the heart of comprehensive programs designed to prevent the prostitution and sex trafficking of children. Children, their parents, and the public need to be educated about the risks posed to children who become involved in prostitution, trafficking, and/or sex tourism.

EDUCATING CHILDREN

Many children who become victims of prostitution, sex trafficking, or sex tourism, whether in the United States or abroad, do so in large measure because they are unaware of the dangers they face when they run away from home, are sent away from home, or are convinced to leave home in search of better jobs and economic opportunities. It is generally recognized that the better educated children are in general, the less likely they are to become victims of commercial sexual exploitation. Part of that observation rests upon the fact that the longer children remain in school, the older they become and the less vulnerable they are to those who would commercially exploit them sexually.

Although general education no doubt plays a role in helping to inoculate children from the lure of involvement in commercial sexual exploitation, there is also a need for education specific to this issue. As the Department of Health in Wales has observed: "Awareness raising and educative programmes are essential in order to prevent harm to young people through entrapment in prostitution. Such programmes endeavour to help children understand the nature of abusive relationships and to empower them to seek help prior to becoming entrapped by abusive adults."[118] Clearly, in most parts of world schools are most readily equipped to provide such educational programs, but as the US Office of Juvenile Justice and Delinquency Prevention has also pointed out, such education cannot be limited to schools. Those charged with getting the message about commercial sexual exploitation to children must "[e]xplore innovative efforts to reach youth in their preferred media venues (e.g., hip-hop stations, teen newspapers and media outlets, schools, the Internet) and consult with children and survivors to determine in which media to place public education ads to best reach youth."[119]

In addition to general education programs, whether conducted in schools, in the media, or elsewhere, educational efforts have been and should continue to be aimed at those children who are at high risk for commercial sexual exploitation. In particular, educational and social welfare agencies and organizations should clearly target runaway children, so-called "thrownaway" children, and those with histories of personal and/or familial problems (e.g., domestic violence, child abuse, substance abuse, psychopathology, behavioral problems, learning difficulties, and so forth) that may increase their vulnerability to commercial sexual exploitation.

Finally, educating children already caught up in such exploitation can also serve as a form of prevention, albeit secondary prevention. Numerous authorities have expressed concern that children who are rescued from commercial sexual exploitation are at a high risk of returning to the same or a similar form of sexual exploitation without major rehabilitative efforts, most of which have a major educational component.

EDUCATING PARENTS

In countries where it is not uncommon for parents to sell or give away their children, parents are often ignorant of the peril their children will face or so economically desperately that they are willing to take that risk. For what many Americans would consider a pittance, in some Asian countries, children are literally sold by their desperately impoverished parents to traffickers who promise additional payments to the parents and greater economic and educational opportunities for the child, who ends up in forced labor (often prostitution) either in her home country or abroad. Numerous international organizations are now making a concerted effort to educate parents to this danger and help provide economic alternatives.

PUBLIC EDUCATION

Members of the public, both in the United States and internationally, need to be educated regarding the prostitution of children, so that they are better able to understand and help prevent it and so they can avoid becoming involved in it as customers or child sex tourists. Public education of this sort has been referred to by Mitchell et al. as "bystander mobilization."[120] In their words:

> Responses to youth involved in prostitution appeared more victim oriented and thus perhaps more compassionate when the cases came from community reports. It may be possible to promote more of such community reporting by actively educating communities—including social workers, teachers, young people, family members, and victim service professionals—to be advocates for youth they believe to be getting involved in prostitution. Such reporting may short-circuit prostitution careers at an early stage in their development.[121]

Educating the general public may also be important as a deterrent to adults who might otherwise become involved in purchasing sex from children. Public education efforts that highlight the problem and its grave consequences for child victims might help and is certainly worth trying. However, a more direct route may prove to be more feasible: educating adults regarding the criminal sanctions they face should they purchase sex with a child. It appears that many (perhaps most) men who purchase sex with adolescents are not seeking sex with juveniles but are simply unconcerned about the age of the person they view as a prostitute. Alerting these men to the possibility that, in addition to the legal risks faced by all "johns" (i.e., minor charges of patronizing a prostitute), purchasing sex with a child might expose them to much more serious charges (e.g., patronizing an underage prostitute, a felony in some jurisdictions; statutory rape; or endangering the welfare of a child), some of which are felonies and could lead to lengthy terms of imprisonment.

This kind of public education has been attempted mainly in the area of child sex tourism. As ECPAT has reported: "In sending countries, tour operators, travel agencies, airlines and other travel and tourism companies have developed information materials to inform their customers that CST is a problem that not only exists in multiple tourism destinations, but is illegal and has dire consequences for children. Information materials include travel brochures, ticket folders, luggage tags, video spots, public service announcements, and other methods to convey messages to travelers concerning CST."[122] Perhaps the clearest example of this kind of public education occurs in Costa Rica, where posters placed in taxis and rental cars proclaim: "In Cost Rica, sex with children under 18 is a serious crime. Should you engage in it, we will be glad to drive you to jail. We mean it."[123]

Changing the Professional Response to the Prostitution of Children

It is not enough to recognize all prostituted children as victims of child sexual abuse, although that alone would be a major accomplishment in the battle to prevent the prostitution of children. These victims must be rescued, treated, and rehabilitated if they are to avoid continued victimization and/or the sometimes lifelong consequences of being prostituted as a child.

Rescue

Although the ideal is to prevent children from being prostituted in the first place, clearly that goal has not been achieved. It appears that thousands of children are prostituted daily around the world. If the damage done to these youngsters is to be mitigated, they first need to be rescued from the world of prostitution in which so many of them are trapped. The most dramatic form of rescue in this context occurs when law enforcement cracks down on pimps and traffickers, arrests them, and removes prostituted children from their control. In 2012, for example, the FBI conducted a nationwide sweep of pimps who were prostituting children. In one 3-day period in June, FBI agents teamed with state and local police to arrest 114 pimps and rescue 79 children who were being prostituted. Even in announcing this sweep, officials acknowledged that "[w]ithout sophisticated shelter/home case management and comprehensive social services combined with adequate living quarters, these children will return to the streets because underfunded and underdeveloped shelter/homes cannot compete with the promises of a pimp."[124] Clearly, rescuing children from pimps and prostitution requires more than physically removing them from the situations in which they have been trapped. Whether in the United States or abroad, these child victims need shelter, adult supervision, treatment, and rehabilitation in order to keep them from returning to abusive and exploitative circumstances from which they have been rescued.

Treatment and Rehabilitation

Although clearly a form of tertiary prevention, treatment and rehabilitation of youngsters who have been prostituted are essential elements in any effort to eradicate the commercial sexual exploitation of children and adolescents. As noted previously in this chapter, these youngsters often suffer from physical injuries and ailments as well as psychological symptoms. These problems frequently limit their functioning and make them vulnerable to further victimization and/or prostitution. If they manage to escape from exploitation, some are reunited with their families, but at least in the United States most end up being placed in group homes, foster care, or residential treatment centers. Many also bounce in and out of youth drop-in centers, homeless shelters, and programs that provide temporary housing for runaways. It is not uncommon for some of these young victims to go back and forth between treatment and rehabilitation programs and prostitution.[125] Sadly, many end up in juvenile detention facilities, where they are treated as young criminals, because there is simply no other safe place to put them.[126]

Treatment and rehabilitation of sexually exploited minors is a difficult task, one that many believe takes months if not years of effort by a host of helping professionals. Under current systems, these youngsters rarely get the intensive treatment and rehabilitation they seem to need. In a report prepared for the US Department of Health and Human Services, Heather Clawson (a psychologist) and Lisa Goldblatt Grace (a social worker) outlined what they and others who work with young victims of commercial sexual exploitation believe is the optimal approach to treatment and rehabilitation.[127]

Clawson, Grace, and the professionals they consulted believe that "minor victims of domestic sex trafficking" require voluntary residential treatment for at least 18 months in a safe and secure facility where they can have their basic physical needs met; receive health and mental health care; have access to educational, life skills, and vocational training; receive case management services; and, in some cases, work toward reunification with their families.[128] They recognize, however, that even such an optimal program would not, by itself, be sufficient to meet the treatment and rehabilitation needs of youth who have been subjected to commercial sexual exploitation, much less serve as an effective means of preventing this insidious form of child sexual abuse:

> While providers and law enforcement stressed the need for residential facilities for this population as a priority, they also recognized that a residential facility alone would not be enough to effectively serve these girls. There was universal agreement that the residential facility needed to be situated along a continuum of care that began with prevention education and outreach to at-risk populations, teachers and school counselors, health and human services professionals, juvenile justice and child welfare systems personnel, parents, and communities at large. The residential facilities also need to be connected to existing community-based programs, including youth drop-in centers and emergency shelters, given their contact with this population and

the importance of these programs as an identification and referral source for the facilities. Finally, providers and law enforcement alike noted the need for long-term aftercare services, including support groups, mentoring, individual counseling, and education. It was believed that once we had in place well-designed and well-funded residential facilities to house these girls, we could begin to work on the other aspects of the continuum.[129]

Conclusions

There is no shortage of ideas for preventing child sexual abuse and exploitation. If every one of the preventive efforts described in this book were effective and implemented, the sexual abuse and exploitation of children would no longer be such a serious problem. Unfortunately, some of these efforts appear to be largely ineffective. Moreover, even among those efforts that seem effective, most have little if any systematic empirical data to establish their efficacy. Also, many apparently effective approaches represent forms of secondary and tertiary prevention, meaning that they are effective (if at all) only after a child has already been sexually abused or exploited.

If the most recent data regarding child sexual abuse are accurate, over the past couple of decades society has made significant gains in preventing child sexual abuse. However, if these apparent gains are to be maintained in the years to come, preventive efforts such as those described in this book will need to be carefully examined using both empirical evidence and logical reasoning. Given the limited resources available, particularly in these times of growing government fiscal austerity, there is a greater need than ever to assess both the efficacy and the cost-effectiveness of strategies for preventing child sexual abuse.

Although it is difficult to assess the efficacy and cost-effectiveness of the initiatives described in this book, some appear sensible, some appear questionable, and some appear ineffective and even counterproductive. For purposes of summarizing the present assessment of these initiatives, they are categorized as (1) probably effective, (2) possibly effective, and (3) probably ineffective or counterproductive.

STRATEGIES THAT ARE PROBABLY EFFECTIVE IN PREVENTING CHILD SEXUAL ABUSE

A number of sensible strategies, most involving education, technology, and alterations to the physical environment, are probably effective in preventing child sexual abuse.

Education Regarding Risk

The foundation of any prevention effort must rest, at least in part, on accurate knowledge of the nature and level of the risk that is to be prevented. Sadly, not all of the information about child sexual abuse that is being provided to children, parents, and members of the community is accurate, but where accurate data are available they should be broadly communicated in an understandable manner. In that regard, for example, efforts to make people aware of the myth of stranger danger have undoubtedly contributed to the prevention of child sexual abuse. Similarly efforts to promote sex offender legislation based upon the myth of inevitable recidivism have made it more difficult for the public to understand the true parameters of the risk of child sexual abuse.

Teaching Children to Protect Themselves

Beyond general education, efforts have long been made to teach children to protect themselves from child sexual abuse. Although these efforts have not been without controversy, nearly all experts agree that even if these efforts have not been proven to prevent child sexual abuse, they promote the disclosure of such abuse when it occurs. Moreover, fears that these efforts might lead to many false accusations or to adverse mental health consequences for children have not been documented. In the absence of data to the contrary, developmentally appropriate efforts to teach children to protect themselves from child sexual abuse are sensible, relatively inexpensive, and should continue.

Educational efforts have also been aimed at teaching youngsters about the nature and dangers of commercial sexual exploitation. It appears that many adolescents who become victims of prostitution, sex trafficking, or sex tourism do so largely because they are unaware of the dangers they face when they run away, are sent away, or are convinced to leave home in search for a better life. Although there are few if any data on the effects of these educational efforts, it seems quite likely that these efforts do make at least some children less vulnerable to commercial sexual exploitation by making them aware of that phenomenon and offering them strategies to avoid becoming a victim of it.

Educating and Accommodating Child Witnesses

Other efforts to prevent child sexual abuse or at least ameliorate its harm have emerged as the courts have struggled to make the legal system more child-friendly and less likely to pose further harm to already injured children. Providing child victims with developmentally appropriate education aimed at helping them become more comfortable and effective as witnesses is sensible, inexpensive, and unlikely to undermine the search for truth or the rights of alleged perpetrators. Similarly sensible and inexpensive, as long as they are not used for purposes of

legal strategy, are alterations to courtrooms or courtroom routine aimed at accom-
modating the developmental needs of child witnesses and making their testimonial experience smoother and less traumatic.

Minimizing Opportunities for Undetected Sexual Abuse

Still other practical methods of preventing child sexual abuse have developed
largely as a result of increasing concerns about such abuse occurring in institutional settings, such as day-care centers, schools, juvenile detention facilities, and
youth-serving organizations. Child sexual abuse almost always occurs in private,
where the perpetrator cannot be seen and is unlikely to be stopped by others.
Thus, efforts have been made to reshape the physical environment of institutions
that serve children, so that private space is minimized, thus reducing the capacity
of a perpetrator to sexually abuse a child without being observed. Similarly, many
of these institutions have installed video cameras on their premises and instituted
policies prohibiting staff members or volunteers from being alone with a child.

These kinds of practical interventions are not without cost, both financial
and social. Physical renovations, video cameras and "never alone" policies create added costs for institutions. Their implementation also changes the nature
of interaction among staff, volunteers, and children. At the same time, however,
these interventions seem bound not only to protect some children from sexual
abuse but protect volunteers and staff from misunderstandings and false accusations of abuse. Such interventions, although sometimes costly, are undoubtedly
effective and likely to prove more than worth the cost.

Severely Punishing Producers and Distributors
of Child Pornography

Draconian punishment for the possession of child pornography is extremely
expensive, not cost effective, and probably does little to affect the market for this
awful contraband. However, severe criminal punishment for the manufacture and
distribution of images of child sexual abuse is justified by both denunciation and
deterrence and may work, in conjunction with other strategies, to reduce both
child sexual abuse and the availability of images of that abuse.

Using Technology to Stop the Production and Dissemination
of Child Pornography

The proliferation of child pornography in the Internet age is largely the result of
technological advances in digital photography and computing. However, other
digital technologies are beginning to catch up with these advances and it is now
possible to detect Internet files that contain images of child sexual abuse without

opening them. Hash values of files known by law enforcement to contain child pornography can be used by Internet service providers (ISPs) to screen files without examining their contents. Those files whose hash values indicate that they contain child pornography may be deleted, rejected, and/or reported to law enforcement authorities. This method of screening is obviously limited to images already known to law enforcement but the government's database of such images is constantly growing.

Although imperfect and subject to privacy complaints, hash value screening shows great promise as a tool to eliminate the distribution of images of child sexual abuse. This methodology obviously requires cooperation from ISPs. Many of them are already cooperating on a voluntary basis, but it may be necessary for government to mandate their cooperation, even though doing so would require addressing privacy issues and perhaps even constitutional concerns.

Currently available technology is also capable of detecting and shutting down child pornography websites. This technology is regularly used by ISPs and law enforcement, and its use could be expanded although most child pornography images are transmitted via peer-to-peer file sharing rather than Internet websites.

Using Technology to Rescue Children Who Appear in Child Pornography

Using a combination of technology, tenacity, and good detective work, law enforcement agents have been able to rescue hundreds if not thousands of children who are being abused in the making of child pornography. These rescues have been made possible in large part by manually searching child pornography images for clues to the location and identity of the victims and/or perpetrators. This is a labor-intensive strategy but one that has obviously been effective in preventing further abuse to many children who have been abused and helping to bring about the arrests of many abusers.

STRATEGIES THAT MAY BE EFFECTIVE IN PREVENTING CHILD SEXUAL ABUSE

Numerous strategies for preventing child sexual abuse appear promising but for one or more reasons must be characterized as only possibly effective.

Parent Education

It stands to reason that educating parents about the dangers of child sexual abuse and ways to protect their children from those risks will help prevent child sexual abuse. Thus, it is not surprising that a multitude of relevant parent education programs have been developed and offered by public and private agencies. What is surprising is that some of these programs have demonstrated no apparent impact on parents' understanding of indicators of child sexual abuse or how they should respond if their children disclose such abuse.

If parent education programs are to be effective as a means of preventing child sexual abuse, they may need to be better designed and implemented so that parents take them seriously but at the same time are not so personally threatened or overwhelmed by the information offered that they ignore it or reject its relevance for them and their children.

Another aspect of parent education that is less well studied, if studied at all, involves informing parents of the risk of commercial sexual exploitation and trafficking. In some nations, where it is not uncommon for children to be sold or given away in the face of economic desperation, parents are often ignorant of the peril these children face or so desperate that they are willing to take that risk. Obviously, educating these parents is not sufficient to protect their children from sexual exploitation and trafficking, but it is probably helpful.

Encouraging Bystander Intervention

Other important initiatives that will undoubtedly have significant preventive impact involve encouraging bystander intervention. Although developed largely in response to child sexual abuse in institutions, these initiatives are important in the prevention of such abuse in all contexts. At the least formal level, these initiatives involve simply encouraging anyone who has any knowledge or suspicion of child sexual abuse to report it to the proper investigative authorities. The cost of such encouragement is minimal and the payoff potentially great.

At the most formal level, bystander encouragement takes the form of legally requiring any person who is aware of, or has reason to suspect, child sexual abuse to report it to the authorities. Such laws are rarely enforced and thus have virtually no cost but might increase the likelihood that some bystanders who know of or suspect child sexual abuse will report it. For that reason alone, states that have not adopted such laws should do so, even if there is no genuine expectation that they will be regularly enforced.

Another form of bystander intervention involves professionals, many of whom are required by law to report reasonable suspicions of child abuse, including child sexual abuse. This is known as mandated reporting and every state has some form of it. However, the efficacy of these laws is unknown and they too are rarely enforced. Still, these laws are worth retaining for at least two reasons. First, they probably result in some reports of child sexual abuse that would not be made without them; in cases where child sexual abuse is suspected but not clearly established, such laws may encourage professionals to err on the side of caution and make a report. Second, mandated reporter laws make it clear that the confidentiality and privilege usually associated with communications between clients/patients and professionals is effectively waived, as a matter of law, when there are reasons to suspect child abuse.

One final form of bystander mobilization worth noting relates to adults who have sex with children who are being prostituted. Clearly, it would be helpful if individuals who become aware of such children recognized what is happening to them as a form of child sexual abuse and reported it as such. It would also undoubtedly be helpful if law enforcement officials recognized that most of these children are not prostitutes who require punishment but victims who require help. A more direct educational route to prevention in this context may be criminally prosecuting adults who patronize underage prostitutes for all the crimes they have committed—not only patronizing a prostitute but statutory rape and child endangerment. Making adults who are tempted to engage in acts of prostitution with children aware of the full criminality of such conduct might help some avoid that temptation and, in some instances, turn would-be victimizers into mobilized bystanders.

Rescuing, Treating, and Rehabilitating Child Victims of Prostitution

In recent years, hundreds of children in the United States have been liberated from pimps and others who have forced them into prostitution. The number of such children rescued outside the United States is unknown but probably even greater. Clearly, rescuing these children from sexual slavery helps prevent child sexual abuse, albeit among a group of youngsters who have already been severely victimized. It also seems clear that rescue, by itself, is not sufficient to keep many of these children from revictimization. Although empirical data are lacking, it seems to go almost without saying that providing child victims of prostitution with shelter, supervision, treatment, and rehabilitation is necessary to keep some of them from returning to the abusive and exploitative circumstances from which they were rescued.

Exercising Extraterritorial Jurisdiction to Prosecute Child Sex Tourists

In recent decades, some Americans have traveled to other countries to engage in sex with minors, often young children. Many of the victims of this phenomenon, known as sex tourism, are locals but some have been transported to the destination country by sex traffickers. Because many of the destination countries had lax laws and limited investigative and prosecutorial resources, and/or because many sex tourists departed before their sexual activities with minors were reported, few were ever held criminally responsible.[1] Since 2003, however, US law has permitted the prosecution of Americans who sexually exploit children abroad if their conduct would have been illegal in the United States, regardless of whether it was a crime in the destination country. As of 2012, a total of 99 Americans had been arrested for sex tourism offenses outside the United States; all were convicted.[2]

Although this number appears small relative to estimates of the number of persons committing these offenses, improved enforcement would likely result in more arrests and convictions which, in turn, would probably strengthen the deterrent effect of the sex tourism laws.

Limiting the Sexualization of Children

It is often suggested that the sexual abuse of children is fueled in part by the way modern society, particularly the media, sexualizes children. It is believed that depicting children as sexually savvy, attractive, and/or seductive tends to normalize sexual feelings toward children and even encourage some adults to act on those feelings. Unfortunately, there is a dearth of empirical data on the effects of the sexualization of children. This is clearly a concern that needs further research. However, given that the sexualization of children might itself be reasonably regarded as a form of child sexual exploitation, society can ill afford to wait for solid empirical evidence before making greater efforts to deal with this problem.

Background Checks for those Who Work with Children

Today virtually all states require fingerprint and criminal background checks on applicants for jobs working with children in public schools and licensed day-care facilities. Many private schools, day-care facilities, and private youth-serving agencies are exempt from these requirements but may choose to impose them. Fingerprint and criminal background checks may prevent some sexual abusers and potential abusers from having access to children, but since most sex offenders are first-time offenders, such screening probably does not exclude most potential sex abusers from being employed or allowed to volunteer in schools, day-care centers, or youth-serving agencies.

Criminal background checks that do not include fingerprints may fail to identify applicants who have criminal records but have changed their names or used aliases on their applications. Even fingerprint checks have been found to be less than perfect in identifying individuals with criminal records. However, the major concern about background checks is their cost effectiveness. Only an extremely small percentage of applicants that submit to criminal background checks, even including fingerprinting, will be identified as convicted criminals, much less sex offenders. Because of the cost of criminal background/fingerprint checks (estimated to be between $18 and $24 each) and the extremely low "hit rate" in identifying applicants with troubling criminal records, the overall cost of identifying each such offender via these checks appears to be in excess of $35,000.

In the eyes of some, keeping even one sex offender from working or volunteering with children is a worthwhile investment, no matter what the cost. As a practical political matter, it seems extremely unlikely that any state will repeal its current requirement regarding employees of public schools or licensed day-care centers, no matter what the cost or who pays it. Thus, the more significant question may be whether youth-serving organizations not required by law to conduct criminal background and/or fingerprint checks should be required to do so or should voluntarily do so. That is a determination that must be made by each state and/or organization. However, in making that determination, it should be kept in mind that these checks are not only costly, far from perfect, and unlikely to identify most potential sexual abusers, but their use may give parents and children a false sense of security.

Psychological and Other Screening of Applicants

In an effort to weed out those who might be at risk for sexually abusing children, the Catholic Church and some other religious denominations have imposed mandatory psychological screening on those who wish to become ordained clergy. Largely because of its costs, formal psychological screening is rarely used in other youth-serving contexts. However, numerous youth-serving organizations use interviews, applications, and reference checks to screen applicants for positions working or volunteering with children.

If formal psychological screening (e.g., examination by a mental health professional and/or psychological testing) identifies individuals not psychologically fit for a clerical vocation, some so identified may be potential child sex abusers. However, there are no psychological tests or procedures that can validly identify a current or potential child sexual abuser. Conversely, simply because an applicant does not appear, through psychological assessment, to suffer from a mental illness or personality disorder does not mean that he or she is not a potential child sexual abuser.

In addition to fingerprint and background checks, youth-serving agencies and organizations have been encouraged to use both a written application and personal interview to screen potential employees and volunteers. However, there is no evidence that using a written application and/or personal interview for would-be volunteers and employees of youth-serving organizations will reduce the risk of child sexual abuse within those groups. Applicants for these positions may lie on an application and/or during a personal interview. More importantly, however, there are no questions that reliably identify potential child sexual abusers and differentiate them from applicants who would not pose a risk to children.

Still, formal applications and personal interviews may not be wholly without preventive value. Applications and interviews that include pointed questions make it clear to applicants that an organization is serious about screening out individuals who might put children at risk. Moreover, the formality of the application and interview may deter some would-be abusers from applying for fear that they might be identified as risks to children and embarrassed by their exclusion.

Similarly, there is no evidence that reference checks on an applicant who wants to work or volunteer with children will be effective in screening out would-be child sex abusers. However, simply making it clear to applicants that they must provide references, and that these references will be carefully checked, may deter applications from some who are seeking to gain access to children for sexual purposes.

Training Employees and Volunteers

In the wake of nationally publicized scandals and lawsuits as well as recommendations from government agencies, many if not most youth-serving organizations now make efforts to train their employees and volunteers in at least the basics of preventing, recognizing, and reporting child sexual abuse. This training ranges from dozens of hours of in-person lectures with ongoing follow-up to a half-hour or less of watching a superficial online video. There is a danger that when organizations publicize such training (especially when it is minimal) parents, children, bystanders, and even other employees or volunteers may let their guard down when it comes to child sexual abuse, assuming incorrectly that this training is generally effective. However, where this training is mandatory, extensive, and ongoing, it is hard to believe that it will not have at least some preventive effect, even if that effect is only secondary or tertiary in nature.

Zero Tolerance Policies

It would seem to go without saying that an employee or volunteer found to have sexually abused a child should be barred from any further involvement with any youth-serving organization. In most instances today that is taken for granted with regard to public schools, juvenile detention centers, licensed day-care centers, and many private youth-serving organizations, at least if the individual in question has a criminal conviction for sexual abuse. However, there are critics of this policy who believe that it does not take into account rehabilitation of sex offenders and the need for forgiveness, particularly in religious organizations. For example, some have questioned the zero tolerance policy of the Catholic Church, which provides that a member of the ordained clergy who admits to, or is found to have committed, "even a single act of sexual abuse" is to be "permanently removed from ministry."[3]

In the absence of empirical data, it is impossible to determine whether zero tolerance policies have helped prevent child sexual abuse. The recidivism rate for child sex offenders is rather low, but allowing known child sexual abusers to work or volunteer with children would almost certainly increase the risk to at least some children and probably increase the discomfort of many others.

Changing the Way Allegations of Child Sexual Abuse are Investigated

It is generally acknowledged that investigating allegations of child sexual abuse has significant potential for further harming a child who has already been traumatized and that particular care must be taken to gather evidence that is likely to be admissible in court and result in criminal convictions. Over the past three decades, in efforts to make child sexual abuse investigations less traumatic for alleged child victims and more likely to develop admissible evidence leading to successful prosecution of abusers, more than 700 Children's Advocacy Centers (CACs) have been opened in the United States. CACs were designed to coordinate all aspects of child sexual abuse investigation and intervention "by bringing together professionals and agencies as a multidisciplinary team to create a child-focused approach to child abuse cases."[4] Today, CACs receive substantial government funding and are often touted as offering state of the art procedures for investigating child sexual abuse allegations.

What little research has been done on the efficacy of CACs has shown mixed results. Parents and other caregivers who deal with CACs appear to be more satisfied with the investigative process than those who work with other agencies, but not significantly more likely to feel better about how troubled their children were during the investigation or about the number of interviews their children experienced. In fact, it appears that children whose cases are investigated by CACs are exposed to more rather than fewer interviews than those whose cases are handled elsewhere. Moreover, investigations conducted by CACs seem much more likely to include potentially traumatic physical examinations of alleged child victims. Perhaps most concerning of all, it appears that processing child sexual abuse investigations through a CAC leads to more prosecutions but not to more convictions—a finding that raises doubt as to whether the CAC investigative model is preferable to other approaches in terms of obtaining convincing legal evidence of child sexual abuse.

If CACs perform as intended, they have great potential for decreasing the risk that child sexual abuse victims will be further victimized, mitigating the psychological and/or physical harm already done to such victims, and assisting in the successful prosecution of individuals who might otherwise continue to sexually victimize children. However, to date, the CAC model has not proven more effective than other more traditional, less well-developed, and less highly funded investigative approaches.

STRATEGIES THAT ARE PROBABLY INEFFECTIVE OR COUNTERPRODUCTIVE IN PREVENTING CHILD SEXUAL ABUSE

Several strategies that have been motivated in part or whole by a desire to prevent child sexual abuse are probably ineffective in that regard. Indeed, some of these strategies may, in the long run, increase rather than decrease the incidence of child sexual abuse.

Extending or Abolishing Statutes of Limitation

In efforts to enable more alleged victims of child sexual abuse to pursue lawsuits or prosecutions against their abusers, many jurisdictions have extended or abolished time limitations for initiating such litigation. These efforts are grounded in the understandable and documented concern that many victims of child sexual abuse do not fully comprehend the nature of their abuse until years, perhaps even decades, after it occurs. Prior to these efforts, this problem was handled in most states by tolling the statute of limitations until the alleged victim reached the age of maturity. Thus, for example, where the limitation for filing a tort lawsuit was 3 years from the date of injury, an alleged victim of child sexual abuse would be allowed to bring a lawsuit anytime within 3 years of reaching legal maturity. There were, however, no similar exceptions for criminal prosecutions.

Laws extending or abolishing time limitations for civil suits and criminal prosecutions in child sexual abuse cases may offer some victims an opportunity for justice they would not otherwise have had. At the same time, however, these laws create hardships for alleged offenders who may be required to defend themselves against charges that are decades old and for a justice system that is required to make just decisions where crucial evidence may be stale, lost, or forgotten. More importantly in the present context, there is no evidence that abolishing or expanding the time periods in which alleged child sexual abusers may be subjected to litigation has any incremental deterrent effect on would-be child sexual abusers. Many acts of child sexual abuse are spontaneous and opportunistic and most unlikely to be affected by considerations as arcane and remote as the statutes of limitation. Abolishing criminal statutes of limitation in child sex abuse cases might result in more abusers being incarcerated and thus unable to reoffend, but even that is doubtful in many cases. Given the difficulties in obtaining convictions even in child sexual abuse cases that are prosecuted in a timely manner, it is hard to imagine a high rate of conviction in criminal prosecutions for child sexual abuse brought many years or decades after the alleged abuse.

Enhancing Criminal Penalties for Child Sex Offenders

Extremely harsh criminal penalties for child sex offenders may serve the purposes of denunciation, retribution, and incapacitation, but do they make a significant contribution to modern efforts to prevent child sexual abuse? Data on crime in general show a correlation between increased rates of incarceration and lower rates of crime. However, that relationship is thought to be largely a function of incapacitation rather than deterrence, because length of sentence by itself seems to be unrelated to recidivism.[5]

Long-term incapacitation of child sex offenders appears on its face to be a worthy goal. It is, however, extremely expensive and often unnecessary because the recidivism rate for child sex offenders is rather low. Thus, while extremely severe criminal sanctions may stop some child sexual abusers from reoffending, the number so affected is likely to be relatively small. In terms of cost effectiveness, sentencing child sex offenders to extremely lengthy prison terms will often mean paying huge sums of money to prevent what is not likely to have occurred without such lengthy confinement.

Also, the extraordinarily severe criminal sanctions imposed upon some child sex offenders both reflect and fuel the growing stigmatization of such offenders in today's world. That stigmatization, which often might be better characterized as demonization, makes it more difficult for child sex offenders to be rehabilitated, which in turn may increase their likelihood of reoffending. Finally, it is possible that if penalties for less serious child sex offenses become too harsh, they may be perceived as grossly disproportionate, and judges and juries may balk at convicting some defendants charged with these crimes, even when the evidence is compelling.

Civil Commitment of Child Sex Offenders

Twenty states and the federal government have sexually violent predator (SVP) laws that allow convicted sex offenders to be court-ordered into indefinite secure confinement after they have completed their prison sentences. Like enhancements to criminal punishment for sex offenders, SVP laws add to the length a time an offender is incarcerated and thus incapacitated from reoffending. SVP laws thus raise the same concerns that were just discussed with regard to enhanced sentences for convicted sex offenders. Confinement under these laws requires multiple costly layers of extraordinary review by mental health professionals and the courts, includes high-priced and constitutionally mandated but unproven psychological treatment, and is much more expensive than imprisonment or parole supervision in the community.

Given the huge costs of implementing SVP statutes, the remarkably low rate of recidivism among sex offenders, the extraordinary difficulties conscientious mental health experts have in predicting which sex offenders are likely to reoffend, and the lack of evidence that these laws prevent future sexual offending, they make little sense as a means of preventing child sexual abuse. Like the extremely severe criminal sanctions just discussed, SVP laws might stop some child sex offenders from reoffending by confining them. However, given what is known about sex offender recidivism, it is more likely that these extremely costly laws are designed to prevent offenses that would not have occurred without them.

Worse, in terms of prevention, SVP laws may have negative effects. These widely publicized and highly popular laws may lead the public to believe that the most dangerous sex offenders have been removed from society indefinitely, lull parents and other child caretakers into a false sense of security, and lead society to be less cautious when it comes to protecting children from sexual abuse. Also, implementation of these laws seems bound to enhance the deep revulsion and enmity the public already feels toward sex offenders and, in so doing, make their rehabilitation and safe return to society more difficult.

Sex Offender Registration and Notification

Under state Megan's Laws as well as the federal Sex Offender Registration and Notification Act, convicted sex offenders are required to register with law enforcement officials annually and may have their photographs, names, offenses, and other identifying information made available to the public on state and federal websites. The ostensible goal of these laws is to prevent sex offending by making the public aware of convicted sex offenders living in the community. It is believed that by publicizing information about these offenders (including their home addresses), members of the public will be warned of their presence, recognize the risk they pose, and make appropriate efforts to avoid that risk to themselves and/ or their children.

Legislatures and the courts have concluded that common sense suggests that these laws will be effective in preventing sex offender recidivism. The first problem with these laws is that many of them were enacted on the basis of grossly inflated estimates of sex offender recidivism. The second problem is that these common sense assumptions are not supported by data. The consensus of empirical research is that sex offender registration and notification laws do not significantly affect sex offender recidivism and thus fail to provide the public protection upon which they are premised.

Third, and perhaps more importantly, sex offender registration and notification laws may *increase* the likelihood that convicted sex offenders will recidivate. As a result of such laws, these offenders may be shunned, ostracized, threatened, and driven from communities, thus making it less likely that they will receive the treatment, stability, and support many need to avoid reoffending.

Occupational, Residency, and Travel Restrictions

As a practical if not legal matter, convicted sex offenders, whether or not their offenses were against children, are barred from most public and many private jobs involving work with children. Public and private rules preventing convicted sex offenders from serving as teachers, school bus drivers, day-care providers, clergy, or even volunteers in youth-serving agencies are undoubtedly overinclusive and needlessly bar some individuals from pursuing careers or avocations. Although the recidivism rate among these offenders is low, these laws and rules are sensible because they probably marginally reduce the risk of child sexual abuse and definitely reduce the likelihood of institutional liability. Schools or other youth-serving organizations that hired a sex offender who then sexually abused a child would almost surely be the targets of successful lawsuits for negligent hiring.

However, the same reasoning does not apply to widespread laws that limit where convicted sex offenders may live or travel. Most states and many municipalities have enacted laws that preclude convicted sex offenders from living in areas near (e.g., 500–2,500 feet from) schools, childcare centers, playgrounds or other places where children congregate. Some have laws barring such offenders from working or even being in these areas.

In many instances, these laws work extreme hardships on convicted sex offenders who would be unlikely to reoffend without them and even more unlikely to reoffend in areas in which they live, work, and are thus known to others. These laws have forced such offenders to move from their homes, prevented them from living with supportive family members, made it extremely difficult if not impossible for them to find housing in some areas, and have driven some into homelessness. In many cases, these laws have also limited employment opportunities for sex offenders, whose chances of finding work are often already severely hampered by their offense records and presence on sex offender registries.

Overall, these residency and travel laws appear to have no demonstrable impact on child safety. Worse, they may have the effect of decreasing child safety because they often isolate sex offenders from their families and support systems, undermine their ability to support themselves financially, and thus interfere with their transition from incarcerated offenders to law-abiding citizens living in the community.

NOTES

CHAPTER 1

1. Bruce Rind, Philip Tromovitch, and Robert Bauserman, "A meta-analytic examination of assumed properties of child sexual abuse using college samples," *Psychological Bulletin* (1998): 124(1), 22–53.
2. American Academy of Child and Adolescent Psychiatry, Facts for Families, No. 9 (March 2011). Available at: http://www.aacap.org/galleries/FactsForFamilies/09_child_sexual_abuse.pdf (accessed May 7, 2013).
3. Sharon LaFraniere, "The relentless scourge of child sexual abuse take an endless toll on girls in sub-Saharan Africa—Africa & Middle East," *New York Times*, Thursday, November 30, 2006. Available at: http://www.nytimes.com/2006/11/30/world/africa/30ihtafrica.3731273.html?pagewanted=all&_r=0 (accessed April 28, 2013).
4. Tulir CPHCSA and Save the Children Sweden, "Doesn't every child count? Research on prevalence & dynamics of child sexual abuse among school going children in Chennai" (2006). Available at: http://www.tulir.org/images/pdf/Research%20Report1.pdf (accessed April 28, 2013).
5. John P. J. Dussich, "Japanese childhood victims of sexual abuse and their social perceptions: Comparisons with children in Germany, Greece and the USA," *International Review of Victimology* (January 2006): 13(1), 99–113.
6. Leroy G. Schultz, "Child sexual abuse in historical perspective," *Journal of Social Work & Human Sexuality* (1982): 1(1–2), 21–35, 21.
7. Carolyn Hilarski, John S. Wodarski, and Marvin D. Feit (Eds.), *Handbook of social work in child and adolescent sexual abuse* (2008): 5, Haworth Press, New York NY.
8. Schultz, *supra* note 6, 21.
9. John Lascaratos and Effie Poulakou-Rebelakou, "Child sexual abuse: Historical cases in the Byzantine Empire (324-1453 A.D.)," *Child Abuse & Neglect* (2000): 24(8), 1085–1090, 1087.
10. Ibid., 1088.
11. Ibid.
12. Hilarski et al., *supra* note 7, 9.
13. Guido Ruggiero, *The boundaries of Eros* (1985): 149–150, New York, Oxford University Press.
14. William Naphy, *Sex crimes from Renaissance to Enlightenment, Gloucestershire, England* (2004): 141, Gloucestershire, England, Tempus Publishing Limited.
15. Karen Liebreich, *Fallen order* (2004): 68, New York, Grove Press.

16. Naphy, *supra* note 14, 141.

17. Ibid., 136.

18. Hilarski et al., *supra* note 12, 15.

19. Ibid.

20. Lynn Sacco, *Unspeakable: Father-daughter incest in American history* (2009): 34, Baltimore, Johns Hopkins University Press.

21. Ibid., 34–35.

22. Ibid., 38.

23. Rebecca Bolen, *Child sexual abuse: Its scope and our failure* (2001): 14, New York, Kluwer Academic.

24. Ibid.

25. Linda Gordon, "The politics of child sexual abuse: Notes from American History," *Feminist Review* (Spring 1988): 56–64, 58 [emphasis in original].

26. Estelle B. Freedman, "'Uncontrolled desires': The response to the sexual psychopath, 1920-1960," *Journal of American History* (1987): 74(1), 83–106, 92.

27. Lauretta Bender and Abram Blau, "The reaction of children to sexual relations with adults," *American Journal of Orthopsychiatry* (1937): 7, 500–518, 514.

28. Edwin H. Sutherland, "The sexual psychopath laws," *Journal of Criminal Law and Criminology* (1950): 40(5), 543–554, 544.

29. Freedman, *supra* note 26, 83–84.

30. Lauretta Bender and Alvin Grugett, "A follow-up report on children who had atypical sexual experiences," *American Journal of Orthopsychiatry* (1952): 22(4), 825–837, 826.

31. Alfred Kinsey, Wardell Pomeroy, Clyde Martin, and Paul Gebhard, *Sexual behavior in the human female* (1953): 121, Philadelphia, Saunders.

32. Erna Olafson, David L. Corwin, and Roland C. Summit, "Modern history of child sexual abuse awareness: Cycles of discovery and suppression," *Child Abuse & Neglect* (January-February 1993): 17(1), 7–24, 15.

33. Bolen, *supra* note 23, 21.

34. Olafson et al., *supra* note 32, 15.

35. Nancy Whittier, *The politics of child sexual abuse* (2009): 5, New York, Oxford University Press.

36. Ibid.

37. Diana Russell and Rebecca Bolen, *The epidemic of rape and child sexual abuse in the United States* (2000): 159, Thousand Oaks, California, Sage Publications.

38. Ibid.

39. Ibid.

40. Ibid., 160.

41. Ibid., 164.

42. Ibid.

43. David Finkelhor, Gerald Hotaling, I.A. Lewis, and Christine Smith, "Sexual abuse in a national survey of adult men and women: Prevalence, characteristics and risk factors," *Child Abuse & Neglect* (1990): 14, 19–28.

44. Ibid.

45. Ibid.

46. Diana E. H. Russell and Nicole Van de Ven, *Crimes against women: Proceedings of the International Tribunal* (1990): 110–111, Berkeley, California, Russell Publications.

47. Judith Lewis Herman, *Sex offenders: A feminist perspective* (1990). In W. L. Marshall, D. R. Laws, & H. E. Barbaree (Eds.), *Handbook of sexual assault: Issues, theories and the treatment of the offender* (1990): 177–190 at 178, New York, Springer Publishing.
48. Whittier, *supra* note 35, 127.
49. Ellen Bass and Laura Davis, *The courage to heal: A guide for women survivors of child sexual Abuse* (1988): 71, New York, Perennial Library.
50. Ibid., 21.
51. Ibid., 22.
52. Carol Tavris, "Beware the incest-survivor machine," *New York Times*, January 3, 1993. Available at: http://www.nytimes.com/1993/01/03/books/beware-the-incest-survivormachine.html?pagewanted=all&src=pm (accessed April 29, 2013).
53. Whittier, *supra* note 35, 128.
54. Olafson et al., *supra* note 32, 18.
55. David Hechler, *The battle and the backlash: The child sexual abuse war* (1988): 7, Lexington, Massachusetts, Lexington Books.
56. Ibid., 9.
57. Jon R. Conte, "Child sexual abuse: Awareness and backlash," *Sexual Abuse of Children* (Summer/Fall 1994): 4(2), 224–232, 228.
58. Ibid., 229.
59. Ibid.
60. Jerry Seper, "System fails to stop repeat offenders," *Washington Times*, December 15, 1993, A7.
61. Washington Revised Code § 71.09.020(1) *et seq.*
62. *See, generally,* Charles Patrick Ewing, *Justice perverted: Sex offense law, psychology and public policy* (2011): 76–81, New York, Oxford University Press.
63. Richard Meryhew, "Hope keeps search for Jacob going: Ten years and thousands of leads have come and gone, but the abduction of Jacob Wetterling still grips St. Joseph and the investigators who have poured their lives and hearts into the case," *Minneapolis Star Tribune*, October 22, 1999, 1B.
64. Mary Divine, "After 20 years, Minnesota still wonders, Where's Jacob?" *St. Paul Pioneer Press*, October 21, 2009, 1.
65. *See* Ewing, *supra* note 62, 76–83.
66. Ibid., 83–92.
67. Susan J. Creighton, "Child pornography: Images of the abuse of children" (November 2003): 1–7, 1. Available at: http://www.nspcc.org.uk/Applications/Search/Search.aspx (accessed May 4, 2010).
68. David Finkelhor, Kimberly J. Mitchell, and Janis Wolak, "Online victimization: A report on the nation's youth" (June 2000). Available at: http://www.unh.edu/ccrc/pdf/jvq/CV38.pdf (accessed April 30, 2013).
69. Ibid., 6.
70. Janis Wolak, Kimberly Mitchell, and David Finkelhor, "Internet sex crimes against minors: The response of law enforcement" (November 2003): 1. Available at: www.unh.edu/ccrc/pdf/CV70.pdf (accessed April 30, 2013).
71. Janis Wolak, Kimberly Mitchell, and David Finkelhor, "Online victimization of youth: Five years later" (2006). Available at: www.unh.edu/ccrc/pdf/CV138.pdf (accessed April 30, 2013).
72. Ibid., 21.

73. 18 U.S.C. § 2422.

74. Pub. L. No. 108-21, § 103(a)(2)(B), (b)(2)(A).

75. Pub. L. No. 109–248.

76. 18 U.S.C. § 2423 (Supp. 2004).

77. *See, generally,* Ewing, *supra* note 62.

78. Human Rights Watch, *No easy answers for sex offenders* (2007): 9. Available at: www. hrw.org/en/reports/2007/09/11/no-easy-answers (accessed April 10, 2013).

79. Jay Albanese, "Commercial sexual exploitation of children: What do we know and what do we do about it?" Washington, DC: US Department of Justice Office of Justice Programs (2007): 1.

80. George Santayana, *The life of reason* (1906): 35, New York, Charles Scribner's Sons.

81. Association for the Treatment of Sexual Abusers, "Sexual abuse as a public health problem" (2011). Available at: http://www.atsa.com/sexual-ab use-public-health-problem (accessed April 30, 2013).

CHAPTER 2

1. Association for the Treatment of Sexual Abusers, "Sexual abuse as a public health problem" (2011). Available at: http://www.atsa.com/sexual-ab use-public-health-problem (accessed April 30, 2013).

2. *See, generally,* New York State Department of Health, "Basic statistics: About incidence, prevalence, morbidity, and mortality—statistics teaching tools." Available at: http://www.health.ny.gov/diseases/chronic/basicstat.htm (accessed April 30, 2013).

3. US Department of Health & Human Services, Administration for Children and Families, Administration on Children, Youth and Families, Children's Bureau, "Child maltreatment 2010," (2010): viii.

4. Ibid., ix.

5. Ibid., 21.

6. Ibid., ix.

7. Ibid., 24.

8. Ibid., 133.

9. *See* Child Maltreatment 2010, *supra* note 3 and Child Maltreatment (annual issues 2000 through 2010, published by US Department of Health & Human Services, Administration for Children and Families, Administration on Children, Youth and Families, Children's Bureau).

10. Harriet L. MacMillan, Ellen Jamieson, and Christine A. Walsh, "Reported contact with child protection services among those reporting child physical and sexual abuse: Results from a community survey," *Child Abuse & Neglect* (2003): 1397–1408, 1399.

11. Ibid., 1399–1400.

12. Ibid., 1400.

13. Ibid., 1402.

14. US Department of Health and Human Services, Fourth National Incidence Study of Child Abuse and Neglect (NIS-4): Report to Congress (January 15, 2010). Available at: http://www.acf.hhs.gov/sites/default/files/opre/nis4_report_congress_full_pdf_jan2010.pdf (accessed April 30, 2013).

15. Ibid., 2–3.

16. Ibid., 3.

17. Ibid.

18. Ibid., 3–7.

19. Ibid.

20. Ibid.

21. Ibid.

22. Ibid., 6.

23. Ibid., 7.

24. Andrea J. Sedlak, "A history of the national incidence study of child abuse and neglect," (2001): 2. Available at: http://www.docin.com/p-371939586.html (accessed April 30, 2013).

25. Fourth National Incidence Study of Child Abuse and Neglect (NIS-4): Report to Congress, *supra* note 14, 3–7.

26. Ibid.

27. "Developmental Victimization Survey," University of New Hampshire, Crimes Against Children Research Center. Available at: http://www.unh.edu/ccrc/projects/ developmental_victimization_survey.html (accessed April 30, 2013).

28. Ibid.

29. Heather Turner and David Finkelhor, "Developmental Victimization Survey (DVS) 2002-2003 NDACAN Dataset Number 126 User's Guide and Codebook," (2007): 3. Available at: http://www.ndacan.cornell.edu/ndacan/Datasets/ UserGuidePDFs/126user.pdf (accessed April 30, 2013).

30. Ibid.

31. David Finkelhor, Sherry L. Hamby, Richard Ormroda, and Heather Turner, "The Juvenile Victimization Questionnaire: Reliability, validity, and national norms," *Child Abuse & Neglect* (2005): 29, 383–412, 406.

32. David Finkelhor, Richard Ormrod, Heather Turner, and Sherry Hamby, "The victimization of children and youth: A comprehensive, national survey," *Child Maltreatment* (February 2005): 10(1), 5–25, 10.

33. Ibid.

34. Ibid., 11.

35. David Finkelhor, Richard Ormrod, and Heather Turner, "Re-victimization patterns in a national longitudinal sample of children and youth," *Child Abuse & Neglect* (2007): 31, 479–502, 492.

36. Diana Russell and Rebecca Bolen, *The epidemic of rape and child sexual abuse in the United States* (2000): 159, Thousand Oaks, California, Sage Publications.

37. Ibid., 33.

38. Ibid., 162.

39. Ibid.

40. Ibid., 161–162.

41. Ibid., 163.

42. David Finkelhor, Gerald Hotaling, I.A. Lewis, and Christine Smith, "Sexual abuse in a national survey of adult men and women: Prevalence, characteristics and risk factors," *Child Abuse & Neglect*, (1990): 14, 19–28, 19.

43. Ibid., 20.

44. Ibid., 21.

45. Noemí Pereda, Georgina Guilera, Maria Forns, and Juana Gómez-Benito, "The prevalence of child sexual abuse in community and student samples: A meta-analysis," *Clinical Psychology Review* (June 2009): 29(4), 328–338, 328.

46. Ibid., 335.
47. Ibid.
48. Ibid., 329.
49. David Finkelhor, Heather Turner, Richard Ormrod, Sherry Hamby, and Kristen Kracke, "Children's exposure to violence: A comprehensive national survey," US Department of Justice, Office of Justice Programs, Office of Juvenile Justice and Delinquency Prevention (2009): 1. Available at: http://www.unh.edu/ccrc/pdf/ DOJ-NatSCEV-bulletin.pdf (accessed April 30, 2013).
50. Ibid., 2.
51. Ibid.
52. Ibid., 5–6.
53. US Department of Health and Human Services, Fourth National Incidence Study of Child Abuse and Neglect (NIS-4): Report to Congress (January 15, 2010): 6. Available at: http://www.acf.hhs.gov/sites/default/files/opre/nis4_report_ congress_full_pdf_jan2010.pdf (accessed April 30, 2013).
54. Ibid., 7.
55. David Finkelhor, Lisa Jones, and Anne Shattuck, "Updated trends in child maltreatment, 2008." Available at: http://www.unh.edu/ccrc/pdf/CV203_Updated%20Trends%20 in%20Child%20Maltreatment%202008_8-6-10.pdf (accessed April 30, 2013).
56. Lisa Jones and David Finkelhor, "The decline in child sexual abuse cases," *Juvenile Justice Bulletin*, Office of Juvenile Justice and Delinquency Prevention, US Department of Justice (January 2001): 5. Available at: http://www.attorneygeneral. jus.gov.on.ca/inquiries/cornwall/en/hearings/exhibits/Nico_Trocme/pdf/Decline. pdf (accessed April 30, 2013).
57. Ibid.
58. Joanna Almeida, Amy Cohen, S.V. Subramanian, and Beth Molnar, "Are increased worker caseloads in state child protective service agencies a potential explanation for the decline in child sexual abuse? A multilevel analysis," *Child Abuse & Neglect* (2008): 32, 367–375, 368.
59. Ibid.
60. Jones and Finkelhor, *supra* note 56, 4.
61. Fourth National Incidence Study of Child Abuse and Neglect (NIS-4): Report to Congress, *supra* note 53, 8.
62. Ibid., 4-2.
63. Finkelhor et al., *supra* note 49, 6.
64. Pereda et al., *supra* note 45, 333.
65. Ibid., 332.
66. S. N. Madu and K. Peltzer, "Risk factors and child sexual abuse among secondary students in the Northern Province (South Africa)," *Child Abuse & Neglect*, (2000): 24, 259–268, 265.
67. Pereda et al., *supra* note 45, 333.
68. *See generally*, William Holmes and Gail Slapp, "Sexual abuse of boys," *JAMA* (December 2, 1998): 280(21), 1855–1862; Elisa Romano and Rayleen V. De Luca, "Male sexual abuse: A review of effects, abuse characteristics, and links with later psychological functioning," *Aggression and Violent Behavior*, (2001): 6, 55–78.
69. David Finkelhor, Heather Hammer, and Andrea Sedlak, "Sexually assaulted children: National estimates and characteristics," US Department of Justice, Office of Justice

Programs, Office of Juvenile Justice and Delinquency Prevention (2008). Available at: ttps://www.ncjrs.gov/pdffiles1/ojjdp/214383.pdf (accessed April 30, 2013).

70. Fourth National Incidence Study of Child Abuse and Neglect (NIS-4): Report to Congress, *supra* note 53, 15.

71. Pareda et al., *supra* note 45, 234.

72. Emily Douglas and David Finkelhor, *Childhood sexual abuse fact sheet* (undated): 1–11, 7. Available at: http://www.unh.edu/ccrc/factsheet/pdf/CSA-FS20.pdf (accessed April 30, 2013).

73. Frank W. Putnam, "Ten-year research update review: Child sexual abuse," *Journal of the American Academy of Child & Adolescent Psychiatry* (March 2003): 42(3), 269–278, 270.

74. Ibid.

75. David Finkelhor, Heather Turner, Richard Ormrod, and Sherry Hamby, "Violence, abuse, and crime exposure in a national sample of children and youth," *Pediatrics* (November 1, 2009): 124(5), 1411–1423, 1414.

76. Fourth National Incidence Study of Child Abuse and Neglect (NIS-4): Report to Congress, *supra* note (2010): 53, 4–12.

77. Ibid.

78. David Finkelhor, Richard Ormrod, and Mark Chaffin, "Juveniles who commit sex offenses against minors," US Department of Justice, Office of Justice Programs, Office of Juvenile Justice and Delinquency Prevention (2009): 1. Available at: https://www.ncjrs.gov/pdffiles1/ojjdp/227763.pdf (accessed May 1, 2013).

79. Ibid., 2.

80. Ibid., 3.

81. Ibid., 4.

82. US Department of Health and Human Services, Administration on Children, Youth and Families, "Child maltreatment 2004," (2006). Available at: http://archive.acf.hhs.gov/programs/cb/pubs/cm04/cm04.pdf (accessed May 1, 2013).

83. Howard N. Snyder, "Sexual assault of young children as reported to law enforcement: Victim, incident, and offender characteristics sexual," US Department of Justice, Office of Justice Programs (July 2010). Available at: http://bjs.gov/content/pub/pdf/saycrle.pdf (accessed May 1, 2013).

84. Erna Olafson, David Corwin, and Roland Summit, "Modern history of child sexual abuse awareness: Cycles of discovery and suppression," *Child Abuse & Neglect* (January-February 1993): 17(1), 7–24, 15.

85. John H. Gagnon, "Female child victims of sex offenses," *Social Problems* (Autumn, 1965): 13(2), 176–192, 188.

86. Ibid.

87. Ibid., 188–189.

88. Ibid., 189.

89. R.S. Kempe and C.H. Kempe, *Child abuse* (1978): 55, London, Fontana/Open Books.

90. Susan A. Clancy, *The trauma myth: The truth about the sexual abuse of children—and its aftermath* (2009): 96, New York, Basic Books.

91. Ibid., 95.

92. Angela Browne and David Finkelhor, "Impact of child sexual abuse: A review of the research," *Psychological Bulletin* (1986): 99, 66–77, 66.

93. Ibid., 75.
94. *See, e.g.,* Marsha Briere and John Runtz "Multivariate correlates of childhood psychological and physical maltreatment among university women," *Child Abuse and Neglect* (1998): 12, 331–341; Bonnie Kessler and Kathleen Bieschke, "A retrospective analysis of shame, dissociation, and adult victimization in survivors of childhood sexual abuse," *Journal of Counseling Psychology* (1999): 46(3), 335–341.
95. *See, e.g.,* Christine Gidycz, Christie Coble, Lance Latham, and Melissa Layman, "Sexual assault experiences in adulthood and prior victimization experiences," *Psychology of Women Quarterly* (1993): 151–168; Sue Boney-McCoy and David Finkelhor, "Prior victimization: A risk factor for child sexual abuse and for PTSD-related symptomatology among sexually abused youth," *Child Abuse & Neglect* (1995): 1401–1421; Barbara Krahe, Renate Scheinberger-Olwig, Eva Waizenhofer, and Susanne Kolpin, "Childhood sexual abuse and revictimization in adolescence," *Child Abuse & Neglect* (April 1999): 23(4), 383–394.
96. *See, e.g.,* Gail Wyatt, Donald Guthrie, and Cindy Notgrass, "Differential effects of women's child sexual abuse and subsequent sexual revictimization," *Journal of Consulting and Clinical Psychology* (1992): 16(5), 67–173; Terri Messman and Patricia Long, "Child sexual abuse and its relationship to revictimization in adult women: A review." *Clinical Psychology Review* (1996): 23(4), 397–420; Louisa Gilbert, Nabila El-Bassel, Robert Schilling, and Ellen Friedman, "Childhood abuse as a risk for partner abuse among women in methadone maintenance," *American Journal of Drug and Alcohol Abuse* (1997): 23(4), 581–595.
97. *See, e.g.,* Bessel Van der Kolk, J. Christopher Perry, and Judith Herman, "Childhood origins of self-destructive behavior," *American Journal of Psychiatry* (1991): 148, 1665–1671; Ronald Winchel and Michael Stanley, "Self-injurious behavior: A review of the behavior and biology of self-mutilation," *American Journal of Psychiatry* (1991): 148, 306–317; Arne Boudewyn and Joan Liem, "Childhood sexual abuse as a precursor to depression and self-destructive behavior in adulthood," *Journal of Traumatic Stress* (1995): 8, 445–459; Sarah Romans, S.E., Judy Martin, Jessie Anderson, G. Peter Herbison, and Paul Mullen, "Sexual abuse in childhood and deliberate self-harm," *American Journal of Psychiatry* (1995): 152, 1336–1342.
98. *See* Wyatt et al., *supra* note 96.
99. *See, e.g.,* Sally Zierler, Lisa Feingold, Deborah Laufer, Priscilla Velentgas, Ira Kantrowitz-Gordon, and Kenneth Mayer, "Adult survivors of childhood sexual abuse and subsequent risk of HIV infection," *American Journal of Public Health* (May 1991): 572–575; Eric Rosenberg, Manuel Bayona, C. Hendricks Brown, and Steven Specter, "Epidemiologic factors correlated with multiple sexual partners among women receiving prenatal care," *Annals of Epidemiology* (November 1994): 4(6), 472–479.
100. *See, e.g.,* Paul Mullen, Judy Martin, Jessie Anderson, Sarah Romans, and G. Peter Herbison, "Childhood sexual abuse and mental health in adult life," *British Journal of Psychiatry* (1993): 163, 721–732.
101. *See, e.g.,* Damaris Rohsenow, Richard Corbett, and Donald Devine, "Molested as children: A hidden contribution to substance abuse?" *Journal of Substance Abuse Treatment* (1988): 13–18; Maria Root and Patricia Fallon, "The incidences of victimization experiences in a bulimic sample," *Journal of Interpersonal Violence*

(1988): 161–173; Judith Stein, Jaqueline Golding, Judith Siegel, Audrey Burnam, M. A., and Susan Sorenson, "Long-term psychological sequelae of child sexual abuse: The Los Angeles Epidemiologic Catchment Area Study," (1988) In G. E. Wyatt & G. J. Powell (Eds.), *Lasting effects of child sexual abuse* (pp. 135–154), Newbury Park, California, Sage; L. Hart, L. Mader, K. Griffith, and M. de Mendonca, "Effects of sexual and physical abuse: A comparison of adolescent inpatients," *Child Psychiatry and Human Development* (1989): 49–56; Elizabeth Pribor and Stephen Dinwiddie, "Psychiatric correlates of incest in childhood," *American Journal of Psychiatry* (1992): 52–56; Bill Watkins and Amon Bentovim, "The sexual abuse of male children and adolescents: a review of current research," *Journal of Child Psychology and Psychiatry* (1992): 197–248; Kathleen Kendall-Tackett, Linda Williams, and David Finkelhor, "The effects of sexual abuse on children: A review and synthesis of recent empirical findings," *Psychological Bulletin* (1993): 164–181; Mark Yama, Stephanie Tovey, and Bruce Fogas, "Childhood family environment and sexual abuse as predictors of anxiety and depression in adult women," *American Orthopsychiatric Association* (1993): 136–141; Gurmeet Dhaliwal, Larry Gauzas, Daniel Antonowicz, and Robert Ross, "Adult male survivors of childhood sexual abuse: Prevalence, sexual abuse characteristics, and long-term effects," *Clinical Psychology Review* (1996): 619–639; Paul Mullen, Judy Martin, Jessie Anderson, Sarah Romans, and G. Peter Herbison, "The long-term impact of the physical, emotional and sexual abuse of children: a community study," *Child Abuse & Neglect* (1996): 20, 7–22.

102. *See, e.g.,* Jon Conte and John Schuerman, "Factors associated with an increased impact of child sexual abuse," *Child Abuse & Neglect* (1987): 201–211; William Friedrich, Robert Beilke, and Anthony Urquiza, "Behavior problems in young sexually abused boys: A comparison study," *Journal of Interpersonal Violence* (March 1988): 21–28; Gail Wyatt and M. Mickey, "Ameliorating the effects of child sexual abuse: An exploratory study of support by parents and others," *Journal of Interpersonal Violence*, (1987): 2, 403–414.

103. *See, e.g.,* Mary Ellen Fromuth, "The relationship of childhood sexual abuse with later psychological and sexual adjustment in a sample of college women," *Child Abuse & Neglect* (1986): 10(1), 5–15.

104. *See, e.g.,* Paul Mullen, Judy Martin, Jessie Anderson, et al., "Childhood sexual abuse and mental health in adult life," *British Journal of Psychiatry* (1993): 163, 721–732; Paul Mullen, Judy Martin, Jessie Anderson, et al., "The effect of child sexual abuse on social, interpersonal and sexual function in adult life," *British Journal of Psychiatry* (1994): 165, 35–47; George Cooney, "Self-esteem, depression, behaviour and family functioning in sexually abused children," *Journal of Child Psychology and Psychiatry* (1995): 36(6), 1077–1089; Anne Stern, Deborah Lynch, R. Kim Oates, et al., "Self-esteem, depression, behaviour and family functioning in sexually abused children," *Journal of Child Psychology and Psychiatry* (1995): 36, 1077–1090; Sarah Romans, Judy Martin, and Paul Mullen, "Childhood sexual abuse and later psychological problems: Neither necessary, sufficient nor acting along," *Criminal Behaviour and Mental Health* (1997): 7, 327–338.

105. *See, e.g.,* Valerie Whiffen and Sharon Clark, "Does victimization account for sex differences in depressive symptoms?" *British Journal of Clinical Psychology* (1997): 36, 185–193; Kendall-Tackett et al., *supra* note 101; Mullen et al., *supra*

note 100; M. Windle, R. Windle, D. Scheidt, and G. Miller, "Physical and sexual abuse and associated mental disorders among alcoholic inpatients," *American Journal of Psychiatry* (1995): 152, 1322–1328; Vaughn Heath, Roy Bean, and Leslie Feinauer, "Severity of childhood sexual abuse symptom differences between men and women," *The American Journal of Family Therapy* (1996): 24(4), 305–314.

106. *See, e.g.,* Pamela Alexander, "Application of attachment theory to the study of sexual abuse," *Journal of Consulting and Clinical Psychology* (1992): 60, 185–195.

107. *See, e.g.,* Kendall-Tackett et al., *supra* note 101.

108. *See, e.g.,* Briere and Runtz, *supra* note 94.

109. *See, e.g.,* David Fergusson, Michael Lynskey, and John Horwood, "Childhood sexual abuse and psychiatric disorder in young adulthood: I. Prevalence of sexual abuse and factors associated with sexual abuse," *Journal of the American Academy of Child & Adolescent Psychiatry* (1996): 35, 1355–1364.

110. *See, e.g.,* Kendall-Tackett et al., *supra* note 101; Joel Paris, Hallie Zweig-Frank, Jaswant Guzder, "Psychological risk factors for borderline personality disorder in female patients," *Comprehensive Psychiatry* (1994): 35(4), 301–305; Arne Boudewyn and Joan Liem, "Childhood sexual abuse as a precursor to depression and self-destructive behavior in adulthood," *Journal of Traumatic Stress* (1995): 8, 445–459; N. Rodriguez, S.W. Ryan, A.B. Rowan, and D.W. Foy, "Post-traumatic stress disorder in a clinical sample of adult survivors of childhood sexual abuse," *Child Abuse & Neglect* (1996): 20(10), 943–952.

111. *See, e.g.,* Johann Kinzl, Christian Traweger, and Wilfried Biebl, "Sexual dysfunctions: Relationship to childhood sexual abuse and early family experiences in a nonclinical sample," *Child Abuse & Neglect* (July 1995): 19(7), 785–792.

112. Bruce Rind, Philip Tromovitch, and Robert Bauserman, "Condemnation of a scientific article," *Sexuality & Culture* (Spring 2000): 4(2), 1–62.

113. Ibid., 9.

114. Ibid.

115. Rind et al., *supra* note 112, 15.

116. Bruce Rind, Philip Tromovitch, and Robert Bauserman, "A meta-analytic examination of assumed properties of child sexual abuse using college samples," *Psychological Bulletin* (1998): 124, 22–53, 42.

117. Ibid.

118. Scott O. Lilienfeld, When Worlds Collide: Social Science, Politics, and the Rind et al. (1998) Child Sexual Abuse Meta-Analysis, *American Psychologist*, 2002, v. 57, No. 3, 176–188 (2008) at 178.

119. Ibid.

120. Ibid.

121. Ibid

122. Ibid.

123. Ibisd.

124. Ibid. at 180

125. Ibid. at 181

126. Ibid.

127. Ibid.

128. H. Con. Res. 107, 1999

129. Lerch, I., Letter to Richard McCarty, October 4, 1999, *Psychological Science Agenda* (1999), 12(6), 2–3.

130. American Psychological Association Council of Representatives, Draft Minutes, August 3 & 6, 2000), unpublished manuscript quoted in Lilienfeld, supra note 118 at 182.

131. Clancy, supra note 90 at 182.

132. Ibid. at 184.

133. Ibid.

CHAPTER 3

1. Pennsylvania Coalition Against Rape and National Sexual Violence Resource Center, "Child sexual abuse prevention and risk reduction literature review for parents & guardians" (2011): 2. Available at: http://www.nsvrc.org/sites/default/files/Publications_NSVRC_LiteratureReview_Child-Sexual-Abuse-Prevention-and-Risk-Reduction-review-for-parents_0.pdf (accessed May 1, 2013).

2. Ibid.

3. "Darkness to light, seven steps to protecting our children: A guide for responsible adults" (2007). Available at: http://www.nsvrc.org/sites/default/files/Publications_NSVRC_LiteratureReview_Child-Sexual-Abuse-Prevention-and-Risk-Reduction-review-for-parents_0.pdf (accessed May 1, 2013).

4. Ibid., 5.

5. Ibid., 8.

6. Ibid., 9.

7. Child Sexual Abuse Prevention and Risk Reduction Literature Review for Parents & Guardians, *supra* note 1, 1.

8. Ibid., 9.

9. *See, e.g.,* Erika Burgess and Sandy Wurtele, "Enhancing parent-child communication about sexual abuse: A pilot study," *Child Abuse & Neglect* (1998): 22(11), 1167–1175; Paul Madak and Dale Berg, "The prevention of sexual abuse: An evaluation of Talking About Touching," *Canadian Journal of Counseling* (1992): 26(1), 29–40; Leihua Sylvester, "Talking about touching: A personal safety curriculum: Preschool to grade 3 curriculum evaluation summary," Seattle, WA: Committee for Children (1997).

10. "Parents as teachers of safety." Available at: http://www2.fiu.edu/~pats/curriculum.htm (accessed May 1, 2013).

11. Committee for Children, "Talking about touching: A personal safety curriculum" (2001): 9. Available at: http://www.cfchildren.org/Portals/0/TAT/TAT_DOC/Scope_Sequence_TAT.pdf (accessed May 1, 2013).

12. Stephen Smallbone, Willia Marshall, and Richard Wortley, *Preventing child sexual abuse: Evidence, policy and practice* (2008): 52, Portland, Oregon, Willan Publishing.

13. David Finkelhor, "Prevention of sexual abuse through educational programs directed toward children," *Pediatrics* (September 1, 2007): 120(3), 640–645, 640.

14. Ibid., 641.

15. Ibid.

16. Ibid., 643.

17. Ibid.

18. Esther Deblinger, Reena Thakkar-Kolar, Eloise J. Berry, and Christine M. Schroeder, "Caregivers' efforts to educate their children about child sexual abuse: A replication study," *Child Maltreatment* (February 2010): 15(1), 91–100.

19. Ibid., 95.

20. *See, generally,* Smallbone et al., *supra* note 12, 144.

21. For a full list of statutes, *see* US Department of Health and Human Services, Administration for Children and Families, Administration on Children, Youth and Families Children's Bureau, "Mandatory reporters of child abuse and neglect" (2012). Available at: https://www.childwelfare.gov/systemwide/laws_policies/statutes/manda.pdf (accessed May 1, 2013).

22. Lisa M. Jones, Theodore P. Cross, Wendy A. Walsh, and Monique Simone, "Do Children's Advocacy Centers improve families' experiences of child sexual abuse investigations?" *Child Abuse & Neglect* (2007): 31, 1069–1085, 1070.

23. Ibid.

24. Kathryn Kuehnle and Mary Connell, *The evaluation of child sexual abuse allegations* (2009): 423–424, New York, John Wiley & Sons.

25. Jones et al., *supra* note 22.

26. Ibid., 1073.

27. Ibid., 1075.

28. Ibid., 1076.

29. Ibid., 1079.

30. Kathleen Faller and Vincent Palusci, "Children's advocacy centers: Do they lead to positive case outcomes?" *Child Abuse & Neglect* (2007): 31(10), 1021–1029.

31. Ibid., 1025.

32. Theodore P. Cross, Lisa M. Jones, Wendy A. Walsh, Monique Simone, and David Kolko, "Child forensic interviewing in children's advocacy centers: Empirical data on a practice model," *Child Abuse & Neglect* (2007): 31, 1031–1052.

33. Ibid., 1045.

34. *See, e.g.,* The Children's Advocacy Center of Gregg and Harrison Counties Protocol (2009). Available at: http://ebookbrowse.com/childrens-advocacy-center-sample-protocol-doc-d112124134 (accessed May 1, 2013); The Montana Children's Justice Center: Overview (2012). Available at: https://doj.mt.gov/wp-content/uploads/cjcreport.pdf (accessed May 1, 2013); What does a CAC do? Available at: http://www.crbcac.com/What_we_do.html (accessed May 1, 2013); Merrimack County Child Advocacy Center (undated). Available at: http://www.merrimackcounty.net/administration/cac.html (accessed May 1, 2013).

35. Aaron Miller and David Rubin, "The contribution of children's advocacy centers to felony prosecutions of child sexual abuse," *Child Abuse & Neglect* (2009): 33, 12–18, 13.

36. Ibid.

37. Ibid., 15.

38. Ibid., 17.

39. Faller and Palusci, *supra* note 30, 1023.

40. Thomas Lyon, Nicholas Scurich, Karen Choi, Sally Handmaker, and Rebecca Blank, "'How did you feel?': Increasing child sexual abuse witnesses' production of evaluative information," *Law and Human Behavior* (October 2012): 36, 448–457, 448.

41. American Academy of Child and Adolescent Psychiatry, "Protecting children undergoing abuse investigations and testimony" (1986). Available at: http://www. aacap.org/cs/root/policy_statements/protecting_children_undergoing_abuse_ investigations_and_testimony (accessed May 1, 2013).

42. *See, e.g.,* Alison Cunningham and Lynda Stevens, "Helping a child be a witness in court: 101 things to know, say and do," London, Ontario: Centre for Children & Families in the Justice System (2011). Available at: http://www.lfcc.on.ca/ Helping_a_Child_Witness.pdf (accessed May 1, 2013).

43. Erna Olafson and Sally Fitch, "Preparing the child witness in sexual abuse cases," University of Pittsburgh (2002). Available at: http://www.pacwcbt.pitt.edu/ Curriculum/203%20Preparing%20the%20Child%20Witness%20in%20Sexual%20 Abuse%20Cases/Content/Outline.pdf (accessed May 1, 2013).

44. *See* American Bar Association, "Integrating technology in child abuse cases: Overview for judges" (September 2010). Available at: http://www.ameri-canbar.org/content/dam/aba/migrated/child/PublicDocuments/integrating_tech_ child_abuse_cases_overview_judges.authcheckdam.pdf (accessed May 1, 2013).

45. *See Maryland v. Craig,* 497 U.S. 836 (1990).

46. American Bar Association, *supra* note 44.

47. New York Criminal Procedure Law § 65.20 (2).

48. Ibid., § 65.20 (8).

49. Ibid., § 65.20 (10).

50. *Maryland v. Craig,* 497 U.S. 836 (1990).

51. *Matter of Nicole V.,* 71 N.Y.2d 112 (1987); New York Family Court Act § 1046(a)(vi).

52. *See, e.g.,* Federal Rules of Evidence 803(2) and 803(4).

53. *See, e.g.,* Federal Rules of Evidence 807.

54. *Crawford v. Washington,* 541 U.S. 36 (2004).

55. Ibid., 52.

56. *Snowden v. State,* 867 A.2d 314 (Maryland, 2005).

57. Ibid., 328.

58. Ibid., 315.

59. Ibid.

60. Deborah Paruch, "Silencing the victims in child sexual abuse prosecutions: The confrontation clause and children's hearsay statements before and after Michigan v. Bryant," 28 *Touro Law Review* 85 (2012): 44.

61. "Sexualizing children / exploitation of children." Available at: http://www.redbub-ble.com/groups/pink-panther-magazine/forums/9540/topics/203602-sexualizin g-children-exploitation-of-children (accessed May 1, 2013).

62. Jessica Valenti, "Sex sells—even to kids: Racy clothing for preteens is sending a troubling and dangerous message," *The Daily,* March 26, 2011. Available at: http:// www.thedaily.com/page/2011/03/26/032611-opinions-column-bras-valenti-1-2/] (accessed May 1, 2013).

63. Lindsay Lieberman, "Protecting pageant princesses: A call for statutory regulation of child beauty pageants," 18 *Journal of Law and Policy* 739 (2010): 745.

64. American Psychological Association, Report of the APA Task Force on the Sexualization of Girls, (2010): 33–34. Available at: http://www.apa.org/pi/women/ programs/girls/report-full.pdf (accessed May 1, 2013).

65. Ibid., 33.

66. Ibid., 34.

67. Ibid., 43.

68. National Coalition to Prevent Child Sexual Abuse and Exploitation, National Plan to Prevent the Sexual Abuse and Exploitation of Children (March, 2012): 14–15. Available at: http://www.preventtogether.org/Resources/Documents/NationalPlan2012FINAL.pdf (accessed May 1, 2013).

69. *See, e.g.,* Bill Chappell, "Penn State abuse scandal: A guide and timeline," *NPR News,* June 21, 2012. Available at: http://www.npr.org/2011/11/08/142111804/penn-state-abuse-scandal-a-guide-and-timeline (accessed May 1, 2013); Mark Viera, "Former coach at Penn State is charged with abuse," *New York Times,* November 5, 2011. Available at: http://www.nytimes.com/2011/11/06/sports/ncaafootball/former-coach-at-penn-state-is-charged-with-abuse.html?pagewanted=all (accessed May 1, 2013); Pennsylvania Office of Attorney General, *Commonwealth v. Gerald Sandusky,* Grand Jury Presentment, November 2011. Available at: http://www.attorneygeneral.gov/uploadedfiles/press/sandusky-grand-jury-presentment.pdf (accessed May 1, 2013); Freeh, Sporkin and Sullivan, LLP, Report of the Special Investigative Counsel Regarding the Actions of the Pennsylvania State University Related to the Child Sexual Abuse Committed by Gerald A. Sandusky, July 12, 2012. Available at: http://progress.psu.edu/the-freeh-report (accessed May 1, 2013).

70. Ibid.

71. S. Daniel Batson and Adam A. Powell, "Altruism and prosocial behavior." In *Handbook of psychology* (2003): 472, New York, John Wiley & Sons.

72. Stop It Now, "What do U.S. adults think about child sexual abuse? Measures of knowledge and attitudes among six states" (2010): 8. Available at: http://www.stopitnow.org/files/RDD_Survey_Report.pdf (accessed May 1, 2013).

73. Ibid.

74. Ibid., 9.

75. *See, e.g.,* Joan Tabachnick, "Engaging bystanders in sexual violence prevention," National Sexual Violence Resource Center (2008). Available at: http://www.nsvrc.org/sites/default/files/Publications_NSVRC_Booklets_Engaging-Bystanders-in-Sexual- Violence-Prevention.pdf (accessed May 1, 2013).

76. Mandatory Reporters of Child Abuse and Neglect, *supra* note 21, 3 [emphasis added].

77. Ibid.

78. Ibid.

79. Ibid.

80. Ibid.

81. US Department of Health & Human Services, Administration for Children and Families, Administration on Children, Youth and Families, Children's Bureau, "Immunity for Reporters of Child Abuse and Neglect," (2012). Available at: http://www.childwelfare.gov/systemwide/laws_policies/statutes/immunity.cfm (accessed May 1, 2013).

CHAPTER 4

1. National District Attorneys Association, National Center for Prosecution of Child Abuse, "Statutes of limitation for prosecution of offenses against children" (2012). Available at: http://www.ndaa.org/pdf/Statute%20of%20Limitations%20for%20

Prosecution%20of%20Offenses%20Against%20Children%202012.pdf   (accessed
May 1, 2013).
2. Ibid.
3. Ibid.
4. California Penal Code § 803(g).
5. *Stogner v. California*, 539 U.S. 607 (2003).
6. Testimony of Deborah Del Prete Sullivan, Office of Chief Public Defender, regarding An Act Concerning the Statute of Limitations for Prosecution of Certain
Sexual Offenses Using DNA Evidence, Judiciary Committee, Connecticut House
of Representatives, April 18, 2007. Available at: http://www.cga.ct.gov/2007/JFR/
H/2007HB-07085-R00JUD-JFR.htm (accessed May 1, 2013).
7. Yair Listokin, "Efficient time bars: A new rationale for the existence of statutes of
limitations in criminal law," 31 *Journal of Legal Studies* 99 (2002): 118.
8. David Viens, "Countdown to injustice: The irrational application of criminal statutes of limitations to sexual offenses against children," 38 *Suffolk University Law
Review* 169 (2004): 188.
9. Marci A. Hamilton, *Justice denied: What America must do to protect its children*
(2008): 109, New York, Cambridge University Press.
10. Ibid., 28.
11. Viens, *supra* note 8, 188.
12. Ibid.
13. *See, e.g.,* Alexander Abad-Santos, "Rep. Dale Kildee thinks he's being black-
mailed with molestation tale," *The Atlantic Wire*, November 21, 2011. Available
at: http://www.theatlanticwire.com/politics/2011/11/rep-dale-kildee-thinks-hes-
being-blackmailed-molestation-tale/45224/ (accessed May 1, 2013); Dale Kildee,
"Sexual abuse allegations are an 'attempt to blackmail me,'" *Huffington Post*,
November 21, 2011. Available at: http://www.huffingtonpost.com/2011/11/21/
dale-kildee-sexual-abuse-_n_1106622.html (accessed May 1, 2013); "U.S. Rep. Dale
Kildee denies sex abuse claim, says relatives tried to blackmail him," *Detroit Free
Press*, November 21, 2011. Available at: http://www.freep.com/article/20111121/
NEWS15/111210352/U-S-Rep-Dale-Kildee-denies-sex-abuse-claim-says-relatives
-tried-blackmail-him (accessed May 1, 2013).
14. National Conference of State Legislatures, "State statutes related to Jessica's Law,"
(2008). Available at: http://www.leg.state.vt.us/WorkGroups/sexoffenders/NCSLs_
Jessicas_Law_Summary.pdf (accessed May 1, 2013).
15. *See Kennedy v. Louisiana*, 554 U.S. 407 (2008).
16. Sharon Otterman, "Therapist sentenced to 103 years for child sexual abuse," *New York
Times*, January 22, 2013. Available at: http://www.nytimes.com/2013/01/23/nyregion/
nechemya-weberman-sentenced-to-103-years-in-prison.html (accessed May 1, 2013).
17. David Finkelhor, "The prevention of childhood sexual abuse," *The Future of Children*
(Fall 2009): 19(2), 176.
18. Matthew R. Durose, Patrick A. Langan, and Erica L. Schmitt, "Recidivism of sex offenders released from prison in 1994," U.S. Bureau of Justice Statistics (2003). Available
at: http://bjs.ojp.usdoj.gov/index.cfm?ty=pbdetail&iid=1136 (accessed May 1, 2013).
19. Alan R. McKelvie, "Recidivism of Alaska sex offenders," *Alaska Justice Forum* (2008):
14–15. Available at: http://justice.uaa.alaska.edu/forum/25/1-2springsummer2008/
g_recidivism.html (accessed May 1, 2013).

20. Lisa L. Sample and Timothy M. Bray, "Are sex offenders different? An examination of rearrest patterns," *Criminal Justice Policy Review* (March 2006): 17, 83–102.
21. Stephen Patrick and Robert Marsh, "Recidivism among child sexual abusers: Initial results of a 13-year longitudinal random sample," *Journal of Child Sexual Abuse* (March-April 2009): 18, 123–36, 125.
22. Andrew J. R. Harris and R. Karl Hanson, "Sex offender recidivism: A simple question," *Public Safety and Emergency Preparedness Canada* (2004): 1–23. Available at: http://www.publicsafety.gc.ca/res/cor/rep/2004-03-se-off-eng.aspx (accessed May 1, 20 13).
23. Ibid., 8.
24. Ibid., 11.
25. *See Harmelin v. Michigan*, 501 U.S. 957 (1991).
26. Silvia M. Mendes, "Certainty, severity, and their relative deterrent effects: Questioning the implications of the role of risk in criminal deterrence policy," *Policy Studies Journal* (February 2004): 32(1), 59–74, 60.
27. Finkelhor, *supra* note 17, 176.
28. Jennifer Bleyer, "Patty Wetterling questions sex offender laws," *City Pages News*, March 20, 2013. Available at: http://www.citypages.com/2013-03-20/news/patty-wetterling-questions-sex-offender-laws/full/ (accessed May 1, 2013).
29. *See* Washington Revised Code § 71.09.010 *et seq.*
30. Dretha M. Phillips, "Community notification as viewed by Washington's citizens" Washington State Institute for Public Policy (March 1998). Available at: www.wsipp.wa.gov/rptfiles/CnSurvey.pdf (accessed May 1, 2013).
31. Charles Patrick Ewing, *Justice perverted: Sex offense law, psychology and public policy* (2011): 76, New York, Oxford University Press.
32. Angie Cannon, "Mother perseveres in Megan's Law effort," *The Philadelphia Inquirer*, May 15, 1996, B1.
33. Ibid.
34. *Doe v. Poritz*, 142 N.J. 1, 14-17 (1995) [citations omitted].
35. Human Rights Watch, "No easy answers for sex offenders" (2007): 25. Available at: www.hrw.org/en/reports/2007/09/11/no-easy-answers (accessed May 1, 2013).
36. Ibid.
37. Ibid.
38. 42 U.S.C.S. § 14071.
39. 64 Fed. Reg. 572, 581 (1999).
40. *Smith v. Doe*, 538 U.S. 84 (2002); *Connecticut Department of Safety v. Doe*, 538 U.S. 1 (2003).
41. Pub. L. No. 104-236, 110 Stat. 3093 (1996) (codified at 42 U.S.C. § 14072).
42. Pub. L. No. 109-248, 120 Stat. 587 (2006) (codified at 42 U.S.C. § 1690).
43. 42 U.S.C. § 16902.
44. US Department of Justice, Dru Sjodin National Sex Offender Public Website. Available at: http://www.nsopw.gov/ (accessed May 1, 2013).
45. US Department of Justice, "Department of Justice Announces improvements and name change for Dru Sjodin national sex offender public website" (Press Release, December 3, 2008). Available at: http://www.ojp.gov/newsroom/pressreleases/2008/smart09009.htm (accessed May 1, 2013).
46. "Sex offenders," *ABC News, World News Tonight*, June 7, 2006.

47. *See, e.g.,* Tex. Govt. Code Ann. § 508.187 (Vernon 2009); Bridget Brown, "Ordinances will affect most sex offenders," *The Facts,* May 10, 2006. Available at: http://thefacts. com/news/article_08e43fef-41bd-54b1-bd42-52221ecce527.html (accessed May 1, 2013); Carol Christian, "New law limits where sex offenders can reside: Violators can be fined $500 per day of offense," *The Houston Chronicle,* April 16, 2009, 1; Texas Department of Safety, "Frequently asked questions." Available at: http://www. txdps.state.tx.us/administration/crime_records/pages/faq.htm (accessed May 1, 2013).

48. Loretta Kalb, "Libraries plan sex-offender response," *Sacramento Bee,* August 29, 2006, B2.

49. *See* Joseph L. Lester, "The legitimacy of sex offender residence and employment restrictions," 40 *Akron Law Review* 339 (2007).

50. Ibid.

51. California Department of Corrections and Rehabilitation, "Jessica's Law." Available at: http://www.cdcr.ca.gov/Parole/Sex_Offender_Facts/Jessicas_Law.html   (accessed May 1, 2013).

52. Katharine Mieszkowski, "Tracking sex offenders with GPS," *Salon,* December 19, 2006. Available at: http://www.salon.com/news/feature/2006/12/19/offenders (accessed May 1, 2013).

53. *Doe v. Poritz,* 142 N.J. 1, 14–17, 13 (1995) at 13.

54. *Doe v. Miller,* 405 F.3d 700, 706 (2005) at 716.

55. Washington State Institute for Public Policy, "Does sex offender registration and notification reduce crime? A systematic review of the research literature" (June 2009). Available at: www.wsipp.wa.gov/rptfiles/09-06-1101.pdf (accessed May 1, 2013).

56. Federal Bureau of Investigation, "National Incident-Based Reporting System." Available at: http://www.fbi.gov/ucr/faqs.htm (accessed May 1, 2013).

57. Ibid.

58. J.J. Prescott and Jonah E. Rockoff, "Do sex offender registration and notification laws affect criminal behavior?" National Economic Bureau of Research Working Paper No. 13803 (February 1, 2008): 1. Available at: www.gsb.columbia.edu/.../ prescott%20rockoff%20meglaw%20jan%2010.pdf (accessed May 1, 2013).

59. L. Shao and J. Li, "The effect of sex offender registration laws on rape victimization," Unpublished Manuscript (2006).

60. Washington State Institute for Public Policy, *supra* note 55, 5.

61. Ibid., 3.

62. Kristin Zgoba, Philip Witt, Melissa Dalessandro, and Bonita Veysey, "Megan's Law: Assessing the practical and monetary efficacy" (December 2008). Available at: www.ncjrs.gov/pdffiles1/nij/grants/225370.pdf (accessed May 1, 2013).

63. Ibid., 2.

64. Jill S. Levenson and Leo P. Cotter, "The impact of sex offender residence restrictions: 1,000 feet from danger or one step from absurd?" *International Journal of Offender Therapy and Comparative Criminology* (2005): 49, 168–178, 170.

65. Ibid., 174.

66. Michael Chajewski and Cynthia Calkins Mercado, "An evaluation of sex offender residency restriction functioning in town, county, and city-wide jurisdictions," *Criminal Justice Policy Review* (2009): 20, 44–61.

67. Ibid., 59.
68. Ibid.
69. Ibid.
70. Paul A. Zandbergen and Timothy C. Hart, "Reducing housing options for convicted sex offenders: Investigating the impact of residency restriction laws using GIS," *Justice Research and Policy* (Fall 2006): 8(2), 1–24.
71. Ibid., 1.
72. Ibid.
73. Ibid.
74. *E.B. v. Verniero*, F.3d 1077, 1102 (1997).
75. Human Rights Watch, "No easy answers for sex offenders" (2007): 87–88. Available at: www.hrw.org/en/reports/2007/09/11/no-easy-answers (accessed May 1, 2013).
76. Ibid.
77. Ibid., 7; "Murdered in the United States—2008: Registered sex offenders & others" (February 18, 2009). Available at: http://sexoffenderresearch.blogspot.com/search/label/%28...Advocacy%20-%20RSOs%20Murdered (accessed May 1, 2013).
78. National Alliance to End Sexual Violence, "Legislative analysis: The Adam Walsh Child Protection and Safety Act of 2006." Available at: www.naesv.org/Policypapers/Adam_Walsh_SumMarch07.pdf (accessed May 1, 2013).
79. Christopher Dela Cruz, "Report finds Megan's Law fails to reduce sex crimes, deter repeat offenders in N.J.," *Newark Star-Ledger*, February 07, 2009. Available at: http://www.nj.com/news/index.ssf/2009/02/study_finds_megans_law_fails_t_1.html (accessed May 1, 2013).
80. "Sex offenders hurt property values, Wright State University study shows," April 12, 2002. Available at: http://www.wright.edu/cgi-bin/cm/news.cgi?action=news_item&id=310 (accessed May 1, 2013).
81. Leigh Linden and Jonah E. Rockoff, "There goes the neighborhood? Estimates of the impact of crime risk on property values from Megan's Laws," Paper presented at American Law & Economics Association Annual Meetings (2007): 1. Available at: law.bepress.com/cgi/viewcontent.cgi?article=1931&context=alea (accessed May 1, 2013).
82. Human Rights Watch, *supra* note 75, 9.
83. States with SVP laws include Arizona, California, Florida, Illinois, Iowa, Kansas, Massachusetts, Minnesota, Missouri, Nebraska, New Hampshire, New Jersey, New York, North Dakota, Pennsylvania, South Carolina, Texas, Virginia, Washington, and Wisconsin.
84. Texas Health and Safety Code, Sec. 841 (Vernon, 1999).
85. *Kansas v. Hendricks*, 521 U.S. 346 (1997).
86. Ewing, *supra* note 31, 222.
87. Ibid.
88. American Psychiatric Association, *Diagnostic and statistical manual of mental disorders, Fourth Edition* (1994), Washington, DC, American Psychiatric Association.
89. Eric S. Janus and Robert A. Prentky, "Sexual predator laws: A two-decade retrospective," *Federal Sentencing Reporter* (December 2008): 21, 90–97, 93.
90. American Psychiatric Association, *supra* note 88, 649–650.
91. John Q. La Fond, *Preventing sexual violence* (2005): 140, Washington, DC, American Psychological Association.

92. *See* Thomas Zander, "Civil commitment without psychosis: The law's reliance on the weakest links in psychodiagnosis," *Journal of Sex Offender Civil Commitment* (2005): 1, 17–82; Michael B. First and Robert L. Halon, "Use of DSM paraphilia diagnoses in sexually violent predator commitment cases," *Journal of the American Academy of Psychiatry and Law* (2008): 36(4), 443–54.

93. Dean R. Cauley, "The diagnostic issue of antisocial personality disorder in civil commitment proceedings: A response to DeClue," *Journal of Psychiatry & Law* (2007): 35(4), 475–497, 488.

94. Association for the Treatment of Sexual Abusers, Brief *Amicus Curiae*, *Kansas v. Hendricks*, 1996 U.S. S. Ct. Briefs LEXIS 553 (1996): 14.

95. American Psychiatric Association, *supra* note 88, 528.

96. Janus and Prentky, *supra* note 89, 94.

97. 2006 Mass. Super. LEXIS 77 (2006): 1–11.

98. Ibid., 3.

99. Ibid., 4.

100. Ibid.

101. Ibid., 5.

102. *U.S. v. Shields*, 2008 U.S. Dist. LEXIS 13837 (2008): 1–7, 4.

103. *See, generally,* Karen Franklin, "Hebephilia: Quintessence of diagnostic pretextuality," *Behavioral Sciences and the Law* (November/December 2010): 751–768; Allen Frances, "DSM-5 rejects 'hebephilia' except for the fine print," *Huffington Post*, May 5, 2012. Available at: http://www.huffingtonpost.com/allen-frances/dsm-5-rejects-hebephilia-_b_1475563.html (accessed May 1, 2013).

104. *U.S. v. Shields*, *supra* note 102, 4.

105. American Psychiatric Association, *supra* note 88, 522–523.

106. Ibid., 525–532.

107. Ibid., 532.

108. *U.S. v. Shields*, *supra* note 102, 5.

109. Ibid.

110. Robert P. Archer, Jacqueline K. Buffington-Vollum, Rebecca Vauter Stredny, and Richard W. Handel, "A survey of psychological test use patterns among forensic psychologists," *Journal of Personality Assessment* (2006): 87, 84–94, 87.

111. *State v. Rosado*, 889 N.Y.S.2d 369, 390-391, 392-394 (2009) [citations omitted].

112. Stephen D. Hart, Christine Michie, and David J. Cooke, "Precision of actuarial risk assessment instruments: Evaluating the 'margins of error' of group v. individual predictions of violence," *British Journal of Psychiatry* (2007): 190, 60–65, 60.

113. Ibid.

114. Ibid., 64.

115. Ibid., 60.

116. *Kansas v. Hendricks*, *supra* note 85, 371.

117. Jill S. Levenson and David S. Prescott, "Treatment experiences of civilly committed sex offenders: A consumer satisfaction survey," *Sexual Abuse: A Journal of Research and Treatment* (2009): 21, 6–20, 6–7.

118. Howard Barbaree, "Evaluating treatment efficacy with sexual offenders: The insensitivity of recidivism studies to treatment effect," *Sexual Abuse: A Journal of Research and Treatment* (1997): 10, 111–128, 112.

119. R. Karl Hanson, Ian Broom, and Marylee Stephenson, "Evaluating community sex offender treatment programs: A 12-year follow-up of 724 offenders," *Canadian Journal of Behavioural Science* (2004): 36(2), 87–96, 87.

120. Robert Prentky and Barbara Schwartz, "Treatment of adult sex offenders treatment of adult sex offenders," *Applied Research Forum* (December 2006): 1–10, 2.

121. R. Karl Hanson, Arthur Gordon, Andrew J. R. Harris, Janice K. Marques, William Murphy, Vernon L. Quinsey, and Michael C. Seto, "First report of the collaborative outcome data project on the effectiveness of psychological treatment for sex offenders," *Sexual Abuse: A Journal of Research and Treatment* (2002): 14(2), 169–194, 181.

122. Ibid.

123. Marnie E. Rice and Grant T. Harris, "The size and sign of treatment effects in sex offender therapy," *Annals of the New York Academy of Sciences* (2003): 989, 428–440, 440.

124. Friedrich Losel and Martin Schmucker, "The effectiveness of treatment for sexual offenders: A comprehensive meta-analysis," *Journal of Experimental Criminology* (2005): 1, 117–146.

125. Ibid., 117.

126. Ibid.

127. Jane Dennis, Omer Khan, Michael Ferriter, Nick Huband, Melanie Powney, and Conor Duggan, "Psychological interventions for adults who have sexually offended or are at risk of offending (Review)," *The Cochrane Collaboration* (December 12, 2012).

128. Ibid., 28.

129. Monica Davey and Abby Goodnough, "Doubts rise as states hold sex offenders after prison," *New York Times*, March 4, 2007. Available at: http://www.nytimes.com/2007/03/04/us/04civil.html (accessed May 1, 2013).

130. Texas Department of State Health Services Council on Sex Offender Treatment, "Civil commitment of the sexually violent predator—Inpatient vs. outpatient SVP civil commitment." Available at: http://www.dshs.state.tx.us/csot/csot_ccinout.shtm (accessed May 1, 2013).

131. Monica Davey and Abby Goodnough, *supra* note 129.

132. Ibid.

133. Jennifer E. Schneider, "A review of research findings related to the civil commitment of sex offenders," *Journal of Psychiatry & Law* (October 2008): 36(3), 463.

134. Ewing, *supra* note 31, 57.

135. Martiga Lohn, "Sexual predator treatment squeezes budgets," *Associated Press*, June 21, 2010. Available at: http://www.nbcnews.com/id/37819608/ns/us_news-crime_and_courts/#.UT0D_I2PVIF (accessed May 1, 2013).

136. Davey and Goodnough, *supra* note 129.

137. Molly T. Geissenhainer, "The $62 million question: Is Virginia's new center to house sexually violent predators money well spent?" *University of Richmond Law Review* (2008): 42(5), 1301–1336.

138. "Bill stuck on sex offender funding," *Minneapolis Star Tribune*, March 9, 2010. Available at: http://www.startribune.com/politics/state/87182192.html (accessed May 1, 2013).

139. Rocco LaDuca, "$30M later, Mid-State facility not yet housing sex offenders," *Utica Observer-Dispatch*. Available at: http://www.uticaod.com/news/

x512367636/-30M-later-Mid-State-facility-not-yet-housing-sex-offenders (accessed May 1, 2013).

140. American Psychiatric Association, *Dangerous sex offenders* (1999): 173–174, 170, Washington, DC, American P{sychiatric Association.

141. Ron Donato and Martin Shanahan, "The economics of child sex-offender rehabilitation programs: Beyond Prentky & Burgess," *American Journal of Orthopsychiatry* (2001): 71(1), 131–139, 132.

142. Ibid., 131.

CHAPTER 5

1. *State v. Berger*, 103 P.3d 298 (2004); 134 P.3d 378 (2006) (affirmed); *Berger v. Arizona*, 549 U.S. 1252 (2007) (cert. denied).

2. 18 U.S.C.S. § 2253.

3. Ashlee Clark, "Lexington house forfeited in child-porn case," *Lexington Herald-Leader*, October 21, 2009. Available at: http://www.kentucky.com/2009/10/21/984943/lexington-house-forfeited-in-child.html#ixzz0nkdmTjOT (accessed May 1, 2013).

4. 18 U.S.C. § 2259.

5. 18 U.S.C. § 2251.

6. US Department of Justice, Child Exploitation and Obscenity Section, "Citizen's guide to United States federal child exploitation laws." Available at: http://www.justice.gov/criminal/ceos/citizensguide_porn.html (accessed May 1, 2013).

7. 18 U.S.C.S. § 2252.

8. Ibid.

9. Ibid.

10. Ibid.

11. *U.S. v. Skotzke*, 2007 U.S. Dist. LEXIS 39352, 1 (2007).

12. Statement of B. Todd Jones (US Attorney, District of Minnesota), US Sentencing Commission Regional Hearing on the State of Federal Sentencing, October 20, 2009. Available at: www.ussc.gov/AGENDAS/20091020/Jones_testimony.pdf (accessed May 1, 2013).

13. 18 U.S.C.S. § 2252.

14. Ibid.

15. *See* US Sentencing Commission, The history of the child pornography guidelines, October 2009. Available at: http://docs.google.com/viewer?a=v&q=cache:WwOlNPEfqZYJ:www.ussc.gov/general/20091030_History_Child_Pornography_Guidelines.pdf+%22history+of+child+pornography+sentencing+guidelines%22&hl=en&gl=us&pid=bl&srcid=ADGEESgCRwdNj1sWJ79xCC1WIlIfEJbSSuxirhMy37N99x7B8UU4e1qfVZhrHXxvRBDKR4GJvS8AFw6ig6-mTONXHZIhnWMUUZX0GcxJgur_lSl5EVEFbnt9kT2yF9UJtl-ao0ipnWwu&sig=AHIEtbQUKp3l-to_lQG3tWVWblyyEDkEew (accessed May 1, 2013).

16. 543 U.S. 220 (2005).

17. US Sentencing Commission, Report to Congress: Federal child pornography offenses (2013): ii.

18. *U.S. v. Paull*, 551 F.3d 516 (2009).

19. *U.S. v. Ontiveros*, 2008 U.S. Dist. LEXIS 58774, 1–2 (2008).

20. Ibid., 16–19.

21. Ibid., 13.

22. Statement of Judge Robin J. Cauthron, US Sentencing Commission Regional Hearing on the State of Federal Sentencing, November 19, 2009. Available at: www.ussc.gov/AGENDAS/20091119/Cauthron.pdf (accessed May 1, 2013).

23. Lynne Marek, "Sentences for possession of child porn may be too high, judges say." *The National Law Journal*, September 10, 2009. Available at: http://www.law.com/newswire/cache/1202433693658.html (accessed May 1, 2013).

24. Ibid.

25. US Sentencing Commission, *supra* note 17, 11.

26. *See* Charles Patrick Ewing, *Justice perverted: Sex offense law, psychology and public policy* (2011): 142–143, Washington, DC, Government Printing Office.

27. Richard Wortley and Stephen Smallbone, "Child pornography on the Internet," May 2006. Available at: http://purl.access.gpo.gov/GPO/LPS70983 (accessed May 1, 2013), 9–10.

28. *See* Eileen Ormsby, "The new underbelly," *Sydney Morning Herald*, June 1, 2012. Available at: http://www.smh.com.au/technology/technology-news/the-new-underbelly-20120531-1zktt.html (accessed May 1, 2013).

29. Ibid.

30. Christopher Williams, "Anonymous hacktivists target child abuse websites," *The Telegraph*, October 24, 2011. Available at: http://www.telegraph.co.uk/technology/news/8846577/Anonymous-hacktivists-target-child-abuse-websites.html (accessed May 1, 2013).

31. US Sentencing Commission, *supra* note 17, 108.

32. Ibid., 90–91.

33. Ibid., 109.

34. Ibid., viii.

35. Ibid.

36. Ibid., xx.

37. Ibid., 328–329.

38. Ibid., 98–99.

39. Ibid., 328.

40. Statement of Deirdre D. von Dornum on Behalf of the Federal Public and Community Defenders before the United States Sentencing Commission Public Hearing on Child Pornography Sentencing, February 15, 2012.

41. Ibid.

42. Ibid.

43. John Carr, Theme Paper on Child Pornography for the 2nd World Congress on Commercial Sexual Exploitation of Children. Available at: http://www.childcentre.info/robert/extensions/robert/doc/67ba32d30c03c842b7032932f2e6ce74.pdf (accessed May 1, 2013).

44. Michael C. Seto and Angela W. Eke, "The criminal histories and later offending of child pornography offenders," *Sexual Abuse: A Journal of Research and Treatment* (2005): 17(2), 201–210.

45. Ibid., 208.

46. Ibid.

47. L. Webb, J. Craissati, and S. Keen, "Characteristics of Internet child pornography offenders: A comparison with child molesters," *Sex Abuse* (2007): 19(4), 449–465, 457.

48. Ibid., 455.

49. Jerome Endrass, Frank Urbaniok, Lea C. Hammermeister, Christian Benz, Thomas Elbert, Arja Laubacher, and Astrid Rossegger, "The consumption of Internet child pornography and violent and sex offending," *BMC Psychiatry* (2009): 9:43.

50. Ibid., 10.

51. Ibid.

52. David L. Riegel, "Effects on boy-attracted pedosexual males of viewing boy erotica," *Archives of Sexual Behavior* (2004): 33(4), 321–323.

53. Ibid., 321.

54. Ibid.

55. Ibid.

56. Ibid., 322.

57. Ibid.

58. Ibid., 323.

59. Kelly M. Babchishin, R. Karl Hanson, and Chantal A. Hermann, "The characteristics of online sex offenders: A meta-analysis," unpublished paper.

60. Ibid., 2.

61. Ibid., 18.

62. Ibid.

63. Ibid., 19.

64. Ibid., 20.

65. Ibid., 2.

66. Michael C. Seto, R. Karl Hanson, and Kelly M. Babchishin, "Contact sexual offending by men with online sexual offenses," *Sexual Abuse: A Journal of Research and Treatment* (March 2011): 23(1), 124–145.

67. Ibid., 133–134.

68. Ibid., 135.

69. Ibid., 136.

70. Austin F. Lee, Nien-Chen Li, Raima Lamade, Ann Schuler, and Robert A. Prentky, "Predicting hands-on child sexual offenses among possessors of Internet child pornography," *Psychology, Public Policy, and Law* (November 2012): 18(4), 644–672.

71. Ibid., 647–648.

72. Ibid., 668.

73. David L. Riegel, *supra* note 52, 323.

74. 18 U.S.C. § 2252(a)(6).

75. VA Code § 18.2-374.4.

76. Ibid.

77. Michelle K. Collins, "Child pornography: A closer look," *The Police Chief* (March 2007). Available at: http://www.policechiefmagazine.org/magazine/index.cfm?fuseaction=display&article_id=1139&issue_id=32007 (accessed May 1, 2013).

78. US Immigration and Customs Enforcement, "123 sexually exploited children identified by HSI during 'Operation Sunflower'—Operation commemorates anniversary of an 11-year-old girl rescued in Kansas; reflects the agency's growing focus on victim-centered investigations" (News Release) January 3, 2013. Available at: http://www.ice.gov/news/releases/1301/130103washingtondc.htm (accessed May 1, 2013).

79. Ibid.

80. *See, e.g.,* Martin Kaste, "A click away: Preventing online child porn viewing," *NPR News*, August 31, 2010. Available at: http://www.npr.org/templates/story/story.php?storyId=129526579 (accessed May 1, 2013).

81. Richard Wortley and Stephen Smallbone, "Child pornography on the Internet," US Department of Justice, Office of Community Oriented Policing Services (COPS). Available at: http://www.cops.usdoj.gov/Publications/e04062000.pdf (accessed May 1, 2013).

82. Treaty Series: Treaties and International Agreements Registered or Filed and Recorded with the Secretariat of the United Nations (Volume 2171): 247. Available at: http://treaties.un.org/doc/publication/UNTS/Volume%202171/v2171.pdf (accessed May 1, 2013).

83. Kaste, *supra* note 80.

84. Wortley and Smallbone, *supra* note 81, 10.

85. Ibid., 28.

86. "National campaign to prevent teen and unplanned pregnancy sex and tech: Results from a survey of teens and young adults," (2008). Available at: http://www.thenationalcampaign.org/sextech/pdf/sextech_summary.pdf (accessed May 1, 2013).

87. A thin line, 2009 AP-MTV digital abuse study. Available at: http://www.athinline.org/MTV-AP_Digital_Abuse_Study_Executive_Summary.pdf (accessed May 1, 2013).

88. Cox Communications, Teen online & wireless safety survey research findings, May 2009. Available at: http://ww2.cox.com/wcm/en/aboutus/datasheet/takecharge/2009-teen-survey.pdf?campcode=takecharge-research-link_2009-teen-survey_0511 (accessed May 1, 2013).

89. Amanda Lenhart," Teens and sexting: How and why minor teens are sending sexually suggestive nude or nearly nude images via text messaging," Pew Internet and American Life Project, December 15, 2009. Available at: http://www.pewinternet.org/~/media/Files/Reports/2009/PIP_Teens_and_Sexting.pdf (accessed May 1, 2013).

90. Andy Phippen, "Sharing personal images and videos among young people," South West Grid for Learning (2009). Available at: http://blackpoollscb.org.uk/contents/documents/sexting-detail.pdf (accessed May 1, 2013).

91. Ibid., 1.

92. Kaitlin Lounsbury, Kimberly J. Mitchell, and David Finkelhor, "The true prevalence of 'sexting,'" *Crimes Against Children Research Center* (April 2011): 4. Available at: http://www.unh.edu/ccrc/pdf/Sexting%20Fact%20Sheet%204_29_11.pdf (accessed May 1, 2013).

93. Marsha Levick and Kristina Moon, "Prosecuting sexting as child pornography," 44 *Valparaiso University Law Review* (2010): 1035–1054, 1038. Available at: http://scholar.valpo.edu/vulr/vol44/iss4/2 (accessed May 1, 2013).

94. *See, e.g.,* Mike Celizic, "Her teen committed suicide over 'sexting,'" *TODAY*, March 6, 2009. Available at: http://www.today.com/id/29546030/ns/today-parenting_and_family/t/her-teen-committed-suicide-over-sexting/#.UYrC4-_D9iE (accessed May 1, 2013).

95. Tamar Lewin, "Rethinking sex offender laws for youth texting," *New York Times*, March 20, 2010. Available at: http://www.nytimes.com/2010/03/21/us/21sexting.html?pagewanted=all&_r=0 (accessed May 1, 2013).

96. Florida Department of Law Enforcement—Sexual Offender/Predator Flyer. Available at: http://offender.fdle.state.fl.us/offender/flyer.do?personId=60516 (accessed May 1, 2013).

97. Grant Schulte, "Iowa court upholds 'sexting' conviction," *USA Today*, September 18, 2009. Available at: http://usatoday30.usatoday.com/news/nation/2009-09-18-iowa-sexting_N.htm (accessed May 1, 2013).

98. Radley Balko, "Prosecutor shaming: Berkshire, Massachusetts Second Assistant District Attorney Robert W. Kinzer III," *Huffington Post*, February 2, 2013. Available at: http://www.huffingtonpost.com/2013/02/28/prosecutor-shaming-berksh_n_2780559.html (accessed May 1, 2013).

99. Miranda Jolicoeur and Edwin Zedlewski, "Much ado about sexting," *National Institute of Justice* (June 2010). Available at: https://www.ncjrs.gov/pdffiles1/nij/230795.pdf (accessed May 1, 2013).

100. *See* National Conference of State Legislatures, Sexting Legislation 2012. Available at: http://www.ncsl.org/issues-research/telecom/sexting-legislation-2012.aspx (accessed May 1, 2013).

101. US Department of Justice, "Youth Internet safety survey," (December 2001). Available at:http://www.ojp.usdoj.gov/ovc/publications/bulletins/internet_2_2001/internet_2_01_6.html (accessed May 1, 2013).

102. Ibid.

103. Ibid.

104. Ibid.

105. David Finkelhor, Kimberly J. Mitchell, and Janis Wolak, "Online victimization: A report on the nation's youth," (June 2000): 2. Available at: http://www.unh.edu/ccrc/pdf/jvq/CV38.pdf (accessed May 1, 2013).

106. Ibid., 4.

107. Ibid.

108. Ibid., 6.

109. Janis Wolak, Kimberly Mitchell, and David Finkelhor, "Internet sex crimes against minors: The response of law enforcement" (November 2003): 1. Available at: www.unh.edu/ccrc/pdf/CV70.pdf (accessed May 2, 2013).

110. Ibid., vii.

111. Janis Wolak, David Finkelhor, and Kimberly Mitchell, "Internet-initiated sex crimes against minors: Implications for prevention based on findings from a national study," *Journal of Adolescent Health* (2004): 35(5), 11–20, 16.

112. Janis Wolak, Kimberly Mitchell, and David Finkelhor, "Online victimization of youth: Five years later" (2006): 16. Available at: http://www.missingkids.com/en_US/publications/NC167.pdf (accessed May 2, 2013).

113. Janis Wolak, David Finkelhor, Kimberly J. Mitchell, and Michele L. Ybarra, "Online 'predators' and their victims: Myths, realities and implications for prevention and treatment," *American Psychologist* (February–March 2008): 63(2), 111–128, 115.

114. 18 U.S.C. § 2422.

115. *See, generally,* Ewing, *supra* note 26, 186–198.

116. Ibid., 202–204.

117. Ibid., 190–198.

118. Naomi J. Freeman, "The public safety impact of community notification laws: rear-rest of convicted sex offenders," *Crime and Delinquency* (OnlineFirst, published on May 18, 2009 as doi:10.1177/0011128708330852).

119. Ibid., 9.

120. Ibid., 18.

121. Kelly M. Babchishin, R. Karl Hanson, and Chantal A. Hermann, "The characteristics of online sex offenders: A meta-analysis," unpublished paper, 2.

122. Wolak et al., *supra* note 113, 111.

123. Kimberly J. Mitchell, Janis Wolak, and David Finkelhor, "Police posing as juveniles online to catch sex offenders: Is it working?" *Sexual Abuse: A Journal of Research and Treatment* (2005): 17(3), 241–267, 245.

CHAPTER 6

1. American Association of University Women, *Hostile hallways: Bullying, teasing, and sexual harassment in school* (2001), Washington, DC, American Association of University Women.

2. Ibid., 2.

3. Ibid., 13.

4. Ibid., 13.

5. Charol Shakeshaft, "Educator sexual misconduct: A synthesis of existing literature" US Department of Education (2004): 17–18. Available at: http://www2.ed.gov/rschstat/research/pubs/misconductreview/report.pdf (accessed May 2, 2013).

6. Ibid., 18.

7. Ibid.

8. Amos Kamil, "Prep-school predators: The Horace Mann School's secret history of sexual abuse," *New York Times*, June 6, 2012. Available at: http://www.nytimes.com/2012/06/10/magazine/the-horace-mann-schools-secret-history-of-sexual-abuse.html?pagewanted=all&_r=0 (accessed May 2, 2013).

9. Shakeshaft, *supra* note 5, 29.

10. Ibid., 24.

11. Ibid., 31–32.

12. Ontario College of Teachers, *Professional misconduct related to sexual abuse and sexual misconduct* (2002): 2. Available at: http://professionallyspeaking.oct.ca/publications/PDF/advisory100802_e.pdf (accessed May 2, 2013).

13. *See, e.g.,* Stephen Smallbone, William L Marshall, and Richard Wortley, *Preventing child sexual abuse: Evidence, policy and practice* (2008): 164, Portland, Oregon, Willan Publishing.

14. United Educators, *Preventing molestation in schools* (undated): 3, cached version. Available at: http://webcache.googleusercontent.com/search?q=cache:pPxjqZU5LYwJ:osig.org/vault/doclib/document.htm%3Fid%3D247+United+Educators,+Preventing+Molestation+in+Schools&cd=2&hl=en&ct=clnk&gl=us (accessed May 2, 2013).

15. *See* Shakshaft, *supra* note 5, 43.

16. *See, e.g.,* Gordon Dillow, "$6.8 million settlement doesn't say 'we're sorry,'" *Orange County Register*, August 3, 2003, B1; Charlie Roduta, "Schools diversify insurance coverage," *Columbus Dispatch*, July 10, 2006, 1A.

17. Review Panel on Prison Rape, Report of Sexual Victimization in Juvenile Correctional Facilities (October 2010). Available at: http://www.ojp.usdoj.gov/reviewpanel/reviewpanel.htm (accessed May 2, 2013).

18. Ibid., 1–2.
19. Ibid., 2.
20. Ibid.
21. Ibid.
22. Bureau of Justice Statistics, "Sexual abuse plagues U.S. prisons and jails," August 27, 2010. Available at: http://www.corrections.com/articles/25688 (accessed May 2, 2013).
23. Review Panel on Prison Rape, *supra* note 17, 17.
24. Ibid., 22.
25. Ibid., 26.
26. Ibid., 6.
27. Ibid., 13.
28. Ibid., 2–3.
29. US Department of Justice, Office of Justice Programs, Bureau of Justice Statistics Status Report: "Prison Rape Elimination Act of 2003, PREA Data Collection Activities," (June 2010). Available at: http://bjs.gov/content/pub/ascii/pdca10.txt (accessed May 2, 2013).
30. Allen J. Beck, Paige M. Harrison, and Paul Guerino, "Sexual victimization in juvenile facilities reported by youth, 2008-09" (January 2010): 3. Available at: http://www.scribd.com/doc/25076850/U-S-DOJ-Report-on-Sexual-Victimization-in-Juvenile-Facilities-2010 (accessed May 2, 2013).
31. Ibid.
32. Beck et al., *supra* note 30.
33. Ibid.
34. Ibid.
35. *See* Christopher Hartney, "National Council on Crime and Delinquency Fact Sheet: Youth under age 18 in the adult criminal justice system" (2006). Available at: http://www.wcl.american.edu/endsilence/documents/youthunder18intheCJ system.pdf (accessed May 2, 2013).
36. James Austin, Kelly Dedel Johnson, and Maria Gregoriou, "Juveniles in adult prisons and jails: A national assessment" (2000). Available at: https://www.ncjrs.gov/pdffiles1/bja/182503.pdf (accessed May 2, 2013).
37. Allen J. Beck, Paige M. Harrison, Marcus Berzofsky, Rachel Caspar, and Christopher Krebs, "Sexual victimization in prisons and jails reported by inmates, 2008-09" (2010): 12. Available at: http://www.wcl.american.edu/endsilence/documents/SexualVictimizationinPrisonsandJailsReportedbyInmates2008-9.pdf (accessed May 2, 2013).
38. National Criminal Justice Reference Service, National Prison Rape Elimination Commission Report (2009): 146.
39. Ibid.
40. Ibid., 147.
41. Beck et al., *supra* note 30.
42. Review Panel on Prison Rape, *supra* note 17, 4–35.
43. Ibid., 13.
44. National Criminal Justice Reference Service, *supra* note 38, 149.
45. Ibid.
46. Ibid., 150.
47. Ibid., 155.
48. Ibid., 151.

49. Review Panel on Prison Rape, *supra* note 17, 11.
50. Ibid., 34.
51. Ibid.
52. Ibid.
53. Ibid., 11.
54. Ibid., 14.
55. Ibid., 21.
56. Ibid.
57. National Criminal Justice Reference Service, *supra* note 38, 119.
58. Review Panel on Prison Rape, *supra* note 17, 34.
59. Bernard Gallagher, "The extent and nature of known cases of institutional child sexual abuse," *British Journal of Social Work* (2000): 30, 795–817, 805–806.
60. Review Panel on Prison Rape, *supra* note 17, 28.
61. Ibid., 19.
62. Smallbone et al., *supra* note 13, 168.
63. Ibid.
64. Doulas Linder, "The McMartin preschool abuse trial: A commentary" (2003). Available at: http://law2.umkc.edu/faculty/projects/ftrials/mcmartin/mcmartinaccount.html (accessed May 2, 2013).
65. Ibid.
66. Ibid.
67. Robert Reinhold, "The longest trial—a post-mortem. Collapse of child-abuse case: So much agony for so little," *New York Times*, January 24, 1990, A1. Available at: http://www.nytimes.com/1990/01/24/us/longest-trial-post-mortem-collapse-child-abuse-case-so-much-agony-for-so-little.html?pagewanted=all&src=pm (accessed May 2, 2013).
68. Ibid.
69. Doulas Linder, *supra* note 64.
70. David Finkelhor, Linda Meyer Williams, Nanci Burns, and Michael Kalinowski "Sexual abuse in day care: A national study" (1988). Available at: https://www.ncjrs.gov/pdffiles1/Digitization/113095NCJRS.pdf (accessed May 2, 2013); David Finkelhor and Linda Meyer Williams, *Nursery crimes: Sexual abuse in day care* (1988), Newbury Park, California, Sage Publications.
71. Finkelhor et al., *supra* note 70, 4.
72. *See, e.g.,* Marcus Erooga, *Creating safer organisations: Practical ways to prevent the abuse of children by those working with them* (2012): 38, Chichester, West Sussex, Wiley-Blackwell.
73. Warren E. Leary, "Risk of sex abuse in day care seen as lower than at home," *New York Times*, March 22, 1988. Available at: http://www.nytimes.com/1988/03/22/us/risk-of-sex-abuse-in-day-care-seen-as-lower-than-at-home.html (accessed May 2, 2013).
74. Ibid.
75. Finkelhor et al., *supra* note 70, 4.
76. Kathy Karageorge and Rosemary Kendall, "The role of professional child care providers in preventing and responding to child abuse and neglect" (2008): 33. Available at: https://www.childwelfare.gov/pubs/usermanuals/childcare/childcare.pdf (accessed May 2, 2013).

77. US Department of Health & Human Services, Administration for Children and Families, Administration on Children, Youth and Families, Children's Bureau, "Child maltreatment 2010" (2010): ix, 84.

78. Finkelhor and Williams, *supra* note 70, 25.

79. Child Care in America 2012 State Fact Sheets: 8. Available at: http://www.naccrra. org/sites/default/files/default_site_pages/2012/full2012cca_state_factsheetbook. pdf (accessed May 2, 2013).

80. Ibid., 10.

81. Finkelhor et al., *supra* note 70, 69.

82. Ibid.

83. Ibid., 149.

84. Ibid.

85. Karageorge and Kendall, *supra* note 76, 41.

86. Finkelhor et al., *supra* note 70, 150.

87. National Child Care Information and Technical Assistance Center, "The 2008 child care licensing study" (2010): 8. Available at: http://www.naralicensing.drivehq. com/2008_Licensing_Study/1005_2008_Child%20Care%20Licensing%20Study_ Full_Report.pdf (accessed May 2, 2013).

88. Ibid.

89. Ibid., 1.

90. Ibid., 42–43.

91. United States Government Accountability Office, "Overview of relevant employment laws and cases of sex offenders at child care facilities," (August 2011). Available at: http://www.gao.gov/new.items/d11757.pdf (accessed May 2, 2013)

92. Child Care Aware of America, "Background checks: It is time to protect children in child care," (March 2013): 13–14. Available at: http://www.naccrra.org/sites/ default/files/default_site_pages/2013/background_checks_white_paper_final_ march_9_2013_0.pdf (accessed May 2, 2013).

93. Ibid.

94. Ibid., 2–3.

95. U.S. General Accounting Office, "Child care: Overview of relevant employment laws and cases of sex offenders at child care facilities," September 13, 2011. Available at: http://www.gao.gov/assets/330/322726.html (accessed May 2, 2013).

96. Ibid.

97. Ibid.

98. Ibid.

99. Ibid.

100. Inspector General, US Department of Health and Human Services, quoted in Finkelhor et al., *supra* note 70, 59–60.

101. *See, e.g.,* Leslie J. Calman and Linda Tarr-Whelan, "Early childhood education for all: A wise investment," (2005): 4. Available at: http://web.mit.edu/workplacecenter/ docs/Full%20Report.pdf (accessed May 2, 2013).

102. Child Care Aware of America, *supra* note 92, 2.

103. Finkelhor et al., *supra* note 70, 71.

104. Ibid., 97.

105. Ibid.

106. Ibid., 97–98.

107. Ibid., 98.

108. Ibid.

109. Karen J. Terry, Margaret Leland Smith, Katarina Schuth, James R. Kelly, Brenda Vollman, and Christina Massey, "The causes and context of sexual abuse of minors by Catholic priests in the United States, 1950-2010" (2011). Available at: http://www.usccb.org/issues-and-action/child-and-youth-protection/upload/The-Causes-and-Context-of-Sexual-Abuse-of-Minors-by-Catholic-Priests-in-the-United-States-1950-2010.pdf (accessed May 2, 2013).

110. Ibid., 9.

111. Ibid., 9–10.

112. Ibid., 10.

113. Ibid.

114. Ibid., 8.

115. Ibid., 32.

116. Tom Roberts, "Critics point to John Jay study's limitations," *National Catholic Reporter*, May. 23, 2011. Available at: http://ncronline.org/news/accountability/critics-point-john-jay-studys-limitations (accessed May 2, 2013).

117. Ibid.

118. "United States Conference of Catholic Bishops, Charter for the Protection of Children and Young People," June 16, 2011. Available at: http://www.usccb.org/issues-and-action/child-and-youth-protection/upload/Charter-for-the-Protection-of-Children-and-Young-People-revised-2011.pdf (accessed May 2, 2013).

119. *See, e.g.,* Karen E. McClintock, *Preventing sexual abuse in congregations: A resource for leaders* (2004), Herndon, Virginia, The Alban Institute.

120. Praesidium Accreditation Standards. Available at: http://www.saintjohnsabbey.org/response/twentyfive.pdf (accessed May 2, 2013).

121. Monica Applewhite and Paul Macke. The Response of Religious Institutes of Men to the Crisis of Sexual Abuse in the Roman Catholic Church in the United States, 221–232, Santa Barbara, California, Praeger..

122. On the Establishment of Safe Environment Programs. Available at: http://www.crookston.org/sep/partonearticlethree.pdf (accessed May 2, 2013).

123. Plante and McChesney, *supra* note 121, 75.

124. Ibid., 45.

125. United States Conference of Catholic Bishops, *supra* note 118.

126. Plante and McChesney, *supra* note 121, 45.

127. Ibid., 234.

128. Ibid., 234–235.

129. Ibid., 200.

130. Ibid., 201.

131. Boy Scouts of America, "Facts about scouting." Available at: http://www.scouting.org/About/FactSheets/ScoutingFacts.aspx (accessed May 2, 2013).

132. Jessica Naziri and Nell Gram, "Boy Scout files on suspected abuse published by The Times," *Los Angeles Times*, December 25, 2012. Available at: http://articles.latimes.com/2012/dec/25/local/la-me-scouts-data-20121226 (accessed May 2, 2013); Files available at: http://spreadsheets.latimes.com/boyscouts-cases/ (accessed May 2, 2013).

133. Janet I. Warren, "Review of the ineligible volunteer (IV) files of the Boy Scouts of America (BSA)," August 25, 2011. Available at: http://www.scouting.org/filestore/youthprotection/pdf/WarrenReport.pdf (accessed May 2, 2013).
134. Ibid.
135. Scott K. Parks, "Boy Scouts shield abuser files used to vet volunteers, *Dallas Morning News*, September 12, 2010. Available at: http://www.dallasnews.com/news/local-news/20100911-Boy-Scouts-shield-abuser-files-used-9797.ece (accessed May 2, 2013).
136. Ibid.
137. Janet I. Warren, Statement of Dr. Janet I. Warren Regarding BSA's Ineligible Volunteer Files, September 20, 2012. Available at: http://www.scouting.org/filestore/youthprotection/pdf/WarrenReportSummary.pdf (accessed May 2, 2013).
138. Ibid.
139. Ibid.
140. Ibid.
141. Ibid.
142. Ibid.
143. Kim Christensen and Jason Felch, "Boy Scout files show suspects got help hiding; Scouting officials in many cases aided accused molesters in covering their tracks," *Los Angeles Times*, September 16, 2012, A1.
144. Ibid.
145. Ibid.
146. Ibid.
147. Ibid.
148. Ibid.
149. US Department of Health and Human Services, Centers for Disease Control and Prevention, "Preventing child sexual abuse within youth-serving organizations: getting started on policies and procedures" (2007): 1. Available at: http://www.cdc.gov/violenceprevention/pdf/PreventingChildSexualAbuse-a.pdf (accessed May 2, 2012).
150. Boy Scouts of America, Youth Protection Guidelines: Training for volunteer leaders and parents. Available at: http://www.usscouts.org/safety/yp_guidelines.pdf (accessed May 2, 2013).
151. Ibid., 8–9.
152. Ibid.
153. Christensen and Felch, *supra* note 143.
154. Warren, *supra* note 137.
155. US Department of Health and Human Services, Centers for Disease Control and Prevention, *supra* note 149, 5.
156. Boy Scouts of America, Adult application. Available at: http://www.scouting.org/filestore/pdf/524-501.pdf (accessed May 2, 2013).
157. Ibid.
158. Boy Scouts of America, "Youth protection & adult leadership" (2012). Available at: http://www.scouting.org/scoutsource/HealthandSafety/GSS/gss01.aspx (accessed May 2, 2013).
159. US Department of Health and Human Services, Centers for Disease Control and Prevention, *supra* note 149, 5.

160. Ibid., 6.
161. Ibid., 7.
162. Ibid., 24.
163. Ibid., 27.
164. Ibid.
165. Ibid., 28.
166. Ibid.
167. Boy Scouts of America, "Youth protection." Available at: http://www.scouting.org/Training/YouthProtection.aspx (accessed May 2, 2013).
168. Freeh, Sporkin and Sullivan, LLP, Report of the Special Investigative Counsel Regarding the Actions of the Pennsylvania State University Related to the Child Sexual Abuse Committed by Gerald A. Sandusky (July 12. 2012): 129. Available at: http://progress.psu.edu/the-freeh-report (accessed May 1, 2013).
169. Ibid.
170. US Department of Health and Human Services, Centers for Disease Control and Prevention, *supra* note 149, 30.

CHAPTER 7

1. End Child Prostitution, Child Pornography, and the Trafficking of Children for Sex (ECPAT) International, *Europe and North America Regional Profile* (1996): 70, Bangkok, Thailand, ECPAT.
2. Testimony of Deborah Richardson, Chief Program Officer, Women's Funding Network, U.S. House of Representatives Judiciary Subcommittee on Crime Terrorism, and Homeland Security Hearing Regarding, "Domestic minor sex trafficking," September 15, 2010. Available at: http://judiciary.house.gov/hearings/pdf/Richardson100915.pdf (accessed May 3, 2013).
3. US Department of State, "The facts about child sex tourism," (2005): 1. Available at: http://2001-2009.state.gov/documents/organization/51459.pdf (accessed May 2, 2013).
4. Janice G. Raymond and Donna M. Hughes, "Sex trafficking of women in the United States," (2001): 5. Available at: https://www.ncjrs.gov/pdffiles1/nij/grants/187774.pdf (accessed May 3, 2013).
5. Unite for Sight, "Child labor and child abuse in developing countries," (2011). Available at: http://www.uniteforsight.org/gender-power/module4 (accessed May 3, 2013).
6. Fair Trade in Tourism, "Child sex tourism: SA travel and tourism industry takes a stance," (2010). Available at: http://www.fairtradetourism.org.za/thecode/resources/media/Industry%20Fights%20Child%20Sex%20Tourism.pdf (accessed May 3, 2013).
7. "Domestic minor sex trafficking," Hearing before the U.S. House of Representatives, Subcommittee on Crime, Terrorism, and Homeland Security of the Committee on the Judiciary, September 15, 2010. Transcript available at: http://judiciary.house.gov/hearings/printers/111th/111-146_58250.PDF (accessed May 3, 2013).
8. National Center for Missing & Exploited Children, "About us." Available at: http://www.missingkids.com/About (accessed May 3, 2013).
9. Testimony of Ernie Allen, U.S. House of Representatives Victims' Rights Caucus and Human Trafficking Caucus, July 19, 2010.

10. Richard J. Estes and Neil Alan Weiner, "The commercial sexual exploitation of children in the U. S., Canada and Mexico, executive summary" (2001): 1. Available at: http://www.sp2.upenn.edu/restes/CSEC_Files/Exec_Sum_020220.pdf (accessed May 3, 2013).

11. Ibid., 2.

12. Ibid., 10.

13. Ibid.

14. Ibid.

15. Martin Cizmar, Ellis Conklin, and Kristen Hinman, "Real men get their facts straight; Ashton and Demi and sex trafficking," *Village Voice*, June 29, 2011 [bracketed material in original]. Available at: http://www.villagevoice.com/2011-06-29/news/real-men-get-their-facts-straight-sex-trafficking-ashton-kutcher-demi-moore/ (accessed May 3, 2013).

16. Ibid.

17. Ibid.

18. Rick Jervis, "Super Bowl draws child sex rings: Law enforcement targets human trafficking near event," *USA Today*, February 1, 2011, 3A. Available at: http://usatoday30.usatoday.com/printedition/news/20110201/superbowlsexrings01_st.art.htm (accessed May 3, 2013).

19. Patricia Leigh Brown, "In Oakland, redefining sex trade workers as abuse victims," *New York Times*, May 24, 2011, A13.

20. Katie McLaughlin, "Moore, Kutcher: Join our crusade to end child sex trafficking," *CNN*, April 15, 2011. Available at: http://www.cnn.com/2011/WORLD/americas/04/14/kutcher.moore.piers.morgan/index.html (accessed May 2, 2013).

21. Cizmar et al. *supra* note 15.

22. Nick Pinto, "Women's Funding Network sex trafficking study is junk science: Schapiro Group data wasn't questioned by mainstream media," *Village Voice*, Mar 23 2011. Available at: http://www.villagevoice.com/2011-03-23/news/women-s-funding-network-sex-trafficking-study-is-junk-science/ (accessed May 3, 2013).

23. Testimony of Deborah Richardson, Chief Program Officer, Women's Funding Network, Hearing of the U.S. House of Representatives, Crime, Terrorism, and Homeland Security Subcommittee of the Committee on the Judiciary, September 15, 2010.

24. Women's Funding Network, The Supply of Commercially Exploited Girls on the Rise in Three U.S. States, (Press Release) August 3, 2010. Available at: http://www.womensfundingnetwork.org/about/news/press-releases/the-supply-of-commercially-exploited-girls-on-the-rise-in-three-us-states (accessed May 3, 2013).

25. The Schapiro Group, "Adolescent girls in the United States sex trade: Tracking results for May 2010," (Report prepared for Women's Funding Network). Available at: http://www.scribd.com/doc/50736028/Adolescent-Girls-in-the-United-States-Sex-Trade (accessed May 3, 2013).

26. Nick Pinto, *supra* note 22.

27. Ibid.

28. Ibid.

29. Ibid.

30. UNESCO, Trafficking Statistics Projects Description. Available at: http://human-trafficking.org/links/83 (accessed May 2, 2013).

31. *See, e.g.*, UNESCO, "Data comparison sheet #1: Worldwide trafficking estimates by organizations UNESCO Trafficking Project," (2004). Available at: http://www.unescobkk.org/fileadmin/user_upload/culture/Trafficking/project/Graph_Worldwide_Sept_2004.pdf (accessed May 2, 2013).

32. PBS Frontline, "Sex slaves: Estimating the numbers," (2006). Available at:http://www.pbs.org/wgbh/pages/frontline/slaves/etc/stats.html#2 (accessed May 3, 2013).

33. Heather J. Clawson, Nicole Dutch, Amy Solomon, and Lisa Goldblatt Grace, "Human trafficking into and within the United States: A review of the literature," (2009). Available at: http://aspe.hhs.gov/hsp/07/humantrafficking/litrev/ (accessed May 3, 2013).

34. UNICEF, "Children on the edge: Protecting children from sexual exploitation and trafficking in East Asia and the Pacific." Available at: http://www.unicef.org/vietnam/childse.pdf (accessed May 3, 2013).

35. Siddharth Kara, *Sex trafficking: Inside the business of modern slavery* (2010): 17, New York, Columbia University Press.

36. UNICEF, *supra* note 34, 3.

37. UNICEF, "Profiting from abuse: An investigation into the sexual exploitation of our children," (2001): 7. Available at: http://www.unicef.org/publications/files/pub_profiting_en.pdf (accessed May 3, 2013).

38. "Official: More than 1M child prostitutes in India," *CNN*, May 11, 2009. Available at: http://edition.cnn.com/2009/WORLD/asiapcf/05/11/india.prostitution.children/ (accessed May 3, 2013).

39. Charles M. Goolsby, Jr., "Dynamics of prostitution and sex trafficking from Latin America into the United States," (2003). Available at: http://www.childtrafficking.com/Docs/cul_bground_latin_america_0108.pdf (accessed May 3, 2013).

40. UNHCR, "2011 trafficking in persons report—Brazil," June 27, 2011. Available at: http://www.refworld.org/country,,,,BRA,,4e12ee9116,0.html (accessed May 3, 2013).

41. ECPAT International, Russian Federation, "Global monitoring report on the status of action against commercial sexual exploitation of Children: Russian Federation," (2006). Available at: http://s3.amazonaws.com/rcpp/assets/attachments/241_306_EN_original.pdf (accessed May 3, 2013).

42. "Trafficking and sexual exploitation between Venezuela and Ecuador," Survivors' Rights International, July 17, 2003. Available at: http://web.archive.org/web/20080515164643/http:/www.survivorsrightsinternational.org/sri_news/alert_sexual_exploit.mv (accessed May 4, 2013).

43. Julia O'Connell Davidson and Jacqueline Sanchez Taylor, "Child prostitution and sex tourism: Dominican Republic," research paper prepared for ECPAT, (1996). Available at: http://www.childtrafficking.com/Docs/o_connell_1996__child_prost3.pdf (accessed May 4, 2013).

44. "Gateways to exploitation," *Globe and Mail*, November 10, 2007. Available at; http://www.theglobeandmail.com/news/world/gateways-to-exploitation/article1089077/ (accessed May 4, 2013).

45. Ibid.

46. UNICEF, "Report reveals Kenyan child sex industry of 'horrific' magnitude." Available at: http://www.unicef.org/infobycountry/kenya_37817.html (accessed May 4, 2013).

47. Willy Pedersen and Kristinn Hegna, "Children and adolescents who sell sex: A community study," *Social Science and Medicine* (2003): 56, 135–147, 1.

48. Ibid., 142.

49. Fair Trade in Tourism, "The Code Workshop," October 26, 2010. Available at: www.fairtourismsa.org.za/.../Code_Training_FTTSA_WSPresentationNo (accessed May 4, 2013).

50. ECPAT International, "Combating child sex tourism: Questions and answers," (2008): 7. Available at: http://www.ecpat.net/ei/Publications/CST/CST_FAQ_ENG.pdf (accessed May 4, 2013).

51. "This could be your kid," *Newsweek*, August 17, 2003. Available at: http://www.the-dailybeast.com/newsweek/2003/08/17/this-could-be-your-kid.html (accessed May 4, 2013).

52. US Department of Justice, Office of Justice Programs, National Institute of Justice, "Commercial sexual exploitation of children: What do we know and what do we do about it?" (2007): 3. Available at: https://www.ncjrs.gov/pdffiles1/nij/215733.pdf (accessed May 4, 2013).

53. Kimberly Mitchell, David Finkelhor, and Janis Wolak, "Conceptualizing juvenile child prostitution as child maltreatment: Findings from the national juvenile prostitution study," *Child Maltreatment* (2010): 15, 18–36, 18.

54. Ibid., 19.

55. Ibid., 25.

56. Ibid., 26.

57. Ibid.

58. Ibid., 27.

59. Testimony of Steven R. Galster, Commission on Security and Cooperation in Europe, 106th Congress, 1st Session, June 28, 1999.

60. Mitchell et al., *supra* note 53, 26–27.

61. US Department of Justice, The national strategy for child exploitation and interdiction: A report to Congress (2010): 32–33. Available at: http://www.justice.gov/psc/docs/natstrategyreport.pdf (accessed May 4, 2013).

62. Kara, *supra* note 35, 19.

63. Heather Clawson and Linda Goldblatt Grace, "Finding a path to recovery: Residential facilities for minor victims of domestic sex trafficking," US Department of Health and Human Services, (2007). Available at: http://digitalcommons.unl.edu/humtraffdata/10/?utm_source=digitalcommons.unl.edu%2Fhumtraffdata%2F10&utm_medium=PDF&utm_campaign=PDFCoverPages (accessed May 4, 2013).

64. Mitchell et al., *supra* note 53, 32.

65. Ibid., 26.

66. US Department of Justice, *supra* note 61, 34.

67. New York Penal Law § 230.04.

68. Ibid., § 230.05.

69. Ibid., § 230.06.

70. Ibid., § 130.25.

71. Ibid., § 130.30.
72. Ibid., § 130.35.
73. Ibid., § 230.07.
74. Ibid., § 230.20.
75. Ibid., § 230.25.
76. Ibid., § 230.30.
77. Ibid., § 230.32.
78. Ibid., § 260.10.
79. Ibid., § 260.20.
80. 18 U.S.C. § 2423.
81. 18 U.S.C. § 2422.
82. 18 U.S.C. § 1591.
83. 18 U.S.C. § 2423(b).
84. US Department of Justice, "Citizen's guide to U.S. federal law on the extraterritorial sexual exploitation of children." Available at: http://www.justice.gov/criminal/ceos/citizensguide/citizensguide_trafficking.html (accessed May 4, 2013).
85. 18 U.S.C. § 2423(d).
86. U.S. Immigration and Customs Enforcement, "Fact sheet: Operation Predator: Targeting child exploitation and sexual crimes," June 25, 2012. Available at: http://www.ice.gov/news/library/factsheets/predator.htm (accessed May 4, 2013).
87. United Nations, "Protocol to prevent, suppress and punish trafficking in persons, especially women and children," (2010). Available at: http://ec.europa.eu/anti-trafficking/download.action?nodePath=%2FLegislation+and+Case+Law%2FInternational+Legislation%2FUnited+Nations%2FUnited+Nations+Protocol+on+THB_en.pdf&fileName=United+Nations+Protocol+on+THB_en.pdf&fileType=pdf (accessed May 4, 2013).
88. European Commission, "Together against trafficking in human beings," January 11, 2013. Available at: http://ec.europa.eu/anti-trafficking/section.action;jsessionid=DMFhRQkMB59pqQk3LsRlcN5g5dpnTh64Gy4PywSRHFlxylbwCJgQ!-656776111?sectionPath=Legislation+and+Case+Law%2FInternational+Legislation%2FUnited+Nations (accessed May 4, 2013).
89. United Nations Office on Drugs and Crime, United Nations Convention against Transnational Organized Crime and the Protocols Thereto (2012). Available at: http://www.unodc.org/unodc/treaties/CTOC/ (accessed May 2, 2013).
90. United Nations Office on Drugs and Crime, Definition of Trafficking in Persons (2013). Available at: http://www.unodc.org/southeastasiaandpacific/en/topics/illicit-trafficking/human-trafficking-definition.html (accessed May 4, 2013).
91. United Nations, United Nations Treaty Collection (Status as at May 13, 2013, 05:21:42 EDT). Available at: http://treaties.un.org/Pages/ViewDetails.aspx?src=TREATY&mtdsg_no=XVIII-12-a&chapter=18&lang=en (accessed May 13, 2013).
92. United Nations Office on Drugs and Crime, "Human trafficking: A crime that shames us all," (February 2009). Available at: http://www.ungift.org/doc/knowledgehub/resource-centre/GIFT_Global_Report_Executive_summaries_all_languages.pdf (accessed May 4, 2013).
93. Ibid., 9.

94. Council of Europe Parliamentary Assembly, "Fighting 'child sex tourism,'" March 14, 3013. Available at: http://www.assembly.coe.int/Communication/Asocdoc16_2013.pdf (accessed May 4, 2013).

95. Mohamed Y. Mattar, "Child sexual tourism: The appropriate legal response," 2003. Available at: http://www.protectionproject.org/wp-content/uploads/2010/09/Sex-Tourism-Response.pdf (accessed May 4, 2013).

96. World Tourism Organization, ECPAT International, Interpol, International Hotel and Restaurants Association, Tourism Authority of Thailand, EMBRATUR, Tour Operators' Initiative for Sustainable Tourism Development, Federation of International Youth Travel Organizations, Japan Committee for UNICEF, "Code of conduct for the protection of children from sexual exploitation in travel and tourism." Available at: http://www.ecpat.net/ei/Publications/CST/Code_of_Conduct_ENG.pdf (accessed May 4, 2013).

97. Ibid., 3.

98. ECPAT, "What experts think on combating child sex tourism: Findings of interviews with selected experts," (2009). Available at: http://www.defenceforchildren.nl/images/13/875.pdf (accessed May 4, 2013).

99. See, e.g., Nicholas D. Kristof, "How pimps use the web to sell girls," New York Times, January 25, 2012. Available at: http://www.nytimes.com/2012/01/26/opinion/how-pimps-use-the-web-to-sell-girls.html?hp&_r=1 (accessed May 4, 2013); Daniel Fisher, "Backpage takes heat, but prostitution ads are everywhere," Forbes, January 26, 2012. Available at: http://www.forbes.com/sites/danielfisher/2012/01/26/backpages-takes-heat-for-prostitution-ads-that-are-everywhere/ (accessed May 4, 2013); Jessica Brady, "Senators take on Village Voice Media over child prostitution," Roll Call, May 2, 2012. Available at: http://www.rollcall.com/news/senators_take_on_village_voice_media_over_child_prostitution-214232-1.html (accessed May 4, 2013); J. J. Hensley, "Adult services ads are targeted," The Republic, May. 19, 2012. Available at: http://www.azcentral.com/arizonarepublic/local/articles/20120516backpage-adult-ads-targeted.html (accessed, May 4, 2013).

100. "Lawsuit accuses Craigslist of promoting prostitution," CNN, March 5, 2009. Available at: http://www.cnn.com/2009/CRIME/03/05/craigs.list.prostitution/ (accessed May 4, 2013).

101. "Craigslist to remove erotic services section, monitor adult services posts," Los Angeles Times, May 13, 2009. Available at: http://latimesblogs.latimes.com/technology/2009/05/craigslist-attorneys-general-erotic-services-prostitution.html (accessed May 4, 2013).

102. See, e.g., The Associated Press, "New bill outlaws prostitution ads," Houston News, April 17, 2013. Available at: http://www.ktrh.com/articles/houston-news-121300/new-bill-outlaws-prostitution-ads-11199118/ (accessed May 4, 2013); Karen Boros, "Minneapolis targets Backpage.com ads in fight against juvenile sex trafficking," Minneapolis Post, August 8, 2012. Available at: http://www.minnpost.com/two-cities/2012/08/minneapolis-targets-backpagecom-ads-fight-against-juvenile-sex-trafficking (accessed May 4, 2013).

103. Letter to Hedda Litwin, National Association of Attorneys General, from Samuel Fifer, SNR Denton US LLP, September 23, 2011. Available at: http://www.thestranger.com/images/blogimages/2011/09/27/1317168662-backpage_response_to_naag.pdf (accessed May 4, 2013).

104. Ibid.

105. Jessica Brady, "Senators take on Village Voice Media over child prostitu-
    tion," *Roll Call*, May 2, 2012. Available at: http://www.rollcall.com/news/
    senators_take_on_village_voice_media_over_child_prostitution-214232-1.html
    (accessed May 4, 2013).

106. "Senators call on Backpage to end human trafficking through adult services
    advertising," (Press Release) April 26, 2012. Available at: http://www.blumenthal.
    senate.gov/newsroom/press/release/senators-call-on-backpage-to-end-human-
    trafficking-through-adult-services-advertising (accessed May 4, 2013).

107. Ibid.

108. Letter to Samuel Fifer, Counsel for Backpage.Com, LLC, from National Association
    of Attorneys General, August 31, 2011. Available at: http://www.tn.gov/
    attorneygeneral/cases/backpage/backpageletter.pdf (accessed May 4, 2013).

109. "Clergy coalition launches campaign to educate Village Voice Media's top 50
    advertisers about sex ads of minors on Backpage.com," (Press Release) April 19,
    2012. Available at: http://wolf.house.gov/uploads/Backpage.com%20Release.pdf
    (accessed May 4, 2013).

110. "Petition: Tell Village Voice Media to stop child sex trafficking on Backpage.com,"
    Change.org. Available at: http://www.change.org/petitions/tell-village-voice-media-
    to-stop-child-sex-trafficking-on-backpage-com (accessed May 4, 2013).

111. Robert Sanborn, "Time to pull the plug on adult ads on Backpage.com," *Houston
    Chronicle*, July 10, 2012. Available at: http://www.chron.com/opinion/outlook/
    article/Time-to-pull-the-plug-on-adult-ads-on-backpage-com-3697366.php
    (accessed May 4, 2013).

112. Pierce Greenberg, "Federal judge issues restraining order against state law aimed
    at Backpage.com," *Nashville City Paper*, January 4, 2013. Available at: http://
    nashvillecitypaper.com/content/city-news/federal-judge-issues-restraining-
    order-against-state-law-aimed-backpagecom (accessed May 4, 2013).

113. Mike Masnick, "Oh look: Police can use Backpage.com to track down, arrest & con-
    vict pimps & prostitutes," *Techdirt*, October 2, 2012 available at: http://www.techdirt.
    com/articles/20121002/07354820569/oh-look-police-can-use-backpagecom-to-
    track-down-arrest-convict-pimps-prostitutes.shtml (accessed May 4, 2013).

114. Elizabeth Stuart, "Companies pull ads from Village Voice Media to protest child
    sex trafficking," *Deseret News*, May 3, 2012. Available at: http://www.deseretnews.
    com/article/865555189/Companies-pull-ads-from-Village-Voice-Media-to-
    protest-child-sex-trafficking.html?pg=all (accessed May 4, 2013).

115. Fisher, *supra* note 99.

116. Olga Kharif, "Prostitution ads return to Craigslist in some markets, report says,"
    Bloomberg News, May 24, 2012. Available at: http://go.bloomberg.com/tech-blog
    /2012-05-24-prostitution-ads-return-to-craigslist-in-some-markets-report-says/
    (accessed May 4, 2013).

117. AIM Group, "Sex ads: Where the money is," September 14, 2010, p. 2. Available
    at: http://aimgroup.com/files/2010/09/sex-ad-report-summary.pdf (accessed May
    4, 2013).

118. New Wales Department of Health, "Safeguarding children involved in prostitu-
    tion," (2000): 41. Available at: http://www.westsussex.gov.uk/idoc.ashx?docid=
    a40649a4-1c0d-4b05-9318-815fe7c68252&version=-1 (accessed May 4, 2013).

119. J. Robert Flores, "Protecting our children: Working together to end child prostitution," (December 2002): 5. Available at: https://www.ncjrs.gov/pdffiles1/ojjdp/204990.pdf (accessed May 4, 2013).

120. Mitchell et al., *supra* note 53, 33.

121. Ibid.

122. ECPAT International, *supra* note 50, 27.

123. ECPAT, "Young person's guide to combating child sex tourism," (2008): 12. Available at: http://www.ecpat.net/ei/Publications/CYP/YP_Guide_to_CST_ENG.pdf (accessed May 4, 2013).

124. Stephanie Lambidakis, "79 rescued in child prostitution sweep," *CBS News*, June 25, 2012. Available at: http://www.cbsnews.com/8301-201_162-57460095/fbi-79-rescued-in-child-prostitution-sweep/ (accessed May 4, 2013).

125. Clawson and Grace, *supra* note 63.

126. Lambidakis, *supra* note 124.

127. Clawson and Grace, *supra* note 63.

128. Ibid., 2.

129. Ibid., 8.

CHAPTER 8

1. "G8 experience in the implementation of extraterritorial jurisdiction for sex crimes against children," April 18, 2007, Child. Available at: http://torc.linkbc.ca/torc/downs1/Extraterritorial%20Jurisdiction.pdf (accessed May 5, 2013).

2. US Department of Homeland Security, "Fact sheet: Operation predator: Targeting child exploitation and sexual crimes," June 25, 2012. Available at: http://www.ice.gov/news/library/factsheets/predator.htm (accessed May 5, 2013).

3. United States Conference of Catholic Bishops, Charter for the Protection of Children and Young People, June 16, 2011. Available at: http://www.usccb.org/issues-and-action/child-and-youth-protection/upload/Charter-for-the-Protection-of-Children-and-Young-People-revised-2011.pdf (accessed May 2, 2013).

4. National Children's Alliance, "Child and family friendly facilities." Available at: http://www.nationalchildrensalliance.org/index.php?s=36 (accessed May 5, 2013).

5. *See, e.g.,* David Finkelhor, "The prevention of childhood sexual abuse," Fall 2009. Available at: http://futureofchildren.org/futureofchildren/publications/docs/19_02_08.pdf (accessed May 5, 2013).

ABOUT THE AUTHOR

Charles Patrick Ewing, JD, PhD, is State University of New York Distinguished Service Professor and Vice Dean at the SUNY Buffalo Law School. Dr. Ewing is a graduate of Harvard Law School, he received his PhD at Cornell University, and he was a postdoctoral fellow at Yale University's Institution for Social and Policy Studies. Dr. Ewing is the author of nine previous books including *Justice Perverted: Sex Offense Law, Psychology, and Public Policy* (OUP, 2011) and President of the American Board of Forensic Psychology.